Heine was a man of disconcerting vitality and passionate individualism whose complicated character was always misunderstood or inadequately appreciated. He was violent both in his loves and hates, outwardly exuberant and confident, inwardly humiliated and utterly lonely. His writing, too, combined tenderness and irony, poisonous wit and sweetness of style. All his life he burned with enthusiasm for a Germany that never was, and scorned the Teutons who harried Jews.

The dichotomy of loyalties in Heine, the product of his time and station, is fully explored in HEINE: THE ARTIST IN REVOLT. The romantic touched by disillusion, the patriot shamed by his own zeal, Heine experienced some of the intensest conflicts of an age of revolution and counter-revolution. Yet in his poetry he transcended all limitations, and despite the barriers of his age and his religion he was able to move men and women of all nations, races, and creeds.

Max Brod has presented a compelling portrait of Heine the poet, the Jew, and, above all, the human being, drawn against the background of his age. Heine is seen as an integral part of the culture in which he lived, a man whose origins and early years prefigured the person he became. With his rich background in Jewish tradition and family lore ever with him, he plunged into the thick of a fermenting society on the verge of disintegration and succeeded in doing what no one else did in his day—emancipating himself from the narrow confines of the Jewish Middle Ages while preserving the continuity of his Judaism.

emancipationist and assimilationist strivings. Dr. Brod has here discussed the poet, his age, and general philosophical and religious problems with the candor and detachment that only the passing of time can bring.

HEINRICH HEINE

HEINE AS A YOUNG MAN

Engraving by E. Mandel after F. T. Kugler

HEINRICH HEINE

THE ARTIST IN REVOLT

BY

MAX BROD

TRANSLATED FROM THE GERMAN BY JOSEPH WITRIOL

*He who does not go as far as his heart urges,
and reason permits, is a poltroon; he who goes
farther than he wanted to go is a slave.* HEINE

The peaks of the mountains see each other.

NEW YORK UNIVERSITY PRESS

Washington Square • New York

1 9 5 7

© 1957 by Max Brod.

Library of Congress catalogue card number: 57-10138

First published in London in 1956 by Vallentine, Mitchell & Co. Ltd.
First United States edition 1957

Manufactured in the United States of America.

TO FELIX WELTSCH
MY FRIEND ON LIFE'S JOURNEY

Contents

Preface

In 1934 my biography of Heine was published by Allert de Lange (Amsterdam). A second, revised edition (4th-6th thousand) appeared in 1935. Both editions remained unknown in Germany. For this English translation, the publication of which is timed to coincide with the centenary of Heine's death (17th February, 1956), I have had to make a number of alterations, necessitated by the tremendous events we have witnessed since 1935. Not only did much factual matter have to be revised, but it was inevitable that a whole outlook and sense of history should be affected. The destruction of a large part of the Jewish nation and the re-establishment of the State of Israel after an interruption of nearly two thousand years has forced us to modify our view of the historical epoch in which Heine lived and worked and to revise our judgment of its emancipationist and assimilationist strivings. Nevertheless, I find myself able to say that I have not been obliged to make any major modification in the general thesis of the book. Certain statements of fact, it is true, simply slid from beneath my feet, so to speak. When (to take an example) I referred in 1934 or 1935 to the existence of a certain Jewish library or to the survival of folk-customs among the masses of East European Jewry, I could not be expected to realise that soon after the publication of the book all would be totally destroyed. It is for this reason, chiefly, that such deletions or alterations as there are have been made. At the same time I have been able to benefit from the progress registered by recent Heine research (cf. the episode, in Chapter I, of the ' Chevalier von Geldern '). I have consulted, *inter alia*, the monumental annotated edition, now completed, of Heine's letters by Friedrich Hirth, whose basic approach to Heine, however, is diametrically opposed to my own, and Felix Stössinger's erudite and perceptive study of Heine, *Mein Wertvollstes Vermächtnis*.

A biographer of Heine cannot shirk the question of Jewish-Gentile relationships which so largely coloured the poet's life and work. In the pages that follow I have dealt with this question at some length. Here I would do no more than conclude this preface by expressing the hope that the day is not far distant when, in the words of one of the *Harzreise* poems,

Alle Menschen, gleichgeboren,
Sind ein adliges Geschlecht.

' All men and women, ennobled by birth, are one noble race.'

TEL AVIV, CHESHVAN 5716/NOVEMBER, 1955.

I

The ' Orientalist '

IN HEINE'S *Memoirs,* after descriptions of his childhood and reminiscences of his family on his mother's side (the van Gelderns), there occurs the following passage:

> The best and most precious find that I ever made in these dusty packing-cases, however, was a note-book written in the hand of a brother of my grandfather. He was called the Chevalier or the Orientalist and my great-aunts were always full of stories about him.
>
> He must have been some queer sort of saint, this great-uncle of mine, whose name was Simon de Geldern, too. His cognomen of 'Orientalist' was given him because he had travelled extensively in the East and was always decked out in Oriental garb on his return.
>
> He seems to have stayed longest in the coastal towns of North Africa, particularly in those of the Moroccan States. Here he learnt the craft of armourer from a Portuguese and practised it with success.
>
> He made a pilgrimage to Jerusalem. On Mount Moriah, in the ecstasy of prayer, he had a vision. What did he see? He never told anyone.
>
> An independent Beduin tribe, which professed, not the religion of Islam, but a kind of Mosaic faith, and which had its base, so to speak, in one of the unknown oases of the North African desert, chose him to be their leader or Sheikh. This warlike community lived at strife with all its neighbouring tribes and was the terror of the caravans. To speak in

1

European terms: my late great-uncle, the pious visionary of
the holy mount of Moriah, became a bandit chieftain. In those
beautiful parts, too, he acquired the knowledge of horseman-
ship and the riding skill which aroused so much admiration on
his return to the West.

At the various courts where he resided for lengthy periods
he was conspicuous by his personal beauty and dignity, as well
as by the splendour of his Eastern dress, which entranced the
women especially. No doubt, too, the esoteric knowledge he
claimed to possess made a powerful impression. No one
ventured to expose the all-powerful necromancer to his exalted
patrons. The spirit of intrigue feared the spirits of the Cabbala.

Only his own arrogance could plunge him into ruin. The
old great-aunts shook their grey locks with an air of deep
mystery when they whispered of the ' Orientalist's ' gallant
association with a very illustrious lady—an association the
discovery of which obliged him to leave court and country with
all speed. Only by fleeing and leaving all his goods and chattels
behind was he able to escape certain death—and this escape he
owed moreover to his proven ability as a rider.

After this adventure he seems to have found a secure
asylum in England, though in straitened circumstances. I
deduce as much from a pamphlet of my great-uncle's, printed
in London, which I once came across by chance when
clambering to the topmost shelves of the Düsseldorf Library.
It was an oratorio in French verse entitled *Moses on Horeb*,
referring perhaps to the vision I have mentioned, but the introduction was in English and dated from London. The verse,
like all French verse, was tepid water, rhymed, but the prose of
the English introduction reveals the dissatisfaction of a proud
man who found himself in need.

I was unable to get much positive information from my
great-uncle's note-book ; it was written mostly—perhaps as a
precaution—in Arabic, Syriac, and Coptic characters, inter-
mingled strangely enough with French quotations, for example,
very often the verse:

> Où l'innocence périt c'est un crime de vivre.

I was struck, too, by several statements likewise written in
French, which language appears to have been the writer's
usual idiom.

He was a puzzling phenomenon, hard to comprehend, this
great-uncle. He led one of those colourful existences which
were only possible at the beginning and in the middle of the
eighteenth century ; he was half naïve enthusiast propagating
cosmopolitan Utopias which were to make the whole world

happy, and half soldier of fortune who, conscious of his own strength, breaks through or leaps over the crumbling barriers of a decaying society. In any case he was a man through and through.

His charlatanism, which we do not deny, was not of the common kind. . . . Be that as it may, this great-uncle exercised the boy's imagination to an extraordinary extent. Everything that I was told about him made an ineradicable impression on my young mind, and I plunged so deeply into his peregrinations and vicissitudes that I often had the queer feeling in broad daylight that I myself was my late great-uncle and that my life was only a continuation of his life who had died so long ago!

At night the same thing happened in my dreams. My life at that time resembled a great daily newspaper, the upper sections of whose pages contained the present with its daily news-items and daily debates, while in the lower parts of the pages the poetic past fantastically revealed itself in continuous dreams like a serial romance.

In these dreams I identified myself completely with my great-uncle. It was a weird sensation, feeling that I was someone else and that I belonged to another age! In my dreams I found myself in places I had never seen before and in situations I had never conceived of, and yet I moved with steady tread and self-assured mien.

People in strange, vividly coloured garments and of a mysterious cast of countenance met me, but I shook them by the hand as if they were old acquaintances ; I understood their completely foreign language, which no one had ever heard before ; to my astonishment I even answered them in the same language, gesticulating in a way that was quite unlike me and saying things which contrasted in a repulsive manner with my usual mode of thought.

This strange condition lasted about a year, and although I became quite one with myself again, it left behind secret traces in my soul. Many a peculiarity, many a fatal sympathy or antipathy completely out of keeping with my natural disposition, many actions indeed which are opposed to my way of thinking, I explain as the after-effects of the dream-time when I was my own great-uncle.

How true these lines of Heine's are he did not know, nor did he ever find out.

A *leitmotif* of his life: He was often wiser, sang and wrote from profounder depths in his soul than his surface consciousness was aware of. 'Ah God! in jest and unwittingly I spake that which I had felt.'

Today we are in a position to check, more closely than Heine could, and in accordance with the facts, the identification of himself with his great-uncle which Heine, almost playfully, projected. The note-book written in Hebrew and in Hebrew characters, which owing to his defective knowledge of the language he could not decipher—of which he could not even recognise the language and the characters—has been preserved and parts of it were published, translated, and annotated by David Kaufmann in 1896. Unfortunately, only parts, as with so many important sources for the history of the Jewish spirit, as with—to take an example—Reubeni's travel journal, which still awaits a complete translation. And when a publication does appear, in what a frame of mind does it seem to be engendered!

The commendably industrious scholarship of Kaufmann's work, *Aus Heinrich Heine's Ahnensaal* (Breslau, 1896), is disfigured by satirical Philistine outbursts against a species of humanity which does not fit in with the Lord's highly respectable *bourgeois* world-system, and by extravagant praise, conveyed in the unctuous tones of the graveside sermon, of Heine's other ancestors who led a more settled life than his great-uncle did. Kaufmann gives the adventurer, Cabbalist, man of the world, artist, beggar, savourer of life, a thorough ticking-off. We, however, see in the clear but anxious glance of this strange creature Heine's forerunner, and we fall in love with his glittering misfortunes which anticipate so much of Heine's destiny.

It must be confessed that in all probability he saw nothing of North Africa, except Egypt, nor has the diary anything to say of equestrian virtuosity or the leadership of a warlike Jewish tribe *à la* Reubeni. But the life presented to us is wild and restless and buffeted from place to place enough. It is a life that has a family likeness in many of its features, and which in its details is really shattering, to the anguishes and upheavals of Heine's own life, so that in comparing the two lives the force of parental influence, of the law of ' him in whose footsteps you trod,' of spiritual inheritance, is made abundantly manifest. . . . I now give the facts ascertained by Kaufmann. Simon von Geldern was born in 1720, the son of Lazarus von Geldern, who seven years later was appointed Court Factor to the Elector of Jülich-Berg in Düsseldorf. The family, the most respected in the Jewish community of Düssel-

dorf, had reached the height of its glory. But the firstborn son—
firstborn as Heine was—deviated from type. He was given the best
teachers, from the age of four he learnt Talmud, at fourteen he ran
away from school to Frankfurt. Frankfurt was for him, as for
Heine, the first station of his exile. Without his parents'sanction he
left Frankfurt with a school friend and wandered through Germany.
His first great love was for a cousin. She appeared to him afterwards in dreams. An illness, fever, and hallucinations. He attempted
to work in his father's business ; the attempts failed. He hadn't the
makings of a ' shop-Jew.' He turned, with the same lack of success,
to selling lottery tickets, an occupation which Heine later
immortalised in the character of Hirsch Hyazinth. His travels
began. His destination was the rich uncle, as with Heine, but this
time in Vienna, not Hamburg. His itineraries were remarkably like
those undertaken later by his grand-nephew. Simon went to
London, then via Munich to Vienna ; his chief interests were the
opera, the comedy, the café, cards. But he always laid aside a tenth
of his income for the purchase of books. This income was derived
partly from language lessons, which he gave to elegant ladies and
gentlemen, but principally from allowances he drew from his rich
relations. In the midst of this sybaritic existence he was suddenly
overcome by a longing to make a pilgrimage to Palestine, at that
time a very unusual and dangerous undertaking. He looked at Italy,
stayed a while in Florence. From then on, that which for his grand-
nephew remained verse-phantasy in the *Hebrew Melodies* became
for him reality. From Leghorn Simon reached Alexandria ; the
port of Acre ; the Cabbalists' city of Safed, over whose rocky
landscape he rode on a young ass. Here he spent his days in study
and prayer ; the man of the world of the Viennese cafés and opera
had become a sage. 1751 was the year of his asceticism, his pious
anchorite's existence. Then fresh travels: Egypt, Safed again, a
stormy crossing that brought him to Smyrna. Here his man-of-
the-world manner opened the doors of all consulates to him.
Repeatedly we see him visiting the French, English, Swedish, and
Dutch consuls and the Dutch ' chancellor.' Salonika, Con-
stantinople. Between Sofia and Nish he was attacked by bandits
and robbed of his money. The journey continued through Belgrade,
Ofen, Pressburg, back to the rich relations in Vienna. Now,
however, he came as an emissary from the Holy Land, demanding

and receiving respect—a familiar figure in Jewish communities of
those days, who always maintained a connection with Palestine,
however tenuous. His occupation was gathering alms. In this
capacity he journeyed to Moravia, Bohemia, stayed for a short
while in his native Rhineland, saw London again, went to Paris
and did the sights, to Versailles, where he made the acquaintance
of the Chief Librarian of the Royal Library, to Metz, to Germany
again, Denmark ; in Berlin he was received by the Prime Minister,
Count Heinrich von Podewils, and his charming daughter, also by
Margrave Karl von Anspach, the brother-in-law of Frederick the
Great. What urge it was that always drove the tirelessly wandering
Ahasuerus to start on his travels anew we are unable to fathom,
but in 1756 he set out for Palestine for the second time. On the
voyage the ship was captured by corsairs and plundered. Simon
lost all the valuable presents he had been given, he lost all his
provisions.

In the night of Wednesday, 6th Elul, his pious mother
appeared to him in a vision. Friendly shapes pass before him,
the dead and the living, his deceased uncle Emanuel von
Geldern and Emanuel's daughter Freudchen, whom he had
once loved and who perhaps would have given his whole life
a new direction had not his marriage with her been prevented.
He was once more among his own, only in his dreams, it is
true ; but so sweet was the memory of it even when he awoke
that it poured oil on the waves of the sea and seemed to quieten
the tempest raging around the ship. The days passed in painful
religious disputations, forced on him by the theologically
inclined ship's captain—he was deaf into the bargain—seconded
by two priests. In strange contrast to this grim symposium are
the idyllic scenes with a young wolf which the captain had
brought on board from Barbary. But this was no messianic
wolf that could be played with for ever. This was an animal
which, when it started to use its teeth and bite, had to be
thrown overboard (Kaufmann).

How many Heine motifs, with the wind of the Flying Dutchman
of the Schnabelewopski fragment blowing around them, speak to
us from these few lines alone!

This book of *Reisebilder* ends with a view of Carmel. But a
few years later Simon de Geldern was noted in the dossiers of the
Paris police as an ' adventurer '—' rabbi and adventurer ' reads

the entry. Afterwards we find him in Amsterdam, Mannheim, Hanover, in 1763 in Prague, in 1764 in Hungary, in Hildesheim, Dessau, Leipzig, Dresden, and London again. He died, aged 54, in Alsace. Apart from the oratorio mentioned by Heine—its correct title is *The Israelites on Mount Horeb*—he published a remarkable book: the testimonials and recommendations he had been given as a pious emissary. A copy of the printed book with handwritten entries is preserved in the Amsterdam city library.

Simon von Geldern's posthumous papers—letters, rough drafts, chits, lists of names—are scattered all over the world. From them Fritz Heymann compiled the main chapter of his vivid and enthralling book, *Der Chevalier von Geldern* (Querido, Amsterdam, 1937), to which I am indebted for much additional informative material on this ancestor of Heine's. This material was not available when the first two editions of my book appeared.

The talented author of *Der Chevalier von Geldern* rightly compared the eponymous hero of his book with Casanova. The former had less luck, it is true. After being thrown into prison in Palestine in 1757 he made his way again to Italy, lost all his money, collected from Jews and Christians, at Faro, took part in a Court concert in the Tuileries, even caught sight of Louis XV. One of his Jewish friends is named as Mardoché Ravel. He lived by gambling and bookselling, associated with speculators and charlatans, came to Cologne, finally to Düsseldorf to the parental home. Thence he went to The Hague, at that time the rendezvous for all political secret agents. On one occasion he talked with Voltaire, whose guest he was at Les Délices. Here, too, there is the parallel with Casanova. Later he tried to pump Voltaire's banker for a loan, but without success. All the time he made unavailing efforts to find suitable employment, whether in the form of diplomatic services, library work, language lessons, or cabbalistic prophecies. He was deported from Vienna by the Empress Maria Theresa's Commission of Morals, imprisoned in Pressburg. A third journey to the Holy Land proved another failure. Plague, famine, national hatreds devastated Palestine. Nevertheless, in spite of all these set-backs he disdained the counsel of a worthy cousin that he should doff his exotic garb and begin to lead a respectable life. He experienced 'signs and wonders,' was set upon by Arabs, escaped with his life. From now on he comported himself as a pious man, as a repentant sinner.

He wished to get to India via Aleppo, Basra, but was warned
against doing so by the Danish explorer Niebuhr, who had just
returned from the desert, where he had lost four members of his
scientific expedition. Simon turned back.

His wanderings continued for another twenty years, this time in
Europe. He suffered many bitter experiences, but had better times,
too. In Wolfenbüttel he nearly became librarian. Someone else was
rightly preferred: Lessing. He taught in a non-Jewish boarding
school in London, had his biblical epic printed. Later, by chance
and through a misunderstanding, he found himself in a circle of
Freemasons ' of strict observance ' to which the Crown Prince of
Hessen-Darmstadt and other exalted personages belonged.
Eventually he was awarded the official title of a ' Court Cabbalist,
Secret Magic Councillor, and Court Factor to his Serene Majesty.'
The last ten years of his life he spent in a castle lodge in Buxweiler
(Lower Alsace) ; an *otium cum dignitate* such as Casanova enjoyed
a little later in Count Waldstein's castle in Dux. ' Two amusing
old fools ' (Heymann). A compound of rationalist admiration of
Voltaire and superstitious mystification such as was only possible
in the age of the so-called ' Enlightenment.' The last phase was the
strangest of all: the gentleman-adventurer became deeply concerned
with the degraded position of his fellow-Jews throughout the world.
He furnished the Abbé Grégoire with material for his prize essay
on the theme set by the Academy in Metz: ' Are there any means
of enabling the Jews of France to lead more useful and happier
lives ? ' Thereby he contributed to the emancipation of the Jews
which a few years later the Abbé wrested for them in the course
of the French Revolution. A few months after Geldern's death
came the storming of the Bastille. Details of the disposition of his
posthumous papers will be found in Heymann.

Simon (or Simeon) von Geldern also left a family tree which
enables us to trace the origins of the family back to the seventeenth
century. Simon's grandfather is Josef or Juspa von Geldern. The
latter's father—the great-great-grandfather of Heine's mother, Betty
(Peira)—can still be traced, too, also the connection by marriage
with the celebrated family of Glückel of Hamelin, whose memoirs
have come down to us.

The father, Josef—or to give him the name by which he
was more frequently called, Juspa—enjoyed a privilege unusual

for those days and confined to specially favoured families. He
was allowed to use a surname. Although such a surname would
be more or less latent, in the sense that it would not be used in
the streets, that is to say, among the Jews, it would be in
evidence whenever its owner needed documentation in his
public life. One of his ancestors must have migrated to
Germany from Geldern in Holland or, as is more likely, have
come to Düsseldorf from the neighbouring city of Geldern,
bequeathing his descendants the name of Geldern or von (i.e.,
from) Geldern.

So writes Kaufmann. The name of Heine's mother, ' von
Geldern,' accordingly has geographical, not aristocratic, significance.
A snobbish remark of Heine's—reported by Laube—in which he
boasted of his noble descent can only be evaluated in the same way
as the reference in his memoirs to the portrait of his beautiful
paternal grandmother: ' Had the artist painted a large diamond
cross resting on the lady's breast none would have doubted that
they were looking at the portrait of some countess-abbess of a
noble Protestant foundation.' Mimicry of this kind is very infrequent
with Heine, but he is not entirely free from it. No doubt the
tendencies of the period exerted too strong a temptation.

Not nobility in the usual sense of the word, but nobility of the
Jewish kind is to be found in Heine's ancestry. They belonged to
an élite, these von Gelderns: an élite of mind, creative energy, and
communal responsibility—a trio of qualities more often in evidence
then than now. Juspa is *Obervorgänger* or President of all the
' protected ' Jewish communities enjoying right of residence
and high taxation under the Elector's wing. He became
Kammeragent or Court Factor to the Elector Johann von Jülich-
Berg and founded by special electoral privilege Düsseldorf's first
synagogue.

A ray of sunshine warmed the heart of the community ;
the Jews of Düsseldorf greeted the erection of the House of
God, built for them by their President, as a sign of electoral
protection and social improvement. This was no temporary
toleration of an individual purchased at a price, no paper
protection affording the right of stay for a limited period.
This—or so it seemed in the bliss of that first enthusiasm—was
a proof of public recognition of the Jewish religion. It was a
monument, rooted firmly in the soil and reaching proudly to

heaven, symbolising a right accorded to the whole religious community to reside permanently in a land they could call their own.

Heinrich Heine, the grandson's grandson, knew nothing of this event that so stirred the souls of Juspa Geldern's contemporaries. He writes merely, depicting the legendary wealth of his ancestor: 'The present hospital in the new city also belonged to him.' Kaufmann comments: 'Evidently Heine had no idea that the Maximilian Joseph Hospital in the new city of Düsseldorf was the synagogue of his ancestor Juspa von Geldern.'

Juspa's son Lazarus von Geldern also attained the position of Factor to the Court of Jülich-Berg and President of the Jewish community. For a time he lived in Vienna, whither he had gone as the son-in-law of the rich and respected Simon Pressburg. He had eleven children, among them the unsteady Simon, but among whom also was Heine's grandfather, the honourable and solid Gottschalk, who graduated in 1752 as a doctor of medicine in the University of Duisburg. (With a thesis on hoarseness.) Gottschalk's eldest son, too, became a doctor, *Hofrat*. The family, then, had been long settled in the Lower Rhineland, was respected by Jew and Christian alike, had attained academic honours and worldly rank without denying its ancestral religion. There was no ghetto in Düsseldorf, the Jews lived in all parts of the city. Compared with the situation in Prussia or Frankfurt, the Jews enjoyed liberty, freedom of movement, unrestricted access to European culture. Moreover, even before Heine's birth, Düsseldorf had come into French possession (1795, General Kléber in Düsseldorf). All these factors contributed decisively to Heine's youthful impressions. He grew up frank and upright. No doubt he came in for some petty bullying in the Catholic school he attended as a boy, but real hatred, real persecution of the Jew, he did not experience until he was nineteen and had left home, when he was involved in a Jewish brawl in Hamburg.

In his memoirs Heine does less than justice to his paternal ancestry, for not unconvincing reasons which he himself gives. His father, Samson Heine, had come from Hanover (or Hamburg), was an outsider with no aunts and great-aunts to sing the praises of this branch of the family to the child. Here, too, modern research has been illuminating—Gustav Karpeles: *Heinrich Heines Stamm-*

baum väterlicherseits in *Gedenkbuch zur Erinnerung an David Kaufmann* (Breslau, 1900). His great-grandfather, David Simon Heine, lived in Hanover and enjoyed the right to a surname. 'The origin of the name (Heine) is not clear. As far back as 1334 there was a Jew in Strasbourg with the name of Heyn.' David Simon's father came from Bückeburg. His name was Isak. The archives have nothing to say of him. On the other hand, the memorial book of the community of Hanover speaks of David Simon as a pious, charitable man who carried out the commandment to love one's neighbour as oneself, who first and foremost encouraged and financially aided those engaged in the study of the Law, who kept holy the religious commandments and was supported in so doing by his wife. His son, Heine's grandfather, in his relationships with the authorities, is Heymann Heine ; in the ' Jewish Street ' his name is Chayim Bückeburg, a name readily transferred by anti-Semitic humourists to the grandson, for no apparent reason and with no particular humour. We do not know much about Heymann Heine. He prospered and married *en secondes noces* the daughter of a rich merchant, Meyer Samson Popert of Altona. The second son of this marriage was Heine's celebrated Hamburg uncle, the banker Salomon Heine, and the third was Heine's father, Samson. Heymann himself is named as one of the eighteen men who in 1762 founded in Hanover a ' Society for the Study of the Divine Teaching, for Visiting the Sick, and for the Practice of Charity,' men who belonged to the most respected and oldest families in the community. His praises, too, are recorded in the memorial book of the Hanover community.

Both on his father's and mother's side, then, Heine came of families whose settlement in North-West Germany went back historically for many generations, who were firmly grounded in Jewish tradition and took an active, indeed, a leading, part in maintaining it, until the Emancipation gave another direction to the entire religious community. The impression that manages to cling to many Heine biographies of nomadic restlessness, huckstering uncouthness, uncivilised ancestry in a word, must therefore be rectified in the light of the results of modern research. The generation to which Heine's parents belonged stood fast by Jewish tradition and Jewish knowledge, even though they had not been unaffected by the revolutionary legislation relating to the Jews

which, coming from France, had reached Western Germany before
the other parts of the country.

A final quotation, from Kaufmann, showing the love of
tradition and the love for things of the spirit which prevailed in
the house of Heine's ancestors:

> From his native Düsseldorf, a city which under an art-
> loving and extravagantly generous Prince was at the height of
> its prosperity, Lazarus von Geldern had taken with him to
> Vienna a feeling for the refinements of life. He endeavoured
> to make his house worthy of the best education and taste of
> the period. A slight memorial to which the fragrance of its
> surroundings still seems to cling has been preserved for us. It
> testifies to the refinement and to the patronage of the arts
> prevailing in the house of Juspa von Geldern. In 1723 he had
> commissioned a Jewish scribe and artist of remarkable skill,
> one Moses Judah, named Löb, son of Benjamin Wolf Broda
> of Trebitsch in Moravia, to write down on parchment the ritual
> for the two evenings of the Jewish festival of freedom, the
> Passover Haggadah. The text was to be decorated with bright,
> gaily coloured pictures illustrating the events recorded in the
> Haggadah. Perhaps the great-grandchild, he for whom it was
> reserved to record in an immortal work of art the distilled
> poetry of those Festival evenings, perhaps Heinrich Heine,
> author of the *Rabbi von Bacharach,* had feasted his eyes as a
> boy in his parents' home on those selfsame pictures which the
> æsthetic urge of his great-grandfather had caused to be painted
> in the family Haggadah.

It may be that the ' scribe and artist ' mentioned here was one
of my ancestors. The facts as they are recorded render this by no
means improbable. The names ' Broda ' and ' Brod ' are identical,
and it is established that among my ancestors were practitioners of
these pious arts. In that case I may pause here in the congenial
thought that once before a member of my family has been in the
service and at the behest of the house of Heine.

II

Youth, Düsseldorf

THERE IS no means of ascertaining the date of Heinrich Heine's birth. The official documents were destroyed in a fire, and the information from other sources varies. And so the first fact of Heine's life is shrouded in the same obscurity that veils *La Mouche*, who appeared towards the end of it ; in spite of all the professional research on the subject, her identity has never been satisfactorily established. That Heine's life, ostensibly so illumined by rationality, so egocentric and cynical, its features, so it is alleged, paraded with such conceit and hardihood in the full view of all and sundry—that Heine's life should be framed in the shadow of these two mysteries may well suggest that the stereotyped characterisations of the poet are open to question.

Heine was not born on New Year's Eve, 1800. He only said so for the sake of his *mot*: ' I am one of the first men of the century.' When he was not indulging in his innate love of leg-pulling he stated that the 13th December, 1799, was the ' authentic ' date of his birth. According to other reports, he first saw the light of day two years earlier, on the 13th December, 1797. As Heine himself writes to his sister, the date of his birth is not correctly given in the archives of the Düsseldorf municipality, ' for reasons which I prefer not to state.' Was this another attempt at creating a mystery ? What were the reasons ? Evasion of military service—a reason naturally adopted with fervour by a certain

13

school of research—or to enable him to start his secondary
schooling in conformity with the age requirements of the Düsseldorf
Lyceum—or to facilitate his migration to Hamburg ? There is
room for endless speculation. The matter is of no importance.[1]

The child was named Harry after a business friend of the
family—' my father's friend, who was an expert in the buying of
velveteens.' ' I still like to be called by the name,' says Heine in
his *Memoirs*. In the family circle he was always known by it, in
spite of the fact that it had been the cause of one of his first painful
conflicts with the surrounding world. Schoolfellows and neighbouring children would shout ' Harr-ee ' at the boy, in imitation
of the cry of the street-sweeper who loaded his donkey-cart with
the refuse piled up every morning in front of the Düsseldorf
houses.

> My homonymy with the street-sweeper's long-eared
> quadruped was a continual nightmare to me. The big boys
> used to go past me shouting ' Harr-ee!' while the smaller
> ones would greet me in the same fashion, but at a respectful
> distance. At school the same theme was developed with
> refined cruelty ; as soon as ' donkey ' was mentioned in any
> context at all everybody would turn and stare at me, which
> never failed to make me flush with vexation. It is incredible
> how schoolboys everywhere can find ways of ' ragging ' their
> unfortunate fellows.

The boy's sensitive nature was easily hurt! Heine, the malicious
mocker, always remained, in fact, over-sensitive to mockery and
ridicule when he himself was its butt. ' When I complained to my
mother, all she said was that I should try to learn and be clever
and then no one would be able to say I was a donkey.'

His mother aroused his ambition ; her methods were rational,
it was from her that the child received, for the first time, the legacy
of French Reason in its most primitive form: learn much, know,
be clever. It was his mother, too, who gave him his first writing
lessons. It was she who supervised the education of her four

---

[1] Friedrich Hirth, the editor of the complete letters of Heine, whose
massive contribution to Heine scholarship is, however, by no means free
from error, considers that Heine saw the light of day before his parents
were officially married, and that they falsified his date of birth in order to
conceal this fact. Hirth's reasoning does not seem to me to be entirely
convincing.

children: Harry, Charlotte, Gustav, Max. It was she who planned for the boy, first, after the fashion of the Napoleonic Empire, a career in the army and in the service of the State; then, after Napoleon's downfall, he was to emulate the Rothschilds; finally, she dreamt of his becoming a lawyer. All castles-in-the-air; it can hardly be otherwise when mothers seek to plan their children's destiny for them.

His love for his mother remained one of the strongest pillars in Heine's life. It mingles touchingly with his nostalgia for Germany. 'Das Vaterland wird nie verderben, jedoch die alte Frau kann sterben.'—The Fatherland would never perish, but the old lady might die.

> Seit ich die Mutter nicht gesehn,
> Zwölf Jahre sind schon hingegangen;
> Es wächst mein Sehnen und Verlangen.
>
> Mein Sehnen und Verlangen wächst.
> Die alte Frau hat mich behext.
> Ich denke immer an die alte,
> Die alte Frau, die Gott erhalte!
>
> Die alte Frau hat mich so lieb,
> Und in den Briefen, die sie schrieb,
> Seh ich, wie ihre Hand gezittert,
> Wie tief das Mutterherz erschüttert.
>
> Die Mutter liegt mir stets im Sinn.
> Zwölf lange Jahre flossen hin,
> Zwölf lange Jahre sind verflossen,
> Seit ich sie nicht ans Herz geschlossen.
>
> . . . .
> Nach Deutschland lechzt' ich nicht so sehr
> Wenn nicht die Mutter dorten wär.
> . . . .

> Since last my mother's face I saw,
> Twelve years have passed, twelve years have vanished;
> I long for her from whom I'm banished.
>
> My longing and my loving grows.
> My mother's spell no limit knows.
> Where'er I go I always see her,
> My mother! Pray God may safely keep her!

My aged mother loves me so,
Each letter costs her grief, I know.
I know she writes with hand that's shaking.
I know her mother's heart is breaking.

My mother's always in my mind,
A dozen years have passed, unkind,
Twelve years have passed since our last meeting,
When 'gainst my heart her heart was beating.

. . . .
I would not long for German air,
Were not my mother living there.
. . . .

He sought to the very end to hide from her the catastrophic turn that his disease had taken. When the news reached Hamburg from Paris that he was confined to his bed, he wrote to her that it was only a publisher's trick to increase the sale of his books. Did she believe him? She was very wise, and sometimes, as we know from *Deutschland, ein Wintermärchen,* she would put ' tricky questions.' A capable, resolute woman. She survived her son. What a picture Heine draws in a few strokes, of their meeting again after all those years. The few terse lines ring wonderfully true:

Und als ich zu meiner Frau Mutter kam,
Erschrak sie fast vor Freude;
Sie rief: ' Mein liebes Kind!' und schlug
Zusammen die Hände beide.

' Mein liebes Kind, wohl dreizehn Jahr
Verflossen unterdessen!
Du wirst gewiss sehr hungrig sein—
Sag an, was willst du essen? '

And when to my mother at last I came,
Near-frightened was her pleasure;
She cried: ' Dear child!' and in her joy
She clapped her hands together.

' Dear child, nigh thirteen years, no less
Have passed without a meeting!
And hungry you must surely be—
What would you like for eating? '

A realist. One has to have known these Jewish matrons personally to appreciate them, to realise what streams of powerful

feeling flow beneath their superficial rationalism. They are still to
be met with today, these Jewish mothers. I fancy I know Frau
Betty Heine as I did my own mother—my own mother, it is true,
was quite different, but I have met Frau Betty Heine more than
once in my life. It was not from her, as Heine himself confirms,
that he inherited his imaginative and romantic disposition. She had
' a dread of poetry,' snatched any novel she found in the child's
hands away from him, forbade him to go to the theatre, reprimanded
servants who told ghost stories in his hearing. All the same, she
was unable to stop an old maidservant who came from the Münster
region, and who had a great store of tales and folk songs, from
early capturing the boy's heart with the sweet horror of the old
German legends. And the adolescent's first puppy love, his first
kiss, were for the red-haired Sefchen, the hangman's daughter.
The pages in the *Memoirs* that tell of ' Red Sefchen,' of her
hangman's sword, of her muffled, almost toneless voice, and of
the strange meals and ceremonies in the lonely hangman's cottage
are—together with the portrait of his father and a few politico-
philosophical passages—among the finest prose that Heine ever
wrote ; serious, balanced, unspoilt by cheap witticisms ; ranking
equally with the classics of German prose, which is definitely more
than can be said of Heine's prose in general.

The father: His portrait, although bathed in the kindly light
of a certain childishness which borders, if truth be told, on frivolity
or even light-headedness, is much more of a ' problem picture '
than that of the mother. Certainly it is a strange pendant to the
sharply defined outlines of the mother. She was a ' strict Deist,
guided predominantly by reason,' the daughter of an educated man
who as a doctor had established his place in German culture. She
herself was highly educated—' even as a very young girl she had
to read Latin dissertations and other learned writings to her father.'

This does not conflict with the fact that her letters which have
come down to us are in German written in Hebrew characters ;
such was the custom in her day. These letters inveigh against
etiquette and convention in the manner of the ' Enlightenment ' ;
Rousseau's pupil exalts ' feelings ' above ' motives,' but is opposed
to the ' so-called fashionable sensibility.' She is all clear pure spirit,
at the same time capable of strong emotion. In the lines she wrote
after her brother's death—in 1796—the vivid style of her son's

writing may already be discerned. ' In vain did my friends seek to console me with the misfortunes of my fellow men and women ; my neighbour's wound does not heal my own. In vain did Reason seek to comfort a heart rent by anguish. . . . Oh, it is astounding how much those can endure whom Fate has seemed to pierce with its arrows, until at length they stand firm and hardened, like living monuments of human suffering and resistance.' Between such a mother and her child spiritual bridges, at any rate, possibilities of understanding, could exist.

No such bridge led to the father, a somewhat ' simple ' man who enjoyed life to the full. Heine *père* was a gallant who never lost his love of military display (as Victualler to the troops he had accompanied the Duke of Cumberland on his Flanders and Brabant campaigns), and who was never so much in his element as when wearing the handsome dark-blue uniform of the Düsseldorf militia, marching at the head of his column past his house in the Bolker-strasse and waving a salute to his wife ' with exquisite grace.' Even his business was only a game to him, which he played ' as children play at soldiers or shops.' The only bridge leading to such a delightfully ' quaint ' father, who still clung to his old-fashioned hair style, was a bridge of love, not understanding. And so the part of Heine's *Memoirs* dealing with his father concludes with a kind of solemn utterance which by its specific wording seems designed to counter any contrary feeling : ' He was of all persons the one I loved most of all on this earth.' And then—see the comparable passage in *Schnabelewopski* :

He has now been dead for more than twenty-five years. I never thought that one day I would lose him, and even now I can hardly believe that I have in fact lost him. It is so hard to realise that people we love so much are dead. But then they are not dead, they live on in us and dwell in our souls.

Since then not a night has passed without my being unable to avoid thinking of my father, of blessed memory, and when I awake in the morning, often I still think I hear the sound of his voice, as if echoing in a dream. And then I feel I must dress quickly and hurry down to my father in the big parlour as I used to do as a boy.

My father always used to get up very early and set about his business, winter and summer, and usually I found him already seated at his desk, from where, without looking up, he would give me his hand for me to kiss. A beautiful, finely-formed, elegant hand which he always washed with almond powder. I still see it in front of me, I see the tracery of every fine blue vein standing out against the dazzling white of that marble hand. The scent of almonds seems to tickle my nostrils, and my eyelashes are wet.

Sometimes my father did not leave it at giving me his hand to kiss. He would take me between his knees and kiss me on the brow. One morning he embraced me with quite exceptional tenderness and said : ' Tonight I had a very beautiful dream about you and am very pleased with you, my dear Harry.' As he uttered these naïve words a smile hovered around his lips, as if to say : However badly Harry may behave in reality, I shall always have beautiful dreams about him, so as to be able to go on loving him.

This naïvely emotional, irrational temperament of Heine's father accounts for the fact that he adhered more closely to traditional Judaism than did Heine's mother, who early changed her Jewish first name Peira (= Zippora, according to Zunz) to Betty. Heine *père,* on the other hand, remained Samson Heine to the end of his days. It has been established that he was President of the ' Society for the Practice of Philanthropy and for the Recital of the Psalms ' in Düsseldorf, an Orthodox Association of the type of the *Chevra Kadisha* or ' burial society.' To have been elected President he must *ex hypothesi* have been an ' Orthodox ' Jew, but this is not necessarily in conflict with the information given by Heine about his father's zest for living and enjoyment of worldly pleasures. Karpeles, from whose previously quoted work on Heine's family tree I take the facts, does not agree. However, I am strongly of the opinion that more credence ought to be given to a poet's autobiographical utterances than the experts are inclined to give. Where there are apparently contradictory statements one should always ask whether the documents and facts adduced by other authorities are not, after all, compatible, in some way or other, with the autobiographer's own utterances, and whether in the final analysis it may not be the other authorities rather than the poet whose information is incorrect. The school usage, on the other hand, always tends to decide against the autobiographer in cases of doubt ; indeed, it tends to manufacture such cases of doubt artificially. It is such a pleasant feeling, is it not, to seem wiser, or at any rate more conscientious, more objective than the autobiographer, to expose his artful dodges and

his caprices. It is such a pleasant feeling, that some writers resort
to violent methods in order to achieve it—but I am going much
further than I wanted to do in joining issue with the fine scholar
who rendered such splendid service in the field of Heine studies.
In what follows I quote Karpeles without reservation :

> Later, it is true, Samson Heine's ' enlightened ' wife caused
> him to become more and more estranged from ' Orthodox '
> circles. By the beginning of the new century he is to be found
> among the exponents of ' Enlightenment ' in his religious com-
> munity ; indeed he had joined the ' Dawn ' Freemasons' Lodge
> in Frankfurt-on-Main. In 1804 we find Samson Heine listed as
> a contributor to the founding of the first, or one of the first
> (German-Jewish)   schools   in   Frankfurt-on-Main—the
> *Philantropin.*

Heine's father, however, never became a Deist in Frau Betty's
fashion ; he kept to the form of Judaism, which was a truer guardian
of Jewish content than the philosophic interpretation of religion,
with its ostensible respect for the ' kernel ' of Judaism, could ever
be. The ' husk ' proved robust, endured more firmly than the so-
called ' kernel ' even when—as happened with Heine *père*—it was
often little more than mechanical practice. In spite of everything,
this husk contained, unnoticed, almost unconsciously, the folk
element of Judaism, its essential life, were it never so petrified and
divorced from current reality. Folk custom and religious practice
went closely together ; indeed, the two were indistinguishable. When
irreligious utterances made by the boy were reported to Herr Samson
Heine he didn't show the ' same indulgence ' that he did in the
case of the hangman's daughter, but delivered that remarkable
' curtain lecture '—' doubtless the longest speech he had ever
delivered '—with the flickering, two-edged irony of which the
Memoirs fragment closes :

> My dear son! Your mother sends you to Rektor Schall-
> meyer to study philosophy. That is her affair. I for my part
> do not like philosophy as it is nothing but superstition and I
> need my wits about me for my business. You can be as much
> of a philosopher as you like, but I must ask you not to say
> in public what you think, as it would harm me in my business
> if my customers got to know I had a son who didn't believe
> in God. The Jews in particular would not buy any more
> velveteens from me, and they are honest people, pay prompt

cash and are right in keeping to religion. I am your father and therefore older than you and hence more experienced ; you must take my word for it, therefore, if I venture to tell you that atheism is a great sin.

In a sense the father was right. Heine belonged to the Jewish community, more particularly to the *kehilla* or Jewish community of Düsseldorf, and more precisely still to a particular stage in the development of this community, which is determined by the epoch —the beginning of the nineteenth century—and by the French domination of the Rhineland. Only against this background can the beginnings of Heine's education and development be properly understood. Which does not mean that his non-Jewish environment, as well, did not assume the greatest significance for him. Both the pious Catholic population and its way of thinking—*Wallfahrt nach Kevelaar*—and the Old German pagan myths in the shape of folk saga and tale found their way into the boy's receptive mind, no less than the many and varied figures of the *Elementargeister* and landscape and historical tradition. Landscape, saga, the history of the homeland . . . even in a late period of his life Heine could write from Paris :

No, memories of the old German religion have not been extinguished. They say there are greybeards in Westphalia who still know where the old images of the gods lie hidden ; on their death-bed they tell their youngest grandchild, who carries the secret in his tight-locked Saxon heart. In Westphalia, the former Saxony, not everything that lies buried is dead. If you walk through the old forest groves there you can still hear voices from the dawn of time, you can still hear the echo of magic spells with profound meaning in them and with more vitality in them than in all the literature of the Brandenburg March. Once, as I was wandering through these forests, a queer feeling of dread took hold of me as I passed the age-old Siegburg. 'Here,' said my guide, 'here King Wittekind once lived,' and he heaved a deep sigh. He was a simple woodcutter and he carried a big axe. I am convinced this man would fight today for King Wittekind if necessary, and woe betide the skull on which his axe fell !

It will be seen that those people who try to suggest that Heine was a *blagueur*, a café-littérateur and materialistic socialist with no sense of history, have no easy task, whether they regard this conception of Heine as praiseworthy or the reverse. What is certain, however, as certain as his innermost connexion with the environment of his German homeland, is that the possibility and the extent of this connexion were determined by the legal and factual conditions prevailing in the Jewish community in which he grew up.

The Duchy of Jülich, of which Düsseldorf was the capital, belonged, with Cleves and Berg, to the Electoral Principality of the Bavarian Palatinate and was occupied by the French revolutionary armies in 1795, which caused Betty van Geldern to give expression to patriotic lamentation in her letters. The town had previously been shelled by the French. The streets were afire, the Palace garden—the same in which Heine was later, on a fine day in May, to read the first book of his 'intelligent boyhood,' *Don Quixote*—was desolate. 'My favourite spot,' writes Betty, 'lying at the end of the garden, is practically in ruins ; all the lovely trees which gave such welcome shade even in the fiercest midday heat of summer have been felled ; in future there will be no cool spot anywhere in the neighbourhood except—the grave. Do not reproach me with deliberately picking on such dismal matters. Whatever I should choose to write about would fill heart and mind with inexhaustible grief. Hopes of a peace have disappeared here entirely. Oh, I fear the torch of war will not be extinguished save in tears and blood ! ' So much as an example of the characteristic style of Heine's mother. The populace, however, seem to have accepted the French dominance, which put an end to the feudal conditions under which they had been living, without any great dismay. After a brief interval—1801 to 1806—in which the territory reverted to the Palatinate, Napoleon's brother-in-law, Joachim Murat, took over the reins of government in the 'Grand Duchy of Berg.' He was a considerate ruler, who did not inflict excessive burdens on his subjects. Generally speaking, there was no dissatisfaction, and French influence became dominant ; it was not until after the Congress of Vienna that the Duchy became part of Prussia in 1815. At the time of Heine's birth, therefore, and during his boyhood, Düsseldorf was part of the French Republic ; afterwards it was a vassal state of the French Empire. In 1811 and 1812 Napoleon himself paid a brief visit to Düsseldorf, about which an account appears in *Buch Le Grand,* where Heine speaks, too, of his native city:

The city of Düsseldorf is very beautiful, and if you think about it from afar off, and if you happen to have been born there, you experience a peculiar sensation. I was born there, and I feel as if I must go home straightway. And when I say home, I mean the Bolkerstrasse and the house where I was born.

In the same book Heine portrays the French troops marching into the city, ' the joyous men of glory who, singing to the music of their bands, had marched all over the world, the gay but earnest features of the grenadiers, the bear-skin caps,' and finally the Emperor, his plain green uniform, his small cap, the white charger, the marble hand gleaming in the sun, the clear eyes and the forehead with shadows flitting over it of creative thoughts, those great seven-league thoughts. Thus had the lad seen him, and thus he was to remain imprinted for ever in the poet's heart.

The French domination affected Heine not merely emotionally, as an unforgettable youthful impression—*The Two Grenadiers* was one of his first poems—but also indirectly through its effect on the status of the Jewish community in Düsseldorf. At this point a frequently repeated error needs to be corrected: that Heine's Bonapartism, which is indeed always flaring up, even at the accession of Napoleon III in Heine's late middle age, is connected with Napoleon's ostensibly benevolent and progressive Jewish legislation. A double error. First, less than justice is done to Heine in attributing his unselfish admiration of Napoleon's genius—an admiration in which, incidentally, he finds himself in the company of Goethe—to narrow racial selfishness. For Heine, Napoleon was always the bearer of the ideas of the French Revolution, the ideas of the Rights of Man, of Liberty, Equality, and Fraternity. He was the ' mortal body of the Revolution, the incarnation of the Revolution.' What did Napoleon's end, what did Waterloo mean to Heine ? He has told us often enough. ' The whole of Europe became one St. Helena, and Metternich was its Sir Hudson Lowe.' And in fact our whole appraisal of Heine's personality will depend on our attitude to the French Revolution. Whether Heine was right or not in claiming Napoleon as a supporter of the revolutionary ideology of a Danton or a Robespierre is another matter. My own view is that Napoleon would have welcomed impartially any ideology which he could have succeeded in enlisting in support of his own brutal, limitless lust for power; that he was quite uninterested in the overthrow of the privileged classes *per se*; in fact he disliked the idea and only exploited it as a starting-point, the best available at the time, for his own career. But Heine's attitude—at any rate, in so far as his enthusiasm for Napoleon's powerful personality does not cause him from time to time to exceed all reasonable limits—Heine's attitude can only be understood with reference to the French Revolution, to whose principles he retained an unshakable loyalty throughout his life. ' I pray thee, gentle reader,' the poet exclaims on the battle-field of Marengo, where he declares the glory of war to be an ' archaic pleasure,' and Napoleon perhaps to be the last conqueror, ' I pray thee, take me not for an absolute Bonapartist ; it is not the man's actions, but his genius, I admire, whether the man's name be Alexander, Cæsar, or Napoleon. My absolute love for the latter does not go beyond 18th Brumaire, when he betrayed liberty. Nor did he betray it out of necessity, but out of a secret predilection for the aristocracy. Napoleon Bonaparte was an aristocrat, a nobleman who was an enemy of civil equality, and it was a colossal misunderstanding that led the aristocracy of Europe, represented by England, to fight him to the death.' We can see here the boundaries that are clearly set to Heine's cult of Napoleon by his (Heine's) attitude to the revolutionary idea, for all that it seems hardly comprehensible to us that now Heine's successors in the French Revolution should have exhausted themselves in sterile hatred of the aristocracy and in anti-clericalism. In any case, Heine's repeated genuflections before the Emperor's image have nothing whatever to do with Napoleon's attitude to the Jews. These genuflections were performed in worship of a genius who Heine thought would redeem humanity.

Secondly must be added the little-known fact that the Emperor and his legislation were anything but friendly to the Jews. On the 3rd August, 1789, the Abbé Grégoire, a Deputy in the French National Assembly, had spoken in favour of the oppressed Jews who were suffering from legal disabilities. Shortly after, Mirabeau thundered against recognising a ' dominant religion.' ' A dominant religion ! May this tyrannical phrase be eradicated from our legislation ! For once you admit such an expression in the religious field, you will have to admit it in all other fields, too. You will have a dominant ritual, a dominant philosophy, and dominant systems. No, justice alone must be dominant.' (As regards facts I now follow S. M. Dubnow's excellent work, *Die neueste Geschichte des jüdischen Volkes*, 1789-1914.) The matter was dealt with in connexion with the granting of civil equality to members of the Reformed (Protestant) Church, but it was complicated by the status of the Jews as a Nation to whom none of the existing formulas applied, and for whom no minority rights existed. State and Nation were regarded as identical ; within the State boundaries *only* the State national group, divided, of course, into several religious denominations, to all of whom it was intended to grant equal rights, was recognised. In addition there were—foreigners. If someone wished to acquire State citizenship, then, in accordance with the notions of the time—still prominent today in many works by West European theoreticians—he had to renounce all connexion with any other national group and with it any possibility of being considered as a member of a minority group. According to this theory, for example, the Germans in Poland or Czechoslovakia would not be entitled to call themselves Germans or to organize themselves as a linguistic and cultural minority group. Nowadays, of course, we have a counter-theory which accords national minorities clearly defined rights within the State without depriving them of their State citizenship, and it is this counter-theory which, although it never fully penetrated into the general consciousness, became the basis of Wilson's Points, the Treaty of Versailles, the legislation of the newly created States, and the League of Nations. At that time, however, the situation was completely new and no one was able to tackle it. The Liberal Deputy Clement-Tonnerre justified emancipating the Jews, granting them the suffrage and the right to public appointments, in the following words which have since become famous: ' To the Jews as a Nation everything must be refused, to the Jews as people everything must be granted. It is said that they themselves do not wish to be citizens ; if they say that, they must be expelled from the country, for there must be no Nation within a Nation. In their petition, however, they ask to be regarded as citizens of the State. The Law is obliged to concede them this right, which only prejudice can deny them.'

It was with the best possible intentions, therefore, that a fundamental confusion arose from which Jews suffered for a century,

and are still suffering today. They were granted individual rights
but denied any rights as a national group ; indeed they were
required to forgo their own national individuality. They were
required to make this renunciation in their own interest, for the
sake of the protection and the equality of rights they enjoyed, or,
as the phrase went in Germany, for the sake of their 'civic
amelioration.' It was the Jews' friends who required them to make
this renunciation. The enemies of the Jews, however, declared
that the Jews *were* a nation, ' with their own laws to which they
have always been faithful,' and made this commendable Jewish
quality the basis of their attempt to bar the Jews in their path
to the Light. I shall examine later in detail—when I come to
discuss the Berlin salons and Heine's Berlin years—the appalling
results this fatal misconception had on the character and on
the condition of the Jews themselves.

Reading the documents of the time today one is forced to the
conclusion that nobody had an inkling of the problem. Jews and
non-Jews alike went wrong with the very best of intentions.
Evidently the new problems posed by the whole question, emerging
as it had done from the night of the Middle Ages, were beyond the
powers of that generation to solve. Not only so, but these problems
gave rise to savage outbursts of hatred which stifled in embryo all
attempts to solve them. To the problem ' State and National
Minority ' was added, in the case of the Jews, the question which at
that period was gradually coming to the surface: 'Religion and
Nation.' It was not known whether these two elements in Judaism—
the religious and the national—were mutually exclusive, or merely
compatible or even interdependent.

On consideration it would appear that some progress has been
achieved at any rate in this field, a fact which may serve to
strengthen the true friend of mankind, whatever his nationality, in
the hope that even in the densest jungle humanity moves slowly but
surely forward. One goal at least is clearly defined, if still far distant,
and those who are aspiring towards it can seek to enlist sympathy
and understanding. In those days, in 1789, no such ideas existed
even in embryo. Nobody knew what they wanted, neither the Jews
themselves, nor their friends, nor even their enemies. The last named,
one would have thought, would have experienced the least difficulty

in knowing the right goal and the right means to achieve it, humanity seemingly being more gifted and efficiently equipped for destruction than for construction. But even the opponents of the Jews were mistaken in the measures they suggested, which, had they been applied, would have achieved the opposite—namely the Jews' moral advancement—of what they intended.

What, then, were the results of the intellectual conflicts regarding the status of the Jews which were then being conducted in such an atmosphere of confusion and lack of understanding on all sides? The French National Assembly confirmed on the 28th September, 1791, the individual—not national—equality of the Jews. Their emancipation was embodied indirectly in the constitution which had been approved by the King a fortnight previously, and which the Constituent Assembly had already discussed for two years, in the general principle that no political discrimination was to be exercised against members of any religious denomination. It had been thought necessary, however, in view of the strong opposition, to lay down, in explicit terms, the application of this general principle to the Jews. In the wake of the French revolutionary armies this principle conquered Belgium, Holland, Switzerland, parts of Italy and Germany, including in the latter country the Duchy of Jülich-Berg, of which Düsseldorf was the capital. Under Napoleon, however, there was a set-back. 'The attitude of the world-conqueror to a nation which could not be conquered by the world was a mixture of baseness and greatness' (Dubnow). Napoleon, unlike his contemporaries, saw in the Jews not a sect but a nation. From this premise, correct in itself, he proceeded to enact as early as 1806 special anti-Jewish legislation. His 'Grand Sanhedrin' was a farce; although enthusiastically greeted by the Jews, its purpose was solely to denationalize them and exercise a sharper control on their call-up for military service. The *Décret Infâme* of 1808 deprived them in important respects of the civil equality and the freedom of movement which had been granted them by the Revolution, and ruined thousands economically. Many Jews, particularly the Notables among them, had believed in Napoleon's love for the Jews till then. The sagacious Dubnow comments:

> The former President, Furtado, and certain other respected members of the Assembly of Notables, heard of the impending

decree. They immediately hastened to the imperial residence at Fontainebleau to protest at this infraction of the law, but they were not received. Napoleon no longer needed the services of the Jewish Notables. Under the cloak of peace and friendship he deprived them of everything he could lay his hands on and later rode rough-shod over them. It was not Napoleon who had deceived the Jews, but the Jews who had deceived themselves by taking his stage décor for reality. The Emperor was true to himself: two years previously he had said in the Imperial Council that it was not the civil, but the political code which should be applied to the Jews, and he now applied his international code of fire and sword to them.

Admittedly the position of the Jews in the territories occupied by France was one of ' liberty ' compared with their position in the rest of Germany, where they were merely ' tolerated,' possessed the right of domicile only as an act of grace, and enjoyed no political restriction of their freedom to marry. Nevertheless, the refusal to grant them their autonomy as a national-cultural group, and the rights except those of paying special dues and taxes and being assimilated which the French policy forced on them, or at any rate made easy for them, were a minor blemish in the French handling of the Jewish question. It is true that at this period there was not—even among the Jews—the slightest understanding of, or desire for, national-cultural autonomy. For the Jews their spiritual existence, assured them by their religious way of life, incursions of the Jewish religion into secular and communal life sufficed. Increasingly it came to be thought that the few existing could be dispensed with ; all that was needed, and what in fact in some cases had been achieved, at least on paper, was civil equality with the surrounding population. At the same time the Jewish religion itself was weakened from within by the prevailing universal religions of Reason and Deism and the belief that all religions had a common basis. Nathan's three rings seemed completely interchangeable. Why cling, then, to the one which differed in no essential respect from the others but was more burdensome in daily life. Only a few customs and ceremonies stubbornly and unreasonably made the answering of such over-astute questioning unnecessarily difficult. Nobody knew really why they had not long since been discarded, these customs and ceremonies. Because of habit, tradition ; perhaps because of a half-unconscious fear of the void. There was nothing national about them, for the Jews were not a nation—'France is our Palestine, its mountains are our Zion,' was the Jewish slogan in Paris—nor could they be essentially religious, for all religion could be expressed in Deism, the religion of Reason, and a few had heard that Deism itself was now a thing of the past. The Jews, after all, read Kant; Moses Mendelssohn made the pilgrimage to Königsberg.

In Heine's youth this whole process of transforming the closely knit ghetto way of life into a new pattern of living, with all the violent upheavals it entailed, had not yet run its course, but everything was ready for it to start; it was in the air. And so we see Harry Heine as a child anxiously keeping all the commandments that had been drummed into him at home, but without believing in them or getting any sense out of them. Invoking the fourth commandment, the child refused to help put out a fire on a Saturday. On another Saturday he bit off the grapes one by one from a neighbour's vine. 'Red Harry!' his playmates exclaimed in horror, 'what have you done?' 'Nothing bad,' he laughed, 'I mustn't pick the grapes with my hand, but the Law doesn't stop us biting them off with our teeth and eating them.'

Empty casuistry of this kind was probably the result of his religious education, both that which he received in the parental home and that which was imparted to him in Rintelsohn's private Jewish school. Before going to Rintelsohn's school Heine had attended the public primary school, which was situated in a Franciscan monastery. In 1811 he passed on to the French *Lyceum* (*Gymnasium*), which was run by Catholic priests. Nevertheless, the early Jewish impressions always retained their hold on him. Witness not only the description of the *seder* (Passover) night in the *Rabbi von Bacharach*, but even more clearly, because he was less consciously striving for effect, passages such as the following (*Die Stadt Lucca*, Chapter X): 'On her way out of the cathedral she dipped her first finger three times in the holy water, sprinkled it on her person each time, and murmured: *Dem Zefardeyim Kinnim*, which she declared to be an Arabic incantation used by sorceresses for changing human beings into donkeys.' These three outlandish words, however, are not and never were an Arabic incantation, but the Hebrew names of the first three of the ten plagues in Egypt.

The recital of the plagues, accompanied by sprinkling (of wine, with the finger) is a feature of the ritual for the two Passover evenings. Incidentally, Heine's Hebrew here is incorrect, like practically everything he quotes from this language. His knowledge of Hebrew must have been extremely tenuous, limited probably to a few conjugations, whose queer sound to German ears he once compared—with not particularly good taste—to the ticking of a clock.

A more substantial result of his early Hebrew education was the inspiration it gave him for his poem *Belshazzar*. Heine told Ludwig Kalisch in 1849 that he took the idea of the poem from the *seder* service when he was sixteen. The original is the magnificent midnight poem with the line: ' He who drank from holy vessels was slain—in the same night.' In fact Heine's poem is clearly inspired by this line, and not by the account in the Book of Daniel, whose climax is the writing on the wall. The very beginning of the poem—

> Die Mitternacht zog näher schon

calls to mind the refrain in the Hebrew: *Va-yehi ba-chatsi ha-layela* (And it came to pass at midnight) and conjures up the tense midnight mood when the pious poet of the early Middle Ages (his name: Yannai) sends all the idols toppling from their pedestals and consigns the oppressors of Israel to oblivion—till the approach of the day which is ' neither day nor night.' There are verses in this ancient poem which for sheer strength and beauty may take their place with the finest lyrical productions of all time. The powerful impression they made on the young poet is not difficult to understand. Moreover, I know more than one Jewish family which has retained nothing of Jewish tradition save only the impressively honest, simple, and rich *seder* night ritual (only that which is completely honest and earnest can unite the normally opposing qualities of wealth and simplicity). Even this meagre and decreasing remnant, however, has sufficed to perpetuate a genuine feeling for Judaism ; even so slender a thread sufficed for the handing down of the treasures of the past to the future.

We shall not go far wrong in thinking of Rintelsohn's school, to which Heine was indebted for the elements of his Jewish knowledge, as a *Talmud Torah* of the type which existed throughout Eastern Europe, with the exception of Russia, until the annihilation

of East European Jewry in the 1939-45 war. Moreover, the language
spoken by the Jews of Düsseldorf contained at least parts of the
vocabulary of ' Yiddish '—or ' Jargon ' as it was called—as well
as the characteristic Yiddish intonation. Their mixed German-
Hebrew vernacular,which Mendelssohn opposed, was another factor
separating the Jews from their neighbours, who spoke High German
or pure German dialects. Berthold Auerbach (' poet and merchant ')
—to take an instance—described this vernacular as a ' bad German
disfigured by Hebrew phrases.' The ' educated ' Jews of Germany,
particularly in Berlin, boycotted it. In the non-German environment
of Eastern Europe and America, however, it crystallized into a fully
developed language with its own grammar and syntax. Such a
development would in any case have been impossible in a German
environment, owing to the fluid nature of the boundaries between
the two languages, and, in fact, no attempt was made to crystallize
the Jewish dialect, so that it petered out without a struggle. With it,
succumbing to the onslaught of secular education, disappeared a
great Jewish tradition ; it is not too much to say, the Jewish Middle
Ages. In Heine's early style, however, traces of the old linguistic
usage are discernible in his frequently jarring syntax and in many
other details (for instance, confusion of cases in the earliest letters).
From the ' Jargon ' point of view Heine's usage is seen to be
consistent and grammatical, incorrect though it is as a ' pure
German.' The numerous Hebrew words in the *Romanzero*, however,
are called for by the poem's subject matter and intentionally introduced by Heine for artistic effect.

Jewish pedagogical methods are brought to mind by Heine in
an episode of the *Romanzero*, although the poet deviates from
biographical fact in ascribing the tuition mentioned in the episode
to his father and not to the paid family teacher. Here are the
opening verses of this episode (the succeeding verses, with their
succinct account of the two leading elements in the *Talmud*,
Halacha, and *Hagada*—instruction and legend—are important, too,
as showing the development of Heine's Jewish education):

> Für Entwicklung seines Geistes
> Sorgte früh der strenge Vater,
> Der den Unterricht begann
> Mit dem Gottesbuch, der Thora.

Diese las er mit dem Sohne
In dem Urtext, dessen schöne
Hieroglyphisch pittoreske,
Altchaldäische Quadratschrift

Herstammt aus dem Kindesalter
Unsrer Welt; und auch deswegen
Jedem kindlichen Gemüte
So vertraut entgegenlacht.

Diesen echten alten Text
Rezitierte auch der Knabe
In der uralt hergebrachten
Singsang-Weise, Tropp geheissen

Und er gurgelte gar lieblich
Jene fetten Gutturalen
Und er schlug dabei den Triller,
Den Schalscheleth, wie ein Vogel.

Father undertook to teach him,
Bringing out his mental powers,
Began with stern insistence
At the book of books, the Torah.

This he read with love paternal,
Read it with the boy in Hebrew,
In those lovely hieroglyphic
Square-shaped Chaldee characters

Springing from the dawn of ancient
History, and to every child appealing,
In these letters seeing, hearing
Man's first child-like undertakings.

And the boy recited sing-song
Fashion, cantillation called,
Finding beauty in the age-old
Story, in the Hebrew Bible,

Warbling like a bird in heaven,
Gurgling gutturals *con amore,*
Lingering on the chain of notes
Whose name in Hebrew is Shalshelet.

The Jesuit *lycée,* French teachers—a complete contrast!
In 1806, when Düsseldorf was incorporated into the Grand
Duchy of Berg, the entire Düsseldorf *arrondissement* numbered

five hundred and seventy Jews—a dwindling minority. Now that the cultural barriers were down and the minds of the Jews receptive to new ideas it was no wonder that their environment began to exert a wholly disproportionate influence on them. From his sick bed Heine, then advanced in years, told a visitor :

As a matter of fact, I have always had a liking for Catholicism which dates from my youth and is attributable to the kindness I received at the hands of Catholic priests. One of these, Schallmeyer, was a friend of my father's and taught us philosophy at school. He got round the school time-table by various means and arranged for me to attend his philosophy lessons when I was only fourteen. I understood everything he said quite well. He was genuinely liberal in his views, but experienced no difficulty in celebrating Mass in his priestly vestments, just like his brother priests, even though the previous day his teaching might have been of the most liberal kind. As a result, from my youth up, I have always been accustomed to seeing nothing incompatible between Freethought and Catholicism. Catholic rites have for me always been something merely beautiful, recalling pleasant youthful memories, and I have never seen in them anything harmful to the development of mankind. I don't know whether you will understand me rightly, but I have always had this feeling. It is something quite personal, something I can do nothing about. There is another youthful memory linked up with it, too. When my parents moved out of the little house we lived in at first, my father bought one of the most imposing residences in Düsseldorf, on the processional route. With the house went the privilege of setting up an altar for the processions, and my father made it a point of honour to beautify this altar as lavishly as his means allowed. The days when the passion-tide altar was decorated were always festivals for me in which I took great pleasure. However, it only lasted till the Prussians came, they took away our privilege from us.

It is evident, therefore, that it is not the dogma of strict Catholicism that prevailed among Heine's teachers and exerted its influence on him, but—together with the whole apparatus of romantic-æsthetic charm and the radiations of Catholic culture and temperament—it was Catholic Enlightenment, Catholic Rationalism that influenced him—the same ideas that in Bohemia found a great leader in the philosopher Bolzano. Eduard Winter's excellent book, *Bernard Bolzano und sein Kreis,* published by Hegner in 1933, gives

a full account of this movement—hitherto insufficiently appreciated
—and of its struggles with official Catholicism.

Winter is opposed to Catholic Rationalism but discusses it
objectively. The parallel between Catholic Rationalism and what
Lessing sought to do for Protestantism and Mendelssohn for
Judaism becomes clear in the following analysis by Winter:

> 'The love of neighbour is the central commandment of
> Christianity—*lex fundamentalis ecclesiæ est lex caritatis*,' writes
> Rautenstreich in his private journal. It is in the active practice
> of love of neighbour that Christianity serves the welfare of
> mankind. All dogmas are viewed in the light of their usefulness
> for the general welfare of the community and are, if necessary,
> softened or placed in the background. And Dobrowsky says in
> a letter of 9th June 1783 to his friend—Helfert—after reading
> the neologist Steinbart: 'I found the abominable doctrine of
> Original Sin and of All-prevailing Grace repellent in the
> extreme.' Dogma, for the Roman Catholic no less than for
> the Protestant neologists, can be only 'submission to happiness
> in accordance with the teaching of Jesus.' In the circles of the
> Roman Catholic Enlightenment efforts were made to achieve
> a 'popular dogma.' In contrast to the Canisian Catechism,[1] this
> popular dogma was intended, by deriving from each individual
> dogma highly fruitful moral lessons, to liberate the whole body
> of Catholic dogma from the sterility into which it had fallen.

It was in this guise, transparent in its simplicity and in its lack
of problems, that Catholicism presented itself to Heine. In his
Hamburg period he adopted a Madonna cult. All this, however,
was quite compatible with his inveighing (*Norderney*) against 'the
old spider of the Cross,' the Roman prelacy.

Heine's education at the *Lyceum* was not only undertaken by
Frenchmen; it was conducted in the very spirit of France. He says
of one of his teachers:

> . . . When the first intelligence of the battle (of Leipzig)
> reached us, he shook his grey head. I know now what that
> shaking of the head signified. Soon there came more detailed
> reports, and we secretly circulated gay pictures showing the
> German generals kneeling on the battle-field and giving thanks
> to God in a most edifying manner. Yes, they could thank God
> —said my teacher, smiling as he used to when he expounded

---

[1] So called after its author, Peter Canisius de Hondt, a Dutch Jesuit
(1521-1597).

Sallust to us—the Emperor Napoleon has thrashed them so often that at last they've been able to learn the lesson he taught them.
Heine was even asked to write French verse. And when he openly admitted his dislike of the metrical system of French poetry and of the *art de peindre par les images,* his teacher of French, the émigré Abbé d'Aulnoi, an elderly little man with an ill-fitting wig, called him a barbarian out of the Teutoburg Forest.

I still recalled with horror having to translate the speech of Caiaphas to the Sanhedrin from the hexameters of Klopstock's *Messiah* (in the professor's chrestomathy) into French alexandrines. It was a refinement of cruelty worse even than the agonies of the Messiah's own passion, and which even the Messiah himself would not have suffered without protest. God forgive me, I cursed the world and the foreign oppressors who inflicted these metrics on us, and I almost became a Francophobe. I could have died for France, but write French verse— nevermore !

And so Heine's early years, although essentially happy and tranquil, prefigured in all their main features the later being whose complicated character was misunderstood, or at best inadequately appreciated, by practically all his contemporaries—not that these complications in Heine's character have been unravelled even now. In these early years there are *Jewish* elements, *Christian* influences, and *French* and *German* impacts on the boy's soul. Nor was the German spiritual impact limited to folk saga and the demons of Teutonic mythology. It was a matter of flesh and blood. Heine was affected by the best kind of German *Mensch,* exemplified in his schoolfriend Christian Sethe, who inspired the youthful verses : ' Du aber standest fest gleich einem Turme ;/Ein Leuchtturm war dein Kopf mir in dem Sturme,/Dem treues Herz war mir ein guter Hafen '—But you stood firm as a rock, you were a lighthouse in the storm-tossed seas, your faithful heart was a sure haven for me.

He was violent both in his loves and hates. The first words we hear him speak he uttered as a four-year-old, a solitary little boy among the little girls in Frau Hinderman's's kindergarten. He had filled Frau Hindermans's snuff-box with sand and had been duly admonished by the teacher. When she asked him why he did it little Harry answered in emphatic tones : ' Because I hate you ! '
An old cook to whom he had been rude—she had refused to

give him the wax candles he needed for his incessant reading—
complained to his father ' and called him a naughty boy who said
anything that came into his head.' Heine's sister and playmate,
Charlotte, relates this story, and it is from her we learn of his
first rhyming efforts and his aversion to violin practice. The old
cook was right in her characterization of the boy. In later years,
too, Heine often—all too often—said anything that came into his
head. He was sorry for it afterwards, wanted what he had done
to be undone. In vain : the enemies he had thus carelessly made
stood firm in a solid phalanx with their weapons poised against
him. These outbursts of hatred remained a part of his personality
he could never eliminate, any more than he could eliminate his
devotion to the cause of the disinherited and the underprivileged
or his proud and noble readiness to help those in need. This
readiness to help shows itself in his youthful love of the ostracized
hangman's daughter (' I kissed her not merely out of tender
affection but also as a demonstration of my contempt for the old
order and its dark prejudices '), and in his intimacy with a school-
fellow disliked by everyone else, one Joseph Levy, the son of a
corn merchant who had a notorious reputation as an usurer. Bieber
(*Confessio Judaica*) says of this fellow pupil of Heine's and Sethe's
at the Düsseldorf *Lyceum* : ' He was badly treated by his father
and avoided by most of his schoolfellows because of his reserved
disposition and peculiar ways. Heine's family strongly disapproved
of their son's association with him.' Heine and he met in secret,
had long talks on philosophy, read the works of Spinoza together.
Heine's letter from Hamburg to Sethe, dated 6th July, 1816,
mentions him : ' Above all, dear Christian, I must beg of you to
befriend poor Levy. It is the voice of humanity you hear. I implore
you by everything you hold holy to help him. He is in the direst
straits. My hearts bleeds. I can't say much ; the words burn in my
flesh.'

There is something symbolic in the fact that this letter comes
at the beginning of Heine's collected correspondence. The actual
circumstances to which the passage quoted refers can no longer
be ascertained, but the words themselves glow brightly with active
sympathy, with the desire to intervene in others' lives, with everything that in a good person may germinate into social feeling and
political passion.

III

The ' Blow to the Heart '

IT WAS DUE to the loving care by which he was surrounded in
the parental home that Harry experienced only two symbols of
out-groupness in his childhood ; Sefchen and Levy, the despised
desperado. Otherwise, all was good breeding, refined manners,
time-hallowed conceptions of propriety. There was a touch of rather
old-fashioned primness about the family circle, for all Betty Heine's
liveliness of disposition. It was indeed Harry's mother who
impressed on her children the rule that when invited out they must
not eat up everything that was put on the table. They must leave
something over, she told them, ' the respect.' And Heine's brother,
Max, tells a charming story of how Harry, who was older than he,
had once ' told on him ' to their mother : ' Mama, would you believe
it, Max ate up the respect.'

It was an age, however, that showed scant respect for ' respects '
and such-like refinements. The parental home that had sheltered
the children so comfortably collapsed. No doubt the different
trading conditions that followed Napoleon's defeat and Heine
père's lack of business ability were equally responsible for this
catastrophe. Heine's father was not a Jew of the resilient, adaptable
type, able to turn lightly from one business to another. At all events,
the 1814 plans for Heine's higher education and university career
had to be suspended. He was sent to a commercial school in
Düsseldorf, and in the autumn of 1815 he had to go to Frankfurt
as a business trainee.

As a potential business man, of course, Heine proved a complete failure, but even in terms of personal experience the Frankfurt period seems to have flitted by leaving barely a trace. He hardly mentions it anywhere in his writings, although as a rule he vividly recalled every place, every station on his life's journey ; with such a subjective writer, always ready to distil his autobiographical experiences into literary form, it could hardly be otherwise. Only on Frankfurt is he almost silent. Apart from the fine poem *Erinnerung*, with its vivid descriptions and its resonant last line, and the second chapter of the *Rabbi von Bacharach*, in which he uses his privilege as an artist to reshape extensively his material, setting the period of action far back into the Middle Ages, I can find scarcely anything of importance to mention. In the romance-fragment which is the *Rabbi von Bacharach* the ghetto atmosphere is faithfully conveyed. The Jews in Frankfurt lived under a far more oppressive régime than did their coreligionists in the comfortable Rhineland. Moreover, after the fall of Napoleon the Frankfurt municipality immediately reverted to its former harshly discriminatory treatment of the Jews, whereas in the Rhineland, even under the Prussians, the French legislation affecting the Jews remained unchanged. The second chapter of the *Rabbi* gives an exceptionally clear picture of the hostility felt towards the Jews in Frankfurt, and of the unfavourable effects which the atmosphere of hatred and fear they breathed had on the Jewish national character. Heine's description culminates in the memorable words which Rabbi Abrahams addresses amid sighs to his wife after their first strange impressions of the entrance to the ghetto. ' See, my beautiful Sarah,' says Rabbi Abrahams immediately the ghetto gates close on them, ' how miserably is Israel protected ! False friends guard his gates outside ; and inside, his guardians are fear and folly.'

There is no doubt that this was Heine's résumé of his unhappy Frankfurt period, viewed though it was in the perspective of his later years when he was better able to evaluate the great happenings of his time. Only once was there a flash, when he described an incident in the reading room of a Freemasons' Lodge to which his father had taken him. A stranger pointed out to him Börne, who had already become famous, with the words : ' That is Dr. Börne, who writes against actors.' On this occasion Heine only stared from

afar ; he was the only one of the two to be affected by this encounter
with the man to whom in later years he was to be irresistibly
drawn ; the man with whom he had so much in common, yet to
whom he was diametrically opposed in so much more. But the
spark caught. Even after a lapse of many years Heine believed he
could ' reproduce with diplomatic precision ' the impression Börne
made on him at the time. He was spellbound. He uses remarkably
forceful language :

> Is there some mysterious aura radiating from exceptionally
> strong personalities ? Do we glimpse some such effulgence with
> our mind's eye, invisible though it be to our bodily eye ?
> Perhaps the moral thunderstorm in an extraordinary personality
> has an electric effect on young people who approach him with
> unblunted minds, as a physical thunderstorm has on cats. A
> spark from this man's eye caught me, I don't know how, but
> I never forgot this contact, and I never forgot Dr. Börne, who
> wrote against actors.

It is characteristic that this one positive impression surviving
from the Frankfurt period should emanate from the spiritual sphere.
Trade and commerce he hated ; he revolted against it and jeered
at the ' big stores, Christian as well as Jewish,' which his father
showed him at the Frankfurt Fair, ' where you buy ten per cent
below factory price and are cheated just the same.'

His dislike of business is expressed in the same unmistakable
terms in a letter he wrote to Sethe in 1816. By now he was in
Hamburg, whither his rich uncle Salomon had taken him as a
junior clerk in the bank of Heckscher & Co. (Salomon Heine's
trading style). He writes to Sethe : ' The Muse has seemingly
forsaken me and has left me to journey North alone. She is a
woman, after all. Or is she terrified of my terrific business activities ?
It's true this is a pretty foul commercial dump, anyway. Whores
in plenty, but no Muses. Many a German bard has sung himself
into a consumption here.' And then follow some verses describing
a visit to Klopstock's grave, beginning : ' Als ich ging nach Ottensen
hin, auf Klopstocks Grab gewesen ich bin '—On a visit to Ottensen
I stood by Klopstock's grave—and ending : ' Meine seele war da
unten tief, wo der heilige deutsche Sänger schlief '—My soul was
deep down there below, where the holy German poet slept.

This youthful letter is clear enough, or so one would have

thought. It seems all the more incomprehensible that a serious
biographer of Heine (Max I. Wolff, 1922), obviously concerned to
assess his subject fairly, can say that in those early years Heine
felt no urge within himself to become a poet. This biographer
declares that Heine had settled down to business very well and had,
indeed, displayed a certain business acumen. At that time he had
' no objection in principle to a business career, even his wooing
of his beloved cousin Amalie was not wholly divorced from business
considerations, he was reckoning on doing well for himself with her
money, etc.'

There must be special motives leading an author to make completely false assertions of this kind when all the documentary
evidence points so clearly to the contrary. One such obvious motive
is the widespread, practically universal belief that all Jews are good
at business and work hard at it. But as well as practical, realistic
Jews, whom I for one do not underestimate, and who constitute
an element by no means unimportant for the preservation of
Judaism's vitality, there have always been numerous Jewish
dreamers and enthusiasts. More important, there have always been
Jews who were pure mind, with a gift for theory or belief or formal
beauty. And, of course, all the gradations and amalgams of
gradations between the two extremes. In the form in which I have
stated it, this is banal. But there is nothing banal whatever in the
frenzied attempts which are continually being made by non-Jewish
observers of Judaism to reduce to *one common denominator* these
two opposite types which are to be found in the Jewish no less
than in other peoples. Nothing banal in asserting this common
denominator, assumed *ex hypothesi* rather than actually experienced,
to be the characteristic quality of Judaism, call this quality
materialism, calculatingness, or anything you like. It's not as simple
as that, but just because of these preconceived notions about Jewish
psychology even well disposed authors can arrive at wrong conclusions in certain particulars. (Among the ' well-disposed authors,'
I include the Heine biographer from whom I have quoted ; he is
not anti-Semitic, and always observes a just proportion both in
praise and blame.) Abstract notions of this kind are particularly
treacherous when attempting to grasp the essence of a nature as
complicated as was Heine's. Unless they are abandoned one runs
the risk of distorting, wrongly evaluating, even those feelings of

the poet which are clearly attested in print, let alone those which are not vouched for, and which often cannot be vouched for, in print.

No, Heine was not calculating, and not of a prudent disposition. The son of a father whose business had failed and a mother who saw everything in the clear light of reason, he was condemned and privileged all his life to seek the mean between the light of progress and a twilight that filled him with foreboding. It is just in the description of this quest of a mean as elusive and impalpable as it was vibrant in its intensity, that perhaps this book will reveal Heine's true significance.

For our present purpose it suffices that Heine had no head for business, precisely because his was not a calculating temperament. His attitude to money was always non-capitalistic, non-Puritan. He liked spending money, not earning and saving it. He enjoyed money, but he valued it only as a means to an end, the end being the enjoyment of life. Money was never for him the be-all and end-all, the creative monster shaping his life. ' Say where have you got to, my golden ducats ? ' is a line in one of his first *Lieder*. Apart from displaying a certain touch of Victorian paternalism towards his beloved wife Mathilde, ' the big spender '— actually he loved her as much for her childish light-hearted spending as for anything else—Heine himself was always light-hearted and extravagant where money was concerned ; always the grand seigneur in relation to lucre, never its slave. This is one of Heine's few invariable traits whose existence is beyond dispute.

Not that Heine was ever indifferent to money. In his German period and at the beginning of his Paris period his love of good living induced in him a financial awareness ; while in his old age, when he was ill and persecuted, he had all too good reason to fear the poverty which was always ' just round the corner.' He knew that the life story of many an author resembled that of ' Philipp Reiser,'[1] and was nothing but ' the tale of a few hundred thalers which the author did not possess, and through the lack of which his whole life became a series of deprivations and " going without." ' For squalid tragedy of this kind he had no taste. Nevertheless— money was never an end in itself for him.

---

[1] Presumably an allusion to Karl Philipp Moritz's (1757-1793) auto-biographical novel *Anton Reiser*.

Uncle Salomon was the very reverse. He was the hero of money, the representative of the ambitious early capitalistic era, the self-made man who had come up the hard way, and who knew quite well that the respect in which he was held in Hamburg was due entirely to his wealth.

For Hamburg, in contrast to Catholic Düsseldorf, was anti-Jewish. Or rather, only the rich Jews were tolerated. Dubnow writes:

> As a result of the occupation of Hamburg by the French troops (1810), the town was incorporated directly into the French Empire, and Jewish emancipation was granted immediately and without a struggle (1811). All restrictions on domicile, acquisition of real estate, commerce, trade and school education were abolished; a few Jews were even elected to the Municipal Council. . . . The emancipation granted by the French disappeared with them, however, when the German Liberation Army occupied Hamburg at the beginning of 1814. The sons of Hamburg Jewry who fought in the ranks of this Army did not suspect that the liberation of the German Fatherland would lead to a renewal of the enslavement of the Jewish people.

The new restrictions affected all Jews except wealthy ones like Salomon Heine or the banker Christian Gumpel who later was a victim of the shafts of Heine's satire—he makes an early appearance in *Buch Le Grand,* and later turns up in *Die Bäder von Lucca.* It is hardly surprising that such men, who knew from experience that their social position, their freedom of intercourse, their dignities, stemmed entirely from their wealth, should have viewed money in an altogether different light from that in which it was regarded by a youth interested only in versifying and a poet's grave. Since Salomon, too, was a strong personality who led his own life, the clash between him and his nephew was destined perforce to be one of fateful violence.

Heine was not prepared to make allowances for the conditioning effects of Jewish history as reflected in the Jews' social position and the altogether exceptional importance of money to them. He took no notice whatever of history as a plea in mitigation; he saw only the contrast between two worlds. ' My mother read *belles lettres,* and I became a poet ; my uncle's mother, on the other hand, read (the bandit chief) Cartouche, and Uncle Salomon became a banker.'

It was obvious that when the uncle got to hear of aphorisms of this kind, which were, moreover, merely a reflection of the nephew's general demeanour, the relations between the two were soon bound to become strained. And all the time Harry was entirely dependent on his uncle's grace and favour ; there had been a drastic worsening in his parents' economic position. They were unable to finance a resumption of his studies once they had been broken off. In any event, owing to Austro-Prussian reaction (Metternich), Jewish prospects in the professions were again far from encouraging, so that a commercial career seemed unavoidable. It is certain that Heine never even tentatively considered the idea of leaving his trainee post in his uncle's bank for another such post elsewhere. It would have needed at best a certain measure of acceptance of the métier in which he found himself for him to have displayed an initiative of this kind. But Heine did not accept this métier at all. And so he found himself imprisoned in his uncle's bank as in a gilded family cage.

Salomon Heine did a great deal for his nephew, but, it would seem, always unwillingly, and without any real understanding. No surer proof of this could be needed than the fact that he set up his nephew in a textile business. In 1817 Heine was in fact the head of 'Harry Heine & Co.' The firm's life was of short duration ; it went into liquidation in 1818. It appears that Heinrich Heine could only seldom be found at his business. He preferred sitting by the bank of the Alster and watching the swans and the stars and the girls passing by, as may be read in more detail in *Schnabelewopski*.

Heine was unhappy in the alien surroundings of Hamburg. The transition from his beloved romantic Düsseldorf, the city of his youth, to this hard-headed business world of Hamburg must have been like plunging into ice-cold water for him. 'It is not foul Macbeth, but Banquo who reigns here.' He felt himself right out of his orbit, he had horror-struck visions startling in their immediacy. Suddenly Hamburg's main street, the Jungfernstieg, would appear to him—

> In that moment I made the appalling discovery that all those faces were blanketed with an expression of impenetrable idiocy, and that all the people passing by seemed to be afflicted with a strange lunacy. The life of these people who visit the Stock Exchange, invite each other into their houses,

move their cheeks, pay their *pourboires,* is based on the axiom that twice two is four. Shocking ! I cried. Supposing while one of these characters was sitting on his stool at the bar he was suddenly to get an idea into his head that twice two made five, and that he had miscalculated his whole life, and that he had spent his whole life in a ghastly mistake.

And at the head of this alien world stood Uncle Salomon, powerful, uncomprehending, sometimes very kind ; at other times refusing to give him what he needed and what he had long come to consider as his just due, of which the most unkindest example was his will, which so darkened Heine's last years. At a time when Heine had achieved a recognized fame, this was bad enough. How much harder must the head of the family's lack of understanding have been for the tyro who was feeling his way and had just published some pseudonymous verses in a local Hamburg paper.

This was in 1818. The pseudonym was Sy Freudhold Riesenharf, an anagram of Harry Heine Düsseldorf. His uncle's remark in later years is well known : ' If the silly boy had learnt something, he wouldn't have needed to write books.' And when Platen's attack on Heine appeared, Salomon quipped : ' Honestly, you know, Henry, old Platen's hit you off pretty well.'

Heine found it particularly vexing that his relatives, the ' family clan ' so often ridiculed by him, should have taken such malicious pleasure in siding with the young author's opponents, and with those who were jealous of him or retailed gossip about him. All the same, this state of war was inevitable, for the nephew and uncle spoke different languages. This was quite literally so ; in Salomon's *obiter dicta* and letters there can still be detected elements of the Judæo-German from which Heine had escaped since his Rintelsohn schooldays and of which the whole of that particular Jewish generation was striving to divest itself. Probably the whole atmosphere in Salomon's household corresponded to his linguistic usage ; they were in the acutely embarrassing half-way stage, fully ripe for assimilation, but completely unassimilated, both socially and in their way of living, in actual fact.

Heinrich Heine must have felt himself to be the more progressive, more sensitive and more perceptive member of the family on all counts, reduced to an unworthy dependence by economic necessity. (The situation was reproduced, though with less intensity

—Heine could afford to be satirical about it—in his association with the Paris Rothschild : ' Ich ward gedrängt von schwarzen Sorgen, ich musste lügen, ich musste borgen bei reichen Buben und alten Vetteln—ich glaube sogar, ich musste betteln.'—I was oppressed by black cares, I had to lie, I had to borrow from rich scoundrels and old hags ; I think I even had to beg.)

It was an intolerable situation, made even worse in Hamburg by the frustrations and disappointments to which youth is so keenly sensitive. Nor were the ' youthful sorrows ' mitigated by the fact that the ' gruff Northern bear,' whom one watched as one did a weathercock, sometimes had his good days. It did not help that, as Heine puts it in a letter to Frau Robert, uncle and nephew were greatly alike in character and temperament—' the same truculence, the same incredible soft-heartedness and unpredictable madness.' It availed nothing that the uncle could be generous, that he had never once left his nephew in the lurch (broadly speaking), and indeed had often supported him in the most extraordinarily liberal fashion.

Salomon was in fact a philanthropist. He had founded that ' hospital for poor, sick Jews ' which inspired one of Heine's finest poems. In the poem the uncle is depicted as a ' dear soul,' as ' wise and lovable '—and it can be taken for granted that the display of these virtues was not limited to this one occasion, but that they were often genuinely in evidence :

> Ein Mann der Tat, tat er, was eben tunlich ;
> Für gute Werke gab er hin den Taglohn
> Am Abend seines Lebens, menschenfreundlich
> Durch Wohltun sich erholend von der Arbeit.

> Er gab mit reicher Hand—doch reichre Spende
> Entrollte manchmal seinem Aug', die Träne,
> Die kostbar schöne Träne, die er weinte
> Ob der unheilbar grossen Brüderkrankheit.

A man of action, he did that which he was able to do. In the evening of his life he gave what he had earned by day for good works, and in helping his fellow creatures he found respite from his labours. His gifts of money were generous, but more lavish than these was the gift of the tear that glistened in his eye ; the beautiful, precious tear he shed for the great incurable disease of his brethren.

How finely Heine limns his uncle in this poem! His portrayal of him as a great, authentically Jewish figure is perfect and irreproachable in its sentiment. It does credit to Heine's Jewish feeling, that Jewish feeling which holds the practice of charity and good deeds in far higher esteem than is usual with other peoples. Many are the praises that have been sung of ' noble misfortunes ' (my book: *Heidentum, Christentum, Judentum* has something to say on the subject) ; Heine's hospital poem is one of the few works of art which deal with what I call ' ignoble ' (curable) misfortune. Yet the very admiration and esteem which Heine in all sincerity felt for his uncle must have made the latter's caprices and his failure to understand the young poet's mind all the more wounding. Hence the ' warning ' he sounds in the *Last Poems* :

> Verletze nicht durch kalten Ton
> Den Jüngling, welcher dürftig, fremd
> Um Hilfe bittend zu dir kömmt—
> Er ist vielleicht ein Göttersohn

> Oh, injure not through frigid tone
> The needy stranger-youth who comes
> Into your home and begs for help—
> Perhaps he is of gods the son.

It was the ' frigid tone ' which acted as a barrier between uncle and nephew, despite the occasions when the monthly remittance was everything that could be desired. In his old age Heine, still smarting with grief, sums up all these ' injuries.' He describes the *Affrontenburg,* his uncle's luxurious villa in Ottensen which is the scene of all the refined snubbing and chicanery and heart-aches he has been forced to endure :

> Die Zeit verfliesst, jedoch das Schloss,
> Das alte Schloss mit Turm und Zinne
> Und seinem blöden Menschenvolk,
> Es kommt mir nimmer aus dem Sinne.

> Ich sehe stets die Wetterfahn',
> Die auf dem Dach sich rasselnd drehte.
> Ein jeder blickte scheu hinauf,
> Bevor er nur den Mund aufthäte.

Wer sprechen wollt', erforschte erst
Den Wind, aus Furcht, es möchte plötzlich
Der alte Brummbär Boreas
Anschnauben ihn nicht sehr ergötzlich.

Die klügsten freilich schwiegen ganz—
Denn ach, es gab an jenem Orte
Ein Echo, das im Wiederklatsch
Boshaft verfälschte alle Worte.

Inmitten im Schlossgarten stand
Ein sphinxgezierter Marmorbrunnen,
Der immer trocken war, obgleich
Gar manche Träne dort geronnen.

Vermaledeiter Garten! Ach,
Da gab es nirgend eine Stätte,
Wo nicht mein Herz gekränket war,
Wo nicht mein Aug' geweinet hätte.

Da gabs wahrhaftig keinen Baum,
Worunter nicht Beleidigungen
Mir zugefüget worden sind
Von feinen und von groben Zungen.

Die Kröte, die im Gras gelauscht,
Hat alles mitgeteilt der Ratte,
Die ihrer Muhme Viper gleich
Erzählet, was sie vernommen hatte.

Die hat's gesagt dem Schwager Frosch
Und solcherweis erfahren konnte
Die ganze schmutz'ge Sippschaft stracks
Die mir erwiesenen Affronte.

Des Gartens Rosen waren schön,
Und lieblich lockten ihre Düfte ;
Doch früh hinwelkend starben sie
An einem sonderbaren Gifte.

Zu Tod ist auch erkrankt seitdem
Die Nachtigall, der edle Sprosser,
Der jenen Rosen sang sein Lied ;
Ich glaub', vom selben Gift genoss er.

Vermaledeiter Garten! Ja,
Es war, als ob ein Fluch drauf laste ;
Manchmal am hellen, lichten Tag
Mich dort Gespensterfurcht erfasste.

Mich grinste an der grüne Spuk,
Er schien mich grausam zu verhöhnen.
Und aus den Taxusbüschen drang
Alsbald ein Ächzen, Röcheln, Stöhnen.

Am Ende der Allee erhob
Sich die Terasse, wo die Wellen
Der Nordsee zu der Zeit der Flut
Tief unten am Gestein zerschellen.

Dort schaut man weit hinaus ins Meer,
Dort stand ich oft in wilden Träumen.
Brandung war auch in meiner Brust—
Das war ein Tosen, Rasen, Schäumen—

Ein Schäumen, Rasen, Tosen war's,
Ohnmächtig gleichfalls wie die Wogen,
Die kläglich brach der harte Fels,
Wie stolz sie auch herangezogen.

Mit Neid sah ich die Schiffe ziehn
Vorüber nach beglückten Landen—
Doch hielt mich das verdammte Schloss
Gefesselt in verfluchten Banden.

The years roll on, the castle stands
With tower and battlements on high.
The castle and all its stupid folk—
I can't forget them, though I try.

Still I see the weathervane
Upon the roof ; it used to creak.
The anxious looks that people cast
Towards it before they dared to speak !

No one spoke until they knew
Which way the wind was blowing up,
For fear the surly Northern bear
Would snap at them and say : ' Shut up ! '

The wisest never spoke at all—
Alas, an echo flew around
In that pleasaunce and gave in spite
To every word another sound.

The castle had a garden fair,
Therein a fountain—ever dry,
Although the fountain basin held
Tears in plenty from a poet's eye.

Accursed garden ! Ne'er a spot
Therein without some shameful scene ;
Each blade of grass bedewed with tears,
What time my heart in shreds has been.

I do not know a single tree
Without its tale of jeers and quips
That fell upon my luckless head
Alike from coarse and dainty lips.

The toad that listened in the grass
Told everything to neighbour rat,
The rat made sure the viper knew,
The viper got the tale off pat.

He told it to his friend the frog,
And all the filthy clan in town
At once the gossip heard, and knew
The insults I had to swallow down.

The garden's roses, white and red,
A lovely fragrance about them shed,
But withered soon, by poison killed.
Alas ! too early were they dead.

Then, too, the nightingale fell ill,
That to the roses used to sing.
Methinks it drank the poison fell
That to the roses death did bring.

Accursed garden ! It seemed as if
A spell was laid upon its trees,
And oft in broad daylight I fled
From phantoms flapping in the breeze.

The foliage green seemed full of ghosts ;
They grinned and cruelly mocked my plight.
The yew trees rattled, groaned and moaned—
In truth it gave me no delight.

The garden had an avenue
That led to a terrace broad and free.
One saw at flood-tide down below
The breakers of the Northern Sea.

Wide out to sea extends the view,
Oft times I stood there wildly dreaming.
The foam surged fiercely in my breast
And tossed and sprayed in endless seething.

In endless seething tossed and sprayed—
Yet powerless as the raging sea
That dashed its proud but helpless waves
Against the rocks still standing free.

I watched with envy ships that sailed
To far-off happier, blessèd lands.
But alas! the accursèd castle stood
And held me tight in cursèd bands.

In these verses, though, we detect another tone. The ' cursèd bands ' are not only financial ones ; they are, with all the entrancing fragrance of the roses in the garden, the bands of Heine's unhappy love for Salomon's daughter Amalie. It is impossible to over-estimate the importance of this love in Heine's life. It determined absolutely the direction that life was to take. It was the cause of his resentful attitude through life and of his contempt for humanity. It aroused in him his pernicious talent for mockery and frivolity. It drove him into a series of easy, unsatisfying liaisons which stimulated his desire for further amorous adventures but which were in their turn quickly abandoned—just as Byron's escapades and Italian adventures were determined by his unhappy love for his sister Augusta.

Not till he found Mathilde did Heine come to terms, on quite another plane, with life, and find peace at last. Even so, the whole relationship with Mathilde can only be understood in the light of the complete contrast it affords to Heine's youthful experience with the blonde, tender, coy, flirtatious nymph who was his cousin. The dynamic Frenchwoman was the exact reverse of all this, and even in Heine's last years his writings bear frequent testimony to the sorrow and the overpowering memory of his great Hamburg love.

Heine was fated to suffer the cruellest blow that can befall a young man of a deeply emotional nature who stands on the threshold of life. He was disappointed in his first love, in which, with all the ardour of a young heart that was new to love, he had set all his trust and all his hopes. It was bad enough that Heine, every whit as much as any Romeo, had to rescue his lady-love in the teeth of a hostile world. True, it was the world of his uncle, of his closest relatives. But this, in view of the social gulf that stood between Heine and his uncle, made things worse, rather than better. For the next few years, which were to be of decisive importance to him, Harry remained the poor cousin, quite insignificant, while Amalie, the spoilt millionaire's daughter, sat enthroned in Affrontenburg 'in all the glory of her diamonds.' Much of Heine's ambition and need for self-assertion can unquestionably be traced back to his humiliation and his desperate struggles for equality in this first love affair of his. To force himself to the top, so as to be equal in rank with the beloved ; to be successful, to get himself talked about : this must have seemed to him the only way in which to bridge the chasm that yawned so dangerously near his heart. He would have needed superhuman firmness and self-assurance not to have followed this path. After all, his special talents pointed in the same direction. Much that is overdone, meretricious, strained and striving-for-effect in Heine's early works—the *Harzreise,* for example—I attribute to this unhappy first love. To the same cause I put down his constant desire, in his letters as in his poems, to pose as if he were standing on an eminence from which he looks down with a contemptuous smile on the swarm of insignificant humanity milling below. The boot was very much on the other foot.

This state of mind was intensified by the oppressive effect which Heine's special position as a Jew had on him. He writes to Sethe :

> Apart from the fact that there is not the slightest feeling for poetry in this town of hucksters—except for doggerel written to order for weddings and christenings—there has been another source of misery for some time now. There is a rather sticky tension prevailing between the baptized and the unbaptized Jews. I call all Hamburgers Jews. The ones I call baptized Jews, to differentiate them from the circumcised ones, are called in popular parlance : Christians.

This pogrom atmosphere, which eventually culminated in street disorders, must have been something new and ominous to one who had been brought up in the comforts of the Rhineland. Moreover, although he had had nothing published at the time, Heine had a presentiment, which turned out to be justified, of the repercussions this antipathy of the populace would have on his career as a poet. ' Things being as they are, it's fairly easy to foresee that Christian love will not leave unmolested the love songs of a Jew.' The nineteen-year-old youth foretells his whole future life, even the peculiar nature of his posthumous fame!

It must have been depressing in the extreme for Heine to find

himself imprisoned in a community with which at that time he had
not the slightest sympathy. His stay in Hamburg was in fact one
of the most un-Jewish periods of his life. The Jewish impressions
of his youth had faded, and he had not yet been affected by the
Jewish renaissance in Berlin. His Jewish feeling seems to have
become completely blunted. His hatred of the Hamburg business
Jews, his relatives, and his disastrous hate-and-love of Amalie
undermined his Jewishness still further. The seeds of Heine's contemptuous and malicious utterances against Jews as individuals,
and particularly against German-Jewish ways, seem to have been
sown in the Hamburg years. They fell on the soil of a vulnerable
soul that was deeply agitated, so that even in later years they bore
bitter fruit. When I spoke of Judaism as a disease, I was only
thinking of the German Jews, Heine once said in Paris.

In Hamburg the parched soul of the young man, thirsting for
love, clung to the German national movement then at its height
after the Napoleonic wars, and to Christian raptures. His beloved
becomes the *wunnevolles Magedein*, the ' blessed damozel ' (which
strikes a highly incongruous note in the early poems), or, more
closely related to his own experiences of the cult of the virgin in
his native Düsseldorf, she becomes the Madonna. Here again the
letter to Sethe is particularly instructive. On account of its
devastating sincerity I prefer it to much in Heine's early lyrics. Its
style, too, is remarkable. It shows a Heine dependent on the young
Schiller and on *Sturm und Drang* models—lines he never followed
again. There is a reference to the Madonna cult in the letter:

> In religious matters I have something very queer to tell you.
> Has Heine gone mad ? you will exclaim. Nevertheless, I *must*
> have a Madonna. Will the heavenly replace the earthly
> Madonna for me ? I *want* to drug my senses. Only in the
> infinite depths of mysticism can I cast off my infinite pain. How
> pitiable *knowledge* seems to me now in its beggar's rags. What
> once appeared to me as transparent clarity now reveals itself
> to me as nothing but nakedness.
> ' Become as little children.' For a long time I thought I
> understood this, oh fool, fool that I was.—Little children have
> *faith*.
> This letter has been lying in my desk almost a month now,
> as I wrote first to Düsseldorf to find out whether you had left
> yet. I've just received your kind letter. By God ! Not *all* my
> joys have died. Forgive me, good, fine Christian, I always loved

you with all my heart, but often, perhaps always, failed to understand you. You were not too proud to write to poor Harry three times without knowing whether you might get an answer? Well, by God ! poor Harry is not so poor any more. From my letter you will see how it is with my heart ; it's still the same. But I'm bearing my pain now in a much *manlier* fashion. Still, I feel as if something were dying away inside me ; poetry, too, seems to be nothing but blurred images in a mist. Oh, M . . ., you cost me much ! I embrace you Christian, but don't press so hard. There's a black iron chain on my naked breast, and just where my poor heart beats there's a black iron cross with many sharp edges. Inside the cross is a lock of M . . .'s hair. Ho! It's burning! . . . oh Christian !

There is a passage in Heine's *Confessions* in which, abjuring his Voltaireanism, he refers obviously to this phase of his life:

I too was frequently overwhelmed in my youth by the infinite sweetness, the mysterious, blessed extravagances of that blissful poesy ; I too adored the most blessed queen of heaven. I put into graceful rhyme the legends of her grace and favour ; my first collection of poems shows traces of this beautiful Madonna period, traces which in later collections I eliminated with ridiculous care.

It seems that at first Amalie was amiably disposed towards her cousin. In any case, the two must have met before, when both were still children, for in 1816 Heine writes to Sethe: ' Rejoice, rejoice : in four weeks I shall be seeing Molly, and with her my Muse returns. I haven't seen her for two years.' But only a few months later follows the decisive long letter to Sethe from which I have already quoted. This letter is remarkable for the warmth of affection for his friend that Heine reveals in it. It is possible to see in it a desperate attempt by Heine to sublimate his own inverse tendencies, and as such it might partially explain and render more pardonable his subsequent attack on Platen's homoerotic poems. Curiously enough, I have never seen a reference to this anywhere. Here is the beginning of this great epistle, in which all the passions of a youthful heart find expression:

She loves me not ! You must pronounce this last mono-syllable, my dear Christian, very very softly. The first three words are eternal heavenly life, but in the last is eternal living hell. If only you could see your wretched friend's face a little, how deathly pale he looks, and absolutely distraught and demented—your justified displeasure at his long silence would soon be appeased. It would be best of all if you could cast a single glance in his inner soul—then you would really get to love me. Actually, dear Christian, you must know that each thought of mine is a letter to you. At any rate, that's the shape it takes. Not long ago I scratched together a boring letter to you a yard long, in which, mid many a sigh, I opened up my whole innermost being to you, from Leda's egg to the fall of Troy. However, I had enough sense to destroy this letter afterwards, as it could have served no purpose but to fall into strange hands, in which case it would have been, perhaps, the end of me straightway. You can't help me in this way, I'm afraid.

I want to tell you something rather amusing. You know, Christian, that from the very first moment I saw you, I was involuntarily attracted to you, and without my being able to account for it to myself you became for ever infinitely dear and precious to me. I think I told you about this a long time ago ; how there was *something* I saw in your features, particularly in your eyes, which in an incomprehensible fashion simultaneously drove me from you and violently drew me back to you, so that in one and the same moment I thought I detected in this something loving well-wishing and again the most bitter, vile, icy scorn. And lo ! I have found this same puzzling something in Molly's eyes. And this is just what it is that is driving me frantic. For although I have the most undeniable, the most irrefutable proofs that she is far from loving me—proofs that even Rektor Schallmeyer would admit were absolutely logical and would not hesitate to put at the head of his system—all the same, this poor loving heart refuses to concede the force of logic, and keeps on saying: What has your logic to do with me, I have my own logic.—I have seen her again—

Dem Teufel meine Seele,
Dem Henker sei der Leib,
Doch ich allein erwähle
Für mich das schöne Weib.

My soul the devil take,
My body take the air,
But I the choice will make
Of a woman wondrous fair.

Ha ! Aren't you shuddering, Christian ? Well you may. I, too, am shuddering.—Burn this letter. God have mercy on my wretched soul.—I have not written these words.—It was a pale someone sitting on my chair who wrote them. All this comes of writing at midnight—O God! Madness does not sin. Hey, you! Don't breathe too hard, I've just put together a wonderfully pretty house of cards. I'm standing right at the top of it and am holding *her* arm.

See, Christian, only *your* friend could raise his eyes to the very highest—do you recognise him by that trait? No doubt it will be his ruin. But you can hardly imagine, dear Christian, how glorious and lovely my ruin looks! *Aut Cæsar aut nihil* was always my motto. *Everything* all the time.

I am a fanatical chess player. I've lost my queen on my first move, and yet I still play. I play for the queen! Shall I carry on playing?

Quand on a tout perdu et qu'on n'a plus d'espoir,
La vie est une opprobre et la mort un devoir.[1]

Silence, accursed, wicked Frenchman, with your craven whinings of despair. Do you not know the German Muse? She stands firm and bold on two eternally unshakeable plinths: manliness and *faith.*—Only preserve me safely, O God, from the dark power of *time.*—To be far from her and to bear an ardent longing in one's heart for many years; that is hellish torture and wrings a hellish cry of pain from one's lips. But, *to be near her,* and yet often to pine in vain through endless-seeming weeks for a glimpse of her who alone can confer happiness—ah—ah—and—oh! oh! O Christian! It's enough to send the purest and most pious of minds into a frenzy of wild demented godlessness.

Oh, well, you are wise, Christian, and you certainly won't want to punish me for my long silence. The dagger-sharp hook that claws every word out of my soul—you don't know the terrible pain it causes. The black dots and dashes come easily to others, they place them here or there as they fancy. They don the buskin the better to walk in the mire. Any buskin you can detect *here* is a gigantic figure of pain rising from the yawning abyss that separates each bleeding wound in my heart.

Don't be angry, Christian, I love you so so much, so much, and am so terribly unhappy withal. Will you too reject me?

---

[1] A misquotation from Voltaire's *Mérope* (end of Act II). The correct quotation is:

Quand on a tout perdu, quand on n'a plus d'espoir,
La vie est un opprobre et la mort un devoir.

Alas, the voice in my heart deceived me sorely, will it prove
false this time too? Christian, say yes or no. By everything you
hold holy, tell me the truth.—Yes? Then I may hope that the
voice in my heart is true for Molly as well. No? Then — — —
Write soon, dear Christian, please, won't you?

Another mortifying thing is that *she* has run down in such
a galling despicable fashion, my beautiful poems, that I wrote
only for her. She has behaved very badly to me in this. But take
my word for it, in spite of all this, I am more devoted to the
Muse than ever. She has become a faithful friend who brings
me consolation. She is so cosy and sweet. I love her with all
my heart.

And so Hamburg becomes the 'schöne Wiege seiner Leiden ' and
the ' schönes Grabmal seiner Ruh '—the ' beautiful cradle of his
sorrows ' and the ' beautiful tomb of his repose.' The queen of his
heart speaks bitter words. A frenzy takes hold of the faithful knight.
It drives him away. He yields his place to another, more fortunate
suitor ; one whose feet are planted more firmly on the ground, who
knows his way about better, who ousts him on every occasion.
Amalie weds a highly respectable rich burgess of Königsberg.

But before this happens many years of torture have still to be
endured. Again and again the friendly gesture, the kindly smile of
the beloved is praised. She promises, she kisses, even—but in the
end it turns out she has said nothing that could bind her. With her
' big, all-knowing eyes ' she looks at him and he admits she is in
the right. She has been good, he has been bad. She was ' charming
and kind and, oh ! even sincere.' Or, as the epigraph to three
different chapters of *Buch Le Grand* puts it with particular
insistence : ' She was lovable, and he loved her ; but he was not
lovable, and she did not love him (Old Ballad).' I have never been
able to read without emotion this simple epigraph, with its prose
rhythm, its queer pseudo-literary attribution, and its repetition that
makes it almost a litany. It is the ' old story,' in the telling of which
the only heart that breaks is the heart of him to whom ' it just
happens.' As far as the girl was concerned, it was nothing more
than what would now be called a flirtation. To the man, however,
it was far more, it was everything that was in his power to feel and
to give. Heine describes in the *Lieder* the phases of this relationship
in all the nuances of their factual development, and yet with all the

continually renewed buoyancy of one whose ardour strives to reach the infinite. In the event it was not given him to achieve the flight into the infinite which this love would have enabled him to accomplish. This failure was destined to be his fate, the great disappointment he never overcame. Even in the late poems, in *Romanzero*, he dreams of the 'cottage high on the mountain slope. We ran a friendly race down the path, Ottilie and I raced hand in hand.' There is a mermaid's twinkle in the sea-green eyes of the beloved, she stands firmly on her tiny feet, her voice rings true and heartfelt, so that you think you can see into the depths of her soul. And the dreaming poet says :

> Heirate mich und sei mein Weib, Ottilie,
> Damit ich fromm wie du und glücklich sei.

> Marry me and be my wife, Ottilie,
> That I may pious and happy be like thee.

She did not marry him. Piety and happiness alike were denied him—that the two would have gone together is clearly stated in the couplet. In actual fact his very personal form of piety only came in the train of the most terrible disasters. The poem ends :

> Was sie zur Antwort gab, das weiss ich nimmer,
> Denn ich erwachte jählings—und ich war
> Wieder ein Kranker, der im Krankenzimmer
> Trostlos darniederliegt seit manchem Jahr.

> What her answer was I never heard again,
> For suddenly I awoke with a start of fear.
> I was a sick man racked with pain
> Once more, and had been many a dreary year.

Do we not feel in the wonderfully irregular, nervous, vibrating rhythm of the two concluding lines, in the 'wrong' accentuation with which they begin and which in each case rolls on through the whole of the verse, something of an overwhelming emotion's desire to 'hold on' for ever ? Here, as in many poems, Heine succeeds in approximating to the expression of inexpressible feelings. He does it with a few quite ordinary words, through sheer rhythm (the counter-point of lyric poetry).

He never recovered. ' I had been studying Roman Law for a
year when I heard on the 1st of May in Göttingen that my betrothed
had wed. It was on the 1st of May ! Smiling spring clothed field
and vale with green. . . . " In both plays, *Almansor* and *Ratcliff,*
and practically on every page of the poems, this betrayal by his
beloved comes to the fore. It is in the breathless ' message ' in which
the peasant is told to ask in King Duncan's castle whether it is the
dark maid or the fair who is the bride. It is in Don Ramiro's phantom
appearance at Donna Clara's wedding. In the poem of the ' loved
one lost for ever.' In ' poor Peter ' who stalks off from Hänsel and
Gretel's bridal dance. In his late years, it comes up in the great
romance of Judah Halevi, in the episode of Ibn Ezra who undertakes a pilgrimage to Jerusalem ' to forget his niece '—to which
Heine adds a drily humorous comment: ' Like so many of his
colleagues, unsettled, no home.' We even think we can discern in
the Frau Abunde of *Atta Troll* the features of the maiden who
laughs in a ' hearty frenzy ' when the poet breaks his neck jumping
out of the window and lies bleeding at her feet. ' Ah, I know that
laughter.' It appears even more clearly in the ' fresco of sonnets '
to Christian Sethe, with its trail of dangerous tittering, locks of hair,
red, kissable lips, beloved gentle angel-minx, culminating in the
cry: ' The world for me was nothing but a torture chamber in
which they hung me by my feet.' The maiden passes by, strikes him
with her golden hammer, is curious to see the poet's death agony.

It has been suggested that sadistic and macabre scenes of this
kind, which are constantly cropping up in Heine's early verse, were
inspired by his romantic love of the hangman's daughter.
Alternatively, they have been regarded simply as being in the then
prevailing romantic fashion. No doubt these explanations have a
certain validity. All the same, I cannot help feeling that it is no
less valid to suggest that the frequent portrayal of the beloved as
actually dead represents a scarcely concealed dream of wish or
revenge fulfilment. Here, in a limited sector, though not over the
whole field of an artist's personality, psycho-analytic methods could
probably clear up certain obscurities. Again and again Heine
converses with the princess, who answers his suit: ' That may not
be, for I lie in my grave, and only at night do I come to thee,
because I love thee so.' Silent shadows beckon him with soft arms
into their misty demesne. ' I wept in my dream ; I dreamt of thee

lying in thy grave.' And the poem *The Stricken Knight* concludes
with this stanza—deleted in the final version :

> Am liebsten möcht er liegen
> Mit Liebchen im Totenschrein.
> Ans kalte Leib sich schmiegen ;
> Der Tod macht alles rein.

> Fain would he lie in coffin shrined,
> And with his loved one death endure,
> Round her cold corpse his arms entwined—
> Death alone makes all things pure.

Here we have entered Tristan's dark territory of death and love.
' It is the dark-powerful country from which my mother sent me.'
One of the many zones in which the worlds of Heine and Wagner
touch. Heine, too, is not lacking in a mother. From love he seeks
refuge with his mother. Again we have two highly revealing stanzas
that were later deleted, this time in the poem *Wasserfahrt* (' Sea
Voyage ') ; it is as if the poet had decided to destroy them because
of their all-too-revealing candour :

> Stolziere nicht, du falsche Maid,
> Ich will's meiner Mutter sagen ;
> Wenn meine Mutter mich weinen sieht,
> Dann brauch ich nicht lange zu klagen.

> Meine Mutter singt mir ein Wiegenlied vor,
> Bis ich schlafe und erbleiche ;
> Doch dich schleppt sie Nachts bei den Haaren herbei,
> Und zeigt dir meine Leiche.

> Vaunt not thy triumph, maiden false ;
> I'll tell my mother, who me befriended.
> When my mother sees my weeping eyes,
> My lamentations will be ended.

> My mother will sing a lullaby
> Till I'll sleep and be deathly white,
> But thee she'll drag by the hairs of thy head,
> And show thee my corpse at night.

Without these two last stanzas the poem strikes an astonishingly
conventional note ; with them, as in the original conception of the

poem, it gains astonishingly in force. In general, Heine gives the impression of tending to suppress or tone down certain passages in the later revisions of his work.

In the *Lazarus* poems he looks back again on his 'lost desires,' speaks of the similarity of temperament by which he and his cousin were mutually attracted. 'Beide ehrlich und bescheiden konnten wir uns leicht verstehen ; Worte waren überflüssig, brauchten uns nur anzusehen '—Both were honest and modest, and could understand each other easily, they needed merely to look at each other. His memories assume highly corporeal forms. For the sake of his adored one he will even learn to smoke cigars—tobacco smoke was always an abomination to him ; he will tell her the Polish anecdotes in Judea's dialect that always aroused her laughter. Then he goes on :

> Und ade! sie sind zerronnen,
> Goldne Wünsche, süsses Hoffen!
> Ach, zu tötlich war der Faustschlag,
> Der mich just ins Herz getroffen.
>
> Golden wishes, golden hopes!
> Fled beyond recall by art.
> Alas, too deadly was the blow
> That struck me truly in the heart!

Originally, the final stanza of the poem was couched in much more drastic language. I doubt whether Heine has anywhere given so definitive an expression to his whole relationship with Amalie and its repercussions throughout the rest of his life as he did in this original final stanza :

> Qualvoll sterb ich hin, die Wurzel
> Meines Lebens ist verletzt—
> Ach, das kommt von einem Fusstritt
> Den man mir ins Herz versetzt.
>
> Racked with pain I die, the source of
> All my life is bruisèd quite.
> Deathly was the blow that swingeing
> Struck my heart with bitter spite.

'The source of all my life is bruisèd quite '—Heine had ample justification for his lament. His association with his cousin was to prove as fateful as Kierkegaard's with Regina Olsen or Grillparzer's

with Katharina Fröhlich. It is an association which shaped the
whole of his life and work, an association the traces of whose first
strong impulse he was never able to shake off. Everything follows
from it. Who does not feel that his exaggerated *amour-propre* is
only a defence, the scar of the wound he received early in his
youth ? Likewise his cynicism : defence mechanism of an all-too-
sensitive spirit ; likewise his revolt against the powerful, the
insolent, the privileged : originally an attack on the rich branch
of his own family. The apparent candour, too ; the talk of
appetite, sweet cakes, oysters, champagne, pecuniary difficulties :
only a particularly subtle ruse to hide the deadly earnestness of
his heart. His wit, too, was defence, a means of making others
keep their distance.

Cabin'd, cribb'd, confin'd as he was, surrounded by enemies,
Heine failed to meet these obstacles by taking the difficult and
painful path of summoning up the imperishably noble qualities of
his innermost soul. Instead, he chose the easier way of direct attack,
not hesitating on occasion to hit out indiscriminately at real or
pretended enemies in his attempt to eliminate what was harmful
to him. In so doing, he showed his character—which I have no
desire to whitewash—to be lacking in harmony and discipline ; in
a word, small. It was this, no doubt, which alienated the finely
sensitive Rahel from him, and, after the Platen controversy, many
others, too.

By striving, as Heine did, to win at all costs, you run the risk
of mobilizing the baser elements in your own nature; of indulging
in self-pity by saying : ' I am the victim of so much injustice that
I have no time to purify myself inwardly. In any case, I have
absolutely no need to. Compared with my opponents' caricature
of me, I am pure, glorious, radiant. . . .' It is precisely this, however, which is the worst injury your adversaries can inflict on you.
The slanders, the nonsense, the lies they spread about you cause
you to react by overstressing your own self, by falling in love with
your own ego. Thus they ruin your character. They defeat you on
another front ; not on the front of the rumours they spread about
you in order to attack you, but, indirectly, on the front of a
pernicious feeling of infallibility which they had no desire to
arouse in you, but the loathsome poison of which they do succeed
in injecting into you.

I think he would have to be a bold man who, in considering
the circumstances of Heine's later years, would declare that the
hostilities to which the poet was continually exposed were not so
intense that he could take no other form of resistance than these
desperate egocentric struggles which, by their disregard of purity,
harmed only himself in the long run. ' He jests at scars that never
felt a wound.' Heine's temporary defeats in the battle, his temporary
depravities, may have been caused by his own weakness. They may,
however, have been equally due to a burden upon his heart that
was *too great,* a world of sorrows that not even an Atlas could
bear. The great disappointment with his young cousin, the ' blow
to the heart ' with which his life as a man began, is responsible
for this excessive weight of sorrow. Particularly in view of the
fact that his Jewishness had a similar effect on him at the time.
Judaism at that time was in its worst stage of development,
between ' Yes ' and ' No,' and Heine felt degraded by all the con-
stricting and irritating manifestations of this transitional Judaism.
I really think I can say: ' It was too much!' It is a wonder—and
points to Heine's nobility of soul in reality—that he did not
succumb entirely, that ' das edle Glied der Geisterwelt '—the
precious part of our spirit world—(*Faust,* transl. MacNeice) at the
end of it all was in fact saved.

It is a commonplace in discussing Heine's general attitude to
say that there was an element of coquetry in the way in which
he portrayed his sufferings ; that his elegant posing and witty *mots*
render it impossible to take them seriously. But what if these
sufferings were so frightful, so utterly beyond his power of direct
resistance, that the only way he was enabled to endure them was
by refracting them through an artistic medium? This wit, this posing
was no game he played, but the last resource of a tortured soul.
Instead of hypocritically condemning it as an unfortunate failing,
we ought to regard it as a clinical thermometer enabling us to read
off the real temperature of his anguish. And simply because someone dons a mask with the rest, jestingly, arrogantly, with an empty
heart—no person of discernment is entitled to deduce therefrom
that masks are always donned only in play, that none is ever
donned because some sorely tried spirit feels the need of a mask
with which he can hide himself in the dark. Those poets whose
gently ironical tone surprises and offends are the most frequently

misunderstood. The oh, so earnest ones, on the other hand, frequently fare better in this respect, at any rate with the superficial critic.

One of the most obnoxious habits of literary historians in general is the way in which they cast doubts, without sufficient reason, on the genuineness of the emotions expressed by poets. As these historians have never themselves experienced a similarly fierce emotion, one that harrows and ravages the whole personality, they cannot credit its existence in others. They have no idea at all of the manifestations of such an emotion ; the unnatural contortions, the masks put on to order, the stiff posturings, the assumed merriment—all of which have only the merest superficial resemblance of form to the carnival masks donned by some ' sunshine children ' as part of an enjoyable game.

Byron experienced the same fate. His *Weltschmerz* was considered a pose, a deliberate way of arranging his cloak, an interesting hero's costume. As if there were not in fact, for every perceptive observer, a stark horror pervading the world, and as if far-fetched reasons were necessary to explain why a man should despair of life, of the whole structure of existence—a man, moreover, whose indestructible love for his sister had driven him from the confines of a sheltered existence into the damnation of Astarte's curse. ' Auf dein Herz und Hirn zugleich kam der Spruch—verwelk, verbleich '—On thy heart and mind together the ban was spoken : wither, perish—so Heine translated the curse that had lit upon the poet whose fate so closely resembled his own. Both sought to escape from their great suffering in sharply felt pleasures and in outrageous eccentricity. Anyone who fails to see in all this the self-defence of beings whose ' source of life was bruisèd quite ' ; who classifies as pure comedy, exhibitionism, caprice, a coolly considered attitude, what in fact was the last self-assertive twitching of a defiance that was desperately struggling for life—does not deserve ever to have read a line of either writer.

At worst Heine can only be reproached with having extricated himself from Astarte's clutches. And it took him many years to do that. In any case, it was a question of choosing between incurring posthumous reproach and committing suicide. Can we blame him for choosing the reproach ? Moreover, the severe biographer may find some solace in the fact that even after the danger of suicide

was over, Heine was never entirely free, to his sorrow, from
Astarte's visitations.

Three years in Hamburg. In the summer of 1819 his business
experiments were brought to a close. The family council had
decided to send him to the University. In Houben's *Gespräche mit
Heine* I find it stated that Heine's uncle provided him with the
means to read law. In the *Memoirs,* however, Heine says: 'When
I took up residence at the University my father's business affairs
were in a very bad way, and my mother sold her jewellery—a
necklace and earrings of great value—to provide for my first four
years at college.' Probably both statements are true.

Heine returned to Düsseldorf in order to bring his classics up
to the required standard, and left for Bonn in the autumn of 1819.
But this was by no means the end of his Hamburg love. In a letter
to H. Straube in 1821 he writes:

I knew it beforehand and I told you beforehand. Hardly
had I entered the outskirts of Hamburg when I had a sudden
feeling of never having left the place, and everything I'd lived
through and thought and felt in the two years I'd been away
from it just vanished from my memory. For an hour I sat in
silence and practically without thinking about anything. In the
book of my life this hour is a dash with no significance, and
yet it speaks volumes. How will the book end? Did the
divine author wish to write a tragedy or a comedy? *Dieu
merci,* I've something to say about that, the *dénouement*
depends on me. All I need is a whiff of gunpowder to send
the hero's cap and bells tumbling off his head.

Yes, but up there in a corner box sits a doll beautifully
dressed up in her Sunday best—the celestial craftsman who
made it surpassed himself. This dearly beloved marionette
ought not to laugh, really, and indeed I would like to see one
or two crystal tears springing from her two liquid orbs. Yes,
there is the rock on which my reason has foundered, and to
which, nevertheless, I want to cling in my deadly fears. . . . .

It was getting on for midnight when I betook myself to
the house of my Dulcinea, to act the part of my Almansor in
real life beneath her window. Unfortunately, unlike my
Almansor, I had no coat, so I had to freeze like a tailor. Also,
instead of a starlit Andalusian summer's night, all I had was
an ash-grey sky, a damp 'Hamburg special' of a wind, and a
drizzle that chilled me to the marrow. The old matchmaker,
who has deceived me so often, had shamefacedly retreated

behind his cloud batteries, and illuminated only with one or two beams the house of all houses.

I hardly need tell you, dearest moaner, how much I moaned there. All the madhouses had let loose their lunatic creatures and driven them hard at my throat. The mad mob celebrated its Walpurgis night in my brain, my chattering teeth provided the dance music, and from my breast gushed warm torrents of red, red heart's blood. The waves of blood dashed eerily around me, I was dazed by the fragrance of her misty presence, and she herself, she herself appeared at the window above, and nodded down at me, and smiled down at me, in all the dazzling splendour of her beauty, so that I thought I would expire in infinite longing and woe and ecstasy. . . .

The letter ends on a harshly discordant note. The ' bitter-sweet be-ringleted little head that so graciously inclined itself in my direction ' proved to be an ' old governess.' Reality breaks through in exactly the same way as in his poems and visions ; cf. the well-known incident of the sea-captain (' Doctor, have you taken leave of your senses ? '). Heine does not pursue his emotions *jusqu'au bout*: he breaks off ; by striking a discordant note he effectively stops any continuance of the emotion ; he forces himself violently into silence. For at bottom Heine was ashamed of his anguish.

I consider reticence to be one of Heine's distinguishing spiritual characteristics. This may sound surprising in view of the fact that it has become traditional for literary critics to cast Heine for the rôle of cynic. I shall not dispute his cynicism, but his mockery is mostly reserved for matters of subsidiary importance, or comes through only momentarily—it does not last. Heine never poked fun at experiences and intuitions which were really important. He never breathed a word about the great love of his life. Amalie's name was hedged round in a profound silence, and the strange aftermath, his love of Amalie's younger sister Therese—' new folly grafted on old '—remained undiscovered for many years after Heine's death. Researches carried out much later provided an insight into this sphere of Heine's life which came as a surprise even to the best students of Heine. They show Heine practising a studied reticence which is deeply moving in a poet assailed on all sides for his immodesty. His holy decency and reticence, traits which still receive all-too-little recognition, find genuinely touching

expression in a conversation which took place between him and
Adolf Stahr and Fanny Lewald in his later years (1850).

Fanny Lewald records:

> I said I had seen and spoken a few times to his uncle
> Salomon Heine in Berlin, at the house of a shipping line
> representative, who later became its managing director, called
> Bloch, and that in my youth I had seen a lot of his cousin
> Amalie Heine, who was married in Königsberg to an educated
> man of private means of very good family, a Herr John
> Friedländer, and that in Königsberg she was thought to have
> been Heine's young love, that I thought her a charming woman,
> and that I had a very soft spot for her extremely handsome
> husband, who was the eldest brother of my girl friends in my
> young days, because he had served as a volunteer in the cam-
> paigns against Napoleon, and in our childhood and youth the
> ' volunteers ' were hero-worshipped by us, more or less like
> Achilles or other heroes of antiquity.
> Heine smiled. ' How young she is!' he said to Stahr, and
> to me: ' I think you see the best in people, although you've
> wielded the lash of satire effectively enough at times.'

Nothing else. Not a word of the ' loved one of his youth.' The
conversation turns to other matters. ' How young she is!' The
remark addressed to Fanny Lewald with which Heine diverts
the discussion reverberates in our ears. And we see the force of
Flaubert's dictum: Through the crevice we can see the abyss.

IV

Universities. Bonn, Göttingen

IT WAS NOT in the cheerful mood of a young student that Heine entered the academic precincts of Bonn after his disappointments in Hamburg. He gives an exceedingly gloomy picture of his state of mind at the time:

> This heart does not burgeon often and easily; to the best of my recollection it has only been in bloom once, and that must have been long ago, a hundred years ago at least. That blossoming, glorious as it was, would have had to wither and perish miserably for sheer lack of sunshine and warmth, I fully believe, had it not been in fact violently destroyed in a dark winter gale.

Hence it is not surprising that the light-hearted tones that characterise Eichendorff's students are missing in Heine.

Added to the personal reasons for his ill-humour came political difficulties. Heine's experiencing of these crucial years in his self-development differs from the way in which they were experienced by the poets who were his contemporaries, or even by the preceding generation of Romantic poets, with whom he had, or at least wanted to have, much in common. We shall look in vain in Heine for an appreciation of University life comparable to Varnhagen's 'inspiring vigour of Halle's academic splendour.' We shall find no counterparts in Heine to Achim von Arnim's 'Cardenio,' the model undergraduate who reads hard, is a bold and skilful duellist, and is popular with professors and students alike. The difference between an inward and an outward reaction to the same set of circumstances becomes very evident in such comparisons.

Heine's attitude to University life was entirely critical, the reason being that he remained outside the circle of those most actively participating in that life, while at the same time he failed to judge it in the spirit of a detached observer. He was an ardent Teutonist at the time, nor did he think of himself at all as an ' outside ' admirer of things German. He felt himself to be fully integrated into German life, with no sense of distinction between himself and other Germans. It is precisely for this reason that he is irascible, as well as being often confused, in his criticisms.

True there is a definite difference of degree in these criticisms of University life. In the Bonn of his native Rhineland the conflict with his environment was not so severe ; its harsh reality only became marked in the presence of the Hanoverian Junkers in Göttingen. ' If I hadn't known from experience how far it was, I really would have walked all the way back to Bonn. Fops in patent shoes and pomaded hair, watery prose-writers in *de luxe* editions, expressionless codfish faces—that's about what undergraduate life here amounts to,' he writes to a friend.

In Göttingen, too, he realized the gulf that existed between himself and the other students. He forcefully expresses the nature of this gulf in *Norderney* :

> If your forebears have been deer hunters from time immemorial, you, their descendant, will enjoy this legitimate occupation too. My forebears, however, were not hunters ; they were very much hunted, and my blood rises at the thought of taking aim at the descendants of their comrades. I know indeed from experience that in a duel I find it far easier to aim at one of these ' sportsmen ' who would like to bring back the days when human beings were the game in a grand hunt. Thank God those days are over. If these sportsmen feel the urge to hunt a human being again, they must pay him for it, as for example they did the runner I saw two years ago in Göttingen. It was on a Sunday, and it was oppressively hot. The poor fellow was already pretty well exhausted with the running he'd done, when some Hanoverian Junkers who were reading *litterae humaniores* offered him a few thalers to run over the course again ; and the fellow ran, and he was deathly white and wore a red jacket, and close behind him raising a

cloud of dust galloped the well-fed aristocratic youths on their fine steeds. Every now and then the horses' hooves prodded the gasping, hunted fellow, and he was a human being.

There is no doubt that at first Heine chose deliberately to ignore the German-Jewish differences that existed. He was a German patriot through and through. He wallowed in German folk-song. He was disillusioned, not by Germanism as such, but by the petty nature of the German life of his day. In one of his first poems (*Deutschland*, 1816) he compares—the comparison is overdone—this petty German life of his own day with the medieval Germany of the 'good old days,' with its castles and 'ladies fair,' 'its ancient love and faith': 'Wo die Sitte und die Tugend/Prunklos gingen Hand in Hand,/Wo mit Ehrfurchtscheu die Jugend/vor dem Greisenalter stand'—where manners and virtue unadorned went hand in hand, where youth stood reverently before age.

It was in this spirit too that in October, 1819, Heine joined his fellow students of Bonn in a demonstration on the Kreuzberg to celebrate the anniversary of the Battle of Leipzig. True, the sonnet *Die Nacht auf dem Drachenfels*, dedicated to the friend of his young days Fritz von Beughem, ends in an ironic anti-climax. The poet finds on returning from 'the night on the Drachenfels' that the flames from the faggots blazing in the midnight air have given him a cold. But to construe this anti-climax as showing Heine's desire to vitiate the preceding verses would be to miss the point entirely. On the contrary, the bathos of the last lines is a measure of the depth of feeling that informs the rest of the poem. The feeling of 'Germany's holy victories,' of 'Germany's weal,' is so strong that Heine is ashamed of it. In his embarrassment he 'soft-pedals' in the sonnet's last tercet; it may be that the consciousness of being an alien, of 'not belonging' is also in some degree responsible.

There was no anti-climax about the factual consequences of the demonstration. The University authorities held a rigorous inquiry. The students were opposed to the Government; patriotism at the time was suspected of being revolutionary, particularly since the time a student named Sand had assassinated the reactionary Kotzebue, in an attempt to undermine the Russo-Prussian-Austrian Alliance, the *System Metternich*. In this atmosphere of suspicion on the part of the authorities Heine was closely questioned about the number of cheers given at the demonstration. When he replied two, one for Blücher, one for German freedom, he was immediately asked the leading question: ' Was there no cheer for the student fraternity ? ' The conditions of the time are illumined in a flash. The student fraternities were hostile to the régime and had been banned since the Sand case.

The victories over Napoleon had failed to bring the German people the changes they hoped for. The citizenry was charged with preserving order as its first duty. Metternich indeed concentrated all his considerable energies after the Congress of Vienna on ensuring that no changes occurred in Europe's political alignments. This should not be regarded as dictated necessarily and exclusively by the interests of the privileged classes. A certain tiredness in the responsible statesmen of the period, a reluctance to tilt the balance in any one direction is not difficult to understand against the background of two decades of bloody warfare which had plunged every *Land* of Germany into mourning and misery.

The revolt against this policy of equilibrium, which the industrial revolution then in progress rendered impossible of attainment in any case, was elemental and spread increasingly among the population. The people had expected other things ; they had fought for a Greater Germany, for reforms, for popular representation. They felt cheated. The popular feeling is conveyed in the patriotic *Deutschland* poem, in which Heine eulogizes the past not merely for its' maidens standing on castle turrets and its men clad in iron, but because no ' *rusé* pigmy despot practised oath-breaking as part of the *System*.'

It was the *Biedermeier* period, a period which, for all its idyllic associations of ' quaintness,' was not lacking in tensions. In his novel *The Epigones* Immermann sums up the situation by saying that the Philistines sat down at the table which the heroes had prepared. The heroes were the people's armies, the free corps who fought against Napoleon. The Philistines were the Congress diplomats with Metternich at their head. Metternich liked to hear himself called ' the physician in the great hospital of the world.' He thought of himself not merely as all-mighty, but as all-wise into the bargain. It was precisely in this period of the young Heine (whose verses he liked to read afterwards), in 1819, that Metternich wrote: ' Twenty times a day I have to say to myself : " *Guter Gott,* how right I am and how wrong the others are." '

During the War of Liberation many had hoped to see the establishment of a unified free Greater German State. Ernst Moritz Arndt even thought in terms of an Imperial Parliament. For Metternich unity of this kind savoured all too much of revolution and would not have been compatible with Austrian hegemony. Thus it came about that conquered France, which was a unitary State, obtained its Chamber of Deputies—admittedly with a Right majority—while Germany remained a collection of fragments ; a loose confederation of thirty-nine sovereign princes with a few Free Cities. The Federal Diet in Frankfurt was not a Central Parliament but an assembly of Government representatives sent by each State. Only in a few Southern German States were constitutions adopted and *Land* Estates set up, as Lessing had demanded fifty years before in his *Kollektaneen* (' German Freedom '). Even so, a statute in one of these constitutions stipulated that deputies must be ' of an equable temperament.' North Germany and Prussia refused to have anything to do with a constitution, in spite of Hardenberg and Humboldt. In Hesse-Cassel soldiers were forced to wear the pre-1806 pigtail, symbol of all the attempts that were being made to force the country back to the conditions prevailing before the French Revolution.

It was only to be expected that many hearts should rise up in revolt at such a state of affairs : the Physical Training Groups under Jahn, the students under Maassmann (later a target of Heine's ridicule, he organized the Wartburg demonstration at which ' anti-student-fraternity books,' a Hesse pigtail, an Austrian Corporal's stick and a Prussian Uhlan's tunic were consigned to the flames).

Feeling was strong even in Schleiermacher's circle of die-hard royalist Prussians in Berlin, and Henriette Herz, whose memoirs elsewhere are so tame, comments :

> It must be admitted that many hopes and aspirations which had provided the people—youth particularly—with a powerful impulse to heroic and successful deeds in the War of Liberation had up till then found no fulfilment. The importance of the people's participation in these wars was belittled ; even, on occasion, made to seem ridiculous. The result was a progressive deterioration in the popular temper. As those on the other side were unable to conceal from themselves entirely that this deterioration was not unjustified, this in turn gave rise to apprehensions. But even if these apprehensions were well

founded, the measures adopted to deal with the public
discontents were inept. These discontents continued long afterwards, with varying intensity of expression, and no one could
say that they had disappeared entirely. I personally could not
but be most painfully affected by much that I saw happen to
men whose former labours for the cause of the Fatherland
and whose pure, indeed lofty, character, I well knew. My
distress was the greater as in the train of these happenings I
saw here and there a moral deterioration take place such as I
would not have thought capable of staining the spirit of any
German, particularly as I felt that the finest results of the
recent wars had been a purification, a sanctification indeed, of
the German character. Espionage and informing penetrated
into circles whose members thought they could speak among
themselves in confidence. Schleiermacher was denounced for
making a remark about the king in such a circle. Actually, it
was not a remark that could have affected his position. It was,
however, couched in a form which would have been objectionable had it been made publicly—not that it ever would have
been—instead of in a circle of people he thought were his
friends. I know all about the matter, as I copied several papers
dealing with it for Schleiermacher's files. It was not a period
I like to linger over. There were days in it that aroused in me
the heartfelt wish never to have experienced them.

The conflicting trends within this opposition to the Metternich
system were not then so easy to disentangle as they now appear
to be to us in retrospect, or even as they were to Heine at the time
of his book on Börne (1840). In his Bonn period everything was
blurred. 'Teutonists' ('*Deutschtümler*') and 'Chartists' ('*Kon-
stitutionsschreier*')—today we would think of them as being in the
opposite political camps of the Right and Left wings (democrats,
socialists) respectively—were at that time opposed in a solid block
to the reactionary régimes of the minor States. As 'demagogues'
all were liable to persecution, to incarceration and to censorship,
which had just been introduced at the beginning of Heine's student
career (Karlsbad Decrees, 1819).

Nevertheless all opposition parties were of the same mind
regarding the unity of the *Reich*. In this instance Heine's voice is
representative (*Norderney*, 1826, and similarly in many later pronouncements. Heine was always consistently 'Greater German,' a
fact which the many who reproach—or admire—him for his lack
of patriotism conveniently overlook):

Our Leipzig Fairs have benefited but little from the Battle of Leipzig. I understand a resident of Gotha wishes to commemorate the battle in epic form, but is at a loss to know how to begin, as he doesn't know whether he is one of the 100,000 souls that Hildburghausen has acquired, or one of the 150,000 that Meiningen has acquired, or one of the 160,000 acquired by Altenburg—unless he begins his epic, perhaps: ' Sing, immortal Muse, Hildburghausen Muse—Meiningen Muse or even Altenburg Muse—anyway sing, sing the iniquitous German redemption ! ' It is impossible to be proud, still less to give utterance to proud thoughts, as long as these traders in human beings carry out their nefarious work in the heart of a Fatherland which lies bleeding in fragments. Our noblest deeds are stultified by these Pyrrhic victories, and while we wrap ourselves in the purple of heroic German blood a knavish politician coifs us with cap and bells.

It was on the question of the polity that was to follow the attainment of the unity of the *Reich,* however, that differences of principle among the Confederate members, who were divided into ' Old Germans ' and Liberals, became manifest. In his book on Börne Heine, contrasting the Hambach and the Wartburg festivals, reproaches ' Old Germans ' with the ' narrow Teutomania ' ' whose love was nothing but hatred of the foreigner, and whose faith consisted only of unreason.' To the cosmopolitan lovers of liberty, on the other hand, ' French Liberalism had addressed its intoxicating Sermons on the Mount.' ' And even if many unreasonable things were said, Reason itself was acknowledged to be the highest authority ; binding, dissolving, and moulding the Law in accordance with her laws.'

Here the fateful question for Heine's development, the question that continually recurs, that gives him no rest, is posed in its clearest form : Should life and the political organization of life be determined by Reason and calculable Utility—or at any rate Utility that can be estimated with reasonable certainty—or must irrational, romantic factors come into play ? I must leave aside the question whether the concepts of ' humanity,' ' world citizenship,' which Heine uncritically equates with ' Reason,' do not in fact contain a supra-rational, a religious element ; whether the ' Jacobinism adapted to German conditions ' can really be reduced to pure Reason ; whether ' life ' and ' political organization of life ' are governed by the same principle instead of being, perhaps, diametrically opposed.

Be that as it may: at this period both German revolutionary parties marched together, united in the common struggle against Metternich. Yet Heine, acute observer of people as he was, was not slow to notice that the ' Teutonists ' echoed the modern catchphrases ' with a sour expression and even sang the Marseillaise . . . with a grimace of distaste.' And he adds the comment:

Nevertheless, there was a common struggle for a common stake, German unity, the only progressive idea evolved by the early Opposition. Our defeat is perhaps a blessing. . . . As brothers in arms we should have fought loyally at each other's side, we should have been firmly united in battle, even in the hour of victory . . . but the next morning irreconcilable differences would have appeared which could only be settled by the *ultima ratio populorum,* that is, the foreign decapitating machine (guillotine). The more short-sighted German revolutionaries, it is true, judged everything by French standards, and at an early stage they split up into Constitutionalists and Republicans and then further into Girondists and Montagnards, and as such they vied in hating and slandering each other, but the better informed knew quite well that in the German revolutionary army there were only two radically different parties, incapable of any joint transaction and preparing in secret for bloody internecine strife. Which party seemed preponderant ? Well informed Liberals made no attempts to conceal from each other that their party, which was dedicated to the principles of the French Revolution, though numerically stronger was weaker in fervour and resources. It was a fact that the regenerated Teutonists, despite their numerical inferiority, were possessed of a fanaticism of an almost religious kind for which a fanaticism engendered only by Reason proved to be no match.

These pronouncements, as I have indicated, were made by Heine in his later years and applied by him in retrospect to the period of his youth under discussion and to the period immediately following (up to the July revolution). The problem, however, particularly in its very personal implications, in its effect on his position in German cultural circles, was already occupying him when he was a student at Bonn. This is shown in his important essay *Die Romantik,* which is to a certain extent the precursor of one of his chief works, the book on the ' Romantic School.'

In a few lines the essay illumines three aspects of Romanticism: the subjective aspect of the Jew, whose inclusion in the ranks of the German people has become liable to question, and who therefore proclaims language, 'das deutsche Wort,' to be the 'holiest good'—'a Fatherland even for him to whom stupidity and guile deny a Fatherland.' It was in the nature of things that the trend towards national separatism should be marked among the Romantics, with their emphasis on the particular as opposed to the general, on historic causality as opposed to abstract concepts, on empiricism and living as opposed to a priori reasoning. How remote this particular tendency was, however, from enlisting all nations in a common humanity, although this ideal still remained alive for most Romantics—how crass the forms were which this tendency took, may be seen from a later remark of Heine's which could serve as a text to the sermon, prompted by his feeling of isolation, which he preaches in his essay on Die Romantik: ' I once had occasion to admire the thoroughness with which my " Old German " friends compiled, in a Göttingen Bierkeller, their proscription lists in readiness for the day they would attain power. Anybody descended even in the seventh degree from a Frenchman, Jew or Slav was condemned to exile.'

The second aspect of Heine's short but tightly-packed essay is the æsthetic one. The poetry of the Greeks and Romans was sensuous, tangible, limited. The ' priceless boon of Christianity ' brings with it new, thrilling emotions of infinity, and for these, new words are needed. ' In this manner arose so-called Romantic poetry, with its loveliest burgeoning in the Middle Ages.' Heine rejects the notion that this poetry, recently revived on German soil, should be less clear and its images less precise than classic poetry, which he calls ' plastic.' He does not accept the antithesis. Characteristically placing Goethe, the uomo universale, in the Romantic group with which he had only peripheral contacts, Heine says: ' Hence it is that our two greatest Romantics, Goethe and A. W. Schlegel, are at the same time our greatest plastic poets.' In dealing with the third, political aspect of Romanticism Heine defines clearly the stand he had always made and was always to make against the political implications of the movement. Heine is ' not playing ' ; he rejects a very powerful offshoot of the movement which in all else still commands his allegiance. His arguments are uneven, but instinctively sound. The young student arrives, in part independently and in part under the influence of Wilhelm Schlegel, at a conception of

Romanticism which embraces revolution and progress: unconsciously his Romanticism approaches the essentials of the French movement. (Cf. the Rakoczy march in Berlioz's *Damnation of Faust*. The Rakoczy strains are by no means a disparate element in the opera, but an organic part of it proclaiming the ideals of the freedom-loving subsidiary group of the Romantic movement.)

Even within the confines of German Romanticism, however, the ideals of freedom were urged far less infrequently than is commonly supposed nowadays. These ideals found powerful support in Bettina Brentano, Lenau, Uhland, in Müller's poems on Greece, etc. Heine, then, early formulated a kind of programme of non-reactionary Romanticism:

> Many of those, however, who have observed to what an enormous extent romantic poetry has been influenced by Christianity, and in its wake chivalry, mistakenly believe that they must provide a mixture of these two elements in their poems to make them 'romantic.' I believe, though, that Christianity and chivalry were only a means of bringing Romanticism to the fore; its flame has long been burning on the altar of our poesy; no priest needs to tend its lamp with holy oil, and no knight needs to keep armed watch over it any longer. Germany is free now; no cleric can imprison German minds any longer, no petty aristocratic tyrant can whip the bodies of his German serfs any longer, and therefore let us see to it that the German Muse becomes a free, lovely, unaffected, honest German girl again and no soulful, drooping nun, and no pedigree-ridden damsel waiting for her knight to woo her.

It is not surprising that this challenge to the hitherto accepted machinery of Romanticism, with the pious prayer of its final sentence, should have led to violent and often unjustified attacks against the two Schlegels. All the same, during the year he spent at Bonn, August Wilhelm Schlegel was without doubt Heine's guiding star. The Hamburg troubles receded into the background, to be replaced by a new and wholesome influence.

Schlegel was the outstanding professor among those whose lectures Heine attended in Bonn. Heine met him socially too; in a letter to Fritz von Beughem he boasts of having 'chatted with him for hours over a cup of coffee.' He showed him his poems. Schlegel praised their originality. 'His first question is always:

"How's the publication of your poems getting on ? " He seems to be most anxious to see them published.' Heine went through his poems and corrected them on Schlegel's advice. Schlegel also suggested that he should translate Byron.

All this took his mind off his love sorrows, which he had already transfigured and put into literary form in his tragedy *Almansor*. Hence the outburst in his letter: ' Oh ! dear Fritz, the thorns pierce me every minute, but they can no longer hurt me so very greatly as they used to.'

While a student Heine was chiefly preoccupied in carrying out Schlegel's suggestions. The law course which he was officially required to follow he found nothing but a burden which his conscience told him he must ' mug up.' Roman Law he detested. Afterwards, it seemed to him that he had wasted ' three good years in the springtime of life studying Roman casuistry, in other words jurisprudence, the most illiberal of all disciplines.' Nevertheless, in spite of his aversion to legal studies he was determined to practise as a lawyer in Hamburg. Bearing in mind this fixity of purpose we can more readily understand the cruel compulsion to which his whole life was subjected ; a compulsion which explains many a dart he threw in retaliation. His mood at this time of ' blasted swotting ' is expressed in an utterance like:

What an awful book the *corpus juris* is, this Bible of selfishness. I've always found the Roman code as detestable as the Romans themselves. These robbers want to safeguard their swag, and they seek to protect by law what they have plundered with the sword ; hence the robber became a combination of the most odious kind, soldier and lawyer in one. Truly, we owe the theory of property, which was formerly a fact only, to these Roman thieves ; and the much vaunted Roman Law on which all our present-day legislations and state-institutions are based is nothing but the development of this theory in all its pernicious implications, in spite of the fact that this Law is diametrically opposed to religion, morals, common humanity and reason.

At Bonn Heine attended Schlegel's lectures on ' History of the German Language,' Arndt's on ' The *Germania* of Tacitus,' Hüllmann's on ' German State-Law,' and Radloff's on ' German Pre-History '—' which by the end of the terms had not got further than the age of Sesostris.'

Evidently he was chiefly interested in German studies, in German history, although he attended lectures strictly appertaining to his law course as well. His relationship to Schlegel was that of an admiring pupil and was expressed in sonnets ; an art-form which, with much else, he took over from his teacher. This teacher had guessed at the ' stab of doubt ' that was piercing his life to the marrow, and with kindly words of healing had bent down over him and stayed the weakly plant. Heine's gratitude at the time was undoubtedly heartfelt. Equally genuine was his eulogy of Schlegel as a poet, who shuns the sham muse and who, intoxicated with love, clasps ' Germany's true muse ' in his arms ; who uncovers ' the Rhine's Nibelunghoard,' and in addition has borrowed treasures of poetry from all languages and countries.

How far removed is Heine the student from the sharply negative criticism of Schlegel which he expressed in his later years, when he refused to concede any ability to Schlegel either as poet or scholar or even as critic ; when he vented his ire on him because in Bürger's poems he had heard only ' the crude shout of an ill-educated schoolmaster ' and not ' the heartrending cries of pain of a Titan whom an aristocracy of Hanoverian Junkers and school pedants had tortured to death.' In this later mood of opposition even the description of Schlegel at the time of his Bonn lectures assumed in retrospect another, very sarcastic tone. The powerful impression made by Schlegel on the young Heine is revealed, however, beneath the element of caricature in the description, as in a palimpsest, and almost against Heine's will :

> With the exception of Napoleon, he was in those days the first great man I had ever seen, and I shall never forget his impressive appearance. I still feel even today the thrill I experienced when I stood in front of his desk and heard him lecture. I was wearing a white pea-jacket, a red cap, and no gloves, and I had long, fair hair. Herr August Wilhelm Schlegel, on the other hand, wore kid gloves and was dressed in the height of Paris fashion. He exhaled the perfume of good society and of *eau de mille fleurs*. He was the very personification of fastidious elegance, and when he spoke of the Lord Chancellor of England he added ' my friend.' His footman stood beside him resplendent in the livery of the Schlegelian baronial establishment and trimmed the wax candles burning in the silver candlesticks which, with a glass of sugared water, stood on the desk in front of this prodigious personage.

Liveried footman! Wax candles! Silver candlesticks! My friend the Lord Chancellor of England! Kid gloves! Sugared water! These things were unheard of in a German professor's lecture. We youngsters were dazzled not a little by such brilliance, and I in particular. I wrote three sonnets to Herr Schlegel at the time, each of which began: ' O thou who, etc.' It was only in verse, though, that I would have dared to address so distinguished a personage as ' thou.' He was in fact genuinely distinguished in his appearance. Only a few straggling silver-grey hairs still shone on his small, narrow head, and his body was so thin, emaciated, transparent, that he seemed to be all spirit, that he seemed almost a symbol of spirituality.

It is undeniable that the attack on Schlegel—I cannot quote it here—which follows this description of him assumes a spitefully personal form which eventually becomes obnoxious in the extreme (similarly in *Bürgerkönigtum*, 1832). On this occasion as on others Heine seems to have had no idea how much he offended the person he ridiculed with his witticisms, which were not always good witticisms. In attack he went far beyond the bounds imposed by differences of opinion and outlook, and did everything he could to bring his opponent down. He dwelt on the more humorous, and irrelevant, trivial side of his opponent's private life. Led astray by the joy of battle he showed no desire to come to grips with his adversary's true character and real qualities, although in his other writings he exalts the principle of justice above all else.

In Schlegel's case particularly, in view of the enthusiastic nature of Heine's youthful utterances, we are in a position to examine the subjective and not merely the objective truthfulness of Heine's attacks. An examination of this kind reveals a degree of frivolousness, of *Schadenfreude,* indeed, indifference to his fellow-man's well-being, which is so distressing that I must anticipate my remarks on the even more violent attacks on Platen, Börne *et al,* and comment on it now.

Heine's aggressiveness, his ruthless mockery, his obvious intention at all times not merely to refute his opponent but to ' crush ' him verbally, is incontestably one of his chief traits. It is an essential part of his make-up. Combined with his own sensitiveness to attacks on himself, it gives us a rather peculiar and not particularly pleasing picture of the man. He trod on people's toes and was highly indignant when they trod on his. It is true that as far as Platen was concerned, Heine was attacked first ; but his defence and retaliation went far beyond permissible bounds.

Literary controversy is, of course, unobjectionable where differences of opinion and outlook are concerned. And only a prig would condemn outright any and every attempt to invigorate the objective arguments on both sides by attacks *ad hominem*. After all, we think in concrete terms and we contend with living people, not with disembodied ideas. St. Augustine's *hominem diligere, errorem odisse* is a counsel of perfection and can only be lived up to approximately, not fully. On a much earthlier plane of human endeavour is Goethe's method of attack which he adopts in his sublime essay on Kotzebue: always seek out what is important and pleasing even in your opponent. It is a ' homely ' method, as the great sage himself does not fail to point out, but it is one which springs from a much sounder, more modest—and hence more just—way of looking at things than does Heine's cruelly offensive method.

Goethe says:

If we examine carefully the history of literature we find that those writers whose aim it is to be of influence through instruction or entertainment are in an unenviable position, for there is never any lack of opponents seeking to wipe out their past activities, belittle their present achievements, and weaken their future influence. Ancient and modern controversies of every kind will convince us that there is no way of retaliating, for everything is lacking in a contest of this kind ; there are no duelling grounds, no seconds, no umpires ; and in every arena, as in the circus of olden days, the mob of impetuous partisans will fling itself on to the side of the greens or the blues. The battle sways in the direction of the greatest mass of people, and what started as a match of skill leads to revolt, bitterness, and ends in violence. The moral man need never be without an aid in such a situation, however, provided he doesn't go too far to look for it, since it lies directly by his side ; indeed, it often demands imperiously to be used. Availing myself of my biographical right, I can mention, for instance, one out of many who opposed my influence. This one made it his particular business to counteract in every possible way my talent, my activities, and my happiness. My temperament is such that I should find myself quite defenceless and in an unpleasant situation had I not for some time now been using against importunity of this kind the homely method whose praises I have been singing ; had I not accustomed myself to regard the existence of him who pursues me with aversion and hatred as a necessary and indeed beneficial ingredient in my own life. I like to think of him as a citizen of Weimar, and am pleased that he cannot deprive the city I hold in such esteem of the merit of having been his birthplace. I like to think of him as a handsome, high-spirited boy who would lay booby traps for me in my garden and often delighted me with his merry pranks. It gives me pleasure to think of him as the brother of a charming woman who always showed herself worthy of respect as a wife and mother. If I review his literary activity I recall with pleasure the cheerful impression made on me by certain passages, etc.

And so Goethe reviews with brilliant humour and complete superiority every facet of Kotzebue's life that he could turn to his own positive account—up to Kotzebue's successful plays which enabled Goethe the theatre director ' to entertain the spectators and help the box office.' And he concludes the description of his suggested procedure with a fine piece of self-criticism and with studied moderation : I should be very glad to have made this confession if as a result I should get to know that many who find themselves in a similar position had also benefited by adopting this method, which is neither highly moral nor still less Christian, but arises from a transfigured egoism ; and that in so doing they had banished from their minds that most unpleasant of all sensations , ineffectual resistance and impotent hatred.

I have quoted all this at length—and I might add my favourite motto, for which I am indebted to Stendhal: *Songez, ami lecteur, à ne passer votre vie à haïr ou à avoir peur*—in order to bring out the more clearly the contrast to the world in which Heine lived.

Even attacks as violent as Schopenhauer's on Hegel, the *summus philosophus,* and on the professors of philosophy with their motto of   *primum vivere, deinde philosophari,* or even Lessing's letters against Klotz or Hauptpastor Goeze, are nearer in spirit to Augustine's maxim than Heine's outbursts of hate. Schopenhauer's and Lessing's attacks are serious onslaughts of great gravity—none would deny the value and importance of these cathartic struggles— but it is typical of them that even in the greatest heat of the battle not a single personal trait of those under attack—Hegel, Klotz, and Goeze—is mentioned.

Goethe's 'transfigured egoism' is unique and inimitable, and I mention it here only as an indication of a possible extreme of conduct, of a different kind from the Church Father's; perhaps hardly within the bounds of human attainment. But Lessing, Schopenhauer? For all the sharpness of their polemic they keep strictly to the point they are arguing. The characteristic feature of Heine's polemical style, though, is that he is always trying to 'get a blow in edgeways,' always trying to 'kill' his opponent with an allusion, a play on words, an aphorism. Impotence, a runaway wife, rouge, belly, the ribbons of his various orders—Heine believes that by thrusts of this kind he is scoring off the older Schlegel. But it is only shadow fencing; very cheap, very mean, proving little or nothing at all, and yet, or rather therefore, hurtful. A tactic of this kind, designed to refute certain ideas, meets with little practical success, and whatever success is achieved is incommensurate with the hurt done to the soul of the person attacked, and hence gives the whole proceeding an air of frivolity; frivolous inasmuch as the weal and woe of a fellow-man are lightly toyed with and he is perhaps driven even to despair, without such torturing being in the least necessary for the purposes of the argument, for genuine controversy.

Kierkegaard confirms this viewpoint in a fine comment he makes on Goldschmidt, the Heine of Copenhagen. In his periodical *Korsar*, Goldschmidt held Kierkegaard up to ridicule, inviting the mob's derision of his lanky figure, his trousers, and so on. Kierkegaard observes:

> A *fille de joie* who decks herself out in her best finery, rouges herself, etc., conveys an impression of youth, life, and joy. But behind it all, abomination; behind it all is the old face; for the features of sin are old. Similarly when calumny decks itself out as altruistic wit and jest, and becomes a kind of mammoth box of chocolates; but inside, abomination, corruption of youth, leading astray of the ignorant; and then, the men who have been hounded to their graves, or if not that, the women who had to share their obloquy with them, etc.

And a further entry in Kierkegaard's journal reads: 'Victims have fallen and quiet tears have been shed by women, the wives and daughters, etc., of the persecuted men; and meanwhile there were exultant grins and an increase in the number of subscribers.'

It is not often that the ruinous effect of polemical writing, and of speculating on the passions of the crowd, has been so acutely observed. And although polemical writing is certainly not in these days the cruellest and most inhuman form that the treatment of our fellow-men takes, it is a source and manifestation of wickedness nevertheless. As such it should not be overlooked, since it contributes more to the brutalisation of men's minds and to the flattering stimulation of their anti-social instincts than is commonly realised.

Kierkegaard sums up the essential nature of this particular brand of wickedness in an account he gives of how he once met Goldschmidt while the attacks in the *Korsar* were in progress:

> One day after I had been subjected to a whole torrent of abuse I met him in the street. He walked past me and I called out to him 'Goldschmidt!' And when he came up to me I asked him to accompany me. I then told him that perhaps he had misunderstood everything I had said to him before, and that he misunderstood my purpose in asking him to give up his *Korsar* activities. He thought perhaps that I was trying to appease him so as not to be exposed myself to his attacks. Now he could see that the reverse was the case. Accordingly I would now repeat to him in all earnestness what I had told him before. And I did. I made it clear to him in all solemnity that he was under an obligation to leave the *Korsar*. It would have been laughable, had it not been so tragic, to see how he was visibly moved and the tears came into his eyes—as is often the case with people of this type—and he said: 'You can talk like that about all my work without mentioning once that at least I have a little talent.'

Talent, yes. But what turn and direction will it take? It is not much use the frenzied admirers which a talent of this polemical kind tends to attract (they are mostly hack writers who feel they are unfairly neglected, and others with ' chips on their shoulders ')— it is not much use these frenzied admirers telling us that it is always possible to find a flaw in someone's total personality by picking on a single detail. The whole personality is to be found in each single detail. In each single detail—granted ; but in fact the personality is only apprehended in all its details or at any rate in the way very many details are presented and combined. But why go on ? ' Intuition ' is wantonly postulated. That suffices the *schadenfroh* claque, be the intuition genuine or not, whether it take account or no of the confusion, the transformations, the

limitations and better elements existing in the human being
exposed to their view ; whether or no it take account, indeed, of
these things as they exist in the nature of humanity as a whole. In
reality intuition, so-called, is nothing but a most unreliable
impression which succeeds in evoking a titillating sensation. Such
a sensation is probably not even justified, is based on a sheer
misunderstanding, on a clumsy photograph. And yet, it is held,
this momentary intuition can be weighed against the whole complex
of motives and counter-motives that have been lived through
' with blood.' Had the age he lived in been technologically
advanced enough, no doubt Heine would gladly have supplemented
with photographs his tirades against the various authors he
carpeted. In fact he made a start in this direction in his attack on
Menzel. He says he would like to see Menzel's portrait (' every
cheekbone a Kalmuck ') as a frontispiece to the next issue of the
Swabian School's *Musenalmanach*.

Heine's delight in mockery and his stooping to intensely personal
attacks when engaged in literary controversy cannot be accounted
for solely by the ' blow to the heart ' and other humiliations which
he had to endure. All these were contributory factors in the
development of his aggressive temperament, but are not sufficient
in themselves to explain it. We are compelled to assume an innate
spiritual predisposition, itself closely connected with his positive
qualities, to the formation of this aggressive temperament. This
should be taken as an indication of the imperfection, inherent and
insuperable, in man's basic structure.

It is tempting to postulate a predisposition of this kind as
residing in the Jewish national character. The overestimation of
words, unaccompanied by deeds, of satire which cannot be sub-
stantiated by reality ; the indulgence in slander and abuse ; the
delight in invective where other nations would resort to arms :
all this certainly characterizes a type frequently to be found among
Jews, though fortunately, of course, neither exclusive to nor
characteristic of the Jewish people as a whole.

The comparison with the sharply personal attacks of
Aristophanes, which Heine himself liked to make, is confusing
rather than helpful. We cannot in our day have any direct understanding of the conditions that prevailed in the Greek city-state ;

of the riotous mood of the Bacchanalian feasts ; of the fact that
Socrates, so badly mauled by Aristophanes, sat amicably with
him at the Symposium, and that Socrates' disciple Plato saw
nothing inconsistent in their sitting together and did not even find
it necessary to comment on it. In contrast to Heine, who
considered—he makes the point in his criticisms of Schlegel—that
' the spirit of the past' was easily comprehensible, I consider the
past to be a book with seven seals, much harder to decipher than
the living present which surrounds us. I am not saying it is *a priori*
impossible to lift the veil from the past ; occasionally the serious
investigator endowed with genius can light upon a truth in his
scrutiny both of past and present. But such ' moments of truth '
are not revealed every day.

Precisely for this reason the ' singing flames ' to which, Heine
says, the satiric poet consigns the contemporaries who provoke
his ire are not nearly so dangerous as Heine, in his overweening
pride, thought they were. ' No God, no saviour ' can redeem from
these flames ? Even the tercets of Dante's hell invoked by Heine
in support of his thesis (*Deutschland ; ein Wintermärchen*) have
had to submit to historiographical reappraisal. And while the
purity of Dante's mind and his great will remain beyond question,
it has long since been recognised that many of his victims were
wrongly singled out by him.

The excessive importance many Jews attach to attacking with
words—far beyond the legitimate functions of such attack, which
are extensive and splendid enough—is connected with the fact that
Diaspora Jewry does not have to contend with the actual exigencies
that would face it if it had a state and national life of its own.
The practically universal political ineptitude of the Jews, in glaring
contrast to their manifold political busy-ness and interestedness and
head for detail, is another consequence of this disastrous word-
fetish, of the illusion of the ' word that kills '—to which must be
added the belief in airy theories. This ineptitude will persist as
long as the Jews are without a country of their own in which
they can learn the ABC of politics again.[1]

Heine's orgies of aggressiveness have a source in his national

---

[1] It is a matter of history that this hard schooling has recently—1948—
begun for the Jews.

extraction, but in addition his own quite personal idiosyncrasy, which tended in the same direction, should not be forgotten. It happens too often that the basic make-up of a poet is overlooked. His opinions are discussed, his moral qualities are appraised, origins and influences are sought for—only on one point are the monographs silent: his unique original talent, his vital powers that are reflected in the highest mental attainments. At a late period in Heine's life, when he was on his sick-bed, a visitor notes (1850):

> Unfortunately I didn't keep a diary, and in spite of my admiration for the poet and my devotion to the man, I was so careless as a youth that instead of carefully hoarding all the fine gold that flowed from the poet's lips I let it slip through my fingers. For he was a spendthrift: wit and imagery poured from his lips in an endless stream which anyone who was not an absolute sieve, as I was, could have caught and retained.

Heine the spendthrift of word and wit! It is important to keep this idea in mind. No doubt it will apply in general to the earlier stages of Heine's life, too. It's one thing to think of someone with a cool head deliberately hatching out spiteful attacks and unloading each one in society whenever the opportunity occurs ; it's another thing to think of someone of an impulsive temperament who is always laying about him without considering the consequences, and as a result causes all kinds of damage, including damage to himself.

A fellow-student and friend, Johann Baptist Rousseau, to whom Heine later addressed two sonnets, describes him as an undergraduate in Bonn:

> A small, somewhat wiry figure ; fair hair touched with white ; a high, imposing forehead ; an ironic, good-humoured smile constantly playing around his lips ; he—Heine—usually puts his hands behind his back and waddles along like a duck. Thinks he's handsome and secretly peeps into the mirror. He speaks well and likes to hear himself talk ; whenever he makes a quip he laughs out loud, and his features, which normally are not particularly oriental, assume a wholly Jewish expression and his eyes, at all times small, practically disappear.

Heine's ' crushingly curt comments or humorous sallies ' are also emphasised by another of his student friends, Neunzig, who, however, declares he found Heine to be more of an observer than a loquacious participant in the general conversation.

Heine's brother Max thus describes him in his Bonn University days: 'He was very mild, gentle, and soft-hearted, but extremely violent when made angry; sometimes in such cases even belying his normal nature by giving way to deeds of violence.' Mitigating all these temperamental outbursts of Heine's is a naïve light-heartedness of whose consequences he seemed to be unaware. In the heat of the moment it led him farther than he wanted to go. When this happened he genuinely attempted to make his peace afterwards, e.g., with Platen. Elsewhere in *The Romantic School,* too, Heine says, with reference to Schlegel, that in appraising him he had perhaps 'gone beyond what was permissible in discussing these people's lives'—an admission which did him credit but which, unfortunately, was not followed by the deletion of the offending passage.

As the years went by Heine's vital instinct for genuine humour without malice, for wholesome, joyous laughter, which is his deepest and most likeable quality and the one most peculiarly his own, enabled him to view the aggressive 'killing' word in its proper perspective. In Paris, for example, he says of Ruge:

> He is very funny but a very decent type. After he had tried to kill me in his *Hallischer Jahrbücher* he visited me in Paris. He told me he had murdered me and was deeply sorry for it. I replied: 'Don't let it worry you, my dear Ruge, I haven't noticed it at all here in Paris.' (Conversation with Stahr and Fanny Lewald, also the parallel passage in the *Confessions.*)

While in his second undergraduate year at Göttingen Heine was rusticated for taking part in a duel. Although his rustication was for six months only, it was nearly three years before Heine returned to Göttingen, a city he disliked and poked fun at in his *Harzreise.* It was at Göttingen that he eventually finished his studies. Meanwhile his enforced temporary separation from the Georgia Augusta University profoundly affected his future career; it led him to go to Berlin and thus opened up a literary career for him, whereas previous attempts from Bonn and Göttingen to secure a publisher for his first poems had been unsuccessful.

Nevertheless, both his first and second period at Göttingen had a brighter side. In spite of their differences in outlook and of Heine's love of pulling the leg of everyone he met, he formed a lively

association with an undergraduate named Wedekind. This Wedekind
has preserved some remarkable conversations with Heine in his
diaries. Somewhat surprisingly, they show that the youthful Heine,
whose early poems often give an impression of slickness and of
being hastily put together, ' deliberately chooses many an apparent
harshness, many an apparent fault, even.' A conversation about a
defective syllable and the importance of this deliberate ' mistake '
in a poem afterwards entitled ' Lament of an Old German Youth '
is reported at length and with great seriousness. It shows a deep
insight into the values of broken rhythm. ' Prosody is about all I
am well up in,' admitted the unhappy law student.

He slates Wedekind's poems so rigorously that the latter
no longer has any stomach for them. He refuses to pass
' double-" e " ' rhymes like *leben-streben, gehen-stehen*. ' There's
no metal in them.'

When he came to Göttingen for the second time Heine was
already famous and was welcomed in many circles. ' Weisse
höfliche Manschetten—ach, wenn sie nur Herzen hätten '—Starched
white cuffs ; if only they had hearts! He became a member of the
' expatriate ' club (*Landsmannschaft*) ' Westphalia.' A pretty barmaid, ' Lottchen of the *Landwehr* ' (the *Landwehr* was a
' respectable pub ' where Heine and his fellow-students liked to
dine), and who had firmly rejected his overtures as long as she
had remained in ignorance of his name, once said to him :
' You're different from the other gentlemen ; you're already as
famous as our professors ; I've read your poems, they're lovely.
I know your " churchyard " poem practically by heart. And now,
Herr Heine, you may kiss me in front of all these gentlemen.
Work very hard, though, and write some more lovely poems.'
Between Heine's first bleak period in Göttingen and his subsequent
return had come the years of fame as a young German poet in
Berlin. Evidently they had not been without their effect on
' Lottchen of the *Landwehr*.'

Towards the end of his life Heine said, referring to this bizarre
yet movingly naïve episode of the waitress : ' That small reward
gave me more genuine pleasure than did all the shining gold pieces
I afterwards received from Messrs. Hoffmann and Campe.'

It was during this second Göttingen period that a lady asked
him : ' You're a platonic lover, no doubt ? ' He replied : ' *Jawohl,*

gnädige Frau; like Platow the Cossack Captain.' He could administer the snub direct to a *gnädige Frau,* but was touched by the fresh unaffected naïveté of a girl from the people.

To superficial observers it might seem that Heine loved nothing better than to jest and to laugh, none louder, at his own jests. They were unable to make head or tail of his ' heartrending poems,' as it was all one to him ' if a girl is unfaithful to him.' But Wedekind, a responsible, serious observer, whose original purpose was solely ' to learn as much as possible from Heine ' (' and that is the chief end I have in view in my association with him '), saw things differently. He notes with surprise one day that Heine's love is not merely an ' idea,' but very truth. Several visits to Hamburg had fanned into fierce flame once more the embers that were still smouldering. ' I have not heard anybody tell me what Ratcliff really is—a madman. Nobody has realised it, and yet it's quite obvious, for he has an *idée fixe.*' The blow to the heart!

The *grand amour* has been destroyed, woman has disillusioned him once for all (it will take decades to heal), the twin star *Amalie-Therese* has spread nothing but utter ruin. Indeed, the numerous sham, sophisticated, ephemeral ' affairs ' that Heine indulged in (and gave poetical expression to in *Seraphine, Angelique, Diane,* etc.) may be regarded as no more than the symptoms of a great and true emotion, approaching Plato's conception of love, which was irreparably destroyed. They are the ruins of a huge, burnt-out pile which is afterwards thrown open to trippers with complete restaurant service provided.

Perhaps as a compensation for the pangs of unrequited love Heine cultivated his friendships with all the greater intensity. His relationship with Christian Sethe varied passionately between better and worse. ' It is a long time since I have had the pleasure of a visit from his Magnificence the State Councillor. Occasionally I see him pass by me in pomp and circumstance and with an elegant inclination of his head,' he writes ironically from Bonn about him. Then fresh protestations of friendship ; they come together in Soest—' a treat once more for this old heart of mine, it seemed as if my Christian had dropped from heaven.' Then, in 1822, a rupture in their relations ; all the same, they continued to correspond. As late as 1843, when travelling in Germany, Heine did not forget the friend of his youth, now an inspector of taxes in the provinces, and he paid him a visit in Münster. 'He had few friends,' writes Ferdinand Osterley, a fellow-undergraduate at Göttingen, who was later to become the city's Chief Burgomaster, 'but once he felt able to trust them he became very fond of them. With few exceptions he was very open-hearted with such friends, was the soul of amiability, showed the utmost delicacy of feeling, and was upright and unsparing of himself. He was very boastful and yet in reality no one thought less of himself than he did ; he liked best of all to joke about his ignorance of law. In spite of the violent headaches with which he was continually afflicted, he had an exceptionally cheerful and lively mind, the quality of which was reflected whenever something struck him as ridiculous.'

In his *Harzreise* résumé of his student years in Göttingen Heine states : 'Although the antipathy I feel to Göttingen in general is stronger than my expression of it, it is not nearly as strong as the respect I entertain for certain individuals there. And I see no reason to deny that I am thinking in particular of the very fine man who took me under his friendly wing at the outset of my University career, and who even then inspired me with a genuine love of historical study ; who later on encouraged me in my enthusiasm for this discipline, so that my mind became more tranquil, my energies were diverted into more wholesome channels, and I was able to experience the consolations of history without which I could never have endured the distressing events of my own day. I am referring to Georg Sartorius, a great historian and a great man, whose eye is a bright star in these dark days, and whose hospitable heart is open to the joys and sorrows of all races, to the cares of beggars and kings, and to the last sighs of declining nations and their gods.' Sartorius is the subject of the sonnet ' To Privy Councillor Georg S.,' one of the serenest and finest of Heine's early poems, worthy of the place it occupies in most editions next to the two immaculate sonnets to his mother.

V

Berlin. First Publications.

'ONE DAY in the second quarter of 1821,' relates F. W. Gubitz in his *Erlebnisse*, 'a young man stood in front of me and asked whether I would receive some poems by him.' It was Heine, who introduced himself with the words: 'I am absolutely unknown to you, but *will* get known through you.'

Six months previously he had sent unsuccessfully, from Göttingen, some poems in manuscript—*Traum und Lied* ('Dream and Song')—to the publishing house of F. A. Brockhaus. 'My address is: Law Student H. Heine, care of Dr. Wyneker in Göttingen.'

This time he had better luck. The publisher read a few verses. The macabre poetry of the *Kirchhof* ('churchyard') verses—'*Ich kam von meiner Herrin Haus*'—I came from my lady's house—bowled him over with all its *Wahnsinn und Mitternachtsgraus*, its eerie midnight madness. The poet's extraordinary appearance added to the effect; 'An unhealthily thin figure draped in flopping clothes, with emaciated features showing signs of premature pleasures.' All the same, Gubitz was sufficiently detached to point out immediately that there were some passages which 'went too far' for the censor. Gubitz observes: 'He (Heine) was ready to re-examine his verses, though not with the best will, I'm convinced; nevertheless, he revised very skilfully.' This process of revision, which was repeated on subsequent occasions, Heine playfully dubbed 'gubitzing.'

91

In his *Letters from Berlin* Heine speaks in highly laudatory
terms of Professor Gubitz, who was not only an editor, but a
practical man of the theatre, a poet, a critic, and a 'master of
the graphic arts' to boot. 'He is perhaps overstrict as regards
correctitude and moral decency. But you are not to think of him
as a pedant. He is a jovial, easy-going man in the prime of life ;
an enthusiast for all that is splendid, and reflecting in his personality
the serene Anacreonism that characterizes his poetry.'

The two men rapidly struck up a pleasant acquaintanceship
based on mutual esteem. In May, 1821, five poems by Heine
appeared in Gubitz's influential magazine *Der Gesellschafter*. They
are: *Der Kirchhof, The Minnesingers, Conversation on Paderborn
Heath, Two Sonnets to a Friend*. These were soon followed by the
Wreath of Sonnets to A. W. v. Schlegel. Heine's entry into literature
was thereby completed, albeit for the moment as magazine con-
tributor only.

The Minnesingers, which, like Heine's other first publications,
was subsequently included in the *Book of Songs* (*Romances*), is
characteristically Heinesque. In the Minnesingers' 'tournament'
the victor is the one with the deepest mortal wound, the one ' whose
songs best gush forth from his heart's blood.' Hamburg yet again !

Another link with the commercial city in the 'Northland' was
forged by a visit which the ever-friendly Gubitz paid to Uncle
Salomon, who happened to be in Berlin. Heine's uncle was dis-
satisfied with his ' unsteady nephew.' He felt he had supported him
long enough. It should be mentioned that he had gradually taken
over the entire care of Heine's sister and brothers, of his mother
and of his now feeble-minded father. Uncle Salomon no doubt now
applied to himself the proverb: ' He who will not listen, must feel.'
Gubitz told him that a poet could not be expected to be in touch
with realities and that such an uncle ought not to abandon such
a nephew. The banker replied: ' I never wanted to. But he's got
to learn that money should be properly employed, whatever a man's
occupation.' He then turned to his business friend, the Berlin banker
Leonhard Lipke, in whose house the conversation took place. ' The
gentleman (Gubitz, that is) says there's a possibility of a great genius
failing. I hope he's right about the genius. Pay my nephew two
hundred thalers now and then five hundred annually for three years.
After that—we'll see.'

Heine's problems both as a student and a creative writer were thus solved, at any rate for the time being. Towards the end of 1821 Heine's first book, *Gedichte von H. Heine,* was published by the *Maurersche Buchhandlung.* Gubitz had again given friendly and active assistance in the publication of the book, which Varnhagen von Ense had also furthered by her recommendation. The initial H. in the author's name is of some interest ; it masks Heine's apparent inability to decide between ' Harry ' and the ' Heinrich ' with which he later signalled—as he thought—his entry into the Germanic world.

The book soon created a stir, though not soon enough for its ambitious young author. It was composed in the main of poems which now form the first parts of the *Book of Songs,* namely *Junge Leiden* (' Youthful Sorrows '—1817-21), with its three sub-sections of *Traumbilder* (' Dream Poems '), *Romances* and *Sonnets,* as well as *Translations from Lord Byron's Works.* Heine carefully edited all his collections of poems and later made many changes of detail in the *Gedichte,* transposing, adding and altering.

For the moment we are concerned only with the facts regarding Heine's first publications ; a critique of the poems and a ' critique of the critiques,' that is of the reception accorded them by Heine's contemporaries, will follow in due course.

In the *Letters from Berlin* which he sent to a paper in his home locality, the *Rheinisch-Westfälischer Anzeiger,* in whose columns they appeared from February to June, 1822, Heine has given us his own description of the new impressions afforded by the city. Later these letters were partly incorporated in the *Reisebilder.* Frankly, there is a lot of tiresome twaddle in them. If, in the collected editions of Heine's works, these fictitious letters published in a newspaper were replaced by the actual letters Heine wrote to his friends from Berlin, they would give us a much more clearly defined and, indeed, a much more authentic portrait of their author. They would reveal the stormy temperament of a personage who was always restless and excited, who suffered continually from ' nervous ' headaches, and whose hyper-sensitivity to noise—he was unable to bear even the ticking of the clock in the next room—foreshadows for us moderns the terrible disease from which he died, although to his contemporaries the complaints he made were ' affectation.'

It has been Heine's fate, indeed, both in his lifetime and after his death, to have encountered incredulity in much that he experienced and lived through in the innermost, most truthful depths of his being. A Berlin lady who was an eye- and ear-witness of the incident related that 'a poem which ended "And loudly weeping I fling myself at her sweet feet" was greeted with such hilarity in the salon of Frau Elise von Hohenhausen, where Heine was reading the poem, that he refused to allow it to be printed.' If Heine were alive today he would have the satisfaction at any rate of knowing that no one listening to this poem in Schumann's deeply felt musical setting would now react to it with 'hilarity,' or indulge in the 'flippancies of Heine's contemporaries about his poetical sentimentality.'

Heine's real letters dating from this period lay bare the tempestuous heart ravaged by passion of one who is a seeker. In the course of a sleepless night he enumerated everything he was still able to love. Five headings only. The first: 'a feminine shadow that now lives only in my poems.'

He was asked for biographical details for inclusion in a 'gallery of poets.' In replying he took up a defensive attitude, 'because at the moment I am not worthy of the name of poet, and have still to prove by my works that I take poetry with exceptional seriousness.' 'I am indifferent to praise or blame; for better or worse I follow the stern path that I have decided is best,' he wrote to his *Landsmann* (originating from the same region), the 'senior Westphalian' Ernst Christian August Keller, whom he praises as one of the many 'fighters for right and truth whose iron voices still resound everywhere—as I can see from men like the doctrinaire of the red earth,[1] who, like a stern usher of God in the great hall of nature, shows everyone to his right place, helping into the seats of humanity the downtrodden worm-like Jew and whipping the laughing clubman out of the soft cushions of privilege in which he reclines embedded in his upholstered chair of idleness.'

There was a strange sequel to this head-in-the-clouds letter: shortly afterwards relations between the two were broken off. Apparently Heine became more and more disillusioned. In his letter

---

[1] *i.e.,* Westphalia, so called because of the bloody activities of the *Feme*, a secret and popular self-appointed criminal tribunal.

to Sethe terminating their friendship he gave vent in bitter terms
to German-Jewish frictions: 'Everything German is repulsive to
me, and unfortunately you're a German.' He will go to Arabia,
write Arabic verses. He must have been shabbily treated, for he
goes on to say: 'O Christian, if only you knew how my soul thirsts
for peace and how day by day it is torn more and more to shreds.
In my dreams I see my so-called friends whispering their tittle-
tattle in each other's ears and it penetrates into my brain like drops
of lead. By day I am followed by eternal mistrust ; I hear my name
pronounced on all sides to the accompaniment of mocking laughter.'

Corroborating this outburst of Heine's is the statement of a contemporary, Immanuel Hermann von Fichte, son of the great
philosopher: 'Heine contributed to the general merriment less by
his own wit than by being a target for the wit of others. Eduard
Gans in particular pursued him with caustic sallies.' In company
it appears he was mostly 'shy, taciturn' (F. Brunold: *Literarische
Erinnerungen*—for many of these contemporary comments on Heine
I am indebted to H. H. Houben's book, compiled with admirable
scholarship: *Gespräche mit Heine*). Friederike von Hohenhausen
paints the following portrait:

> He was small and slight in stature, blonde and pale.
> Although there was nothing outstanding about his features
> individually, their general cast was distinctive, so that one
> noticed him immediately and did not forget him again easily.
> His disposition at that time was essentially mild ; he had not
> yet developed the sarcastic sting which was later to prove the
> thorn in the rose of his poetry. He was himself more sensitive
> to raillery than disposed to practise it on others. In those days
> the wholesome feelings he afterwards ridiculed found a
> harmonious echo in his soul.

Some lines in one of the *Letters from Berlin* devoted to Heine's
friend Eugen von Breza, who inspired him to write his essay on
Poland, tally with the foregoing:

> He was the only person whose company I did not find
> irksome, the only one whose original witticisms enabled me to
> recapture my joviality, and in whose sweet, noble features I
> could clearly see how once my own soul looked in the days
> when I 'wore the white flower of a blameless life' and was as
> yet free from the stains of hatred and lying.

The letter continues with one of those puns in which the writings
of innumerable third-rate scribblers have since abounded. Regarded
purely as harmless little witticisms and not as the acme of linguistic
virtuosity and penetrative insight into the heart of language, these
puns would be endurable—not otherwise (actually, far from
revealing a mastery of language, they indicate a certain ignorance
of, and lack of feeling for, the real, natural values of language).
Schmerz beiseite,[1] continues the letter—the Heine filing his official
reports was a different person, evidently, from the reserved, unhappy
being revealed in his private correspondence. Outwardly, to 'his
public,' he passed for a somewhat blasé bon viveur who found the
Jagor restaurant's 'inspiration' of truffles-and-ice-cream neither
more nor less worthy of notice than Weber's new opera *Der
Freischütz* or the green velvet trousers Spontini wore at the last
levee. He writes not only for his public, however, but without doubt
primarily for his cousin, when he says in the same letter: 'I am
very peevish, sulky, cross and irritable today; my ill-humour has
put a brake on my imagination and all my *mots* are in black
mourning. Don't get it into your head that feminine unfaithfulness
might be the cause . . . these days that could only affect my muscles
of risibility.'

I don't like these crowded *Letters from Berlin* with their high-
pressure humour. I'm bound to admit, though, that what finally
emerges from the hundreds of confusing *faits divers* reported in
them (and held together only by 'association of ideas,' like so many
'pieces' and causeries for which they were the model) is a powerful
impression of the Prussian metropolis after the Napoleonic wars.
In addition there is much in them that reflects credit on their author's
powers of observation and on his sound grasp of values. Heine
was always a good *flâneur*; later in Paris, too, one of his keenest
pleasures was to survey the inhabitants of the big city; there was
a contemplative side to his temperament which acted as a beneficial
though often contradictory complement to his aggressive tendencies
. . . 'and I watched as in a dream the bustling people' he says in
one of his poems.

Furthermore, the letters show a proper appreciation of values.

---

[1] Translator's note. A play on the words *Schmerz* (pain) and *Scherz*
(jest). *Scherz beiseite*=jesting aside, *blague dans le coin.*

The quotation with which the *Letters* are headed is from Kleist's *Prinz von Homburg*, and show that Heine early recognised in Kleist the *genius loci*. The first letter reports baldly: 'Heinrich von Kleist's *Prinz von Homburg* will not be performed.' Berlin was strictly controlled. Politics were forbidden. As a result theatrical and other cultural manifestations assumed an exaggerated importance. A little later (1825), the Royal Theatre singer Henriette Sontag's popularity assumed the proportions of a cult (*Sonntag-Fieber*, 'Sunday fever'). The star system in all its odiousness had started. During Heine's stay in Berlin the 'bridal wreath' (*Jungfernkranz*) from the *Freischütz* had become the rage, errand boys whistled it; in his second *Letter* Heine noted its all-pervasiveness in an extravaganza which has since become justly famous.

Berlin was a military town, full of officers, whom Heine viewed with notable objectivity. 'Although I'm no particular friend of the military I must admit I enjoy watching the groups of Prussian officers in the *Lustgarten*. Fine, strong, vigorous, zestful men.' And on conscription he writes: 'Our youth is thereby saved from decadence.' He speaks admiringly not only of the king, but of his family:

> I feast my eyes on these splendid equestrian figures. They include our royal princes. What a fine, strong, princely breed, with no hint of deformity or unsoundness anywhere in the line. There go the two elder princes, full of joyous life, with courage and nobility written in their fine features. The handsome youth with the clear blue eyes whose countenance bespeaks goodness is the king's third son, Prince Charles. But now there gallops by a radiant, majestic woman erect in her saddle and accompanied by a glittering retinue. That is our—Alexandra. In her brown, closely fitting habit and round hat with plumes, a riding crop in her hand, she resembles those female figures in the old tales of chivalry that still cast their gracious spell on us, and about whom we cannot make up our minds whether they are statues of saints or Amazons. I believe the sight of those wholesome features has made me better.

In thinking of 'Heine the Revolutionary' we should take care not to forget utterances like this. They indicate the great breadth and complexity of a receptive spirit.

It was a spirit which turned away from the Stock Exchange. 'This is where those professing the Old and the New Testaments

do their haggling. Don't let's come too near them. O God, what
faces. Greed in every muscle. When they open their traps I fancy
they're shouting at me " Give me all your money ! " ' It will be
seen that Heine had not forgotten the bandit chief Cartouche about
whom he had quipped in Hamburg.

Old, New Testament—it made no difference. In the same cosmopolitan spirit of freedom from prejudice was his description, for the
benefit of the German students, of the Polish undergraduates in
Berlin as ' models of kindly and courteous behaviour.' Among these
undergraduates was Heine's previously mentioned friend Count
Breza. ' You can tell straightway in their faces that no rude tailor's
heart beats beneath the coarse serge of their jackets . . . when you
see so many fine foreigners you really have to be a pretty staunch
patriot to remain convinced that God's greatest gift to humanity is
a German ! ' Heine had become increasingly estranged, evidently,
from the ' Old Germans,' the ' dilettanti of revolution with their
Physical Training clichés ' as he afterwards called them in the
Harzreise, where he portrayed one such in the peculiar outfit of
his fanatic sect, with long hair hanging down, beret cocked at a
rakish angle, and wearing a locket containing hair from the mane
of Blücher's white charger.

It was not ' religious scruples ' which estranged him from the
reactionary advocates of a Christian-German State. Neither did he
share the ' malice towards Christianity ' of the rationalist Saul
Ascher. In matters of religion he was indifferent. ' All I believe in
now is the theorem of Pythagoras and the King's Prussian Law.'

In this attitude he was decisively influenced by Hegel's
philosophy, which was then in the ascendant in Berlin, though he
confessed he only ' rarely ' understood it. He interpreted it as pure
atheism, an interpretation in which he was confirmed, apparently,
by his personal intercourse with Hegel himself. In his Confessions,
written in his last years in Paris, he recaptured the atmosphere of
his Berlin University years and of his Hegelian studies :

> Hegel's conversation was always a kind of flat-toned
> monologue jerkily delivered and punctuated by sighs ; I was
> often struck by his odd modes of expression, a great many of
> which have remained in my memory. One fine starlit night we
> were both standing by the window. I was a young man of
> twenty-two at the time. I had just finished a good meal and

drunk my coffee, and was waxing lyrical about the stars. I
called them the abode of the blessed. ' Hm, the stars,' growled
the master, ' hm, the stars are simply a bright excrescence in
the sky.' ' Good heavens,' I exclaimed, ' is there no happy realm
there then where virtue may be rewarded after death ? ' Hegel,
however, fixed me with those pale eyes of his and observed
cuttingly: ' So you want a tip for looking after your sick
mother and not poisoning your brother ? '

He wrote even more trenchantly elsewhere about Hegel the
' Master,' in his *Letter on Germany* which followed his *Notes on
the History of Religion and Philosophy in Germany*:

Many people have blamed me for tearing asunder the
curtains from the German heaven and revealing that all the
divinities of the old religion have vanished therefrom, and that
only an old maid with leaden hands and sorrowful heart
remains: Necessity. Alas, I only announced earlier what everybody was bound to find out later. The news that sounded so
strange then is now shouted from every housetop on the other
side of the Rhine. And in what fanatical tones are the anti-
religious sermons sometimes preached ! We now have atheistic
monks who would like to roast M. Voltaire alive for being a
dyed-in-the-wool Deist. I must confess to finding this music
distasteful, but I am not frightened by it. I stood behind the
Master when he composed it, admittedly in very obscure and
involved notation, so that not everybody would be able to
decipher it—I used to see him anxiously looking round sometimes in case he was being understood. Once, when I was
irritated by his ' Everything that is, is reasonable,' he smiled in
a peculiar way and observed: ' It could just as well be:
Everything that is reasonable, must be.' He looked hastily about
him, but soon recovered his composure, for only Heinrich Beer
had heard him. It was not till later that I understood this kind
of saying. In the same way it was only later, too, that I understood why he had said in his *Philosophy of History*: ' Christianity represents progress inasmuch as it teaches of a God who
died, whereas the heathen gods knew nothing at all of death.
What progress it is, therefore, if God never even existed ! '

In spite of this emphasis on irreligiosity, however, it was during
his Berlin period that Judaism aroused an ardent response in the
slumbering depths of his soul.

Henriette Herz's *Reminiscences*, recorded by I. Fürst (*Henriette
Herz. Ihr Leben und ihre Erinnerungen. Herausgegeben von I.*

Fürst, 1858), gives a good picture of the general conditions and cultural outlook of German, chiefly Berlin, Jewry, at this time. Henriette Herz's was the typical career of a Jewess of outstanding talent, seriousness, and beauty. In the Berlin environment in which she grew up it was inevitable from the start, one could say their upbringing made it inevitable, that Jewesses should become completely assimilated to their German environment and divorced from Judaism. Henriette Herz was no more to blame for her apostasy than was Dorothea Schlegel, Mendelssohn's daughter, whose best friend she was, or Rahel Levin, Varnhagen von Ense's wife, who was her junior by a few years, or the Meyer sisters. These latter, though less important, are to be regarded from the historico-cultural viewpoint as analogues of these other assimilated Jewesses. One of these sisters afterwards became Frau von Grotthuis, the other Marianne von Eybenburg (she married Prince Heinrich XIV Reuss morganatically—Johannes Urzidil's *Goethe in Böhmen* gives decisive documentation on Goethe's 'little extempore romance' with Marianne v. Eybenburg).

All these Berlin Jewesses had arrived socially. At the turn of the century and for the next three decades their 'salons' were the focal point of German cultural life. Their lives had assumed the form they did in spite of the opposition—half-hearted, according to Henriette Herz—of their tradition-minded parents, who 'considered a German education inseparable from a Christian basis,' and also 'were against their children doing anything, unless in the exercise of a profession, which would detach them from the family circle and interests, which till then had been organised on patriarchal lines.'

The parental opposition failed. We cannot regret it. What Judaism had these parents to offer their children? It was a crumbling Judaism, no longer aspiring as a matter of course to permeate the whole life of every individual Jew and of the entire Jewish community. It was restricted to the performance of particular functions, to the isolated observance of the religious law or to rational speculation about the 'real core' of Judaism, or to both aspects together, even though these aspects in combination fail to provide a unity. Max Wiener, in his penetrating study *Jewish Religion in the Age of Emancipation*, rightly remarks that neither more nor less was at stake than a 'complete break with the unity

of Jewish culture, the religious colouring of which had been a
source of incomparable strength to it.'

The break was painful but historically necessary. It gave rise
to the whole complex of problems which confronts modern Jewry.
The provisional solution of these problems is now taking shape in
Zionism, which is faced with new tasks of immense magnitude in
restoring to Jewry not merely its own political, national character,
but also its own religious and social essence.

As far as the decisive parting of the ways at the turn of the
eighteenth century was concerned, however, it would have made no
difference in principle whether Judaism had continued to evolve on
Orthodox or on Liberal-Reform lines. The great, terrible break had
to come anyway. For German-Jewish Orthodoxy, too, had abandoned the unity of Jewish living; it had waived the right—to take
an example—to its own civil courts, and renounced the distinctive
Jewish garb. ' Hence an East European Jew surveying the West
from the viewpoint of his own Jewish totality found—with complete
justification *sub specie historiae Judaicae*—that the gap between
Right and Left in Jewry was of far less importance than German
Orthodox or Reform Jews imagined ' (Max Wiener). The difference
in the methodology of assimilation and disintegration was one of
degree only: to what extent could and would the Jews permit
themselves to be absorbed in their environment ? To what extent
did Jews believe they could answer for such an absorption to their
Jewish conscience or religious beliefs ?

It need occasion no surprise that in the general defection it was
the Jewesses who went farther. Whereas the men did at least rack
their brains—and the best of them broke their hearts—in an earnest
endeavour to seek some solution to the problems of Judaism in the
modern world, the girls and young women no longer knew anything
of Judaism, not even in Orthodox families; for while Orthodox
Judaism trains its daughters in prayer and ceremonial
observance, in imprinting the seal of Judaism on their household
tasks, it does not instruct them in the basis of Judaism, in Jewish
teaching, which is regarded as an essentially masculine discipline.
The position of the Jewess is characterized by Henriette Herz's
biographer. Praising his heroine for her linguistic studies (French,
English, Italian, Spanish, Swedish, Hebrew, Greek, Latin), he
observes that she ' regarded all these languages as the best means

of attaining a knowledge of the corresponding national literatures,'
but adds, ' except Hebrew, which she learned because it formed
part of her religious instruction.' And so while on all sides vistas
of radiant, magnificent living were opened up, Hebrew led to a
dead-end, to a religion whose dignity, whose power to reveal the
divine and the human and the national, remained hidden for lack
of proper teaching. But did any of these women who hungered for
education ever make a serious effort to obtain instruction in
Judaism ? Making every allowance for the historical inevitability
of the phase of decadence through which Jewry was passing at the
time, one is forced to observe that as far as Judaism was concerned
these much-admired and celebrated Jewesses of the Berlin salons
behaved like—I shall hazard the word—ninnies.

Into the vacuum thus created these women poured with all the
greater intensity the foreign culture which surrounded them and
into which their feminine spirituality gave them a sympathetic
insight. I can appreciate fairly accurately the situation in which the
German Jewess found herself about 1800. I have a special reason
for being able to do so ; I experienced it myself. The paradox here
is only for those who do not know that the corresponding wave of
assimilation reached Eastern Europe about a century later. This
time it did not achieve the same full measure of destructive effect.
In the intervening years Judaism had developed a new cohesive
force, Zionism, endued with powers of resistance, though far from
possessing inner maturity, and still incomplete religiously and
socially.

During the First World War a stream of Jewish refugees, former
inhabitants of Austria's Eastern provinces of Galicia and Bukovina,
poured westwards in their flight from the Czarist army. A comprehensive school system in which I helped as far as I was able was
organized for their children in Prague. In a class I had of highly
gifted young women, I found the same cultural climate prevailing as
that in which the Berlin Jewess of Heine's day would have been
living. The fathers and brothers of these young women were still
living entirely in the Jewish world, some as Orthodox Jews, some
as militant opponents of Orthodoxy. For these young women, however, Judaism had remained something outside them. As such some
of them loved it, while others had already rejected it, but all were
united in a passionate admiration of the Polish and Russian litera-

tures—that is, of the cultures geographically nearest them—to which was allied some knowledge of German literature. The wonderment, and soon the ever-increasing joy, of these young women knew no bounds when, in the course of a series of lectures on world literature, I began to speak of the Bible and pointed out to them that in importance, beauty, and grandeur these Hebrew scriptures of which they were ignorant could at least sustain comparison with Mickiewicz and Slowacki. . . . I shall never forget being called on by a tall, red-bearded Orthodox Jew who came for the express purpose of looking more closely at the person who taught his daughters things which were so extraordinary and obnoxious, but yet were in a certain sense commendable or at least worthy of consideration. Only gradually was I able to dissipate his mistrust. There is no need for me to elaborate the analogy with the Berlin salons.

The Berlin Jewesses, though, were instructed by Schleiermacher, who combined gravity with becoming elegance (Friedrich Schlegel and Henriette Herz called him ' our bijou ') in his *Religion for the Educated* and were initiated into his sphere of ' feeling of simple dependence ' and ' pious emotions.' Henriette Herz deferred her baptism only while her mother was alive ; she did not wish to offend the old lady. After her mother's death she took the first step to which her heart had long impelled her. Henriette Herz's mother, good soul that she was, was the archetype of those old Jewesses who are as unversed in Judaism as their daughters. In contrast to their daughters, however, they cling passionately with every fibre of their being to this Judaism of which they are indeed ignorant and which they can apprehend only dimly, but which enfolds them snugly in its warmth and outside of which life is, quite simply, inconceivable ; or if conceivable, only as something rather queer. They are still with us, these Jewish mothers. My own mother, of blessed memory, was just such a simple soul.

Henriette Herz was herself not uncritical of the peculiar ' mental outlook ' of the young Berlin Jewesses. After referring to the then fashionable novels by Voltaire and English authors she observes :

It is true that this mental outlook had proceeded on the one hand from the literature of the modern nations, but the seed had fallen on absolutely virgin soil. Nowhere was there any link with tradition, with an education perpetuating itself from generation to generation and keeping pace with the mind and the knowledge of the age. At the same time the prejudices engendered by such an educational process were completely lacking too. The consciousness of these factors accounts for the exuberance, the arrogance, the disregard of accepted conventions in intellectual intercourse which were the hall-mark of this outlook, but it was an outlook that was undoubtedly highly original, powerful, piquant, stimulating, and combining astonishing flexibility with great depth. Somewhat later this outlook reached its efflorescence in Rahel Levin. She was about six years younger than I and most of my female friends, but the warmth of her heart and mind combined with misfortune had brought her to early maturity. I knew her from her earliest childhood, and so I knew how soon in her life she aroused those high expectations which she later fulfilled.

Rahel Levin, too, was conscious of the lack of tradition. In 1811 she writes to Fouqué :

I have never suffered from indifference. If I have been indifferent to anything, it was because I did not know of it, and it did not affect me. . . . My education, which was non-existent, is no doubt to blame. I was taught *nothing* ; I grew up as it were in a forest of people, whereupon Heaven took me under its wing ; not much dirt or falsehood reached me. But I can't learn anything now either. Not even religion ; I am just waiting for it from above, by which I mean either a name for the religion I now profess or the revelation of a new one.

It will be seen that this absence of tradition was not responsible for loosening the hold of religion. It was only with the *old* religion of her fathers that Rahel had no point of contact. The injunction ' Be a Jewess ! ' which she hears in a dream seems to her to be a curse, a stab in the back (' and now my whole life bleeds away '). Otherwise her religious attitude is one of naïve expectation and patient hoping for her individual salvation.

The soul of these women who were divorced from Jewish and new to German tradition was practically *tabula rasa,* rendering them peculiarly prone to the dangers to which their inner uncertainty exposed them. Nevertheless, this state of *tabula rasa* enabled them also to acquire the authentic romantic feeling of exaltation and of untrammelled development of the ego, and it enabled them to appreciate without prejudice the great new values of the time.

The great new world-spanning idea of the day was called—Goethe. Rahel, obeying an innermost need, allowed herself to be fashioned by this idea. It is to her credit that as a result of much heart-searching she kept her distance from Goethe the man, except for a few brief encounters. She did not foist herself on to the great man as so many who were inferior to her in rank did. The spiritual radiation that emanated from him sufficed her, filled her with happiness and gratitude, hovered always as a beneficent and regulating power over a life that, open to all pleasures as it was, was yet filled with so much sorrow.

The faults and virtues inherent in a unique historical situation jostle each other so closely in the lives of these Berlin Jewesses, are so inextricably intertwined, that anyone who aspires to an unequivocal judgment must feel his heart sink within him. In the pages that follow I shall feel constrained by my own sympathies to dwell more on the reprehensible and dark sides of this Diaspora culture. Accordingly, as a corrective, I quote a characteristic passage from Margarete Susman's *Frauen der Romantik,* a book which preserves an admirably poised balance between the many happy insights of its authoress and which brings out the brighter side of the whole era :

> It was precisely here, in this circle, that, as nowhere else in Germany, an aristocracy of birth rubbed shoulders with, and paid homage to, an aristocracy of the spirit ; it was precisely here that there was an intoxication with the things of the spirit ; pure, liberated spirit such as could only be conceived of at that particular moment in history when the spirit was discovered in all its self-revolving glory, when a new world was born in the spirit. We beings of today who are everywhere oppressed and trampled under by reality can with difficulty form an idea of the supreme importance of the spirit and of the purely spiritual in the lives of these people. Their lives were determined not by prosaic realities but by the creations of the spirit, by great thoughts and philosophies and works of art, so that in a strange but none the less certain fashion they soared beyond the confines of actual everyday reality. It was in this Berlin circle that all these intensely eager young Jewish women experienced their emancipation. Their spiritual qualities and their beauty soon attracted to them all the most brilliant men of the day, and it was in this circle that there took place the great blazing efflorescence of Rahel's spirit,

whose fragrance was the quintessence, as it were, of all the spiritual life of the time.

In the salon of Henriette Herz, wife of the physician, naturalist, disciple of Kant, and author of philosophical works, Marcus Herz, there would assemble the writers Ramler, Engel, Moritz, Nicolai, Reichardt the musician, Schadow the sculptor, the brothers Humboldt, who were young men at the time, Count Christian Bernstorff, Gentz, and Count Alexander von Dohna-Schlobitten, who was to become a Prussian Minister and who wanted to marry the beautiful Henriette after Marcus Herz's death.

Henriette was known as the 'tragic Muse' and the 'beautiful Circassian.' Her classic Greek profile was generally admired, as was her tallness, in which her contemporaries could compare her only to Queen Luise. In the nineties v. Brinckmann, Friedrich Schlegel, and Schleiermacher were the most frequent visitors to her salon ; we also hear of Dohm and Carl Laroche, the son of Sophie Laroche, who was a friend of the young Wieland. Her acquaintances became so numerous that in 1819 she was able to enter in her journal the not particularly creditable comment: 'I came across a Fräulein Reizenstein at the *table d'hôte* in Schwalbach. She knows everybody, like me.'

There was plenty of scandal. Even the favourably disposed Margarete Susman had to stigmatize it as the 'spiritual disease of the important personages of the time' and observe :

> It is remarkable that the greater freedom of the age, as illustrated by the purely personal decision taken by so many women to ignore the hitherto recognized social conventions, should have provided such rich nourishment for tittle-tattle among those who were in sympathy with the new style. It was as if the repressed but only partially overcome bourgeois elements were forced to choose this particular outlet for their violent eruption.

'Reading circles' were organised. Henriette stresses the modest nature of the refreshments served on these occasions, nor does she forget the tallow candles which 'shed little more than a half-light in a room that was as long and narrow as a drainpipe.' This austere atmosphere seems to have prevailed only at meetings outside the Herzes' home, however ; the Herzes themselves did things in grander style, with 'food and wine.' When the guests had eaten there were

dancing (the 'Queen's minuet' had just been introduced), party
games in the open air and lawn tennis. At his home Marcus Herz
delivered 'lectures on philosophy to a very select audience.'
'Subsequently papers on physics, illustrated by experiments, were
enthusiastically received . . . even the younger brothers of the King
attended these lectures, and Delbrück, tutor to the Crown Prince,
then fifteen years old, brought his royal pupil along to watch some
interesting experiments.'

The appearance of Goethe's *Götz* and *Werther* split the intelli-
gentsia in two. The older generation, which included Henriette's
husband and the Jewish 'Reformer' David Friedländer, rejected
Goethe ; they missed Lessing's clarity and transparency. The women
stood up for Goethe. Henriette relates a characteristic incident:

> Once when Karl Phillip Moritz was visiting me Herz came
> in holding Goethe's poem *Der Fischer* in his hand. 'It's cool,
> no heart at all ! ' he exclaimed, ' I wish someone would tell me
> what it's all about ! '—' But who wants to know what such a
> poem is about ! ' retorted Moritz, placing his forefinger
> on his brow. Herz looked at him open-eyed.

The split was sharpened by the emergence of the Romantic
school. Novalis was simply an object of ridicule for Marcus Herz ;
Henriette enthused over his writings without understanding them
except ' as a whole.' ' All this was untrue and incomprehensible to
Herz, and not unnaturally so . . . the purely scientific outlook has
no means of appreciating mysticism.'

The foregoing remarks may account for the enthusiasm with
which the Jewesses, who were bound by no tradition and were free
to roam where they pleased, hailed the startlingly new style of
intellectual intercourse and conviviality which had come into being.
But what induced Christian society, the Prussian nobility, to mix
in circles which legally were so far beneath them ? Henriette Herz's
testimony does not give us the complete, objective truth, which
might well repay a sociologist's investigation, but it faithfully
presents a picture all the more vivid and graphic of the effect of
the upheaval in the mind of one of its chief participants. She points
out that scholars in Berlin either used to stay at home in strict
family seclusion or would meet each other in a tavern over a glass
of beer. Women would not be present at their gatherings. The sole
exception was Nicolai, who entertained occasionally.

Of only one scholar in Berlin could it be affirmed that he had a home, if in one's definition of the word one includes the dispensing of hospitality to friends and acquaintances, even if uninvited. By profession this one and only scholar was a member of the commercial classes. His name was Moses Mendelssohn. In spite of his meagre earnings as a silk merchant's manager, scantily supplemented by the proceeds of his writings, and the six children for whom he had to provide, this admirable man kept open house. Foreign scholars seldom visited Berlin without getting someone to take them to him. His and his family's friends came without invitation, hence his daughter's brilliant female friends. Orthodox old Jews, to whom Mendelssohn always acted as a friendly coreligionist, came along too, but they were the most intelligent in the city. Mendelssohn dispensed this wide hospitality regardless of the real sacrifices it entailed for his family, although in the material pleasures he offered his guests it was a rule that the strictest moderation be observed. As a close friend of the daughters I can vouch for the fact that the good lady of the house used to count out the raisins and almonds, a delicacy which was then *de rigueur*, in a definite proportion to the number of guests present, before placing them in the dish and taking them into the drawing-room.

Court circles at the time were confined to the King's closest confidants. There were the usual great court festivities and levées, and at carnival time there were routs organised according to prescription for the high civil and military functionaries. Otherwise nothing, except deadly boredom, particularly for the young noblemen. These could already feel blowing in their faces the revolutionary winds from France which had been formed by the Encyclopedists' writings. In Germany Goethe had opened up for them the possibility of a new intellectual future. What had ' society ' to offer them, what could their homes offer them, even though they might be able to find some intellectual sustenance in them ! In these homes Haller, Hagedorn, Gellert, Ewald von Kleist, and the dramatists à la Gottsched and Bodmer were still the heroes of German belles lettres. Lessing was a free-thinking modern.

Even in the family circle there was indifference to things of the spirit, and boredom ! Alexander v. Humboldt, when he used to write to a mutual female friend and myself from his family castle in Tegel, would usually date his letters from : Castle Ennui. True he only did so in the letters which he wrote in Hebrew characters. I had given him and his brother Wilhelm their first lessons in this script. Later someone else continued to teach them and achieved great success. They wrote it extremely well. To have written in those days, in letters which could have been understood by all, that they enjoyed themselves more in the society of Jewesses than at their ancestral castle would not have been a matter about which a young nobleman could have afforded to be unconcerned !

Was it to be wondered at, then, in such circumstances, that when opportunities of intellectual companionship proffered themselves they should have been eagerly seized by those who sought intellectual stimulus through the *viva voce* exchange of ideas, the anti-Jewish prejudices of the time notwithstanding ? It is equally understandable that it should have been the younger men who first began to mix in these circles, for theirs was the spirit of a New Age whose representatives in the early stages, by a happy chance, included some very beautiful young girls and women. It lay similarly in the nature of things that it should have been the intellectually aspiring element among the youthful nobles who first joined these circles ; the nobility as such were too far removed from the Jews in the class system to mix with them on the same footing.

Gradually, as if by some spell, every youth and young man of any importance who lived in Berlin, or who even just found himself on a visit to it, was drawn into these circles. The consciousness of their own worth and their zest for living made it impossible for these young pioneers to hide their light, once they had set it up, under a bushel, and soon it shed its rays to far-distant horizons. Like-minded feminine relatives and friends of the young men gradually came in. They were quickly followed by the elder men of liberal views who had heard of this new kind of ' society.' In the end we achieved the hall-mark of smartness, for even the Diplomatic Corps did not disdain us. Hence I don't think I'm exaggerating when I say that there was not a single man or woman in Berlin at the time, among those who later distinguished themselves in one way or another, who was not a member of one of these circles for a longer or shorter period, according to their situation in life. Even the Royal Family can hardly be excluded, for at a later period the brilliant young Prince Louis Ferdinand mixed a great deal in these circles.

So the new spirit penetrated to the highest ranks of Berlin society, declares Henriette ; but she concludes her observations on the subject with the crucial sentence: ' Nevertheless, in nearly all parts of the territory conquered by this spirit could be found extensive gaps.'

No one who bears in mind the precarious legal situation of these Berlin Jews, in whose salons the élite of the German aristocracy of intellect and of birth felt at home, will wonder at these ' extensive gaps.' Substantially, Frederick the Great's ' Regulations for Jews,' which laid down two classes of Jews, ' protected ' and ' tolerated,' still applied. The protected Jews comprised three groups. Of these, only the upper group of ' Jews with general privileges ' possessed unrestricted domiciliary and occupational rights for themselves and their dependants. This thin upper crust was composed of families whose fortunes had been built on army contracts, banking, minting, and manufacturing. Lower down the scale there was a progressive curtailment of legal rights. The Jews had to pay enormous sums to the Exchequer. Heavy tolls were imposed on marriages, births, changes of residence, travelling. Consequently each one of these activities was in the nature of a luxury which very few could afford.

> The ingenuity of Frederick the Great's Government reached its peak in 1769 in the notorious china-export tax which was levied on all Prussian Jews. Every Jew contracting a marriage, buying a house, or entering into any other civil obligation was forced to buy a specific amount (up to the value of 300 thalers) of chinaware from the royal manufactory and to export it even at a loss. In the short space of eight years (1779-87) this compulsory promotion of the home industry involved the Jews of Prussia in a loss of 100,000 thalers ; those Jews without sufficient capital to pay for the goods that were dumped on them had their houses mortgaged and sold. Even in spite of all these exactions the Jews still owed the Exchequer a considerable amount (52,000 thalers in 1786). It was not till 1788 that the Jewish communities were able to commute the china tax for a lump sum. The china manufactured in the royal factory in Berlin was ironically known in Prussia and abroad as ' Jew-china.'
> The King zealously guarded all the curiosities, even, of the old legislation affecting the Jews. Invoking a ridiculous decree of 1737 by which all married Jews had to wear beards he rejected the petition of a Jew who wanted to take his off. (Dubnow.)

In 1790, under Frederick William II, a few unimportant alleviations were proposed. The Jews were to be free, *inter alia,* not to refer to themselves as such but to call themselves ' Mosaists ' or ' Deists,' as certain enlightened Berlin Jews had claimed the right to do. They were to be granted a measure of commercial freedom, but only in districts where there was an insufficient number of Christian merchants. The Jewish community, led by David Fried-länder, Mendelssohn's pupil, had enough spirit to reject the draft of an ordinance which would not ensure them complete equality before the law. If the supreme governmental authority had decided indeed to give the Jews ' better facilities for gaining a livelihood,' but not ' to restore their civil honour,' then the Jews were compelled ' with bitter hearts to utter a wish—a terrible wish, but one in which the entire colony was united—that your Royal Majesty deign to leave the position unaltered, although we see quite clearly that matters will become more unendurable from day to day.'

It was not till 1812 that an edict was issued proclaiming that the Jews who till then had been living in Prussia by virtue of special privilege were henceforth to be ' Prussian nationals and citizens.' This was before the decisive struggle against Napoleon. Many Jewish soldiers fell at Leipzig and Waterloo, many received the Iron Cross ; a few dozen were even commissioned. But soon after the victory a counter-emancipation movement set in on all fronts—literary, social, economic, political. Dubnow states that the Prussian edict granting the Jews their freedom remained in full force for only three years ; after that there were again discriminatory ordinances that tore in shreds the fabric of legal equality which the Jews had barely wrested and which did not triumph again till 1848. As a result Heine's years in Berlin and the whole of the rest of his life inside Germany were lived under the impact of renewed assaults on the Jewish position. For the Jews themselves these attacks were all the more distressing as it had seemed to them, during the last phases of the anti-Napoleonic struggle, that their uncertain situation was already yielding to their final liberation.

Meanwhile the vanguard of educated Jewry—it was implicit in the whole situation that in the Jews' over-intense struggle for education much that was half-education should have made itself manifest, too—had gained so firm a hold of German culture that there was an increasing reluctance to accept Jewish legal disabilities. Moses Mendelssohn was called ' friend ' by Lessing and ' one of our worthiest men ' by Goethe (*Dichtung und Wahrheit*, 15th book). Lessing asked for letters from him as ' an act of real charity,' and looked forward to a talk with him ' with all the restless urge of

a visionary awaiting celestial manifestations.' But the same
Mendelssohn, whom Kant embraced, at the gates of Berlin still had
to pay the degrading 'body-tax' prescribed for Jews only. The
unchanged legal situation of the Jews was all the more galling, the
resulting chicaneries the more vexatious and out-of-date, like some
fossil surviving into modern times, in that the spirit of the age, both
among Jews and, of late decades, among Christians, too, definitely favoured emancipation.

There were of course many anti-Jewish groupings at the time
as well, but it was the cosmopolitans who were impelled by the
greater dynamic. Not only Jews, but Christians, spoke of the bright
dawn of universal tolerance. An instance: As far back as 1792
the *Posthumous Poems* of the ' Jewish Scholar and Poet, Ephraim
Moses Kuh,' had appeared (two slim volumes in a handsome leather
binding, with the imprint: Zürich ; Orell, Gessner, Füssli & Co.).
The final redaction of these poems, and their ' correction ' before
printing, emanated from Ramler, the 'German Horace.' Ramler
does not wish his labours on the *œuvre* of this German-Jewish poet
(Heine's earliest precursor, since Süsskind of Trimberg, to warrant
serious attention in the field of German culture) to be regarded as
a mark of personal friendship. In a letter to the editor of the poems,
printed in the preface, he expressly states that he had ' only rendered
this service to the German muse out of love for the Jewish nation.'
Ephraim Moses Kuh lived in Breslau (cf. Berthold Auerbach's
admittedly very mediocre novel *Dichter und Kaufmann,* ' Poet and
Merchant ' ; the biography printed at the head of the poems is more
instructive). As an indication of the mood of the time an extract
from the introduction (by Moses Hirschel) to the poems may be
quoted :

> The barbaric days are over (thanks to this philosophical
> century of ours) when we had to be afraid that people would
> scornfully turn up their noses at the mention of the word Jew.
> The torch of philosophy has spread its beneficent beams among
> us Silesians too, and in our country as elsewhere has lighted a
> path for divine tolerance to tread. A sincere and talented man,
> whatever his religious views and his faith, can now confidently
> claim, and be certain of receiving, the love and respect of
> someone whose views differ from his. Christian and Jew can
> now love, esteem and honour each other as brothers. Those

noble minds which are the glory of mankind, which unite society in the furtherance of human bliss, etc. . . .

Turning over sentiments such as these, which seem diametrically opposed to the ideas we hear nowadays (1934), one is quite able to follow the argument of my friend Felix Weltsch, which he once expressed to me in conversation in roughly these terms:

> To a certain extent—but only to a certain extent—it depends on the Jews themselves whether they wish to assimilate or not. Not the least part of the Jewish tragedy lies in the fact that from time to time nations imperiously demand that the Jews living in their midst should integrate themselves into these nations, should become absorbed in them. They open their arms to us, they *want* us. In times of prosperity, when there is ample living space for all, or at any rate when cultural development is proceeding apace we are just sucked into the gaps which exist in the economy of the nation harbouring us. We *have* to fill these gaps; to put it at its mildest it is made very difficult for us to stand aside from them, they attract us with the force, almost, of a natural law. If the nation harbouring us is in a bad way, however; if it hasn't enough resources to feed its own people, or if all classes in it have reached a certain degree of educational repletion (for the question is definitely *not* one of economics *only*), then the alien body that has been harbouring us ejects us with the same inevitability that it had previously accepted us. Every period of expansion, of spiritual and economic roominess in the history of the nations surrounding us, when their ' drawing powers ' can have full play, is followed by a period of retrenchment, of autarchy and contraction necessarily entailing our extrusion from them. Such is the rhythm of our history in the Diaspora, which never permits us to achieve a tranquil self-development of our own.

So that when after so many centuries Germany's ' drawing powers ' were for the first time given full rein, how could the Jews there be expected to be cool-headed and far-seeing enough not to accept the hand that was offered to them in all honesty as the hand of brotherhood? How could they be expected to accept it, even, subject to certain reservations; for example, minority rights —an idea that had not even been thought of at the time? It was too much to ask! There was a fanatical rush of Jews bursting to feel the handshake of which they had been deprived for so long. It is true that in the process many Jews displayed a shocking lack of dignity. But to preserve one's dignity in a situation of this kind

makes more than average demands on even trained diplomats. And
Jews have been and are anything but politicians. It was precisely
the political instinct which they then—and always—so desperately
needed of which their stateless life in the Diaspora had robbed them.
Diaspora Jews tend far too much to think in terms of final achievements. Politics, however, is the art of short-term achievement.

Hence many were transported into flights of delirious enthusiasm
by their expectations that perhaps the ghetto walls could fall. Had
not Moses and Christ based their religions on the same principles ?
The story of the three rings—excellent in intention and in the final
analysis perfectly valid, but taking no account of vital nuances !
The story still persists. It is ineradicable even today. When I wrote
my book *Heidentum, Christentum, Judentum* (' Paganism, Christianity, Judaism ') about just these clearly definable *differences*, I
found to my astonishment that my well-meaning publisher had
embellished the title-page with the three symbolic rings.

If, then, the Jews could be absolved from certain Christian
' truths of history ' other than ' truths of reason '—the dogma of
the Son of God as understood by the Church, for example—they
would be prepared to accept ' certain ceremonies ' of the Protestant
religion. Thus proclaimed an anonymous pamphlet published in
Berlin in 1799, the *Open Letter to the Right Reverend Church
Councillor and Provost Teller in Berlin, by certain fathers of
families professing the Jewish religion.* This was the Christianity
satirized by Heine in his *Confessions,* ' the very enlightened
Christianity from which all superstition had been strained off, which
could be had in Berlin's churches at that time without even the
divinity of Christ, like turtle soup without turtle.' Well, a Christianity
of this kind could be had only in Heine's imagination and that of
the ' fathers of families.' The Right Reverend Church Councillor
at any rate did not accept such stipulations. Even Schleiermacher
came out against the proposal. It was going too far; it would
emasculate both religions. ' What a sore blow this must be in
particular for our worthy Friedländer,' Schleiermacher lamented.
Meanwhile everybody in Berlin knew that David Friedländer, who
had behaved so courageously only a few years before, was the author
of the pamphlet. Great was the scandal.

The reforming zeal of Israel Jacobsohn in Brunswick, among
many others, was similarly, though more circumspectly, directed to

bringing about an approach to both the outer and inner *mores* of the Gentile environment. It was felt that such a *rapprochement* would promote the desired liberation from the vexatious yoke of the anti-Jewish laws, and would consolidate such scattered gains as had already been achieved in this respect.

The Jewesses of the Berlin salons, however, unlike the ' fathers of families professing the Jewish religion,' did not engage in prolonged wrestling with their consciences. They went to the font straightway, without preliminary quibbling over specific dogmas. In any case, their knowledge of Judaism was limited to a little ritual, the meaning of which they did not understand. Just at that time, though, both the German and Christian cultures were at their zenith and full of youthful vigour, having within them the stuff that wins and fills human souls. Consequently the Jewesses, and soon after their sons, like Veit, the young artist, had no difficulty in seeking the font out of conviction, and felt no need to justify their action on opportunistic grounds. As Frau Schlegel, Dorothea Mendelssohn became a devout Catholic. And Henriette Herz, who had herself become a Protestant, felt a ' certain jealousy,' when she met the friend of her young days in Rome again, at the way in which the German Catholics in Rome, particularly the newly converted among them, stuck together. And it is quite true that on her deathbed Rahel Levin uttered the famous words that are always quoted by her Jewish admirers :

It is with a lofty thrill that I think of my origin and the whole pattern of my destiny, in which the oldest memories of mankind are interwoven with the newest situations, and extremes of time and space are interlinked. What was so long my greatest shame, my bitterest sorrow and disaster, being a Jewess, I would not now miss at any price.

The utterance loses something of its confessional value, however, if read in its context in Varnhagen von Ense's book, *Rahel. Ein Buch des Andenkens für ihre Freunde.* Which goes to show—once more—that quotations should always be read in their context. Very often a picture emerges from such a reading which is quite different from that conveyed by the isolated quotation. Varnhagen writes :

Remarkable, too, are the following words spoken by Rahel on March 2nd. I felt impelled to write them down *verbatim*

directly she uttered them: 'What an extraordinary story,' she
exclaimed with deep emotion, 'I, a fugitive from Egypt and
Palestine, find help, love and care in your midst. It was through
this working of God's will, dear August, that I was sent to you,
and you to me ! It is with a lofty thrill, etc. . . .'

and the famous quotation follows. This is the continuation,
however:

> ' Shall I not feel the same about these sufferings I have
> endured in my illnesses, shall I not have the same lofty feeling
> that I would not want to miss them at any price ? Oh, dear
> August, what a comforting thought. What a momentous
> parable ! In this manner let us go forth ! '

Judaism, then, is merely a parallel to her mortal illness—is
suffering; true, suffering she now would not want to miss. How
little there is to choose between Rahel's outlook, even where she
appears to be *closest* to Judaism, and Heine's ' thousand-year-old
family bane, the unhealthy religion of ancient Egypt,' his hospital
poem which, for all the tenderness pervading it, represents Heine
at his *farthest* from Judaism !

This, then, was the state in which Heine found Berlin Jewry;
a state of dissolution, decadence, helplessness. The honeymoon of
German benevolence towards Jewish society was over. The anti-
Jewish leaflets of Grattenauer, Paalzow and Bucholz had already
made the rounds in Berlin. The salons had reached their zenith
and were starting to decline. Unhappily it was no longer possible
to stop people talking politics, wrote Henriette Herz in her old age.
Still, at Varnhagen's and Rahel's the young Heine could still meet
Humboldt, Schleiermacher, Chamisso and Hegel, who were daily
guests; occasionally, too, Bettina, Frau von Cotta, Arnim. And at
Elise von Hohenhausen's (the translator of Byron), he often drank
tea with Gans and Bendavid, the radical exponent of Jewish
enlightenment, as well as with Varnhagen, Chamisso, ' whose long
grey locks flowed fantastically round his emaciated but distinguished
features '; the historian Leopold von Ledebur; the poet Apollonius
von Maltitz; Count Georg Blankensee, a pinchbeck successor to
Byron; Rahel's ' surpassingly beautiful sister-in-law,' Friederike
Robert; Helmina von Chezy; Frau v. Bardeleben, and others.

Polite intercourse of this kind made neutrality still possible, but
what in a previous generation had been taken for granted as part

of the bond uniting mankind, what had brought Lessing and
Mendelssohn spiritually together—long before the French Revolution—was now exposed once more to the harsh light of conscious
thought, of argument, of special pleading. How did Jewry react?
It attempted to salvage the German-Jewish synthesis which had been
recently evolved and was now threatened once more, by sacrificing
the vital parts of its own make-up, without differentiating, in its
haste, between what had been abused in it and what was sublime
in it. Away with it, away with it all! David Friedländer wrote:
' Our ancient liturgy is full of hymns mourning the loss of the Jewish
people's ancient homeland and of its political liberty. Today,
however, we have only one Fatherland, Prussia, and this is the only
land for which we ought to pray ; we have only one mother-tongue,
German, etc.' By completely assimilating with the German spirit
Jewry desired to demonstrate that it was worthy of emancipation.

This was the exact situation described by the Hebrew writer
Achad Ha-am as ' outer freedom and inner servitude ' in a penetrating essay which appeared in 1891: a hundred years back the Jews
had sold their natural *amour propre* for their ' rights ' and thereby
placed themselves in a position of humiliating dependence on every
passing mood of the nations harbouring them. He, the persecuted
Russian Jew of the Czarist era, who enjoyed fewer rights than did
his brethren in Western Europe, proudly affirms:

I would like to forget for a brief moment the frightful
material and spiritual misery that surrounds me in my native
Eastern Europe and seek consolation *outside* the Pale, in those
countries where there are Jewish professors, Jewish members
of the Academy, Jewish officers and Jewish holders of decorations—but when I do so I find, flickering between all these
decorations and titles, a double spiritual servitude, one which
is moral *and* intellectual. And if someone were then to ask me
whether I envied my fellow-Jews their ' rights,' I would answer
firmly and resolutely with an emphatic, decisive ' No ! ' Leave
me alone with your ' rights ' ! I may not enjoy any ' rights,'
but I haven't sold myself for any either ; *I* can say out loud
that I love my fellow-Jews in every country and in every State,
without apologizing for it with all kinds of pitiable excuses ;
I can remember Jerusalem apart from the liturgy ; *I* can read
the Lamentations of Zion in public without anybody asking
me: ' What's Zion to me, and I to Zion ? ' ; *I* don't have to
praise my people to the skies and claim that it is a schoolmaster

to the other peoples of the world in order to prove that it has
a right to exist ; *I* know quite well ' why I remain a Jew,' or
rather, I understand the question as little as I would the
question why I remain the *son of my father*.

Accurate as Achad Ha-am's analysis was, *one* factor must be
borne in mind : the frightful nature of the situation, mocking all
human efforts to overcome it, into which Heine's own generation
(' first fruits of assimilation,' as another Hebrew writer called them)
suddenly and without preparation found itself plunged.

It is quite true that the ghetto had developed its own firmly
rooted culture and that in it there was a feeling of unity and national
solidarity. The people's leaders and the people's literature had come
into being by natural processes. There was, too, the *spernere se
sperni* pointed out by Nietzsche, though exaggerated by him.
(Nietzsche in general simply never bothers to evaluate properly his
impressions.) But the ghetto, too, had experienced a spiritual decline.
Steinheim, who had experienced the effects of this decline in his
own person, excoriates it all the more vividly (*Moses Mendelssohn
und seine Schule,* 1840) :

> Every prayer and every biblical passage had degenerated
> into meaningless chatter and mechanical muttering. . . . The
> unsavoury visitors who came to us from Poland in wave after
> wave, like plagues of grasshoppers,[1] were entrusted not merely
> with the direction of our religious affairs, but with the
> instruction and education of our children, particularly the boys.
> The girls had practically no education at all.[2] These uncivilized
> people were taken into our families. They ruled their flock with
> a rod of iron, particularly the rising generation. Their discipline
> was as uncouth as their manners, and the punishments they
> administered were unjust and barbaric to such a degree, that not
> infrequently the children's health and lives were endangered
> by the rough handling they received, etc.

Hence emancipation made a breach in a structure which was
already in decay, though still firm in some of its parts. It should
not be forgotten that the ghetto was held together not merely from
within, by the solidarity of its inhabitants, but primarily from
without, by force. The ghetto walls locked the Jews in a *grip of
hatred*. To unlock this grip was a task worthy of the greatest

---

[1] There is a corrective to this in the next chapter, p. 141.
[2] Cf. *ante*, pp. 101 and 102.

exertions of the noblest Jews, if only because it *was* a grip of hatred and the axiom applies that hatred harms not merely the hated but the haters.

All hatred is spiritually damaging to both sides. It gnaws at and gradually consumes the decent instincts of the one who hates, too ; its evil effects know no limit. Hence the efforts of Friedländer, of Jacobsohn in his mixed school for Christian and Jewish pupils at Seesen, and later of Geiger, Holdheim and others were, for all their many mistakes, not merely intended to benefit Jews, but also non-Jews and—without exaggeration—humanity as a whole.

The ' first fruits ' were perforce lacking in experience. For the first time—at any rate, for some centuries—a situation had arisen in which it seemed as if no price could be too high for liberation, however insecurely based. Much can be said in excuse of the ' first fruits.' No such excuse can be made for our present-day assimilationists, who have all the unmistakable lessons of the whole of the last century to learn from.

The generation of the ' first fruits ' were confronted with a problem whose difficulty can hardly be overestimated. They were called upon to undertake two contradictory activities at the same time : to loosen the grip of hatred and yet to maintain, even to love a measure of separatism which till now had been inspired by, and given rise to, hatred only. They were called upon to leap over the abyss into an alien world and yet maintain their identity. No wonder that the best of them gave up the practically impossible task, and that to an unsympathetic eye the whole generation presents a sorry picture. Perhaps it was necessary at first for them to go too far in the one direction, in the leap over the abyss, and for their mistakes to be rectified much, much later. This seems to be the way of mankind in general—a zigzag, a series of swings of the pendulum that are always too far to the right or left and are always trying in vain to balance out through ever fresh mistakes. In vain—for how can mistakes, be their number never so great, ever cancel each other out ? The just mean in all its golden vitality is something quite other than this arithmetical balancing out of opposites. Only very rarely in the history of man, in Moses, Lao-Tse, Plato and Goethe, has this mean revealed itself.

Let us be frank : the generation of ' first fruits ' were not equal to the greatness of their task. Perhaps it was because—we don't know—the task was a gigantic one; perhaps the men who set about it were to blame as well. In seeking to avoid the Scylla of Jewish imprisonment within ghetto walls they foundered on the Charybdis of self-dissolution with its concomitants of hypocrisy and hysteria gradually rising to self-hatred. The assimilationist is always in his own way but can never get away from himself, and is agitated to the end.

It is against this murky background that Heine must be viewed ! Only then can his greatness be appreciated. In absolute terms Heine is anything but a Titan. Compared to his Jewish contemporaries, however, he appears a larger-than-life, astounding figure. And should we not try, in the last analysis, to measure every human being from the level in which he lived ; not seek to measure him in the abstract perspective in which we see a mountain from some distant point on the sea level ?

Heine succeeded in doing what no one else did in his day: in striding out in opposite directions. He did it almost unconsciously, almost as if it were child's play. He walked out of the Jewish Middle Ages into the modern era laughingly, even, to a certain extent, frivolously, and yet succeeded in preserving his continuity with living Judaism. He had nothing to help him in so doing ; his fellow-Jews of the Enlightenment, in particular, could not help him. With the best will in the world, they could not. For all Heine's noisy inward and outward exuberance, where his most intimate secret was concerned there was utter quiet and loneliness. The secret of the path he had to take, of the decision which only he could carry out, only he could manage—he had to find it alone, all alone.

His Jewish contemporaries certainly could not assist him. And it was not only when he instinctively sided with the Orthodox Chacham Bernays against the Liberal Temple Reformers, with whom of course his uncle's sympathies lay, that the Jews took a dislike to him and denounced him to this same uncle again. They opposed him on many other occasions as well. Eventually he came to look upon them as his enemies pure and simple. He had to go his own way alone, a way of errors, of the disastrous baptism. Nobody could understand him. He himself could not understand what it was that was really directing him. If it weren't again rather misleading one could say that it was first and foremost his light-heartedness, his laughing conceit that helped him. He just didn't notice the problem of the opposite directions; he leapt the abyss with a laugh, full of a naïve self-confidence which, in exception to the rule, led him this once aright. In the world of spiritual grace there are no rules; at least, none that we know. . . .

I make the necessary correction at once. It was not laughter alone that guided him ; there was earnestness, too. He had a faithful guide: the books of the Old Testament, which at various times of his life he read and re-read, appreciating them more deeply each time. Jewish history with all its human, social-ethical, and, irradiating the whole, mystical-religious riches accompanied him on his narrow, dangerous path. It was not for its religion, which at first meant nothing to him, the ' scorner of all official religion,' that he read the Bible. But it was not simply for the sake of its historical worldly interest that he read it either. ' Sweet, tranquil plains of the East gleaming in the sun ! How wondrous peaceful lie thy tents ! ' (From his book on Börne.) Nor can Heine's enthusiasm for the Bible be explained purely as a poet's love of romanticism. Early on he sensed that the people of the Book were the bearers of a spirit that was universal, but needed to be expressed by a particular nation ; nation not as a step downwards to bestiality, but as a step upwards to humanity, for the sake of the divine justice —' beneath the hard stone breathes the tenderest moral feeling.'

I have suggested naming this trend of ideas—since the concept of nationalism is tarnished—' national humanism.' More of that anon ! Meanwhile, during his years in Berlin Heine, as well as giving expression in his letters to several not particularly creditable pleasantries about Judaism, wrote his lively study of Poland and worked out his preliminary studies for the *Rabbi of Bacharach*. Heine's superiority to Börne shows itself clearly in the attitudes of the two men to the Bible. The insight of Heine, joyously assenting to the grandeur of life, contrasts with the narrow, abstract, though sincere arguments and Voltairean witticisms of Börne, who saw in the Bible nothing but jejune tales, a parody in the style of Blumauer.[1] In the same way the two men's positions *vis-à-vis* Goethe illustrate the contrast between Heine, with his vital instincts and responsiveness to all that went on in the world, and the dismal,

---

[1] Johannes Aloys Blumauer (1755-1798) was known for his parody of the *Aeneid*.

insensitive outlook of Börne. Thus Heine stands head and shoulders
above his contemporaries of the emancipation.

Meanwhile, Heine had perforce to come to terms and mix with
these contemporaries of his. He had to plunge into the thick of a
fermenting society that was on the verge of disintegration, and to
establish himself against innumerable petty and not so petty rivals,
against false friends and real enemies. As has been said, he did not
succeed in cutting any very good figure in the process. He was far
from being the centre of attraction in the salons and at ' æsthetic
tea-parties ' ; more frequently he was a ' figure of fun.' Later he
took his revenge in a witches' scene set on the Brocken precipice
(in the *Harzreise*):
    ' Indeed, a young poet travelling from Berlin to Göttingen who
rode past the Brocken on the night of the first of May was able
to notice, even, some bookish ladies holding an æsthetic tea-party
on a corner of the mountain. They were reading the *Abendzeitung*
to each other with evident enjoyment and saying what world
geniuses their poetical nanny-goats who were prancing around the
tea table were, and they pronounced final judgment on the latest
developments in German literature. But when they came to *Ratcliff*
and *Almansor* and declared that the author of these works was
completely lacking in piety and Christian feeling the young man's
hair stood on end.'
    Heine came off worst in Grabbe's coterie as well, which used
to meet in Stehely's café and in Lutter and Wegener's wine-shop,
etc. Köchy, v. Uchtritz would also be there. ' Grabbe was always
on top with his coarse witticisms.' On one occasion Grabbe is alleged
to have gone to the extent of threatening Heine physically. ' Heine's
debaucheries with Grabbe and the other bloods exist solely in the
imagination of certain Heine biographers,' wrote Houben. ' Heine
drank very little and did not smoke at all.' A comment of Grabbe's
on Heine has been recorded : ' This chatter about Heine, a rubbishy
Byron I threw down the stairs. The chap's too skinny and too ugly.
This accounts for his sentimentality, which makes him unable to
touch a girl, and is good only for cheap satire.' All of which accords
with what Heine wrote in a letter ; he was living in Berlin, ' ill,
lonely, treated as an enemy, and incapable of enjoying life.'
    Grabbe's hostility to him never affected Heine's admiration of

the ' drunken Shakespeare ' in the least. Heine always considered him a poet of genius. It says much for Heine, and in my view considerably lessens the force of the charges of conceit that are often brought against him, that he did not allow his genuine admiration of poetical and human values to be affected even when the objects of his admiration failed to treat him with any particular cordiality. This applies to Grabbe and even more to Goethe. Heine took the manuscript of Grabbe's *Gothland* to Rahel Varnhagen. ' For I had already seen from the little I had read of it that here was a poet. One can tell poetic game by its scent. This time, though, the scent was too strong for feminine nerves, and at a later hour, towards midnight, Frau von Varnhagen sent for me and implored me for God's sake to take back the horrible manuscript, as she couldn't sleep a wink while it was still in the house.'

Heine liked to think of himself as a Hellene, and unquestionably his actual life, and particularly those occasions in it on which he was cheerful and serene, afforded some justification for regarding him as such. Many visitors confirm this impression. Schumann, foi example, who as a seventeen-year-old student had been commended to Heine in München, and with whom Heine had spent several hours in showing him round the galleries, wrote: ' He came up to me as a friend ; like a kind, Greek Anacreon.' In the unhappy and ill-famed moments when he stood before Goethe (who seemed a Zeus to him) in Weimar, no doubt he felt himself to be a Dionysus. There was a definite period in Heine's life in which he saw his ideal in Goethe the Greek god (the ideal faded only with Heine's illness), in much the same way that Börne used to dream of his hero Lord Byron.

Yet I fancy that it was only during his Italian journey and in his early Paris period that Heine fully conformed to the ideal, as he conceived of it, of the serene pagan Hellene. Certain triumphal but untrue observations, according more with the biographer's wishes than with the actual facts, must be removed from his biography, just as layers of paint have to be scraped off certain pictures. When this is done the heart of the picture is seen to be ' Affrontenburg ' once more. Heine's life is uncovered and we see it to be the life of an afflicted and deeply humiliated man who has had to fight grimly against unfavourable circumstances. Within him no doubt there existed the sketch of a Sunday's child, but it remained a sketch. The finished portrait was different ; it showed a self-conscious, gauche person of great talent but little fortune, and hence justifiably piqued in his *amour propre*; a person, moreover, who was always ill, in spite of the shower-baths—'useless, though they cost a fortune '—he was taking even then in Berlin. There is ample evidence confirming the unfavourable impression he made in his Berlin period.

And Rahel ? A contemporary (Brunold) thought that she too had failed at first to recognize Heine's talent. But this is refuted by her letter to Gentz:

> As he (Heine) is sensitive and queer, I frequently understood him, and he me, where others could make nothing of him. This won him over to me and he accepted me as a patroness. I praised him as did all the others, generously, but would let nothing slip by if I saw his manuscript before it went to press. This seldom happened, however; though when it did I was severely critical of what I saw.

The patroness was indeed severe. 'Don't be a Brentano, I can't stand it,' she said to him, expressing her distaste for romantic extravaganzas and waste of energy. And Varnhagen, too, said he frequently had to remonstrate violently with Heine ' to stop him clambering up to the dizziest heights and then falling to the ground and risking breaking his neck.'

No doubt these warnings were amply justified. Referring to the persecution of the Jews in Hamburg, Heine had said in Berlin: ' There can be no repetition of these incidents, for the Press is a weapon, and there are two Jews who have a German style. I'm one, Börne's the other.' A ridiculous exaggeration of the power of the pen ; cf. the discussion on polemical writing in Chapter IV. Rahel wrote, probably in allusion to other fantasies of Heine similar to the one quoted: ' Heine must become realistic even if it means he has to take a thrashing. Man, be realistic ! ' Varnhagen's comment shows deep insight: ' He must see to it that he keeps himself in a good spiritual atmosphere, for there is much in him that can easily go bad.'

There is no reason to doubt the sincerity with which Rahel exercised her educational functions. She was a mature woman at the time, having reached the age of fifty when Heine arrived in Berlin. She herself practised, and induced others to practise, Goethean restraint and the Goethean clarity of formulation which had enabled her to subdue, painfully enough, her own unruly life, which, left to itself, would have brooked no limitations of any kind.

It is not true that Heine was initiated into the Goethe cult by the Varnhagens. The essay he wrote on Romanticism while still at Bonn reveals his veneration of Goethe. On returning home to Düsseldorf in the Bonn vacation he gave his young brother Max a copy of Goethe's *Faust* and expressly commended it to him in contradistinction to other German dramas. What is true is that Heine's appreciation of Goethe took on added strength through his association with Rahel and her husband, and that he was frequently rebuked for jibbing at the Varnhagen *mores*. 'He must pull himself together,' wrote Varnhagen, 'and make up his mind he is going to stand with both feet firmly planted on the ground, otherwise he'll run the risk of wasting his life in frivolousness and disillusionment. I've told him so myself, and though he didn't like me any the more for it, that doesn't matter.'

Heine was profoundly grateful to the 'little woman with the great soul.' He accepted many, though not all of her admonitions. For reasons not unconnected with the uniquely despotic manner in which she sought to impose her taste Heine once wrote to her that he wanted to wear a dog-collar inscribed: *j'appartiens à Madame Varnhagen*. She constantly strove to 'make him more earnest and to moderate his humorous outbursts.' Whereupon they would outdo each other in entertaining the company with 'follies,' *aperçus*. Once, for instance, Rahel made a very wise observation about the waltz, 'which so frequently seemed not to make sense when people danced it; when they waltzed after every serious struggle, for example. I've always liked and enjoyed it, though, without ever quite knowing why: after every sorrow, struggle, confusion, accomplishment—on with the waltz ! What more can anyone want: whirling, living, being, ending ! Heine tumbled right out of his armchair, helpless and red as a beetroot from laughing. Involuntarily he exclaimed: " Mad," he cried out, " mad, quite mad ; oh, how mad ! No, not madness, stark lunacy ; nobody's ever said anything so idiotic before," and he continued to laugh. Directly he had recovered he was purely and simply all envy. I told him so, too: " You'd have liked to say something as idiotic as *that*," and I laughed. I had to *explain* the last bit, about the waltz. He asked quite seriously, and then he thought it was very good.'

Much as I admire Rahel I must say that in this account she
strikes me as being unduly pleased with herself, whereas Heine's
action seems genuinely that of an artless character who sees no
reason to resist the impulse of the moment.

To Varnhagen, however, who was always Rahel's loving echo,
Heine's laughter seemed little less than *lèse-majesté*. He writes to
his wife about this really very trifling incident in measured tones
which show how precarious Heine's position was even then:

Your news about Heine could be better ; I had indeed hoped
it would be. So many and such rich aptitudes, but Nature in
her haste omitted some important additions, with the result that
his brilliantly illuminated defects are now there for all to see.
There is only one cure for him. He must seek firm ground on
which he can feel absolutely secure within himself. He can
then send his talent out raiding—and come back with all the
loot and mischief he likes. If, however, he has not this firm
ground as his base of operations, he will soon find himself
without anywhere to rest at all. He will have nowhere to leave
all that he has won and will have to risk losing his gains and
himself into the bargain ; eventually he will be arrested as a
common disturber of the peace and will come to a miserable
end. Warn him, if he is still prepared to listen. Yes, it is indeed
difficult to live one's life physically, spiritually and morally in
such a way as to be able to earn the approval of Nature ; how
much harder is it to earn the approval of God and man !
Nevertheless, convey my heartiest greetings and tell him he
can count on me. The other day (13th March), for example,
when we were dining at the Electoral Princess's, Schlegel, like
a coward, wanted to play safe and disclaim the public tributes
Heine had paid to him. He wanted to dissociate himself from
him altogether, but I wouldn't allow it.

Between such opposing temperaments tension was inevitable.
Once, indeed, after a visit from Heine, Rahel writes : ' Open the
windows after him ! ' so much did he get on her nerves. She told
him that he would ' keep on defiling ' himself, as he was quite
satisfied ' to cause irritation, even if it meant he himself had to
play the dirty harlequin or hangman.' Nevertheless, she thought a
gorgeous bunch of roses Heine once sent to her when she was ill
' the first signs of a welcome improvement.' She was a woman with
a genius for frequently changing course, and for all her devotion to
Goethe's noble mean she rather cultivated her unpredictability.

Loyalty was not her strong suit, as Henriette Herz points out, 'although she had a lively feeling for friendship.' Now and then a passing mood would result in one or other of her friendships petering out. In such cases she would say : ' Well, things can't last for ever.' Margarte Susman comments : ' This aspect of her nature frightens us. This emphasis on the personal, all-too-personal, repels us even in its very greatness. For our modern taste the great figure of Rahel seems what is called in sculpture " overmodelled," its lonely tragedy inherent in her nature, her spirit and her fate.' Nor should her own percipient self-criticism of her make-up be forgotten: ' You, Varnhagen, misunderstand my strength. It is one manifestation of a seven-and-seventy-fold sorrow ! This week I have discovered a paradox. A truth that has still to find room in which to assert itself, that presses violently into the world and dislocates a joint in bursting through it—such am I, alas ! Herein lies my death ! '

I quote all this so that the reader may be aware that the disharmonies existing between Heine and Rahel were not all attributable to Heine alone. It is possible that Rahel also, just because of her ' dislocated joint,' saw things wrongly. For her definition of a paradox, too, is wrong. A genuine paradox arises necessarily when the Absolute, which can never be comprehended by the finite understanding, demands entry and breaks into the finite world. That is Kierkegaard's paradox. The paradox that troubled Rahel partook no doubt of the nature of this infinite, but was also finitely determined in considerable measure by her wrong attitude to her repressed Judaism, and to this extent it was, historically speaking, ephemeral, removable and by no means ' eternal ' : no ' truth ' in the strictest sense of the word.

Nevertheless, Rahel was the most important of all those with whom Heine had personal contacts on a serious level. It is for this reason that I have examined in some detail her assessment— negative, on the whole—of the poet. To a peculiar degree certainty and balance were the features of Rahel's character. Yes, she had certainty. But Rahel's life was plotted—with certainty—on a *wrong* system of co-ordinates, German-Christian co-ordinates. Heine had no system of co-ordinates at all ; at the time he swung violently from one extreme to another. This had the disadvantage of uncertainty, and did not make him a particularly attractive figure, but it was perhaps better than being definitely on the wrong track. In considering Rahel's judgments on Heine this peculiar feature of their relationship must always be borne in mind. Where the judgments she passes tend to be unduly severe she always tones them down with one of those sage remarks that we are constantly surprised to find scattered among her capricious fatuities : ' Don't think that I personally have anything to complain of (in Heine) ; in putting one's criticisms into writing they tend to become harsher than they ever really should ; in life itself everything flows together as in a mighty river.'

Heine, who was not distinguished for showing deference, never uttered a disrespectful word about Rahel. And, noting with some surprise the highly official position occupied by our Rahel Levin, the little paradox, we may read in the first edition of one of Heine's books : ' The author dedicates these twenty-eight poems of the *Homecoming* to *Frau Legationsträtin* Varnhagen v. Ense.'

His letters to her pluck deeper at the heart-strings. He writes in April, 1823, for example :

I'm leaving shortly and would like to ask you not to consign me utterly to the lumber-room of oblivion. Honestly, I couldn't retaliate ; even if I were to say to myself a hundred times a day: ' You *shall* forget Frau von Varnhagen '—it wouldn't work. Forget me not ! I cannot allow you to plead a poor memory in excuse. Your spirit has concluded a contract with Time, and when in a few centuries I have the pleasure perhaps of meeting you again as the loveliest and most splendid of flowers in the loveliest and most splendid of celestial valleys, please be kind enough to greet the holly leaf that I shall be— or shall I be something worse ?—with your friendly glow and gracious presence, as you would an old acquaintance. After all, you did as much in 1822 and 1823, when you treated the sick, embittered, sullen, poetical, and unendurable person that I was with a courtesy and kindness that I certainly never deserved in *this* world and could owe only to your kind recollections of me in a previous acquaintanceship. I am, *gnädige Frau*, your respectful and devoted H. Heine.

VI

The Kulturverein

'I expect much of his (Zunz's) forthcoming book of sermons. Not, indeed, edification and spiritual soft soap, but something much better; the creation of a dynamic. It is this that is lacking in Israel.'

Heine.

IN THE MIDST of all this turmoil the *Verein für Cultur und Wissenschaft* (Society for Culture and Science) was formed in 1819 in Berlin. The founders were Leopold Zunz, who afterwards became an eminent Jewish historian; the erudite but fundamentally cold and self-seeking lawyer Dr. Eduard Gans, who was the first member of the Society to forsake Judaism—for a University professorship ('And you crawled to the Cross, to the Cross you despised . . .' sang Heine in *To a Renegade*); and finally Moses Moser, who was closest to Heine's heart, whom he described as 'a living epilogue to Nathan the Wise,' 'a faultless *édition de luxe* of a real human being,' 'a second Marquis Posa.' Heine lost this valuable friendship in the Platen controversy.

Moser, a prosperous merchant and friend of the sciences, was, as Heine wrote retrospectively in his memoir on Ludwig Marcus, 'the most active member of the " Society," its very life and soul.' In this essay he is praised 'not only for the thorough knowledge which was already his at an early age, but for the great love he bore suffering humanity and for his longing to convert knowledge into

healing action. He was indefatigable in philanthropic endeavour,
he was very practical, and he took part self-effacingly in all
charitable enterprises. The great public never heard of what he did;
he fought and bled incognito. His name has remained quite unknown
and is not recorded even in the directory of self-sacrifice. The present
age is not so impoverished as people think ; it has produced an
astonishingly large number of such anonymous martyrs.'

The essay in which this tribute occurs was written in 1844 and
dedicated to another member of the Society, 'little Ludwig
Marcus,' a tragic figure who died in a mental home. He was a
Semitics scholar born in Dessau, and he became a professor in
Dijon. In addition to Gans, Moser, and Zunz—'who in a period
of fluctuating transition always manifested an unshakeable stead-
fastness '—Lazarus Bendavid, a veteran Kantian and a radical
opponent of Hegel, is mentioned as a member. Writing of the
' Society ' itself, viewed in the perspective of ' twenty years after,'
Heine says that ' it soared high in pursuit of a lofty but impracticable
idea. Men of brilliant intellect and good hearts attempted to save
a long-lost cause. The most they succeeded in doing was to unearth
on the battlefields of past history the bones of the fighters who had
preceded them.' Nevertheless, says Heine, the ' ideals and illusions
of the society ' were the finest hour in little Marcus's bleak existence.

According to the essay (which first appeared anonymously in
the *Augsburger Allg. Zeitung,* but was included ten years later by
Heine himself in his writings, with an additional ' Note '), the aim
of the ' Society ' was ' to combine historic Judaism with modern
science, which it was assumed would sooner or later dominate the
world.' And Heine continues with an onslaught as sharp as it is
witty against what has for some time been known as ' Liberal
Judaism.' (The era of Liberal Judaism is now over. Whatever was
valuable in it has been discussed by Max Wiener with a loving
though strictly unbiassed perspicuity that has yet to be surpassed,
in his book, *Jüdische Religion im Zeitalter der Emanzipation,* from
which I have previously quoted.) Heine did nothing to merit being
claimed as a spokesman for the bloodless abstraction of ' Reform
Judaism,' which is what Georg I. Plotke, after an initially sound
analysis of Heine's national Judaism, finally called him in his
book (1913) *Heinrich Heine als Dichter des Judentums.* In order
to refute this common misinterpretation of Heine's position, I quote

his own words (without further reference to the otherwise excellent study by Plotke, who testified to his faith in Germany by giving his life in the [1914-18] War):

> There was no question here (sc. in the *Kulturverein*) of any schismatical bogus 'enlightenment,' still less of that emancipation which nowadays is frequently the subject of chatter so nonsensical and so nauseatingly devoid of any intellectual basis that it is hard to retain one's interest. In particular the Israelite friends of emancipation have succeeded in enveloping the question in a grey, watery cloud of boredom that is calculated to be more harmful to the movement than is the stupid poison emitted by its opponents. We now have Pharisees who boast cheerfully of their lack of talent as writers and who think to defy Apollo by taking up their pens for Jehovah. It is to be hoped that the various German governments will take aesthetic pity on the public with the minimum delay by speedily emancipating the Jews and thereby putting an end to all this twaddle. Sooner or later emancipation will have to be granted, anyway.

One cannot help being struck by Heine's failure to assess at its true worth the *Kulturverein* and its 'long-lost cause.' He had, after all, served the Society enthusiastically from the time he joined it in 1822 until it broke up in 1824. There can be no doubt that to the very end its impelling force made itself felt in all his creative writing. One has only to read Heine's letters to Moser, in which he is always asking Moser and Zunz for source material for the *Rabbi von Bacharach* and reporting on the progress of his ' sombre martyr's lay,' to see how strongly his work was influenced by this society for the scientific study of history.

It is possible indeed to specify the sector in which this influence was most marked. Heine's predilection for the Moorish and Spanish era in Judaism is of a piece with the views persuasively set forth by Zunz in his first contribution to the *Zeitschrift für die Wissenschaft des Judentums* (one of the most valuable of the Society's achievements). The essay by ' Zunz Dr.'—which is how this remarkable man regularly signed himself at the time—is entitled: *On Hispanic place-names in Hebrew-Jewish writings*. It is a characteristic example of the modest and unassuming way in which this great scholar would tackle a problem from its extreme periphery and work inwards. The geographical names are explained with strict objectivity ; this is the actual subject of the essay. *En passant,* however, a new conception of Jewish history and historiography emerges, that which stresses ' native forces, freely expressed, and deeds,' and not the ' foreign element, passive defence, and suffering.' Zunz seizes the opportunity to observe that ' every pulp volume of the Polish period ' was printed, while the Spanish period was neglected. For Zunz it is particularly the Spanish period, only the Spanish period, which is the golden age of Judaism.

The traveller in the wastes of German-Polish barbarism casts his glance at the friendly oasis of the Hesperian lands . . . here above all should the study of Jewish literature be concentrated, for it was here that such a literature did in fact exist. Since the political decline of the Jewish people no period has rivalled the Age of Spain in the field of Jewish endeavour ; an age in which Jewry stood on the same level, indeed not infrequently on a higher level, than Europe. In Spain lived Jews worthy of the highest recognition. There existed not only a dead language as an honoured ancestral legacy, but also a living, understood, developed one. Jewish literature and science, vying with that of the Moors, had its admirers. Even the outer history of Spanish Jewry is more important, stronger, and, after the barbaric epoch of the West Goths, more attractive than elsewhere.

We shall not go wrong in detecting the ever-present influence of Zunz's eulogies of the Spanish-Jewish setting in Heine's choice of Hispano-Jewish and Spanish subjects (in the poem *Donna Clara* written at this time, in the third chapter added later to the *Rabbi* ; in *Disputation,* too, even in *Vitzliputzli* ; in the landscapes of Salamanca and Saragossa which appear in so much of the verse, and in the four-footed trochaic romance-rhythm beloved of Heine). In a work of his late period, also, in the *Hebrew Melodies,* Heine lists some great Jewish poets and quite in Zunz's manner evidently takes it for granted that this ' history of literature ' is the stuff of the history of Judaism.

And yet this tone of resignation when he speaks of the *Verein* in the memoir ? Possibly the personal disillusionment of Gans's baptism had something to do with it. Heine had already before this—in his letters—characterised Gans as a hero too fond of blowing his own trumpet. ' His defection was the more repulsive as he had played the rôle of an agitator for the cause and assumed

certain presidential duties. It is traditionally the captain who is the
last to leave the ship.' Then came Heine's own baptism, then his
'Hellenic' phase, in which, following a wrong theory, he felt himself ideologically opposed to the basic philosophy of Judaism. All
this had tended to modify his outlook and his Jewish enthusiasm
of the *Kulturverein* days. Nevertheless, there must have been a
fault inherent in the structure of the Society to account for its later
affecting Heine only sub-consciously (admittedly there was a
glowing eruption of this sub-conscious influence in Heine's final
affirmation of the Bible), whereas his active memory could only
register the failure, the complete drying up of the hopes that had
once been held. The intellectual basis of the Society was in fact
self-contradictory. There was no clearly defined programme that
could have imprinted itself strongly on Heine's memory. The Society
had in it the promise of great things, of breadth of view and justified pride ; but there was a good deal of opportunism as well, and
ghetto-fear. The latter of two kinds : fear in and fear of the ghetto.
Only the muffled echo of an occasional elemental outcry—immediately silenced by expressions of loyal moderation—which one or
other of the Society's members, usually so respectable, was unable
to repress, reverberated long afterwards beneath the surface. It was
this far-off echo that ever and anon found a response in Heine's soul.

The aim of the Society was defined in its statutes as 'to bring
the Jews into harmony with the age and the countries in which
they live by means of a programme of internal education developing
outwards.' In addition to those already named, the following were
members : Immanuel Wolf, the educationist (known as Wohlwill
and nicknamed 'Monas' from his programmatic article in the
Society's *Zeitschrift*; in this article he considered the fundamental
idea of Judaism lay in the 'idea of divine unity') then there were
the Syndic of the Berlin Jewish community, I. Rubo, and Joseph
Lehmann, editor of the *Magazin für die Literatur des In- und
Auslands,* as well as the veteran David Friedländer. The latter,
although giving the Society an enthusiastic welcome, had in the
very first number of the *Zeitschrift,* in his *Letters on the Reading
of Holy Scripture,* preached a completely disembodied Judaism
(p. 82). Instead of allowing Jewish youth to read the Five Books
of Moses—admittedly they would have hardly been able to understand them in the original—he desired, with the best of intentions,

to give them a diluted ' History of their Ancestors ' and a ' Text-
book of Ethics.'

The ' science ' in the ' Society's ' name and in the name of its
journal had the power of a panacea ascribed to it. Science, according
to the programmatic article by Wolf with which the first issue of
the noteworthy *Zeitschrift* opened in 1822, was to treat its subject,
Judaism, ' purely for its own sake, not for a specific purpose from
a specific point of view.' Since, however, ' the standpoint of
scientific enquiry is the one that characterizes our age,' Wolf
concludes his article with the words :

> Jews must show once more that they are valiant
> co-operators in humanity's common task ; they must place
> themselves and the principle they represent (sc. that of
> monadism previously mentioned) on the scientific plane, for this
> is the plane on which European life is lived. On this plane the
> hitherto existing alienation of Jews and Judaism from the
> outside world must disappear. And if ever the whole of
> humanity will be united in a single bond, it will be the bond
> of reasonableness, of truth.

It is extraordinary how much power Jews attributed once more
to a theory, a mere method of thought. And history may well
record as worthy of note that at one of the most critical junctures
of their history the Jewish people sought to lean on the aid of
pure science.

It would be wrong to interpret this as simply a belated manifestation of the ideology of the Enlightenment. I should be the
last to deny that Jews as individuals are often modern in their
outlook. As a people, however, they are usually a couple of decades
behind the times. This explains why they tended to interpret their
religion and history in the spirit of the Enlightenment *then,* in the
Age of Romanticism, of Fichte, Schlegel, Schleiermacher ; in an
age which was already making other demands on mankind and
giving other answers to its questions. In the same way a large section
of Jewry today regards the materialistic outlook as the firmest basis
for the judgment of intellectual trends, although even in the natural
sciences experts regard this outlook with some degree of scepticism
(coincidence and probability instead of the causal necessity of
natural laws). By adopting philosophies and systems which are well
to the rear of the intellectual battle-front of the day, by displaying

a queer mental rigidity, Jews sometimes compromise the noble cause of progress, of justice. Quite unnecessarily. A socialist philosophy of society may very well be derived from other than materialistic premises, for example. Popper-Lynkeus has argued for such a philosophy purely in terms of intellect and responsibility.

A similar process may have been at work in the propositions deriving from a superannuated Age of Enlightenment which were expressed in the writings of the Jewish Reformers around 1820. Nevertheless, " Jewish science " was not enlisted simply to provide the supposed omnipotence of Reason with a new triumph. It would above all be an injustice to the most responsible and the most steadfast of the Society's members, Zunz, to place his efforts on this purely superficial plane. His seminal labours came from much deeper layers in the soul and their effect was that much the more novel, violent, and persistent.

In his great work *Die gottesdienstlichen Vorträge der Juden, historisch entwickelt* (' Sermons of the Jews, historically treated '— the unassuming title covers an exhaustive study of Jewish literature from the time of Ezra), Zunz says : ' We find that from the earliest times the Jewish people made provision for the divine to be brought near to those of their number who were immersed in daily toil or error or who were fettered by sensual appetite and crude lust.' It was first and foremost the Jews themselves that ' Science ' was to acquaint once more with the nature of this historical ' provision.' Thereby it would restore Jewish self-respect and establish the claim of original Jewish culture to be regarded as a valuable component of world culture as a whole.

For this reason Zunz—quite unlike Friedländer—deplored in his very first publication, *Some Remarks on Rabbinic Literature*, the ' decrease in Hebrew language instruction.' He is critical of the literary tradition, but, unlike several other reformers and followers of the current fashion, he does not condemn it lock, stock, and barrel. He hopes that ' the illustration of the best that has been produced in rabbinic literature will help to dispel the general prejudice that is entertained against it.' He gives a pithy description of this prejudice in commenting on a certain author's tendentious outlook : ' What he calls noble patriotism and courage in the Samnites, Spartans, Carthaginians, Peruvians, and Germans becomes miserable defiance and despair in the Jews.'

True, immediately afterwards he says: 'Thanks be to Eternal
God, those days are over! Pens as powerful as they are respectable
now spread true enlightenment among the people, and still greater
rulers lend their dignity and their might to these pens.' Apart from
the queer phraseology—'powerful, respectable pens'—Zunz's
optimism in the middle of the age of the Holy Alliance seems
peculiar. At a time when the achievements of the emancipation were
once more threatened, was he perhaps not so much recording and
eulogizing the attitude of the governmental circles as suggesting it
to them ? Was his optimism in fact too sober to allow of his
deceiving himself and others ? It is difficult to credit such deception
in a man who in the ninety-two years of his life (it projects
astonishingly almost into our own era—he died in 1886) always
gave signal proofs of strength of character. In spite of his poverty
he resigned a number of posts—as preacher, as editor of the
Spenersche Zeitung, as Director of the Berlin Jewish Teachers'
Seminary—directly they brought him into conflict with his convictions. Heine's sincere tribute to him, in a letter he wrote to Wohlwill
in 1823, may be quoted here:

> I like him, and I find it most distressing that such a fine
> man should not be recognized at his true worth simply because
> of his harsh, forbidding exterior. *I expect much of his forth-
> coming book of sermons. Not, indeed, edification and spiritual
> soft soap, but something much better, the creation of a dynamic.
> It is this that is lacking in Israel.*

And yet, in spite of his purity of soul, his scholarship, and his
love, how far behind Heine's sound instinct for and matter-of-course
grasp of the Jewish situation did Zunz, the leading member of the
'Society,' stand! It is remarkable, for Heine brought with him
nothing of what Zunz had in such overflowing measure. Heine is
distinguished neither for scholarly care nor for humble love of
Jewish values. Nevertheless, such is the fact! For all his frivolity,
for all his frequent groping and oscillating, Heine's intuition and
courage put him head and shoulders above, not merely the Jewesses
of the Berlin salons who were estranged from everything Jewish,
but also the men who were working heart and soul at the time for
a Jewish revival. In Jewish matters Heine's judgments were
sounder than theirs. At any rate in his good moments he pronounced
sound Jewish judgments *en passant* as it were, with effortless ease.

Without thinking much about it he points out the future line of development. With his inspired genius he is generations ahead of his time simply because everything weak, half-and-half, was detestable to him. Inevitably he felt himself driven to a clear affirmation of his Jewishness. Measure him by comparison with his timid Jewish contemporaries, by comparison with the dismal Jewish decadence of those days. Against this murky background his greatness immediately stands out clear and luminous. Faults he has in plenty, but in this one crucial point they leave him and us unaffected.

It is instructive to see how in the *Gottesdienstliche Vorträge* the admirable Zunz aimed at ensuring that the ' science ' of the great Jewish past, which he opened up by his own toil, should not only enable the Jews to feel more respect for themselves, but should simultaneously increase the respect in which the other nations, the ' harbouring ' nations, held them.

By acquiring greater intellectual culture and gaining a more thorough knowledge of their own affairs the Jews would have succeeded not merely in gaining increased acceptance, that is, a greater measure of legal rights ; much faulty legislation, many a prejudice against the Jewish past, many a condemnation of new endeavours are a direct consequence of the neglected state of Jewish literature and science during the last seventy years or so.

This is the clearest formulation possible of one trend of the Society's aims. All the ambiguity and dichotomy inherent in this trend, though blissfully unsuspected by the sincere ' Society ' workers at the time, comes up in Zunz's formulation. The Jews were to ' acquire a greater intellectual culture '; on a Jewish basis, certainly, but only in order to attain thereby the general European, that is, in Germany the German, level of culture, and to fuse with it. What was it that was important in this process: the Jewish basis or the goal that was aimed at: the European, that is German, level ? Should it be found possible to achieve the fusion without any Jewish basis, some of the ' Society's ' members might feel tempted to dispense with the basis and think only of the ' goal.' Gans and Heine succumbed to this temptation ; the one completely, the other momentarily.

The fundamental error of the *Verein*, however, lay in its failure to come to grips with the Jewish problems confronting it. All its fine language and high-sounding words cannot excuse this.

Zunz, too, thought only of assimilation. ' In the civilized countries of the world the Jews are nearer emancipation than ever before,' he again proclaims in his monograph on ' Jewish names.' He adds a magnificent: ' The opponents of emancipation are crushed and silent.' In this treatise Zunz wished to show in particular that the Jews had never restricted themselves to biblical names but had always borrowed names from the peoples among whom they lived as well. The Prussian authorities at the time wished to forbid Jews to use Christian first names. Thus for the purposes of temporary apologetics Zunz discovered a new field of Jewish research. This was typical of his way, which somewhat resembled Columbus's—Columbus, too, had not intended to discover a new world. Zunz unlocked for the first time a whole treasure-chest of ancient documents, although his actual intention had been only to cover the new assimilation by the old.

Zunz's dichotomy is not always as clearly revealed as this in his writings. Often someone wiser than he seems to guide his heart, his intellect, his industriously writing hand. But on the face of it his writings frequently give the impression that because of his great love for Judaism he wants to grant us a patent of nobility. We *had* a Jewish poetry, a Jewish science ; *ergo* we are worthy—not of remaining Jews, but of becoming Germans with equal rights. Zunz does not seem to see the contradiction of appealing to the cultural glories of one's nation and seeking at the same time to surrender to, immerse oneself in—albeit in freedom—another nation.

And in the programmatic article previously quoted, *Some Remarks on Rabbinic Literature,* he does indeed eulogize ' the honourable remnants of the golden age of the ancient Hebrews,' but goes on to say:

> In our day, however, we see Jews applying themselves with increasing earnestness to the German language and to German education—to speak only of German Jews. In so doing they are helping to bury modern Hebrew literature, often perhaps without wanting to do so or suspecting that they are doing so. Precisely for this reason science appears on the scene and demands the accounts of that science or body of knowledge whose reign is *over*. Now, when nothing new of importance is likely to distort our view . . .

Evidently he considers he is officiating at an interment.

Here we see another function of 'science' in the 'Society';
its most flattering and most dangerous function. Science looks up ;
it closes a gate behind it. Its last backward glance is a glance of
pity, not of self-confidence ; it is a glance, not of life, but of death.
'Science' never realized that knowledge of the past can never be
a substitute for vital activity. Just as in Mendelssohn's general
religion of reason thinly coated with Judaism, there was a special,
revealed, very holy mass of commandments which, however, were
never *felt*, but existed simply as 'trimmings,' so the men of the
Kulturverein added to general education and morality a body of
specifically Jewish knowledge whose historic value they lauded
with seeming enthusiasm but did not put to practical use for the
present and future.

It was in this, unhealthy, spirit that Heine assisted in the
'Society's' seminars. He had been recruited by Gans. He taught
French, German, and German history. A student at the seminars,
I. L. Braunhardt, has given us a description of Heine's history
lectures : Heine had an excellent delivery, he described the victory
of Arminius the Cheruscan over the Romans in the Forest of
Teutoburg with great enthusiasm.

Hermann, or Arminius, was for him the exemplar of a
great hero and patriot who risked his life, his all, to win
freedom for his people and to cast off the Roman yoke. When
Heine, raising his voice, cried out, as once did Augustus:
'Varus, Varus, give me back my legions!' his heart exulted,
his fine eyes sparkled, and his expressive manly features
radiated joy and ecstasy. We, his audience, were most
astonished, shattered indeed ; never before had we heard him
speak with such enthusiasm. We could have kissed his hands,
and our admiration for him increased considerably and
remained with us all our lives. It goes without saying that on
this occasion he spoke of the Germany of our own day as
well. I remember quite definitely that he took the opportunity
to lament the fragmentation of our Fatherland at the time and
said—his actual words: 'Whenever I look at the patchwork
map of Germany I am overcome with real horror. One asks in
vain, who really rules Germany ? . . . '

In other words, Pan-German politics, Pan-German enthusiasm.
Nothing of Judaism. That was to be promoted indirectly, very
indirectly, by imparting cultural values to the coreligionists.

Nevertheless, Heine's zeal was great. He was minuting secretary to
the *Verein*, proposed the formation of a women's society. In 1824
he wrote to Moser from Lüneburg, whither he had gone to escape
the din of Berlin and get down to his swotting again (his parents
having settled there after the failure of his father's business in
Düsseldorf):

> You tell me little about the *Verein*. You don't think, do
> you, that the cause of our brethren is less precious to me than
> it has always been? If you do, you're making a profound
> mistake. In spite of the headaches which are getting me down,
> I haven't given up working for the Society. 'May my right
> hand be withered if I forget thee, Yerusholayim,' are the
> words—roughly—of the Psalmist, and they are still mine, too.

Whence came this love of living Judaism, so oddly at variance
with Heine's actual activities, with that lecture of his on Varus, for
example? Whence the emotion, so unusual in the unemotional
circles of the 'Society'? For their part, they never tired of saying
they had forgotten Jerusalem completely, also that they considered
the Jewish Messiah to be simply 'the incarnation of the wishes
of all sincere persons' (Zunz, Works, I, 28), or that they identified
him with 'our glorious sovereign, King Frederick William IV'
(Zunz, Tabernacles Sermon, 1840)!

The solution to the puzzle seems to me to be that Heine drew
from *deeper* sources than the *Verein's*. The *Verein* stimulated him;
together with other factors it ensured that the wound of Heine's
Judenschmerz did not heal up. But the wound itself, with all the
grandeur and dignity shining from it, was felt far more intensely,
more directly by Heine than by all those around him who
encouraged him to engage in Jewish activities.

Even before he came into contact with the *Verein* personalities,
he had immunized himself—as if by a presentiment of what might
happen—against their well-meant tepid poison in a highly original
way; by a journey to Poland undertaken on the spur of the
moment, to visit Count Breza, his fellow-undergraduate.

The Jews of Berlin, who were busily engaged in divesting themselves of everything that was specifically Jewish in their way of
life and in their general philosophy, found the Jews of Eastern
Europe a source of embarrassment where they did not detest them.
Steinheim, for example, launches out into the most violent abuse

of the *plica polonica*, the Polish elf-lock. He denounces in their
entirety the Jewish way of life and Jewish methods of study in
Poland. Even Zunz speaks of 'two centuries of ignorance,' of
'scholastic-talmudic logomachy,' while an anonymous writer in the
Zeitschrift cannot resist getting in a dig at Polish rabbinism, 'which
degenerated in Poland's Jewish schools into a permanent quagmire
of ignorance and uncouthness.' Heine judged differently. His
penetrating eye saw beyond the accidents of time and place, into
the depths, into what mattered.

In his essay *On Poland*, after describing the three estates
(nobles, depressed peasants, and the Jews who constituted the
middle class), he writes:

> In those early days the Jews were culturally and intellec-
> tually certainly well in advance of the nobility, which engaged
> only in the crude work of war and lacked the saving grace of
> French manners. The Jews, however, never ceased to study
> their Hebrew books of science and religion, for whose sake
> they had indeed left a Fatherland and the comforts of life.
> Obviously, however, they have not kept pace with European
> progress. Their intellectual world has stagnated and become a
> mass of unedifying superstition continually added to by a
> thousand-and-one forms of hair-splitting scholasticism. All the
> same, in spite of the barbarous fur cap on his head and the
> still more barbarous ideas inside it, I think far more highly of
> the Polish Jew than I do of certain German Jews with their
> top-hats on their heads and their Jean Paul inside them. In
> his rigid isolation the character of the Polish Jew became a
> whole and when he began to breathe the air of toleration this
> character received the stamp of freedom. The inner man did
> not become a mixed rag-bag of heterogeneous feelings. His
> better qualities were not crushed between the ghetto walls of
> Frankfurt or by infinitely wise municipal ordinances and
> benevolent legal restrictions. The Polish Jew, for all his dirty
> fur cap, his teeming beard, his smell of garlic, and his Jewy
> speech, is more pleasing to me than many a seigneur proud of
> his paper rights.

In truth, Dr. Steinheim may have been a better and more
responsible theologian, a more consistent thinker: Heine understood a hundredfold better than he the meaning of the living
totality of Jewish existence.

Heine's essay *On Poland* made him, as he wrote to Sethe, very
unpopular with the gentry. 'I'm in pretty bad odour in higher

circles, too.' He remained in bad odour, could not shake off the
dislike in which he was held. His naïveté was indeed surprising.
In spite of his sharp attacks on the Prussian officials in Poland—
to say nothing of his epilogue to the *English Fragments*—he still
hoped to appease the authorities and even to obtain a State post,
a professorship in Berlin or Munich. Nor were the doubts he cast
on the ' paper rights ' of which the Jews of Berlin and Hamburg
were so proud exactly calculated to arouse their delight. Remarks
of this kind could never win over to his cause the ' Emancipation-
Jews,' who were then the rising, and in some cases the leading,
members of German Jewry. In Hamburg, where he had family
connexions, they set up a vigorous opposition to him. That is the
way of the world. But Heine was indignant about it. He declared
he hated and despised the *Steinweg,* Hamburg's Jewish quarter at
the time. ' Never will I tell the Steinweg first if I propose doing
something for it, never let it expect anything from me, and never
let it say I have not fulfilled its expectations.' And in another
letter :

> Me, me they have to embitter! Just when I've calmly faced
> the waves of Jew hatred and stand ready to let them hurl
> themselves against me. Truly, it is not the Kleys and the
> Auerbachs[1] that are hated in dear old Germany. I'm feeling
> the effects of this hatred from all quarters. And it's still
> practically in its beginning. Friends with whom I've spent the
> greater part of my life turn from me. Those who used to
> admire me, now despise me ; those I love most hate me most,
> everybody tries to harm me.

Almansor had just appeared. In spite of Heine's protests and
denials (letter to Immermann, 10.6.1823), the general tendency of
the play, which is not precisely Christian, was unmistakable, and
some who had at first rapturously hailed the young poet now felt
quite differently towards him. Heine felt that at this juncture he
was entirely without allies, cut off from Jews and Christians alike.
In one of his last letters to his mother (May, 1853), he sighs: ' I
have never wished to share your aversion to the Jews, mother dear,
but they've made life devilish hard for me. Our Lord and Saviour
must really be a God to forgive these Pharisees their persecution
of me.'

---

[1] Jewish " Reform " preachers.

Heine realized, then, that his radical adoption of a vital Judaism welling up from its original sources, as opposed to the pale ghost of Reform Judaism, could not enhance his popularity with either Jews or Christians. Nevertheless, he never ceased to ridicule half-measures and to hope for ' the creation of a dynamic. It is this that is lacking in Israel,' he writes, as previously quoted, in a letter to Wohlwill which is his most forceful piece of writing at this period. Similarly in his *Gedanken und Einfälle* (' Thoughts and Ideas '): ' One Jew says to another: " I was too weak. This could serve as an epigraph to a History of Judaism." ' And in the letter to Wohlwill his appreciative words about Zunz's ' creation of a dynamic ' are followed by a vivid excoriation of the Reformers, the ' few dozen Solons,' as Zunz himself scathingly described them.

A few chiropodists (Friedländer & Co.) have sought to heal Judaism of its putrescent skin troubles by blood-letting, and as a result of their clumsiness and their cobweb rationalistic bandages Israel has to bleed to death. May they soon come to their senses and realise that there is nothing particularly glorious in weakness, in surrendering all that made us strong, in being the only side that feels called on to make denials, in idealistic Auerbachism. We no longer have the strength to wear a beard, to fast, to hate, and out of our hatred to suffer: that is the motive of our Reformation. Some, who have received their education and enlightenment from actors, want to give Judaism a new décor and a new stage. The prompter is to wear white cuffs instead of a beard. They want to pour the ocean into a pretty fountain made of papier mâché. They want to dress up the Wilhelmshöhe statue of Hercules in Cassel in little Marcus's jacket. Others want to turn evangelical Christianity into a Jewish trading concern. They make a talles (Jewish praying-shawl) out of the wool of the Lamb of God, a doublet out of the feathers of the dove of the Holy Ghost, and underpants out of Christian love, and they go bankrupt, and their successors trade as God, Christ & Co. Unfortunately this firm won't last long. Its drafts on the bank of philosophy are returned dishonoured, and Europe has made a receiving order against it.

Admittedly Heine quickly tones down—in the same letter—what he has just said:

I, too, haven't enough strength to wear a beard and to let them shout ' Abie ' at me and to fast. etc. I haven't enough

strength to eat matzes (unleavened bread) properly. I'm staying
with a Jew, opposite Moser and Ganz, and get matzes instead
of bread and crack my teeth over them. Still, I comfort myself
with the thought that we're in Gohless (exile) after all! And
my digs at Friedländer mustn't be taken too seriously, only a
little while ago I had an excellent pudding at his place. . . .

This is a characteristic example of the way Heine applies the
brake to his emotion, controls the volume of utterances which he
feels have been expressed in too loud a voice. He is a little ashamed
of the fact that what he has said may have been insufficiently
modulated, may have been too much of a simplification, may have
been too stridently one-sided. This aspect of Heine's style will be
discussed later. It is usual to say that he indulges in irony at his
own expense, that he is cynical, even. There is some justice in this.
All the same, in considering this mannerism of his we ought not
in fairness to overlook a particular manifestation of probity, of
intellectual sincerity and reticence to which it gives expression.
Heine's tendency is to prefer self-denigration to posing and self-
glorification.

In any case, it has to be admitted that although Heine was able
to expose with deadly accuracy the errors of Reform Judaism, its
attempts to achieve respectability at the cost of Jewish individuality,
he was unable to offer positive guidance for the future. After all,
it is true (though critics strenuously deny it) that to criticize is much
easier than to improve, or rather that criticism functions on an
entirely different, lower plane than creation and guidance. Flaubert
was quite right when he said: ' If critics knew how hard it was
to write one single simple sentence, such as   " Shut the door," or
" He fancied sleeping," they would give up criticism.'

If this is true of literature, it is no less so of politics. Heine saw
clearly that Jews who sought to deny the ' rock whence they were
hewn ' presented a sorry spectacle. But he was less concerned about
what was to happen to the Jews once their medieval pattern of
living in all its rigidity and totality would be irremediably broken
up. It was not till his life was drawing to its close that he attempted
to grapple with this question, at least as far as it concerned himself.
His answer, necessarily incomplete, took the form of a renewed
pietism. It would seem that the time was not yet ripe even for the
realization of the problem's existence. At any rate, one proposal

that fell from the skies at a meeting of the *Verein* had a slightly comic-opera touch about it.

An American, Mordecai Manuel Noah, rejoicing in the titles of ' Citizen of the United States of America, formerly Consul of these States in Tunis, High Sheriff in New York, Justice of the Peace, and by the grace of God a Leader and a Judge in Israel,' issued a proclamation calling on the Jews of ' the whole world ' to form in America a ' colony of Ararat,' a political state of their own based on American principles of freedom. (The idea was suggested to him, possibly, by the writings of the early English socialist Robert Owen and his communal settlements in New Lanark—though New Harmony was not founded till 1825.) M. M. Noah was made an honorary member of the *Verein*. Zunz and Gans wanted to disseminate his proclamation in Germany.

It was a fantastic, Utopian project midway between the pseudo-Messianic claims of the seventeenth and eighteenth centuries and the first serious plans for Jewish colonization adumbrated by Moses Hess, Kalischer and Pinsker. Heine dismisses it with good-humoured raillery. In a letter to Moser he speaks ironically of ' Ganstown ' and of a ' happier generation by the Mississippi, where a new Jewish literature would flourish.' Rather less objectionable than Berthold Auerbach's designation—forty years later !—of Moses Hess's high-minded and grandly conceived colonization schemes. The only word Auerbach, displaying a strange mixture of fear and self-betrayal, can find for Hess's ideas is ' incendiarism ' (Moses Hess, *Rom und Jerusalem*, note to third letter).

Heine always retained his dislike of ' semi '-Jews. In *The Baths of Lucca* he draws for us a ruthless portrait of the Marquese Gumpelino, prototype of all ignoble stupid assimilationists, easily identified as a ' deserter ' by his long nose. Gumpelino gives his valet Hirsch-Hyazinth ' instruction in education.' He kneels in front of a great crucifix. ' When he is in Rome, he even has his own Chaplain, in the same way that when he is in England he patronizes the best race-meetings and when he is in Paris he supports the prettiest dancing girls.' It is not often that Heine's characterization is as successful as it is in the case of this odious snob and *nouveau riche*. The very intonation and speech peculiarities of the Marquese are drawn with such unerring skill that one immediately

senses the authenticity of his character, even though one may not
have chanced to come across this particular specimen of the large
assortment of run-away Jews in real life. Equally successful is the
delineation of servant Hirsch-Hyazinth, the lottery agent. ' In
education he has progressed with the strides of a giantess.' In
Hamburg he is all for the new Israelite Temple, which ' holds
religious services of pure mosaics, with orthographic German
hymns, and touchingly sentimental little prayers so necessary for
a religion.'

In *The City of Lucca* Heine maliciously declares the Berliners
to be ' too sensible ' for Christianity, which, however, they need for
reasons of State.

In their predicament they avail themselves of the zeal for
service displayed by the poor Jews. The Jews have to be
Christians for them, and as they are a people who will do
anything for money and kind words they have trained themselves so well for their Christian duties that they are now
scandalized by Christian irreligion. They are prepared to fight
to the death for the Trinity and in the dog days even to believe
in it. They thunder against the rationalists. As missionaries and
spies for the faith they infiltrate into all parts of the country
and distribute the jolliest little tracts of a most edifying nature.
In church no one can equal them in the way they roll their
eyes and in the sanctimonious expressions their countenances
assume. The piety they display is so dazzling that some
professional jealousy has been aroused, and the older practitioners have already started complaining among themselves
that the Jews have made a corner in Christianity.

There is a similar outburst against the criminal lawyer Hitzig,
formerly H. Itzig (in the *Hebrew Melodies*). ' Als er noch ein Itzig
war/träumte ihm, er säh geschrieben/an dem Himmel seinen
Namen/und davor den Buchstab H.'—When he was still an Itzig
he dreamt he saw his name written in Heaven, with the letter ' H '
in front of it. He was uncertain whether the ' H ' stood for *Herr*
or *Heil'ger* (' Saint '). ' *Heil'ger* is a fine title, but not suitable for
Berlin. In the end, tired of pondering the problem, he decided to
call himself Hitzig.' The depressing background to these verses
too, was provided by baptized Berlin Jewry.

Heine's withering scorn of emancipation Jewry rose to its
climax in the ' Damascus ' letters of 1840. His anger reached white
heat when he saw how indifferent the emancipated Jews of France

were to the Damascus ritual murder myth propagated by the French
consul in that city, Count Rotti-Menton. The Jews were accused
of having killed a Capuchin monk, Thomas, and his brother. Under
torture some 'confessed'; many died from the treatment they
received. While public opinion in Europe was divided for and
against, Heine wrote:

> Truly, we would regard it as a matter for praise rather than
> for blame if the Paris Jews had shown such great zeal on behalf
> of their unhappy co-religionists as the North German papers
> report them to have done, and if they had in fact spared no
> financial sacrifice to vindicate their maligned religion. But this
> is not the case. The Jews of France have been emancipated
> too long for the bonds uniting them with their fellow Jews
> not to have become loosened.

Heine no longer jésts. He has worn the jester's mask long
enough. Now he assumes the authentic tones of a prophet rebuking
his people. He praises the noble Crémieux and other Jews who have
placed their position and their fortune at the service of justice, but
at the same time he castigates with savage ferocity those who stand
aside:

> Some time ago a former Prussian tradesman who had
> adapted his Hebrew name of Moses (= 'drawn out of the
> water,' Italian *del mare*) to the more euphonious one of a
> Baron Delmar founded an educational institution for impover-
> ished young noblemen in this city. It cost him more than a
> million-and-a-half francs. It was a noble deed. He is so highly
> thought of in the Faubourg Saint-Germain for it, that even the
> most doddering aristocratic old dowagers there and the
> youngest of the pert débutantes no longer make fun of him
> openly. Has this nobleman ever given even a penny to a collec-
> tion in a Jewish cause? I am prepared to guarantee that
> another Baron who has been drawn out of the water, who plays
> the *gentilhomme catholique* and distinguished man of letters
> in the aristocratic Faubourg, has never done anything for his
> fellow-jews either with his money or his pen. Here I must
> interpolate a comment perhaps the bitterest of all. Among the
> baptized Jews there are many who out of cowardly hypocrisy
> abuse Israel more slanderously than do Israel's born enemies.
> In the same way, certain writers who wish to conceal their origin
> denigrate the Jews or even refrain from mentioning them at all.
> This is a well-known, tragically absurd phenomenon. But it
> may be useful to draw the public's special attention to it at
> this moment, as not only the North German papers I have

mentioned but a much more important organ has been
insinuating that everything that has been written in favour of
the Damascus Jews has emanated from Jewish sources, as if
the Austrian consul in Damascus was a Jew, as if the other
consuls there except the French were all Jews. No, all the
consuls in Damascus are Christians, and the fact that the
Austrian consul is not even of Jewish extraction is attested by
the thoroughly open manner in which he protected the Jews
against the French consul.

What was it that enabled Heine to reach such confident conclusions in the matters that vitally affected Judaism ? What was it
that enabled him to give practical expression throughout his life
to these conclusions (apart from a few theoretical errors of no great
importance, his dichotomy of Hellene and Nazarene, for example) ?
Above all, why was Heine of all men so much ahead of his time
in Jewish self-assuredness, whereas others who were far superior
to him in knowledge and logical thinking were completely lacking
in it ? The answer to these questions must be that the others were
afraid, while Heine had courage. His unbounded confidence in
himself included within it as a matter of course the affirmation of
his Jewishness and showed itself in his sound Jewish instincts and
in his manly Jewish bearing. He once wrote of Uncle Salomon, who
after all had not been particularly good to him : ' He is a fine man
and has an innate strength. That's the chief thing, you know '
(Letter to Wohlwill, April, 1823). Here Heine sounds an elemental
note, from the depths ! Strength, the dynamic that he wishes Israel
to have too. Side by side with the claims of the various ethical
systems with which Heine's and succeeding ages—Heine's age in
particular—sought to justify Judaism (and whose great value is
beyond all question), a new sound made itself heard, for once. It
was a sound unlike the others, and seemed essentially called for to
make them complete. It was the sound of elemental life, of defiance,
of embattled resistance. It is heard at its clearest in the poem, *To
Edom* (Edom = Esau, then Rome, and subsequently all non-Jewish
peoples):

> Ein Jahrtausend schon und länger
> Dulden wir uns brüderlich,
> Du, du duldest, dass ich atme,
> Dass du rasest, dulde ich.

Manchmal nur, in dunklen Zeiten,
Ward dir wunderlich zu Mut,
Und die liebefrommen Tätzchen
Färbtest du mit meinem Blut.

Jetzt wird unsre Freundschaft fester,
Und noch täglich nimmt sie zu ;
Denn ich selbst begann zu rasen,
Und ich werde fast wie du !

A thousand years we've borne each other,
And in brotherly love we live,
Graciously you bear my breathing,
I your fury must forgive.

Sometimes, though, throughout the ages,
Passing moods have filled your head,
And your loving Christian claws pounced,
Dyed themselves in Jew-blood red.

Now our friendship's growing firmer,
Daily grows for all to see ;
I too have started raving, killing,
Now I almost rave like thee !

There is no sanction in these verses for combat, which even in
self-defence is *Raserei,* fury, raving. In their bitter irony there
already lies the hint of a suggestion that only when the strong and
virile and the ethical-universal elements of Judaism are brought
together in a harmonious synthesis do they offer a norm of dignified
human conduct.

It may well be that in the context of German literature and
German politics Heine's work is distinctly uneven. Against what
is genuine, great, finely conceived in his achievements must be set
much that is questionable. In the history of the Jewish spirit,
however, where he properly belongs, Heine's portrait is seen in a
different light. Against this background all his achievements are
seen to acquire meaning and to represent organic growth. In their
time and place even his mistakes have their legitimate significance.
They pin-point the mistakes or at any rate the problems of a given
stage in Jewish development. At the same time, they demonstrate
how an outstanding personality was able, by sheer force of his
genius, to break through the barrier of these mistakes and problems,
soar far beyond them, and to indicate, vaguely and instinctively

maybe, the path of a better future for his people, in which they might at least have a voice in their own destiny.

Such intimations, when they occur in Heine—or in others—reflect their author's idiosyncrasy. The form is often strange, open to every kind of misunderstanding. Zunz's tendency, for example, on the upper level of his consciousness, was towards rational-assimilation. To justify this tendency he undertook certain researches which, however, led him into quite different territory, the unexplored regions of the Jewish spirit. This was not fortuitous, of course. Unknown to Zunz himself it was his passionate love of his people which was the mainspring of his researches.

In exactly the same way Heine often appears on the surface to be a mocker and a destroyer of Jewish values. He seems indifferent to Judaism, a militant though shallow rationalist. In reality he passionately desired to arouse, to reawaken Jewry; witness his influence, which is still powerful within the Jewish renaissance. Is not his influence often *malgré lui* ? There are times when we have the impression that the Jewish people, whose great love of Heine is undimmed, understand him better than he ever understood himself.

This peculiar relationship between a people and its hero has been given definitive expression by Franz Kafka in his story *Josephine and the Mouse-people*. The mice in the story, eternally persecuted, with no one to protect them and nowhere to rest their heads, will be readily identified with the Jewish people in the Diaspora, though the wider symbolism will also be apparent: *all* mankind, in a higher sense, are homeless and unprotected before God. (This is always Kafka's way. What is specifically Jewish serves as a symbol of all mankind, is meant to illumine the universal fate, *exemplar vitae humanae*.) It seems to me that in Kafka's description of the endlessly complicated misunderstandings arising between the mouse-people and its great representative Josephine, the tribe's overspoilt star, and in his description of the frequent strains to which their relationship is subjected, we have the best possible biography of Heine; just as Kafka, in fact, has recorded in his own secret cipher everything that needed saying about the Judaism of our age, its decline and its renaissance.

VII

Verse and Prose to 'Buch der Lieder'

BERLIN REMAINED Heine's most important spiritual base for
many years, until 1829 in fact, when he saw the city for the last
time. Since 1823, however, he had been living there only inter-
mittently. In 1823 he moved into his parents' home in Lüneburg
so that he might at last be able to finish his legal studies in peace.
In a letter to Moser he describes his parents' home—their business
failure had left them ruined—as the 'residence of ennui.' However,
his stay in Lüneburg, unprofitable though it was for the most part,
brought with it one gain, his friendship with the 'Goethean' Rudolf
Christiani, a lawyer who later became a Town Clerk. Heine took
him into his confidence. Years later he dubbed him 'The Mirabeau
of the Lüneburg Heath,' as a tribute to his work on the reform of
constitutional law. Heine's letters to him were 'letters in negligée,'
which Heine himself 'preferred a thousand times to the letter in
full-dress uniform.'

Heine found little understanding within his family circle. Of
the reception they gave his works he wrote: 'My mother has read
the tragedies and poems without particularly enjoying them, my
sister barely tolerates them, my brothers don't understand them,
and my father has not read them.' He himself read 'the whole of
Goethe' while in Lüneburg. He reported as much to the Varnhagen
circle, evidently seeking to justify himself in answer to their previous
reproaches. 'I am no longer a blind heathen, but one who sees.
Goethe pleases me very much.' Shortly afterwards his preoccupation
with Pustkuchen's attacks on Goethe led him to adopt a militant
pro-Goethe attitude. This positive feeling of admiration for Goethe
was to predominate in Heine's life and work, in spite of frequent
misgivings about what seemed to him to be Goethe's quietism. 'Ah,

151

how I should like to serve as a volunteer rifleman in the Goethean War of Liberation, but I am up to my neck in the morass of Roman Law. I have no private income and have to worry about my bread-and-butter ' (letter to Ludwig Robert, Rahel's brother).

Bread-and-butter worries induced him to turn his gaze on Hamburg. The result was a repetition of his previous misfortune in his uncle's house, the cause this time being Amalie's younger sister, Therese. A trip to the bathing-resort of Cuxhaven brought temporary alleviation. He wrote the two cycles of the *North Sea* poems. Today their free rhythms still enjoy a high literary reputation in general. I find them the most impersonal of all Heine's writings. True, Heine loved the sea and always sought to liberate himself in it from the ills that oppressed his soul and his body ; true, his storm-tossed heart felt kinship with the sea in its ebb and flow. But the expression Heine gave this love was conventional in the extreme. It is one of the mysteries of the process of artistic creation that frequently what has been felt by the artist in all sincerity should, when transmuted by him into a particular art form having its own laws, be found to be completely lacking in sincerity. This seems to me to be exactly the case with Heine's sea-poetry, which quantitatively accounts for no small part of his *œuvre*. It is because that which is sincere in Heine's poetry appeals to our innermost being, warms us, deeply moves us and, in the highest sense of the word, instructs us, that we must be all the more rigorous in setting aside its insincere elements. Professional critics tend all too easily, however, to confuse genuine perfection, the inspired capture of the substance of a subject in an art-form, with the use of big words or even with the mere attempting of great and sublime themes, as particularly exemplified in these *North Sea* poems of Heine. The whole of this note of reservation applies, by the way, only to the *North Sea* cycles, in which Heine is so to speak the consciously professional poet of mighty ocean ; it does not apply to the quiet miniature poems of rare beauty which occur almost incidentally in the *Homecoming* and elsewhere.

Let us briefly run through the external events in Heine's life up to the time of its first creative high-lights which were embodied in the first two editions of *Reisebilder* and in *Buch der Lieder*.

In the beginning of 1824 Heine matriculated at Göttingen for the second time. This was the period of his association with the undergraduate named Eduard Wedekind which we have already mentioned. In the summer vacation came the *Harzreise*, a journey in the Harz mountains which, later to become famous, at the time resolved itself into a pilgrimage to the throne of Goethe, with a disconcerting and unhappy outcome from whose effects Heine only gradually recovered. Then a short stay in Berlin followed by the resumption of his studies at Göttingen. In 1825, at long last, came the passing of Heine's doctor's examination, his dissertation and graduation and his baptism, prompted solely by considerations of a professional career and without the slightest trace of any change of conviction. (This will be discussed at greater length in the chapter after the next.)

Norderney, Lüneburg, Hamburg, Cuxhaven provided the background to the young man's subsequent efforts to repair his health, which had early been impaired, and to secure a position in which he could make a living. His uncle gave him a letter of credit for four hundred pounds sterling ' for purposes of representation ' in London, together with an introduction to Rothschild. He was to manage strictly on the money given him for the journey. His uncle impressed on him at their leave-taking that the letter of credit was purely ' a formal endorsement of the introduction.' Heine had barely been a moment in London (relates his brother Max) when he presented the letter of credit in Rothschild's counting house, cheerfully pocketed the large sum of money for which it was made out, dined with Rothschild, and for a time at any rate lived as he had always fancied living, in the grand style. Result: the *English Fragments*, which later appeared in the second volume of *Travel Sketches*. On Heine's return there was a violent scene between the nephew of genius and his irate uncle. ' His uncle taxed him with reckless extravagance and threatened never to be reconciled with him again—to all of which Heine listened with the greatest calmness. When his uncle came at last to the end of his sermon, the nephew's only reply was: " You know, uncle, the best thing about you is that you bear my name," and walked proudly out of the room.' The uncle never forgot this scene, as is shown by a letter in which he refers to himself as ' Salomon Heine, the man who bears your name,' to which he adds the word *Spass*, which in the Jewish usage indicates contempt. As late as 1843 the uncle signed: ' Uncle, whose name is Heine, too.' The wound rankled.

The young poet's never-ending financial and professional difficulties were relieved in the nick of time by a *deus ex machina* in the shape of Campe, the Hamburg publisher. Heine formed varying estimates of him, as did the publishing cognoscenti of later generations. Friedrich Hirth, who has edited the great Heine correspondence, has a blistering denunciation of Campe's publishing methods and of the way he paid his authors. Heine, too, wrote from Paris: ' The fact is, in spite of all my German reputation, I would have to rot if Hoffman and Campe were my only paymasters.' Nevertheless, there can be no question that at this particular stage of Heine's life, at any rate, Campe's intervention was a decisive piece of good fortune and helped him in his development and in his rise to fame. Not only the delighted words of praise which Heine lavished on his publisher at all times testify to this—an almost childlike gratitude to the few people who ever showed him a kindness is one of Heine's most prominent, endearing qualities —there is also the evidence of the commercial success Heine's works now began to achieve, a success in which the efficient publisher played no small part. When Heine toyed with the idea of finding another publisher Julius Campe was justified in writing—to a third party—' What I did for Heine and his reputation a Cotta will never do.' In any case, the permanence of their author-publisher relationship, to which Heine remained loyal with few exceptions throughout his life, proves clearly that both parties were aware of the advantages it brought them.

Julius Campe was not only Heine's, Börne's, Immerman's, Gutzkow's, Wienbarg's, Hebbel's—among others'—publisher. He also published books as ' stiff ' and as little likely to succeed commercially as the previously quoted *Moses Mendelssohn und seine Schule* by Dr. Steinheim, a concise theorizing work which is still insufficiently appreciated today. At that time he was the most influential as well as the most progressive publisher in Germany. His books were frequently confiscated in the various states of the German Confederation, but he remained undeterred. The story goes that Heine, whom Campe did not know personally, met him in Campe's bookshop when he (Heine) was buying a book of his own poems. Heine spoke of them very deprecatingly. Campe defended the poet warmly, spoke of the originality of his style, whereupon Heine, taking him at his word, offered him a manuscript which he had ready. Campe agreed on the spot and in 1826 the first volume of the *Reisebilder* appeared.

It contained verse and prose, the much overrated *Harzreise* inset in the *Heimkehr* and *Nordsee I* verse-sequences. (Heine's excellent Czech biographer, Professor Otokar Fischer, rightly points out that the very popular but, on the whole, mediocre *Harzreise* has deflected attention from Heine's good late prose.) A second volume followed in 1827, with more *North Sea* poems, the prose piece on Nordeney, and its fateful supplement of *Xenien* by Immerman. These were satirical epigrams, some of them aimed at Platen. Heine declared that 'with few exceptions, which I have indicated with an asterisk, I shall be quite pleased to adopt them as representing my own views,' thus starting the Platen controversy. The volume ended with the autobiographical sketch *Buch Le Grand* brilliant, dreamily meditative, many-sided, and with a controlled discursiveness. This year, 1827, was an exceptionally fruitful one for Heine. In it came the stay in England, which contributed greatly to his political development, and the edition of his collected lyrics which, under the title of *Buch der Lieder,* was to bring him lasting fame.

Campe did not expect, or so he said, to achieve any success with the book, and Heine sold him the perpetual copyright for a single payment of fifty louis d'or. In fact, it appeared in a new edition every other year and is still today the core of Heine's *œuvre*. Had he been paid fairly for it, the income from the book, combined with the income from Heine's other publications—he was an assiduous writer—would have given him financial security for the rest of his life and saved him all the miseries and humiliations of his Paris period. Campe tarnished his name by insisting on the letter of the agreement and allowing Heine to suffer while he himself became rich.

The *Buch der Lieder,* a great symphony made up of many and varied sounds, assembled the entire lyrical output of Heine's early period, up to 1827. Nothing new, but the panoramic view afforded by the bringing together of all the poems clearly revealed for the first time the disconcerting vitality and the passionate individuality of the unhappy lover. For all the wealth of sound the symphony has a single theme. The formula of the lost leman, the fair, false, faithless woman covers the whole content of the book. Even when the poet turns to other subjects, mockingly or seriously, or turns indeed to other women ; when his one all-consuming love emits a confused echo, as it were, in the shape of a pale attachment to the beloved's sister ; even when, much later, it sends out a solitary bud in the shape of a posthumous poem to her daughter (*kleine Kusinenknospe*)—we feel it is still the same torment, which knows no anodyne. It seems to me that it is this unity of theme, together with extraordinary power of detail, which makes Heine's love poetry so effective (cf. Immerman's appraisal, which will be quoted later, of the *Heimkehr*).

The *Buch der Lieder* brought together the poems that had appeared in Heine's four previous books, though with many alterations and omissions. Heine eliminated some verses he found distasteful ; these have now been readmitted in the present-day Heine editions. Heine scholarship is hard put to it to decide on matters of text and sequence and general composition of the book. For the moment the historical fact must suffice that Heine assembled the lyrics of *Buch der Lieder* from the two volumes of the *Reisebilder* ; from his first book of poems, *Gedichte*, published by Maurer ; and from the *Tragedies together with a Lyrical Intermezzo* which had been published by Dümmler in 1823.

The two tragedies, *Almansor* and *Ratcliff*, were not included in the *Buch der Lieder*, to its advantage. It is difficult to make anything of them. Turn them and twist them as one will, even the sharpest eye will be unable to detect signs of an approach to artistic perfection in the crudely garish scenes and in the petty mistaken-identity and child-swopping *motifs*. Even the reader with a penchant for discovering that the real genius of great authors resides in neglected, little-known works by them is unlikely to be able to make any startling reassessment of Heine by reference to these tragedies. So much for the artistry of these pieces, which is enhanced neither by the effectiveness of their juxtapositional contrast (the scene of the one is set in southern sunshine, that of the other in northern mists) nor by the high opinion the author himself entertained of them. Heine thought highly of *Ratcliff* in particular. As late as 1851 he wrote in a preface to a new edition of the play, *à propos* of the short scene in Tom's thieves' kitchen : ' The great soup question, which a thousand incompetent cooks are now skimming with their spoons and which now daily boils over more furiously,

was already simmering in honest Tom's oven in *Ratcliff*.' In
Ratcliff Heine feels he has ' openly proclaimed his last word ' on
this subject. ' Since then this word has become a battle-cry at whose
sound the pale features of misery take on a purple flame and the
red-cheeked sons of privilege turn white as chalk.' Evidently, this
' word ' is expressed in the lines spoken by Tom (as well as in
Ratcliff's speech immediately preceding them):

> . . . und teilte ein die Menschen
> In zwei Nationen, die sich wild bekriegen,
> Nämlich in Satte und in Hungerleider.
> Weil ich zu letzterer Partei gehörte,
> So musst ich mit den Satten oft mich balgen,
> Doch hab ich eingesehn, der Kampf ist ungleich.

> . . . divided all the world
> In a pair of warring, killing nations,
> The one pot-bellied, the other hunger-suffering.
> Because I found myself a hunger-sufferer
> Often I had to brawl with the pot-bellied.
> I see now, though, the fight is all uneven.

There is an anticipation here of the inspired vision of Heine's
later *Rattenballade*, but it has to be admitted that to the reader of
Ratcliff the passage quoted seems little more than a fleeting
description of milieu having little organic connexion with the rest
of the play.

The preface of 1851 concludes with a purple patch which most
will think is hardly justified by the work itself:

> I wrote *William Ratcliff* under the lime-trees in Berlin, in
> the last three days of January, 1821. The sun shone with a
> certain lukewarm benevolence on the snow-covered roofs and
> on the despondent leafless trees. I wrote it in one stretch,
> without doing it in rough first. While I was writing it seemed
> to me that I heard a noise above my head as of the beating of
> wings. When I told this to my friends, the young Berlin poets,
> they looked at each other with a peculiar expression and
> unanimously assured me that nothing like that had ever
> happened to them in the course of their poetic writing.

The biographical significance of the two tragedies is, indeed,
greater than their artistic significance. Unsuccessful in their work-
manship as they are, Heine's own unhappy situation shows through
them in heart-gripping clarity. These two pieces, too, echo the

theme of ' the lost leman.' In both cases it is quite a different world
from Heine's ; in it the bride is snatched from the yearning grasp
of her lover (Christianity opposed to Almansor the Moor, the
nobility opposed to Ratcliff the highwayman), but this serves only
to intensify the feeling of separation between Heine the poor
proletarian poet and the Hamburg plutocracy of the ' Steinweg.'
This is, in fact, autobiography delineated with the crudest penman-
ship. Heine had every justification for saying in his dedication of
Ratcliff to Christiani : ' From the red book of love I tore off its
seven secret seals.'

Moreover, we may find another biographical clue on an entirely
different level, in the mere fact that Heine's dramas—his epics, too—
were incomplete, fragmentary in their nature. There can be no
doubting the sincerity of his effort, the creative joy he felt in both
works. Of *Ratcliff*, which he describes in a letter to Immermann as
' a great act of confession,' he says this ' poem ' is ' true, or I
myself am a lie ; everything else I have written and still write may
and will perish.'

I am well aware, of course, that quotations from letters bring
with them their own problems ; much in them is written with an
eye on the recipient of the letter or for some other specific purpose,
and needs correcting in the light of the objective facts. All the
same, I feel some weight must be given to the passionate tone of
an utterance like this.

Rather more sceptical is Heine's comment on *Almansor* (letter
to Steinmann). He considers that the ' glorious work ' which he
himself had ' gazed at and idolized ' was ' not only not a good
tragedy, but doesn't deserve even the name of a tragedy.' Very
acutely he gives his reasons : he had made the dialogue too smooth,
had tried to combine the Romantic spirit with severely classic
form, etc. Yet here the earnestness and ardour with which Heine
went to work are unmistakable. One sees all the more clearly
that life itself has knocked the grand form out of his hand ; more
precisely, the difficulties he had to contend with in his life have
burst this form from within. When to all the unhappiness of the
artist, who in any case reacts a hundredfold more sensitively to
every act of unfriendliness than does the ordinary man, another
specific trouble is added—in this case, defenceless poverty and the
fact that he was a Jew in the midst of a hostile environment—then

the tension becomes too great. The ripe meditation, the deep breath indispensable for the dramatist and epic writer, are then no longer possible. It seems as if this aspect of Heine's life is mirrored in the two dramas not only in their form but internally in their action. The substance of each drama is an individual struggle against an overwhelming majority, in both cases unsuccessful. 'Here stands the man with the giant's heart who despises Great Britain's peoples and laws, who strives defiantly with heaven itself—and he is powerless to prevent Earl Douglas lying in his beloved's arms this night.'

It is interesting to note, too, that both plays begin with criticisms of costume; more precisely, of the way in which the national costume had been adapted to foreign manners. It is not difficult to see in this the reflex of the contemporary assimilationist strivings, Heine's resistance to the indignity of Berlin's Jewish baptisms. Almansor is rebuked for wearing Spanish instead of Moorish clothes: ' Who has decked the noble Berber steed with this hypo-critical coloured snake-skin ? Cast off this poisonous skin, O Son of Abdullah, tread on the serpent's head, O noble steed!' The resistance to alien ways increases in intensity till the famous passage is reached: ' Like plague spots, flee the house where a new faith rears its head.' Similarly Douglas is praised by his father-in-law in *Ratcliff* for wearing the traditional Scottish, and not the English, dress:

> Da lob ich mir mein Plaid und meine Mütze.
> Ihr tatet gut, dass Ihr die Narrenkleider
> Vom Leib geworfen habt. Ein Douglas muss
> Im Äussern auch ein Schotte sein, und heute
> Lacht mir das Herz im Leib, wenn ich Euch schaue,
> Euch alle, in der lieben Schottentracht.

> Give me old Scotia's plaid and tartan bonnet.
> Right well you did to strip the Sassenach motley
> From off your limbs. The clan of Douglas must
> In their outward garb be Caledonians too—
> My heart rejoices when I see you all
> Apparelled in our national garments dear.

This is the characteristic note of the play, which is moreover rich in biographical suggestion. The castle conjures up *Affronten-burg* for us once more, with its familiar maiden who at first rains hot kisses on her lover's lips and then with a 'mocking curtsey' utters an 'icy' no. Her mother's name is Schön-Betty (after Heine's mother ?), and the two 'wraiths' who always approach each other with outstretched arms, then separate and disappear, offer a fruitful field for the psycho-analyst.

Almansor was played at the Brunswick Court Theatre, the only time one of Heine's plays was ever performed. The piece was well received right up to the last scene, when a rumour spread that the author was an unpopular Brunswick Jewish money-changer named Heine. The ensuing uproar was such that the curtain had to be lowered and the play could not be completed.

Thus, even in such remote externals, Judaism proved of fateful import to Heine's dramatic efforts, which he saw condemned to failure. Another stone was placed on the wall which eventually was to bar completely his way into German life.

The *Lyrical Intermezzo*—the whole of Heine's lyric work, indeed—calls for an entirely different kind of appraisal from that appropriate to the tragedies with which the *Intermezzo* was coupled.

The tragedies are prentice efforts ; the lyrics belong to the incomprehensible realm of perfection. The tragedies are of interest to us, they provide us with biographical clues ; the lyrics reveal the eternal idea of beauty which we can approach only in awe and rapture, having divested ourselves of all trivial attachments to the inadequate world below.

That such an attitude of unqualified admiration applies only to some, not all of the poems, is so obvious that I mention it only to forestall criticism. It is of little importance, though, *how many* of the poems are completely beautiful, how many are not ; we are now entering a sphere in which measurements and quantities no longer avail. All that counts are the poems that are beautiful in an absolute sense. Everything else that Heine may have written then loses interest. In theory a single poem, a single verse-pattern, even, would be sufficient to confirm Heine's claim to the bays, to erase all his less finished writing. For here, where a sheer artistic experience is concerned, we can only perceive ; we can neither weigh nor measure. In such moments we can feel neither pain nor insufficiency, whether the pain be that of our own or of Heine's life. In the plays, in much of the prose, and, of course, in much of the verse, too, we can sense how the difficulties of Heine's life influenced and marred his literary style ; but in the really and completely beautiful poems no trace of any such influence can be detected ; they are free of, have outsoared, all earthly dross. They are the real miracle in his life ; inexplicable ; his deepest secret, which, like all true artists, he took with him into the grave. Whence did they come to him, from what impulse, these moments of liberation ? No one will ever be able to tell us anything about this veritable ' noumenon.' And yet for a poet it is these peak moments which alone are decisive.

Recently I read a biography of Kleist in which his temptations, aberrations, weaknesses, delusions and destructive tendencies were recorded with so much psychological penetration that in the end one asked oneself : ' Did he ever have one peaceful minute ? ' And yet it is not the *chaos* in Kleist's life which is important in the final analysis, but the fact that from such disordered vital functions could emerge, in spite of everything, such a world of disciplined order, a cosmos of self-controlled sweetness, as the *Prinz von Homburg* or the long short stories.

Let us be clear on this point, then : it is wrong to think of the artist as being a perpetually tortured, badgered individual whose nerves are always on edge. Transcending all his limitations and soothing all his irritations is the halcyon tranquillity of the creative process. Here, and only here, the poet is beyond ordinary human criteria and can be approached only with admiring awe. The poet has so much surplus energy, as it were, that for the moment all the evil and wickedness of life can touch him not at all, it is simply not there, has been conjured away, is powerless—he is free. In the portrait of Heine that I have been sketching till now, the obstacles he had to contend with, his failures, the almost impossible situations in which his German-Judaism placed him have predominated. Now that I come to discuss his masterpieces it is no more than fitting that I should make due acknowledgment of the way in which he trampled over every inner and outer barrier and crushed all difficulties. The force with which the Absolute in a work of art conquers the hazards and tricks of human life may be compared perhaps with the power of death emanating from the Universe; with the supreme cosmic force that, in the moments of the dying man's last feeble struggles, not so much overpowers him as with a slight gesture reduces him to a cipher.

In what follows, then, I may be venturing to pronounce on something on which it is not really possible to pronounce. In that case, the most that can be hoped for is to have perceived some approximation to truth.

With this qualification in mind, let us now consider what it is that continually places the artistic effect of Heine's poetry in jeopardy. There are two danger zones:

1. A harshness of utterance which, though sometimes witty, is nevertheless in poor taste. Not that wit is *always* inimical to the lyric quality, but that there is always a danger that it may be. This peril, like all perils, can only be avoided of course by taking special counter-measures. When this is done the final effect may well be extraordinarily fine. In Goethe, Moerike, this is frequently the case. In Heine it occurs often, too ; in the remarkable Montmartre-cemetery poem, for example ('Keine Messe wird man singen'—No mass will be sung), *Gedächtnisfeier*—'Memorial Service.' Here earthly mourning and crystal-clear angelic wit, simple human affection and loyalty and ironic super-terrestrial gallantry fuse into an inimitable, unforgettable whole. In contrast an example of Heine's wit which is quite intolerable: 'Die Thore jedoch, die liessen/ Mein Liebchen entwischen gar still ;/ Ein Thor ist immer willig, /Wenn eine Thörin will'—The gates, though, let my beloved quietly slip through them ; one fool is always willing if the other is. Here a pun, a fatuous one into the bargain (*Thor* = 'gate,' 'fool' in German) simply turns the poem into nonsense. As I pointed out before, there is no justification for thinking that puns indicate mastery of language. In fact, it's nearly always a sign of linguistic uncertainty when an author goes out of his way to advertise his power over language. Heine is not free from highly suspect boasting of this kind when he often proclaims his mastery of the German tongue (Nietzsche is a similar case).

2. The second danger to which Heine's lyric poetry is subject is that of pretty-pretty word-jingling. Rose, lily, dove, sun, spring, little cheeks, nightingales, dreams, elves, mermaids, 'die Kleine, die Feine, die Reine, die Eine '—the little one, the lovely one, the pure one, the only one—these are only a few of the symbols and epithets that come all too trippingly and practically devoid of content from his pen. Heine cannot be blamed of course for the way in which his lesser imitators have abused this vocabulary ; indeed, he often infuses an

astonishing vitality into images so conventional that in other hands they would seem petrified. All the same, there is danger in this small stock of vapid, stereotyped figures, though—to repeat myself —it can be countered like any other danger. The danger does not lie in the poverty of the images, be it noted. In Eichendorff's poems, too, a small number of similar experiences is continually repeated without ever being exhausted. It would seem as if there were something wrong from the start in Heine's typical word-patterns. Flaubert brilliantly described word-schemes of this kind, which to the Philistine seem to be the quintessence of poetry, as *pohésie*.

The nadir is reached, probably, in the poem: ' Mutter zum Bienelein: Hüt dich vor Kerzenschein '—Mother to little bee exclaims: ' Guard against candle flames.' Here, in a few verses all the defects of the Heinesque lyric manage to come together— including the intensely irritating ' olde German ' (*Deutschtümeln*) of his youthful period, which kills verses like that of the *wunnevolles Magedein* ('blessed damozel'). Fortunately, Heine saw how dangerous this kind of versifying could be—it would scarcely be too harsh to call it simply doggerel—and he himself described its perils in precise terms (his artistic sensibility is indeed beyond praise):

Wenn der Frühling kommt mit dem Sonnenschein,
Dann knospen und blühen die Blümlein auf ;
Wenn der Mond beginnt seinen Strahlenlauf,
Dann schwimmen die Sternlein hinterdrein ;
Wenn der Sänger zwei süsse Äuglein sieht,
Dann quellen ihm Lieder aus tiefem Gemüt ;—
Doch Lieder und Sterne und Blümelein,
Und Äuglein und Mondglanz und Sonnenschein,
Wie sehr das Zeug auch gefällt,
So macht's doch noch lang keine Welt.

When the spring-tide comes and the sun's in the sky,
Then flowers bud forth and shoot on high ;
When the moon begins its pale light to shed,
The stars in the heavens leave their bed ;
When the poet beholds two lovely blue eyes,
Then poems from the depths of his soul 'gin arise ;
But poems and stars and moon and sun,
And flowers and eyes, when all's said and done,
For all the pleasure they give,
Are not the stuff by which we live.

Capable of self-criticism of this kind as he was, it is not surprising that in his later works Heine increasingly cut down his use of stock poetic diction ; the self-consciously literary ghost passages in the early poems should be compared with his later verse on similar themes, in which voices from beyond can almost be heard groaning, and with the fine, taut prose of the *Elemental Spirits* and the *Gods in Exile*.

It might be as well at this point to dispose of the erroneous view, frequently put forth, that *only* Heine's late poems reach the topmost heights of the lyric. On the contrary, as early as the *Book of Songs* we find verses whose perfection is, quite simply, unsurpassable, often next to others which are commonplace in the extreme. It is not possible to lay down any rule, even that of the maturing and developing of genius ; perfect beauty is not bound by human laws, the wind bloweth where it listeth. It is wrong to suggest, even, that Heine achieves perfection in the poems which avoid the perils I have described. Where there is perfection there can be not even the slightest suggestion of peril, and so there can be no question of avoiding perils. In this region of the incomprehensible, of rapture, all earthly difficulties seem infinitely far away. In such a region there reigns a peace seeming to have hardly anything left in common with the ' absence of sorrow ' which is its earthly equivalent.

I wish to make myself as intelligible as possible. I have selected, therefore, three examples of Heine's lyric writing which seem to me as if they will last for all time and may claim a place in the sphere of the Absolute. I have no desire to wriggle out of trying to say whatever can still be said by pleading ' non-subjection to ordinary laws ' and similar—entirely justified—negations of our normal reasoning processes. Although I am well aware that quoting examples in this way always starts a number of hares—there is the thorny question of individual taste, of personal associations—I prefer to take as my guide Goethe's sublime and sound maxim, for which I am indebted to Paul Friedländer's book on Plato :

> It makes all the difference whether I strive to emerge from the light into the dark, or from the dark into the light ; whether, finding clarity uncongenial, I shroud myself in obscurity, or whether, convinced that clarity lies at the bottom of depths that have been plumbed with difficulty, I do my best to bring up all that is possible from these depths that are always so hard to put into words.

The three examples are intended to serve for many. The poem that sets before us the vision of Hamburg, the place ' wo ich das Liebste verlor '—where I lost the most-beloved. 'Am fernen Horizonte/Erscheint, wie ein Nebelbild,/Die Stadt mit ihren Türmen,/In Abenddämmrung gehüllt.'—The city with its towers shrouded in the twilight mist looms on the distant horizon. And then the quiet, very simple, mysteriously revealing lines: ' Ein feuchter Windzug kräuselt/Die graue Wasserbahn '—a drizzling wind is curling the grey waterway. There is more reality here than in many a long novel, and more invocation of the heavenly powers —which are not mentioned by so much as a single word—than in many a prayer in the liturgy. The sun itself, source of life and light, is invoked in elemental fashion, if not as helper, then as witness:

> Ein feuchter Windzug kräuselt
> Die graue Wasserbahn ;
> Mit traurigem Takte rudert
> Der Schiffer in meinem Kahn.

> Die Sonne hebt sich noch einmal
> Leuchtend vom Boden empor,
> Und zeigt mir jene Stelle,
> Wo ich das Liebste verlor.

> A drizzling wind is curling
> The grey waterway ;
> With dismal rhythm my oarsman
> Rows on as best he may.

> The sun once more shines forth and
> Radiant rides in the sky,
> And shows me the city where
> I bade my beloved good-bye.

No one with an ear for the minor key of these verses can ever forget them. And yet only the most ordinary words are used to give us a landscape imperishably quivering between reality and dream. (Schubert's musical setting, though often surpassing Heine's verses, fails to do justice on this occasion to the full force of the poem, though the middle movement does not fall far short of doing so.) Another poem, foreshadowing *Tristan*:

> Der Tod, das ist die kühle Nacht,
> Das Leben ist der schwüle Tag,
> Es dunkelt schon, mich schläfert, etc.

Death is the cool night, life is the sultry day, darkness approaches, the poet feels sleepy. . . .

It is primarily the irregular metre of this poem that casts its spell, its apparent awkwardness (*e.g.*, in the last line). Apparent— both 'irregular' verses have in fact the same scansion and rhyme- scheme. Even the single dactyl, as well as the peculiar assonance of the second and fourth lines and the rhyme of the first and second lines is repeated. Yet in spite of this pattern the poem's effect, sensually as well as linguistically, is that of a feverish stammering. It really has been evolved on the borderland of waking and dreaming, of order and decay. It shows us the secret of Heine's form, as the other poem quoted shows us the secret of Heine's soul. Yet even this emphasis is only apparent. In reality form and content contribute equally to the beauty of both poems, and in the last analysis are indistinguishable. As Novalis put it: 'The outward appearance is the inner core elevated to the status of a mystery— and perhaps *vice versa* too.'

The third example may serve to illustrate how the sublime harmony of a single line or group of lines can irradiate a whole poem, including even the preceding verses, and raise it into the Eternal. The poem is called *Erinnerung* ('Memory'). Much in it seems prosaic, unresolved, though the unqualified appreciation of Goethe is certainly fine:

> Frankfurt, du hegst viel Narr'n und Bösewichter,
> Doch lieb ich dich, du gabst dem deutschen Land
> Manch guten Kaiser und den besten Dichter.

> Frankfurt, fools and knaves in thee do live,
> Yet were noble emperors crowned within thy gates,
> And to Germans their greatest poet didst thou give.

But the really magical lines don't come till the end, when the strange, profoundly true and profoundly human story of the street- girl, reminiscent of Flaubert's *November*, has been told, and nothing remains but the memory of the beautiful girl and her unhappy love:

> Fort ist der alte Wahn, jedoch das Bildnis
> Des armen Kinds umschwebt mich, wo ich bin.
> Wo irrst du jetzt, in welcher kalten Wildnis?
> Dem Elend und dem Gram gab ich dich hin.

The poet's infatuation is a thing of the past, but the picture of the poor child haunts him still. In what ' drear-nighted December ' was she wandering now ? The poet had abandoned her to her misery and pain.

It's the last line of the German that does it :

' Dem Elend und dem Gram gab ich dich hin.'

I know of little that can compare with it in its earnestness, its poignancy and its vowel music. But I feel that if I were to attempt to analyse it further I should become incoherent. . . .

It goes without saying that there are hundreds, perhaps thousands of these ' beauties of Heine.' But everything I have just said will have been misunderstood if the beauty of Heine is sought only in details, in single phrases, lines, poems. This would be to show an insensitivity to the peculiar essence of Heine which, though sometimes sadly diluted, pervades nearly all his work ; a veritable *hic et ubique,* an impalpable phantom like the ghost of Hamlet's father. Not only so, but in their great cohesion lies one of the special beauties of Heine's lyrics. The extraordinary effect they had on his contemporaries may be partly attributable to this fact. More of this later.

It is rather remarkable that the poet who achieved only a partial success in the epic form itself (a few chapters, a few personages) should in his lyric poetry have developed a unity of theme of a quite exceptional, almost epic kind. The experiences of the hero of the poem-sequences form such a consistent whole, the action of the poems develops so progressively, that one could almost speak of verse novels which might be entitled ' The Lover,' ' The Rejected Suitor ' ; subsequently ' The Exile,' ' The Fighter,' and ' The Invalid.' It would seem that this unity of treatment was suggested by Wilhelm Müller's *Müllerlieder* and *Winterreise* (the latter well-known in Schubert's musical settings). Heine himself was aware of this influence, though in a very cordial letter written to Müller in terms of unstinting admiration he suggested other possibilities for the provenance of his (Heine's) style. He openly admits (in his letter, 1826) that ' the similarity of the light metre of my Intermezzo and the metre usually employed by you is not simply adventitious ; probably my Intermezzo is indebted to your lyrics for its innermost accents.'

We can, if we wish, follow the thread of the inner reality of the
Intermezzo somewhat in this fashion: In the first poem we live
through love's beginning (' Im wunderschönen Monat Mai '—in the
wonder-lovely month of May). Thereafter we can go through all
the stages of youthful joy in a love that is returned. For the moment,
the joy is unmarred (' das Himmelslicht, das aus den frommen
Augen bricht '—the heavenly light shining in those kindly eyes).
Then comes the peak of ecstasy in ' wunderbar süsser Stund,' in the
' wonderful sweet moments ' ; the first quarrel (' Du hassest, hassest
mich sogar '—you hate, yes hate me) ; and the pseudo-triumph over
the maiden, when we hear the first harsh note of irony. Soon afterwards the dissension between the two, the incompatibility of their
temperaments, can no longer be hidden. ' You haven't a good
character,' says the world, perhaps rightly, although the world
doesn't know ' how sweet your kisses are, with what a benediction
they burn.' Perhaps rightly, for in the very next poem there is no
longer any talk of ' kindly eyes ' but of ' false hypocritical glances,'
and so it remains. The false maiden marries, the poet is brought face
to face with stark reality reflected in a naturalism of style that
invades the delicate flower-language of the preceding poems. The
conflict between two different worlds leads to jangling disharmonies :
' I bear no malice ' ; ' I believe only in your eyes and in your wicked
heart ' ; the ' hide-and-seek ' poem ; the verses about the kind lady
who had ' secured him his passport for his journey.' Once more
there are graveside visions and death-wishes : ' Ich aber verhänge die
Fenster/Des Zimmers mit schwarzem Tuch ;/Es machen mir meine
Gespenster/Sogar einen Tagesbesuch.' The poet puts up black
curtains, his ghosts visit him in broad daylight.

One of the poems that approach perfection is No. 48. It tells
of an ' island of ghosts ' and ends with the magically musical lines :

Wir aber schwammen vorüber
Trostlos auf weitem Meer.

' But we swam cheerlessly past on the broad sea.'

I like very much, too, the next poem (' Aus alten Märchen
winkt es '—the land of fairy tales). I once half-jokingly called it ' the
glorious national anthem of all Romanticism.' And Schumann's
supremely beautiful musical setting of the poem left me in no doubt
that : ' In spite of the differences between the German and the

Jewish soul, which I do not deny, there are also affinities, mutual
understanding in the innermost, truest, and holiest regions.' 'Were it
not so, Schumann would not have been able to find in certain of
Heine's poems that to which his own soul could respond.' (Cf. my
book *Die Frau, die nicht enttäuscht*, pp. 151 ff.)

In the ensuing poems the poet looks back. In retrospect his
relationship with the faithless woman acquires a different, starkly
horrible aspect. 'She never hated me, and she never loved me.'
'My songs are poisoned—how could it be otherwise?—you poured
poison into the vial of my young life.' The poet's anguish shows no
sign of abating. 'I see you every night in my dreams.' The end of
it all is despair, dead-men's fingers, the abyss, Stygian night, a great
coffin for his great agony.

In the *Heimkehr* sequence the biographical elements are even
more clearly and dramatically in evidence and point to the individual even more precisely. The cycle begins with a (figurative)
burial, like Mahler's Fifth. The sweet figure of the poet's beloved
has disappeared into the night. Like a child in the dark the poet
sings to dispel his fears. In the light of this introduction the second
poem of the sequel, the *Lorelei*, appears as something far deeper
than the picture-postcard verses of popular taste. The lethal power
of the 'false hypocritical glances' of which the Intermezzo sang is
here seen in a highly personal context. 'Die Luft ist kühl und es
dunkelt/Und ruhig fliesst der Rhein,'—the Rhine flows peacefully
in the cool twilight—these beautiful lines are an infinitely tender
résumé of the evening, the fears, the comfort-in-singing of the first
poem. They are beautiful enough to atone for the solecism of the
inversion in the first line of the poem, which may really be, as
Heine's opponents point out with malicious pleasure, an unconscious
relapse into the 'Yiddish' jargon of his youth.

Heine's poem has become a folk-song. In his version the Lorelei
has become a semi-mythical saga-figure, in spite of the fact that in
the Rhineland itself no such local saga was known. That Heine was
able to achieve this must, I think, be due to the fact that for the
nonce he was overpowered by an emotion stronger than was aroused
in him by contemplation of his individual fate, an emotion that left
no room for consideration of the individual but forced him to adopt
an imagery capable of a universal application. The student of Heine
who knows and appreciates how the poet loved the treasury of

German saga and folk-lore cannot fail to be touched by the fact that once, at any rate, this deep love was rewarded. The nation to whom he was so grateful for what it had given him of language and literature accepted the gift of his poem, and in this great unconscious gesture it would seem that it gave him back some of his own gratitude. For once, and exceptionally, overcoming the natural barriers, that which is practically impossible in the realm of the spirit has here become reality. ' Das Unzulängliche/Hier wird's Ereignis.' The unattainable here becomes fact. A passionate longing has here found fulfilment.

It is worth repeating that the Lorelei legend is not based on folk-tale, but was the fruit of Clement Brentano's imagination. His novel *Godwi* has a poem *Die Lore Lay* (' based on the ancient name of the rock *Lurlei* '). It begins : ' Zu Bacharach am Rheine/Wohnt eine Zauberin.'—In Bacharach on the Rhine there lives an enchantress. The poem continues : ' Der Bischof liess sie laden/Vor geistliche Gewalt/Und musste sie begnaden/So schön war ihr' Gestalt.'—The bishop summoned her before a spiritual court but had to acquit her, so beautiful she was. This original version seems to me to be much finer, more powerful than Heine's poem—' but this has nothing to do with the case.' Brentano's novel appeared in 1801 ; subsequently his *Lorelei* poem was either adapted or rewritten by Eichendorff, N. Vogt, Count Löben (1821) and—as late as 1823—Heine.

We continue our journey through the *Heimkehr*. After a few terse, melancholy traveller's impressions, after the eerie description of the gamekeeper's lodge, we meet the beloved's family. ' Auch nach der vermählten Geliebten/Fragte ich nebenbei ;/Und freundlich gab man zur Antwort,/Dass sie in den Wochen sei.'—I asked in passing after my beloved, who had wed, and they replied amiably that she was expecting a child. The beloved's little sister interjects something symbolically nonsensical into the conversation—something about a puppy who later went mad and had to be drowned. And the whole thing starts again. The moment is captured with tremendous power. ' Die Kleine gleicht der Geliebten,/Besonders wenn sie lacht ;/Sie hat dieselben Augen,/Die mich so elend gemacht.'—The little one is the image of the beloved, particularly when she laughs ; she has the same eyes that plunged me into such misery.

As one reads further on, it becomes hard to understand why historians of literature should have found it so difficult to uncover Heine's love for Amalie's sister, Therese. True, Heine himself was the soul of discretion, but if instead of looking for evidence in Heine's letters and private papers his long-published poems had been more closely read, the true state of affairs would have been bound to come to light. Poems 58, 62, and 66 repeat the Therese situation ; the gradual transition from ' acting ' to deadly earnest finds clear expression in Nos. 47, 49, and 60.

Printed before the ' Therese ' poems are the sea-shore verses, the short poem about the ' old path ' and the ' familiar streets ' and the *Doppelgänger* poem (' Du Doppelgänger, du bleicher Geselle '— the poet apostrophises the pale youth who is his double). The old sorrow, the solitary tear appears. The ballad is vivid, bringing the scene to our eyes. And there's another poem, graphic reportage, of which I have always been very fond from my earliest youth. I don't know to what extent my predilection, which I am loth to explain, will be shared. This is the poem about the hulking lazy daughter whose mother goes out to buy flour and eggs and butter with which to bake her cake. The old woman waddles down the street with her lantern. ' The weather is foul, it rains and blows and snows.' But the daughter—

> Die liegt zu Haus im Lehnstuhl
> Und blinzelt schläfrig ins Licht ;
> Die goldnen Locken wallen
> Uber das süsse Gesicht—

The daughter lies at home in the armchair, she blinks sleepily at the light ; her golden locks flow about her sweet face.

Such moments of impersonal contemplation of women who were not near and dear to him, such ' breaks ' in his passion, only serve to act as a foil to the violence of his new passion for Therese. ' Thou little one with big eyes '—this love, strangely reticent and reserved, is even more disastrous than the first. Did recollections of his first love seal his lips when he wrote of his second ? Amalie was never ' little one ' to him ; the slightly contemptuous epithet always refers to Therese. He finds some distraction in memories of childhood : the three Magi, children's games with his sister, the good old days. But thereafter the catastrophe can no longer be stayed. Heine saves himself by his wit, by his contempt of his fellows and by escapades ' under the limes.' This last part of the sequence has something of the quality of a brightly coloured picture-book about it. It grips our heart almost too tightly, with its unexpected contrasts, its fragmentariness, its hasty confusion, its irony through which, however, notes of sincerity can still be detected (' bei dir sitzen, mit dir schwatzen '—to sit with you, chat with you—how captivating is the assonance of this line, is the whole poem . . . or : ' Von schönen Lippen fortgedrängt, getrieben/Aus schönen Armen, die uns fest umschlossen '—pushed away, driven from lovely lips, from lovely arms that held us tight enfolded—how close to the accents of Goethe's Pandora . . . or : ' Uber die Berge steigt schon die Sonne '—now rises the sun over the mountain tops—married to the genuine inspiration of Mendelssohn's melody). The Tristan-like chords to which I previously referred close the sequence in night and dreaming. But there is no release. ' And this slim volume is the urn, with the ashes of my love.'

At first, Heine's poems were favourably greeted by his contemporaries with joy, enthusiasm, affection. And the Göttingen barmaid's exclamation : ' Ach wie herzlich schön ! ' expressed a feeling that at the time probably animated the hearts of many Germans of all classes.

Afterwards there was a change, and up till now Heine has remained one of the writers whose merits have been most fiercely disputed in German territories ; it is not too much to say that in these territories he has remained one of the most hated of writers. Before examining more closely the impact he made on his contemporaries, I think it might prove illuminating to consider the fate that was later to overtake the estimation of Heine and his work. After all, of all the men of letters who wrote in German at the beginning of the last century only two have experienced this peculiar mixture of fame and unpopularity, this peculiar lasting publicity value.

I do not wish to imply that this particular form of immortality has any greatness about it or is in any way desirable. I merely state as a clearly defined fact that such is the immortality that has been the lot of these two authors. Mere fame, *fame without unpopularity*, without eternal arguing and wrangling, could never have brought about the peculiar kind of posthumous significance that has attached to these two men.

The two German writers, then, who have been equally fated to incur both unpopularity and fame, are not otherwise alike. And they are very different in stature. Who of the moderns can stand beside Goethe ! Indeed, it seems almost ironical that chance should have paired these two : the one, quickly overcoming his own initial resistance, admired the other all his life ; the other hardly noticed his admirer's existence. I speak of Heine, I speak of Goethe.

The controversies raging round these two men, Goethe no less than Heine, have still not subsided, but are continually flaring up in the pages of newspapers, periodicals, and pamphlets. Other minds—profound, great, splendid minds, but whose influence has been less widespread—have left their peaceful traces in the pages of weighty tomes and ' standard works.' The critical estimate of these minds may vary with time and place, but at least they are not the subject of noisy warfare. Goethe and Heine, on the other hand, are exposed to public censure as if they were still alive. Goethe, until quite recently, was in bad odour with the Right. Now he tends to come under fire from the Left, who foolishly see in him nothing but a Court lackey. Heine is continually being shot at with unabated fury by the Right. Not that the Left would be anything but highly displeased with him if they knew him better.

Heine's fame and the reasons for it are the subject of my book. Perhaps I may be permitted to devote a short interlude to the study of his chronic unpopularity.

Unpopular ? The word is too weak. All his life he encountered hatred, disgust, anger. This man who was so fond of life was not always sure of it. He was shadowed, spied on ; the reports of Metternich's Paris agents have been preserved. Also there were personal quarrels, duels. In Prussia there were prison cells ready prepared for him. (But the Prussian officers who were plotting to murder him in Paris were a hoax inflicted on him by certain estimable practical jokers.) And even after his death the campaign against him continued unabated. No living author was so vigorously lampooned as the dead Heine. Even when translated into memorial marble he could never achieve any real stability. The history of the Heine memorials in Germany—and in Corfu—suggests nothing so much as an epilogue written by Heine himself to *Germany, a Winter's Tale*. He continues to versify in his grave. Each footprint of his continues to afford material for literature.

A glance at the writings of our much-maligned author, however, will soon reveal the reasons that made him so intensely disliked. A few quotations. First of all there are his revolutionary leanings. Are sentiments such as the following supposed to command general approval ?

> Nicht die Geister zu vertreiben,
> Steht des Volkes Geist jetzt auf,
> Nein, dass jedem freier Lauf,
> Jedem Haus ein Geist soll bleiben :
> Nein, dass adlig all auf Erden,
> Muss der Adel Bürger werden.

It is not against the life of the spirit that the nation's spirit is now aroused ; on the contrary, the nation wants to assure a full spiritual life to every single man and woman. So that all citizens may be able to lead noble lives the nobleman must become a burgess.   (1)

And what was it really, this 'life of the spirit'? As might almost be expected as a matter of course in a Jew, it was the life of individualism, of facile libertarianism. This, for instance :

' That spirit is healthy which contains the pure form of
    individuality.'   (2)

Or, more sharply :

' Only liberty can make the life of the spirit possible, only the
    spirit can make liberty possible.'   (3)

Elsewhere :

' The word " liberty " sounds so beautiful that we cannot do
    without it, even if it were to denote error.'   (4)

Or in verse :

Jene Menschen sind toll, so sagt ihr, von heftigen Sprechern,
Die wir in Frankreich laut hören auf Strassen und Markt,
Mir auch scheinen sie toll, doch redet ein Toller in Freiheit
Weise Sprüche, wenn ach! Weisheit im Sklaven verstummt.

' They are mad, you say, those people who have swallowed
the rantings of the mob orators in France. I think them mad,
too, but a madman at liberty to speak his mind may utter
words of wisdom, though wisdom herself perish, alas, in the
mouth of the slave.'   (5)

In this last quotation there are traces of another Heinesque
tendency which explains why his unpopularity among such a large
section of the German people has been so extraordinarily unaffected
by the lapse of time. I refer to Heine's tendency to exalt France at
Germany's expense and while criticizing the conditions prevailing
in Germany ; indeed his criticisms very frequently assume the form
of a highly disrespectful denunciation of everything German :

> Nothing is more depressing than to think of the heights
> which the German intellect could have attained. But the
> German people has deliberately chosen to be stupid, and that
> for nearly a thousand years. Nowhere else have the two great
> European narcotics, alcohol and Christianity, been more
> scandalously abused. The German intellect ! How unbearably
> ponderous, lame, soggy, down-at-heels, beery it is ! The rise
> of Germany as a great power coincides with the ascendancy
> of France as a cultural power. Already much that is new in
> the sphere of serious thought, much new intellectual excite-
> ment has moved to Paris. Everybody knows now that in the
> most important respect of all—which is and always will be
> culture—the Germans are nowhere. People ask : ' Can you lay
> claim to even one mind of European calibre ? '   (6)

Even admirers of Heine recoil from outbursts of this kind,
finding them strident, subjective, unjust. But does he not frequently
say the same thing in more moderate, and hence more persuasive
and dangerous, tones ?

> ' O France, thou noble brother of Germany, who hast
> poured out thy blood for both countries, who in the delirium
> of fever hast alone turned the perilous crisis for both ! '—And
> previously : ' Nor need we Germans be so proud of our whole
> skins. To risk them so little is not our greatest virtue. The
> disease is in us too. For we are indeed in a sorry state as we
> are now ! And if nothing else happens, and we remain as we
> are now, then the great name of German Nation is nothing
> but a hypocritical cloak concealing the basest weakness and the
> most depraved tendencies. We are a lump of greasy dough
> incapable of being fermented either into enthusiasm for what
> is great or into passionate scorn of what is mean and con-

temptible.' And on Napoleon : ' In what awe would not Europe
have stood of him had he remained true to strict republican
principles. How great would his spiritual stature have been
seen to be. And what a wonderfully rich harvest would we not
with shame have seen flourishing in the neighbouring country
to which we impute every vice. . . . But he chose not to give
us this example of a greatness that would have overwhelmed
us in its earnestness. He pulverized the sacred morality represented by all those wonderful, beautiful and bloody sacrifices
made in the cause of the Revolution, and in its place, he glued
together again with blood the royal throne that had been
struck down.'   (7)

Well, we might be prepared to accept Heine's zeal for liberty
and his strict republican principles if only those principles had been
of unassailable integrity. In point of fact there were too many
breaches made in them by his loose living and by the frequent
vulgarity of his writing, with its seeming predilection for cynicism
and its tendency to dwell unnecessarily on the lower regions of
the body. This is more a question of style, it is true, and we would
remind the reader that for the moment we are in any case not
concerned to pronounce value judgments, but are merely trying
to ascertain why it is that Heine gets under so many people's skins,
particularly German skins. Still, it must be admitted that not
everyone likes to be continually reminded of our bodily necessities
and all that is connected with them. Many people find this sort of
thing revolting, particularly when they find a writer dragging in these
allusions quite irrelevantly, as Heine does. The pointlessly vulgar
Hammonia chapter (26) of *Deutschland* with its purely, or rather
impurely, capricious reference to the *chaise percée*, is an example.
Similarly Heine informs us :

' A mind which hobbles in a sack of prejudices cannot run to
    its destination. . . .'

This idea is quite liberal enough, one would have thought. In
order to drive it home, was it necessary to employ the analogy
of an army of the sick, the lame and the halt that sets out with
its crutches ?

So as not to fall out, with an easy-chair for the Lord's Day,
with a ewer of holy water for sprinkling against evil spirits
and keeping them out of the way, even—begging your pardon

—with a private portable contraption designed for convenience
and decency.   (8)

An unnecessary comparison, quite unnecessary—though
perhaps not inaccurate ! Add to this Heine's complete lack of
inhibitions in other matters of nature, above all his frivolous
attitude to love-making. This is one of his most conspicuous traits.
It reaches a climax in poems like the notorious *Teilung* (' sharing '),
in the satire on the ' Junker Bogoslav Dietrich Karl Ferdinand '
(' of indeterminate sex ') who, we are told, sat by the side of his
sweetheart, ' Fräulein Christinchen '

> ' And like all his Pomeranian compatriots behaved in horribly
> witty and gallant fashion.'

In fact, in his ruttishness he undertakes to snap the slender waist
of his beloved with two fingers ' like the stem of a clay pipe.'
The fair one understandably resists. But the swain's youngest
brother, ' a boy full of mother-wit,' emerges from his corner by the
fire. They had completely forgotten him. He had watched the whole
lubricious scene with wide-open eyes and ears. Now he takes the
Junker aside.

> ' Halt ! ' schrie er, ' Bruder ! Auf ein Wort ! '
> Und zog den Bruder mit sich fort :
> ' Zerbrichst du sie, die schöne Docke,
> So nimm die Oberhälfte dir !
> Die Hälfte mit dem Unterrocke,
> Die, lieber Bruder, schenke mir.'

' Stop ! ' he cried, ' brother, a word.' And he dragged his
brother away. ' If you do break the tasty wench in two, take
the top half for yourself ! Leave me the bottom half with the
petticoat, dear brother ! '   (9)

Clear enough, and understandably annoying ! Nor is there less
cause for annoyance when, in addition to being vulgar, Heine jeers
at the Germanic tribes—in the example quoted, at the Pomeranians.
Indeed he ridicules all German patriots. He is quite capable of
imputing to them, for instance, the manifesto of one ' Nightwatch-
man Germanicus Valhalla.' This remarkable character created by
Heine declared in his manifesto that he had written all the poems
of Herwegh and other political poets.

'I have been deprived of my liberty. In our village this is
the name we give a strip of pasture on which my nightwatchmen
predecessors had the right to graze a beast or two.'
      'I wrote my poems under assumed names in order not to
lose my place. They created a stir.'

In future, though, he wants to be the 'peaceful citizen' again—

that I was and am in prose, however criminally I may have
degenerated in the frenzy of writing poetry and in the worry
of earning my food and clothing.

He subscribes himself

> Everybody's most obedient
> Germanicus Valhalla,
> Sacristan and Nightwatchman in the
>   unfinished Cathedral
> Of Cologne on the Rhine.   (10)

It will be seen that in a few lines Heine succeeds with consummate skill in ridiculing a whole series of the German people's
favourite dreams. At that time the completion of Cologne cathedral
was one such dream. His revulsion against much that was known
in the 'Biedermeier' period as 'altdeutsch' is comprehensible, and
indeed it is possible to give him credit for good will in his attacks
on some of the more deplorable errors of taste then prevailing.
But what is one to say to the following skit on German patriotism
(four Germans named Deutsch, Deutscherig, Deutscherling,
Deutschdich indulge in a 'deutsching' contest)?

> Neulich deutschten auf deutsch vier Deutschlinge deutschend,
> Sich überdeutschend am Deutsch, welcher der Deutscheste sey.
> Vier deutschnamig benannt ; Deutsch, Deutscherig, Deutsch-
>   erling, Deutschdich ;
> Selbst so hatten zu deutsch sie sich die Namen gedeutscht.
> Jetzt wettdeutschten sie deutschend in grammatikalischer
>   Deutschheit,
> Deutscheren Comparativ, deutschesten Superlativ.
> 'Ich bin deutscher als Deutsch.' 'Ich deutscherer.' 'Deutsch-
>   ester bin ich.'
> 'Ich bin der Deutschereste oder der Deutschestere.'
> Drauf durch Comparativ und Superlativ fortdeutschend,
> Deutschten sie auf bis zum—Deutschesteresten ;
> Bis sie vor comparativisch und superlativischer Deutschung
> Den Positiv von Deutsch hatten vergessen zuletzt.   (11)

Let me repeat, we are not discussing whether or no Heine's criticism was justified. All we are concerned with is that it should be realised how unfavourable—more, provocative—its effect must have been and in fact still is.

On top of it all there was a dash of early socialism. We have reportage like this:

> The father weaves the cloth for bed-linen and shirts and trousers and jacket and hose, but he is shirtless himself. He is barefooted and wrapped in rags !
> The children are naked, they warm themselves against each other on their straw mattress and shiver with cold.
> The mother winds bobbins from early daybreak to the fall of night. Her toil consumes oil and wick, but she doesn't earn enough to feed her children properly.
> The State exacts tolls from the man, and he must pay the rent or his landlord throws him out and the police lock him up. The children starve and the mother despairs.
> The Poor Law administrators have deaf ears, etc.   (12)

Always there are diatribes, quite crude invective, like the following highly malicious utterance, in verse for a change:

> ' Nur Kraft allein ist wert und ehrenhaft!'
> Ruft Deutschland aus in neu erworbner Hoheit,
> Doch da man Kraft sich nicht so leicht verschafft,
> Begnügt es sich indessen mit der Roheit.

' Only power is worth anything and is honourable!' cries Germany in its newly won sovereignty. But power not being so easy to acquire, it makes do with brutality.   (13)

Or:

> Da die Deutschen noch bescheiden nach alter Weise,
> Sagt ich gern ein Wort zu ihrem Preise,
> Nun aber, da sie sich selber loben,
> Fühl ich mich fürder der Müh enthoben.

As long the Germans were modest I gladly said a word in their praise, but now that they've taken to praising themselves I no longer feel under any obligation to do so.   (14)

Obviously all this is not the sort of thing that comes from a real German heart, and it cannot be a matter for surprise if real Germans refuse to take it to their hearts. In verses of this kind one

feels the foreign element speaking, the attitude of someone outside
Germany ; in a word, Heine's emigration. There is a pathetic as well
as a satirical side to emigration, the one not less offensive than the
other :

> Das ist der Fluch des unglücksel'gen Landes,
> Wo Freiheit und Gesetz danieder liegt,
> Dass sich die Besten und die Edelsten
> Verzehren müssen in fruchtlosem Harm,
> Dass die fürs Vaterland am reinsten glühen,
> Gebrandmarkt werden als des Land's Verräter,
> Und, die noch jüngst des Landes Retter hiessen,
> Sich flüchten müssen an des Fremden Herd.
> Und während so die beste Kraft verdirbt,
> Erblühen wuchernd in der Hölle Segen
> Gewalttat, Hochfahrt, Feigheit, Schergendienst.

This is the curse of the unhappy land where liberty and law
are laid low : that the best and noblest must wear themselves
out in fruitless grief : that those who love their Fatherland the
most are branded as traitors, and that those who but yesterday
were hailed as their country's saviours must now flee to foreign
shores ; and while the best are left to rot—violence, arrogance,
cowardice, and tyranny flourish in their country's hellish
soil.   (15)

Nor are such outbursts rendered more palatable by a materialistic
background—so it is generally felt—which is hardly less extreme
than that of a Bert Brecht (*Dreigroschenoper* : ' Erst kommt das
Fressen, dann kommt die Moral '—grub first, ethics afterwards).
Witness verses such as the following, entitled *Dignity of Man* :

> Nichts mehr davon, ich bitt euch. Zu essen gebt
>   ihm, zu wohnen ;
> Habt ihr die Blösse bedeckt, gibt sich die
> Würde von selbst.

No more, I pray you. Give him food, shelter. Once you
have covered his nakedness, his dignity will appear of itself.   (16)

I should like to ask the reader who has followed me thus far to
pause now for a moment or two. The couplet just quoted, as far as
the feelings expressed in it are concerned, might well have come
from Heine, culpably enslaved to his impulses and earth-bound as

he was. (In content it is in fact to be found in the concluding verses of Heine's revolutionary ballad about the sated and the hungry rats.) *Might have* come! Actually does come, though, from Friedrich Schiller, whom no one has ever accused of excessive materialism. Look it up in Schiller's poems! Similarly I have had a little joke in all the preceding quotations. My only excuse is that my little joke may have a result which I wish to achieve in all earnestness: that of inducing a measure of scepticism with regard to the alleged traits of an author, whether these traits are propounded in slick but unsubstantial critiques or in ponderous literary histories. The joke consists in the fact that *none* of the quotations I have given is from Heine. The first of the series—which I have numbered for the reader's convenience—has been taken by me from a poem of Achim von Arnim's ; 2 and 3 are sayings of Frau Rat Goethe, quoted by Bettina Brentano ; 4 is from Goethe himself, likewise 5, which is one of Goethe's *Venetian Epigrams*. The particularly anti-German quotation (6), which I characterized when citing it as ' strident, unjust,' I have borrowed from Nietzsche (to whose opinions I certainly attach no great significance). I return to Bettina Brentano in her apotheosis of France (7), her risqué description of the army of ' old crocks ' (8), and her piece of reportage (12)—all taken from her fine work, *Dies Buch gehört dem König*. The poem about the Pomeranian who wants to break his sweetheart in two is by Lessing. The ' Germanicus Valhalla ' and the two caustic quatrains (13, 14) are Grillparzer's property, herewith restored to him. Similarly I hand back the ' deutsching ' verses to Rückert and the noble blank-verse quotation to Uhland (it is from his drama, *Duke Ernest of Swabia*).

That, then, is that. Except for one trifle. Many parallels could easily be found in Heine's writings for all sixteen pseudo-quotations. But does this explain Heine's unpopularity for us ? Far from it. For all the authors I have quoted—Arnim, Rückert, Uhland, Bettina Brentano, Lessing, Grillparzer (with the single exception of Goethe, who is, however, a special case)—are held in the highest esteem throughout Germany. One of them, Nietzsche, is actually grossly overrated. At all events, none of them is disliked. Only Heine is disliked. Yet after all, he said nothing more than his colleagues who enjoy such esteem.

We have made no progress. The extreme difficulty of the task we have undertaken has only become the more apparent. We are still in the dark as to why Heine should have been, and still is, so ' famous and disliked.' This dislike of Heine is evidently a serious problem. I mention it merely to reassure those who are apprehensive about continuing to read a book that has inflicted on them this ' scherzo-intermezzo.'

The basis of the favour Heine's work found with his contemporaries is sufficiently indicated in the publisher's ' blurb ' to his first *Poems* : they were written in the very spirit and in the simple accents of German folk-song. This is true only with many reservations, but the fact remains that it was their folk-song qualities which most impressed the society on whom Heine's lyrics first made their impact. So much so, that subsequently some of Heine's poems were admitted into the canon of German folk-song.

Heine's first book of poems was particularly well received in the author's home country. In May, 1822, the *Rheinisch-westfälische Anzeiger* carried a review by Karl Immermann for which Heine remained grateful all his life. Immermann wrote, *i.a.* :

> Throughout most of Heine's poems there runs a rich vein of life ; he has the first and last prerequisite for the poet ; heart and soul and that to which these give rise : an inner story. You can tell that at one time or another he must have intensely felt and lived through the content of his poems himself. He possesses the true spirit of youth, which is a lot in an era when people are born old.

The same number of the *Anzeiger* published another critique of the poems which is of considerable interest : No German poet since Bürger had succeeded so well in capturing the authentic note of folk-song (quoted from Elster, *Heine's Collected Works, I*). The critique goes on to qualify this praise, though in measured terms :

> What is lacking to give his poems the imprint of genuine folk-song is the fact that their subject matter does not derive from the history of our people. If Heine's *Grenadiers* had been written in French it would have been a genuine French folk-song.

I quote all these views, of course, not because I subscribe to them, but solely for the sake of completeness in considering and describing Heine's impact on his contemporaries. I need hardly stress that for me the merit of Heine's lyric poetry does not lie at all in its imputed affinity with folk-song, either German or French ; nor would it have been in any way improved in this respect had its subject matter been taken from German history (and how many there are of Heine's earlier and later poems which do in fact treat of German history !). On the contrary, it might well be the case that the undoubted popularity of Heine's poems is due to the *difference* between them and genuine folk-song. True folk-song has a quality of obscurity and muffled beauty ; it is disconnected, uneven, jagged. Heine has a certain smoothness, polish, lucidity of feeling and diction, and a clarity of meaning quite alien to folk-song but which by virtue of its greater intelligibility contributed perhaps to the poems' success. Heine himself, with his powers of self-criticism, was quite well aware of the gulf between his own poems and true folk-song. He wrote to Wilhelm Müller, in the cordial letter previously quoted, characteristically :

> I yielded very early to the spell of German folk-song ; later, when I was an undergraduate at Bonn, August Schlegel unveiled many of the secrets of metre for me, but it is my belief that it was not until I had read your own poems that I found the note of genuineness and the true simplicity for which I had always striven. How pure, how clear, your poems are, and all of them folk-poems. In my poems, on the other hand, it is only the form which is somewhat akin to that of the folk-song ; their subject matter belongs to conventional society.

At the same time, there are in Heine's works, and in his letters, passages in which he expresses his complete identification with the German character. All we can do is to note that in this respect— as in many others—Heine was unable to resolve the contradictions within him and was unable to win through to a final integration.

Heine's *Lyrical Intermezzo* also had a good press. Soon the Heinesque mode was paid the most powerful of all tributes—widespread imitation. Again critics were not wanting who noted the ' accents of the old German folk-song '—an important statement from the viewpoint of the history of criticism, wide of the mark though it may seem to us. The faithful Immermann was again to the fore with an article on the *Heimkehr* sequence. He showed remarkable insight in describing the qualities making, if not for the lyric poet in general, at any rate for the lyric poet Heine in particular :

' It is impossible for the lyric poet to practise too much restriction; the narrower his feeling, the more it gains in intensity, and in the intensity of his feeling lie the seeds of success.' A critic in the *Gesellschafter* referred to the ' mixture of tenderest feeling and bitterest irony ; the unique combination of pitiless, penetrating, indeed poisonous, wit and captivating sweetness of style.' Parallels with Lord Byron and Jean Paul were drawn. There was censure, too, for the ' scandal ' and the ' insolence ' of this poetry ; the poet was rebuked for ' technical carelessness,' ' confusion arising from frantic endeavours to be original at all costs.'

In the end the edition of the complete poems, the *Buch der Lieder*, silenced all criticism. Meanwhile, however, a growing opposition had been gathering round *Almansor*. The anti-Christian tendency of the play, implicit in its subject-matter, was felt to be too near the bone—although in point of fact the play was not an attack on Christianity itself but on the spineless Moors (*sc.* Jews) who adopted Christianity from motives of expediency. Hence there is only an apparent contradiction between Heine's statement (in a letter to Immermann), on the one hand : ' I am absolutely disgusted at what I hear of the scandal that is being retailed about the play's general tendency,' and his telling his publisher, on the other hand, that the subject-matter of the play was ' religious-polemical ' and of ' topical interest.' Heine was perfectly justified in repudiating any anti-Christian bias while at the same time emphasizing the topicality of the play, *vis-à-vis* the assimilated, baptized Jewry of the day. The two things are quite different, though in the stormy setting of the play and in the projection of ideas then current on to a medieval background they not infrequently seemed to commingle and can be disentangled only by a subtle and, above all, willing critical intelligence. At all events, *Almansor* made many enemies for Heine in the Rhineland, where till then he had had an admiring following. The consequences were to be serious for him. Again and again he was to be made to realize the difficulties of a Jewish writer in a German cultural environment, how impossible it was for him to avoid being misunderstood on all sides. Eventually it was to lead to self-imposed exile.

VIII

Folk-poetry and Romanticism

'In fact we should do well to look upon each other as people who are just recovering from an illness, since we are all of us a long way from having reached complete health in our spiritual lives yet. But we always forget this.'

RAHEL VARNHAGEN

IT IS NOT DIFFICULT to see that the appeal of Heine's lyrics had little to do with their real or supposed folk-song qualities. Far more powerful as a factor in their success was a new kind of emotion which Heine expressed in his verse; an emotion sharply individual and peculiar to the poet himself, and yet capable of arousing a general response. It was the emotion of someone who was very lonely; who felt himself being ruthlessly pressed to the wall. The wit, by the way, with which Heine seeks to mark this emotion in many of the poems should not be mistaken for coldness nor confused with the dry matter-of-fact-ness of a modern song hit. The original emotion, the mortal injury to the soul, is merely strengthened by the wit which is placed in diametrical opposition to it. The laughter and the frequent emotional posturings in which Heine takes refuge are all a function of his one great, true, rejected love. Often Heine's irony can be seen to be a last desperate attempt to achieve on a negative, cynical plane an equilibrium which he could no longer hope to attain on any serious level. Only the pachydermatous reader will dub this wit and irony 'frivolous'; in truth it is a terrible necessity, a cruel compulsion of which Heine was the victim.

185

It is true that, once having discovered this means of equilibrium,
Heine later on indulged in it on occasion without any compelling
necessity. His temperament, his rapid changes of mood, his conceit,
finally his powerful, quick, always alert sense of humour would no
doubt often have tempted him to alternate imaginary disasters with
real ones. We are not in a position to say in each particular instance
which is which, nor is it necessary for us to be able to. The light
with which Heine started out, the original flower-like purity of soul
of a poet who was to endure most grievous suffering, sheds its
atoning radiance over all the tortuous paths he trod later on in life.

It is his suffering, his experiences which are at the heart of his
poetry. It was this that was new, peculiar to him. He lacked the
far-ranging quality, the power of contemplation, of quietly taking
in what was going on around him that he admired in Goethe ;
Heine once pointed out, very rightly, that Goethe, ' with his clear
Greek eye,' ' never colours things with his own feelings ; he portrays
land and sea for us in the true outlines and colours that God has
clothed them in. That is a merit of Goethe's which only posterity
will appreciate.' The exact opposite, an over-sensitive subjectivity,
is characteristic of Heine. He faces the world like a wafer-thin
vibrating metal sheet. He has nothing but himself, and hardly that.
Nevertheless, he gives everything ; he holds nothing back. Truth to
say, he probably gave more than he could afford to give, for he
really had no reserves at all.

On this question of ' reserves ' one might compare Heine's situation with that described in Brentano's story, *Vom braven Kasperl
und dem schönen Annerl.* Here the blind, doom-laden, harrowing
course of events is made barely endurable for the German narrator
of the story by his ' reserves ' derived from folk-pieties, from the
figure of an old peasant woman, a walking treasury of folk-song who
is only half-conscious of what she is doing. It is true that these
' reserves,' though rendering suffering endurable, at the same time
render it fated to be incurable, for in itself the course of events
described by the author was not as inexorable as he would have had
us believe.

Heine has no such deep reserves ; he is only an individual.
Nevertheless he finds another depth, *his* depth, the depth of bound-
less solitude and isolation. His special isolation as a Jew gives his
love-sorrows, which he could normally have shared with others,

with non-Jews, a new note of poignancy. The others can assuage
these sorrows within a community, they can accept its norms and
fuse their own melancholy with that of their community (as
Brentano's story shows). Heine stands alone, without a background.
The Jewish community as it then was afforded him no possibility
of identification with it ; it could give him no comfort. Rather,
Heine's special position as a Jew increased the sense of isolation
induced by the spurning of his love ; hence the strident tones in his
verse, the effect of personal experience always just underneath the
transparent surface of the poetry and floodlighting it. So that it is
true to say, in the full significance of the words, that in Heine's case
Jewish destiny, as determined by the spatio-temporal configuration
of contemporary Jewry, became the destiny of a poet.

But how is it then that Heine, despite the barriers of the age,
of his Jewishness, has been able to move, directly and deeply, all
men and women, including his contemporaries who were alien to
his race ?

We should be at a loss for an answer but for the very remarkable
fact, which we have constant opportunities of verifying, that the
Jewish situation is merely a symbolical reproduction, exceptionally
clear because of its sharpness of detail, of the general human situation. The Jew in the Diaspora is lonely, rootless, restless. But deep
down is not every human being lonely ? In the endless flow of
Being into eternity is not every bond, all tranquillity, seen to be
untenable ? In one emotional region which we all have to pass
through, for a while at any rate (I am not saying it is the last, best,
highest region), we are all Diaspora-Jews. ' Fremde sind wir auf
der Erde alle/Und es stirbt, womit wir uns verbinden '—We are all
strangers on this earth and that which binds us together dies
(Werfel). Of course there are boundaries separating the specific
Jewish situation and the general human situation, but they must
not be made absolutely rigid (though on the other hand their existence should not be lost sight of). Unless we assume that the fate
of the Jew reveals to us in a special, easily comprehensible way—
because of the sharpness of its outlines—the fate of every human
being, of the human being as such, we shall be able to account
neither for the universal effect of the Old Testament texts to
Handel's great oratorios and to Bach's cantatas (*De Profundis*), nor
for that of Kafka's novels, whose central character (K., or the

' surveyor ') is a Diaspora Jew with his anxieties and his ' non-belonging ' at the same time that he is a human being *tout court,* Everyman.

Of all the favourable criticisms of his verse, Karl Immermann's was closest to Heine's heart. It provided the *point d'appui* of a firm friendship that was to endure. One of Heine's finest letters is that in which he thanks Immermann for the ' words that reconcile one to humanity ' of his review of his (Heine's) poems. The long letter, written unhurriedly, for Heine had honourably spent several months in ripe consideration of Immermann's writings, ends :

> Fools think that because your being a Westphalian provides a point of contact between us (they've taken you for a Westphalian up till now), I ought to compete with you. They don't know that the fine diamond with its clear radiance is not to be compared to the black stone which is simply queerly shaped and from which the hammer of time strikes wild, savage sparks. But what have we to do with fools ? From me you will always hear the admission that I am unworthy to be named in the same breath with you. Professor Gubitz asked me recently to get you for the *Gesellschafter,* but I can't advise you to dissipate your energies in the pages of periodicals, admiring as I do your literary activity. Nature must have endowed you, in addition to poetry, with the beautiful gift of good health. You can do a great deal, an infinitely great deal, of good. The other day I came across a student-fraternity pamphlet : *A Word to his Contemporaries by Immermann.* I believe you wrote it, and was glad to see from it that you early manifested an intense desire for that which is good and right. Down with age-old injustice, with the rule of folly and with badness ! I shall be happy to hold out my hand to you if you will accept me as a brother-in-arms in this holy struggle. Poetry is only a pretty trifle when all's said and done.

Heine's gratitude and enthusiasm were unstinted and sincere. He eulogized Immermann as ardently in letters to others (*e.g.,* Sethe) as he did when writing direct to Immermann himself. He wrote to Steinman : ' Do you know Immermann ? Both of us ought to take off our hats to him, and you first of all. His is a powerful, radiant poetic personality such as few others can show.' In the *Journey from Munich to Genoa* (*Travel Sketches*) he exalts him as the ' eagle in the German Fatherland.' And towards the end of August, 1840, he wrote from Granville to Heinrich Laube :

Yesterday evening I learnt quite by chance, from the *Journal des Débats*, of Immermann's death. I wept the whole night through. What a disaster ! You know how much Immermann meant to me. He was an old brother-in-arms of mine. We made our literary début at the same time, arm in arm, you might say. What a great poet we Germans have lost without ever having properly appreciated him ! We, I mean Germany, cruel old mother that she is ! And he was not only a great poet, but decent and honest, and that's why I loved him. I am prostrate with grief.

No worthier elegy on the great poet can be imagined. And it is gratifying that there should have been a bond between Heine the émigré and the most significant, spiritually richest writer among his contemporaries, the German-to-the-core author of *Oberhof* and *Merlin*. Immermann's German patriotism, his emphatic Prussianism, in any case did not prevent his entertaining friendship for Jews. The long dedicatory poem in his verse epic, *Tulifäntchen,* is devoted to Michael Beer the writer, Meyerbeer's brother ; he (Immermann) was co-director of the Düsseldorf City Theatre with Felix Mendelssohn, who managed the theatre's operas.

There was no very fundamental agreement between Heine's and Immermann's views. Nevertheless, they accorded in many particulars ; in the admiration of Goethe, in the repudiation and parodying of certain romantic and ' Old German ' effusions (cf. Immermann's *Memorabilien* on Jahn), in the beginnings of a bourgeois realism, in the Platen controversy. The correspondence in which the friends exchanged counsel in such matters as the principles of art and prosody, as well as in the more mundane realm of publishing problems, had come to a close before Immermann's death.

Heine was unable to establish any relationship with Goethe. No reply came to the gushing letter (' I kiss the sacred hand, etc.') which Heine sent to Weimar with his first publication. This was a fate that Heine shared with many other writers; with Immermann too, as it happened. On the 1st October, 1824, Heine asked to be received, having reached Weimar after his journey across the Harz Mountains. ' On the Brocken I was seized with a desire to make the pilgrimage to Weimar in honour of Goethe. I have now made the pilgrimage here in the true sense of the word ; that is, on foot and in travel-stained clothing, and I await the granting of my request.

Admiringly and devotedly—H. Heine.' The sole entry relating to
the interview in Goethe's journal, under date 2nd October, reads:
'Heine from Göttingen.' Heine was nervous in the presence of the
great man. 'On many a winter night I had pondered all the
sublime and profound things I would say to Goethe if I once saw
him. And when I did see him at last, I told him the Saxon plums
tasted very good. And Goethe smiled.'

It is not true that Heine later touched up and embellished this
visit in his writings. The version that appeared in 1833 in *The
Romantic School*, from which the above quotation is taken, agrees
with what he says in the letters he wrote immediately after his visit,
except that in the account intended for the public eye there was no
mention of the aged Goethe's bodily frailties. In this we can detect
Heine seeking, consciously or unconsciously, to adhere to the
principle of Goethe's life and art, thereby revealing how deeply
he venerated him and was influenced by him. In *The Romantic
School* he writes:

> He had the calm eyes of a god . . . People say his lips have
> a cold, egotistical line; such a line does indeed characterize the
> gods, and particularly the father of the gods, the great Jupiter,
> to whom I have just compared Goethe. Of a truth, when I
> visited him in Weimar and stood in front of him I turned my
> glance involuntarily aside, lest I see next to him the eagle with
> the lightning in its beak. I almost addressed him in Greek.

And there follows the story of the plums.

That Goethe asked Heine what he was working on, and Heine
replied: 'A *Faust*,' whereupon Goethe 'stiffened,' rests solely on
the testimony of Heine's highly unreliable brother, Max. Heine's
ballet-scenario ('dance-poem'), *Doktor Faust*, was conceived more
than two decades later, though it is true another *Faust* plan dating
from the Göttingen years is mentioned by E. Wedekind. There is
no mention in Heine's letters to Christiani and Moser of any ill-
feeling of rivalry. Such a feeling would not have been in keeping
with the spiritual stature of either of the two men: quite the
contrary, Heine praises Goethe's 'friendly and affable' conversation. 'I was touched by Goethe's profoundly humane concern for
my health.'

The emotional contrast between what Heine (mistakenly) called
Goethe's 'egotism' and Heine's own 'enthusiasm' ('captivated to

the point of self-sacrifice by the idea ') is apparent, but Heine
continues immediately: 'I shall always belong to the Goethean
Free Corps.' Heine kept this promise. So much so, that for his own
'Greek' period, soon to follow the period of unhappy love, Heine
took Goethe (but misunderstanding him) as his model. It should be
borne in mind, in any case, that Heine never failed to acknowledge
Goethe's head-and-shoulders supremacy. His criticisms are never
of his writings ; always of his diplomacy only, his 'quietistic
influence,' the political sterility of his writing, the 'sage veteran of
literature' as he calls him in the poem to Christiani;'the ministerial,
mediating, appeasing Goethe,' as he describes him in the report on
the affair of Fichte's atheism,[1] where, however, he immediately
proceeds to acquit Goethe of all 'ugly motives.'

I need hardly say that, with all Heine's admiration of Goethe,
he was never able to understand fully Goethe the man and his
perennial significance ; however, he implicitly withdrew, when
himself rejecting the idea of literature *à thèse* (*Atta Troll*),much of
what he had said against him. He always did justice, however, to
Goethe the writer ; never tired of paying homage in violent parallels,
in comparisons with Homer and Shakespeare, to the man on whose
critics he was ready to pounce with 'they would have seen the
spots on the moon through their highly polished lenses ; these
keen-eyed observers ! The spots they saw are lush forests, silver
rivers, lofty mountains, smiling valleys.'

It is misleading to suggest that Goethe had a marked antipathy
to Heine, that his opinion of him was coloured, even, by anti-
semitic prejudice. Certainly the overflowing fullness of Goethe's
life, of his work, left him little time to notice or encourage Heine,
and it is true that Goethe commented adversely on the *Reisebilder*.
It would have been strange had he done otherwise, since in his later
writing he rigidly eschewed anything remotely resembling caricature.
No doubt Heine was piqued. He had expected more, a spiritual
echo. 'What on earth do you mean, my dear Varnhagen,' he wrote
later in a letter, 'I, I write against Goethe! If the stars in the sky
become hostile to me, am I to say then that they are nothing but
will-o'-the-wisps ? It is always foolish to say anything against really

---

[1] In 1798 Fichte had been forced to give up his professorship at Jena in
consequence of an accusation of atheism.

great men, even if what one could say was true. I can't abide
Goethe's present way of thinking, his narrow German nationalism
and his shallow pietism—all the more reason why I must hold fast
to Goethe the great pagan.'

This affinity of mind which Heine felt so keenly was not appreciated by Goethe, or not felt by him to be of any importance. This
was due, however, to the reserve he felt called upon to maintain in
his late age; to the stiff formality of the courtier, in reality nothing
but a defence mechanism which Grillparzer describes so movingly.
Henriette Herz, in the memoirs from which I have quoted, tells
many delightful stories about this defence mechanism. With great
understanding she describes how Goethe was ' cheated of precious
time ' by frivolous visitors. ' But,' she goes on, ' I've seen him on
occasion surrounded by a circle of undoubtedly able men and
aspiring youths of promise, all of whom, influenced by the desire
to hear him give expression to some viewpoint, or merely to utter
an opinion, have hung on his lips, without being able to carry away
from a long evening to which perhaps they had been eagerly looking
forward all their lives any greater prize than a long drawn-out
" *Ei—ja*!" or " *So* ? " or " Hm," or at the best   " I quite agree." '
Platen, too, gives an account that tallies with this of a visit he and
a companion paid Goethe. After praising Goethe's kindness, he
says: ' The air of formal ceremony that seems to emanate from
him precluded any real conversation, and after a time he dismissed
us.'

The same thing seems to have happened to our Heine. Nevertheless, it is a fact that Goethe considered him to be one of the
' higher natures,' as the conversation with Eckermann of 14th March,
1830, shows. Goethe first repudiates the attacks made on himself
(' As they cannot deny my talent, they start on my character.' Does
this not sound uncannily like an answer to Heine's reproaches, which,
though, he had never heard ? Likewise Goethe's ensuing remark:
' One moment I'm too proud, next I'm conceited, then I'm rankly
jealous of young talent, then again I'm immersed in sensual
pleasures, etc.'). Then he goes on to recall the martyrdom of men
like Rousseau and Byron, and directly after mentioning these great
names he says: ' And even if the narrow-minded masses did
persecute higher natures ! Even gifted men, men of talent, persecute
each other. Platen vexes Heine, and Heine Platen, and each tries

to denigrate and vilify the other. And yet the world is big and broad enough for people to live and work in it peacefully, and we all have an enemy, in the shape of our own talent, that will fully occupy our energies!' To which it must be said that there was no room in Germany for Heine to live in, nor was there any post of any kind for him to work at; which accounts, partly, for his bitterness. More of this in the next chapter. Expressed in my terminology: his ignoble misfortune prevented his coming to grips with the noble Goethean misfortune of having to fight his own talent.

Finally, as for Goethe's alleged antisemitism, it is sufficient to refer to his distaste for generalizations of any kind, to his relationship to Spinoza, Moses and Felix Mendelssohn, to his conversations with Henriette Herz, Rahel Levin and others. True, he disapproved of the Frankfurt emancipation; perhaps he would have been better disposed to a better solution, a just system of minority rights. Certainly the proposals for dealing with the Jewish question and the measures adopted at the time were far from perfect. The famous passage in the *Wanderjahre* which is always quoted to show Goethe's antisemitism should be looked up in its context, when it will again be seen that a quotation out of context has as little life in it as a fish out of water. The passage occurs in Book III of the *Wanderjahre,* in which it is proposed by the 'superiors' that a model community be formed. After *all* religions are conceded to have a moral value (Chapter XI), the Christian religion is chosen 'after much hesitation' to be that of *this particular community.* Accordingly, Jews who reject the Christian faith are to be excluded from the community—a measure which evidently caused Goethe some embarrassment. He describes it as a kind of pedantry (' in this sense, which might perhaps be considered pedantic '). The very next sentence reads: ' This is quite at variance with our own morality.' In its full context the provision about the exclusion of the Jews is seen to be a subsidiary part of a utopian plan, not a statement of principle, least of all of racialist principle. Concerning another, only apparently antisemitic remark of Goethe's, made by him in conversation, I have written at length in my novel, *Die Frau, die nicht enttäuscht,* pp. 160, 163, 168ff.

There was some doubt about Heine's right literary ' label ' from the moment the very first critiques of his verse appeared. Heine himself accepted a Frenchman's witty description of him as a *Romantique défroqué*, considered his *Atta Troll* to be 'the last free wood-notes of Romanticism.' ' I am the last Romantic poet ; I mark the close of the old lyric school of the Germans while at the same time inaugurating the new school of the modern German lyric. This dual significance of mine is attributed to me by German historians of literature.'

Yet it was precisely this new school, the political-realistic ' engaged ' literature of ' Young Germany,' that Heine fiercely attacked in his *Atta Troll*, after having himself written ' engaged ' poems to his heart's content. *Atta Troll* was to be 'a protest against the plebiscites of the tribunes of the day, against the heroic upholders of character, these Romans who accused me not merely of literary, but of social reaction, of ridiculing the holiest concepts of mankind, even . . . I wrote it for my own pleasure, in the dreamy, capricious mood characterizing the Romantic school in which I spent the happiest years of my youth, and whose schoolmaster I ended up by giving a sound drubbing.' Here we have the key to *défroqué*.

It is not surprising that throughout his life Heine had to endure the most violent attacks and misrepresentations from both Left and Right. Deep down he was one of those people with a sense of responsibility who seek a ' middle way,' though he felt and groped rather than consciously pursued his way towards it. At all events, he was instinctively ill at ease at both extremes, at both poles, no matter how powerfully they expressed themselves ; the high poesy of German Romanticism and the ardent longing for freedom of the German artisan societies in Paris, the first Communists, alike. Hence the hostility, persecution, he encountered from both extremist parties. Hence, too, Börne's remark that while everybody had only *one* back for flogging, poor Heine had two.

I shall deal later with the political significance of Heine's unique position between two extremes. For the moment I wish to deal with his divergence *poetically* from German Romanticism. Heine's poetry has many details in common with German Romantic poetry, but is lacking in the profound, limitless darkness of its ground-tone. We can best see, before we read any further, what this dark tone is by listening to or, better, ourselves playing Schumann's F Sharp Minor Sonata. We shall then hear how the darkness of tone can combine with passionate day dreaming, often expressed with great cheerfulness. It is as if the cheerfulness necessarily follows from the abysmal darkness and fearlessly plunges into its depths, for ' a heavy heart wears a cheerful countenance.' Or we may let the *Davidsbündlertänze*,[1] also by Schumann, op. 6, sound in our ears. ' Eusebius then said what really needed no saying ; there was a great happiness in his eyes '—where we have a transition from the Romantic to the purely Platonic ; in that keenly felt joyous springtide the two were hard to distinguish. Or, considerably diminished in intensity, the great *Fantasy* that takes its epigraph from Friedrich Schlegel, and matches its first theme to it almost syllable for syllable :

> Durch alle Töne tönet
> Im bunten Erdentraum
> Ein leiser Ton, gezogen
> Für den, der heimlich lauschet.

For him that has ears to hear a gentle note is heard persisting through all the notes of our joyous dream-like earth.

Yes, music expresses more clearly than words the many-sided nature of German Romanticism. And as far as words go, I much prefer to any definitions the passionate, frequently incoherent utterances that burst from the lips of those caught up in the Romantic movement itself. For instance, Bettina's intense :

Something new happens every day, things stupid and ridiculous ! But greatness comes only in man's longing, it must not be illumined by the light of day. Everything sublime is a chimera to the common understanding ; what I say, too, will seem hocus pocus to the pastor. The world is full of prophetic fire, which here and there bursts into flames. People think it's just a fire of straw, but had they let themselves be ignited by it, the flame would have purified them, and the greatness they think is a chimera would have become true in them. The flame burned once, though. It will become true without them, too.

---

[1] The *Davidsbündler* or hosts of David were an imaginary body of artists or friends of art created by Schumann. One of the *Davidsbündler* was ' Eusebius,' under which pseudonym, among others, Schumann wrote his musical criticisms.

Novalis discusses Romanticism in *Heinrich von Ofterdingen*, not only when he speaks of the famous ' blue flower,' but when his business men explain as best they can what they sense to be the significance and nature of poetry. ' We've never bothered about the secret of the poet's magic,' they say, ' so long as we've enjoyed listening to his song. . . .' Unlike painting and music, poetry had no instrument at its disposal, no physical basis, nothing external, ' for it is not the mere hearing of the words that really affects us in this magic art. Everything happens inside us . . . the inner sanctuary of the mind. . . . He—the poet—can arouse these magic powers in us at his pleasure, and through the medium of words enables us to experience an unknown, glorious world. Out of their cavernous depths times gone by and times yet to come rise up before us— innumerable people, strange regions and the most fantastic happenings—and take use of the familiar present.'

The Unknown, then, not that which appertains to the present, to everyday existence, is the Romantic domain. Superficially, indeed: remote regions, exoticism, the ' romantic costume ' in Delacroix's paintings, in the oriental travels of Flaubert the ' sheikh.' But, on a deeper level, as Bettina sensed: ' Greatness comes only in man's longing; it must not be illumined by the light of day.' Not what is remote—what is un-actual, what is nocturnal. It is in this sense that Goethe's: ' Classical is healthy, Romantic sickly ' must be understood (a maxim which Goethe himself subjected to frequent justification and revision).

This much appears certain: that in all Romanticism there is an appeal from reason to a higher power, to something uncontrollable—to dissolution, death. Thomas Mann's *The Magic Mountain* illustrates this with crystal clarity. It was Novalis, however, who confided most resolutely in death, as being the other pole of day. Novalis makes it clear, it should be said, that it is not the negative aspect of death which is loved. It was a degenerate offshoot of the Romantic movement which became enamoured of the negative, diabolical, horrific ; of the ' flowers of evil.' Novalis sings of death, however, because for him life on this side is not real life, but ' something upside-down.' Death appears to him as a *plus* quantity, as the deepest truth, as love, as the real life which has been obscured and talked out of existence by the intellect ; as the Unconditional, Whole, Unanalysable, Absolute. So with

Clemens Brentano, who exclaims in a magnificent outburst of transcendent conviction:

> In uns selbst sind wir verloren,
> Bange Fesseln uns beengen,
> Schloss und Riegel muss zersprengen,
> Nur im Tode wird geboren.
>
> In der Nächte Finsternissen
> Muss der junge Tag ertrinken,
> Abend muss herniedersinken,
> Soll der Morgen dich begrüssen.
>
> An Ufers Ferne wallt ein Licht,
> Du möchtest jenseits landen,
> Doch fasse Mut, verzage nicht,
> Du musst erst diesseits stranden.
> Schau still hinab, in Todes Schoss
> Blüht jedes Ziel, fällt dir dein Los.
>
> Ich sinke ewig unter
> Und steige ewig auf
> Und blühe stets gesunder
> Aus Liebesschoss herauf.
>
> So kann ich nimmer sterben,
> Kann nimmer untergehen;
> Denn um mich zu verderben
> Müsst Gott selbst untergehn!

In ourselves we are lost, hemmed in by fetters of anxiety. Lock and bolt must burst apart; only in death can we be born.

The bright day must expire in the darkness of night. Evening must fall if morning is to greet thee.

A light gleams on the distant shore, thou wouldst like to land there. Courage! thou must first be stranded on this shore. Look calmly down; in the lap of death thou canst achieve all things; there thy lot is cast.

I fall and rise for ever and aye, and emerging from the lap of love shoot up in strength increased.

So can I never die, never sink, for to cause me to perish God himself would have to sink!

We shall seek in vain for accents like these in Heine. How ' this-sided ' he is with all his elves, mermaids, sprites, and dead loves!

These loved ones, dead and corpses though they are, fit more
easily into the familiar world, far from having anything to tell us
about the unfamiliar one! How 'this-sided' Heine remains even
on his death-bed! All his horrible afflictions notwithstanding, he
sings of the pleasures of living in this snug and pleasant terrestrial
nest. 'Being stranded on this shore' was no 'landing on the other
shore' for him, but a disaster pure and simple, to be saved from
which he cried aloud to his helping God. He was, in this, literally
heavens apart from Romanticism.

But there are two sides to Romanticism. On the one hand it
was essentially an exploration of the depths of the self, a
'nostalgia for the sources and motives of life' (Susmann). It
sought to grasp 'real' life as opposed to everyday life. Hence it
clung inevitably to night and death. With the same inevitability,
though, it clung also to what was individual; to a free, capricious
life-pattern; to what was historical, to the reality of history, to the
unpredictable event that might have violent repercussions—to all
those things that mocked at reason just as Death and the Beyond
were outside its orbit. With this aspect of Romanticism, that threw
down the gauntlet to the supremacy of reason, Heine certainly had
much in common.

This second aspect of Romanticism contains the historical
element on the one hand and the concrete personal, individual
element on the other. Heine displays the historical element in his
Elemental Spirits and *Gods in Exile,* two works which I consider
to be among his finest. The subject is irrational: popular beliefs,
superstition. The treatment likewise; 'To compress popular
beliefs into a system, as many think they can, is as little feasible
as to frame the fleeting clouds.' The basic idea was Romantic, too,
that 'the mania for the Middle Ages' (which Heine rejects) 'was
really only a secret predilection for the old-German pantheism, as
remnants of this old religion survived in the popular beliefs of the
Middle Ages. I've mentioned before how these remnants, though
distorted and mutilated, survived in sorcery and witchcraft. Indeed,
they live on in the people's memories, in its customs, its language.
. . . The German baker imprints the old druidic pentagram on
every loaf he bakes, and our daily bread still carries the sign of
the Germanic religion. What a profound contrast between this real
bread and the dry, tasteless pseudo-bread provided by the cult of

the spiritual!' Just as the pagan-Germanic gods still survived as dwarfs, goblins, sprites, and salamanders, so the gay Greek gods were not dead either ; and Heine traces them in German folk-tales and in Italian ruins, not least in the magnificent Tannhäuser poem, which he gives twice, in a literal translation and in a free verse-rendering. Heine claims to have been the first to describe in clear, comprehensible terms the transformation of the old nature-cults into Satan-worship and of the heathen priesthood into witchcraft, this 'bedevilling of the gods.' Before him these matters had been treated only 'in the venerable folio and quarto volumes of compilers and antiquaries, in the catacombs of scholarship,' and in the 'confused, abstract language of science.' Heine claims the 'merit of initiative' in this regard, and complains that his successors had 'forgotten' to mention his work. Not that Richard Wagner was any less forgetful in acknowledging Heine's indisputable priority in the 'Tannhäuser' and 'Flying Dutchman' themes. It is indeed remarkable how many motifs of the Wagnerian music-drama are anticipated by Heine. In addition to the two mentioned, there are the Nibelungen hoard, young Siegfried with his sword, the Valkyries. They are a sufficient indication, in any case, of Heine's attachment to the world of Romanticism.

Just as deep as his sense of history was Heine's equally anti-rational preoccupation with the self, with the staunchless flow of the transient moment, with the individual's own experience. Heine's writing is indeed distinguished by an exceptional firmness of outline, by a clarity, by an exceedingly concrete view of life at times bringing him close to Goethe. He shares Goethe's aim, too, of, 'convinced that clarity lies at the bottom of depths that have been plumbed with difficulty, endeavouring to bring up all that is possible from these depths that are always so hard to put into words,' an aim which in the last resort decisively separates Goethe from the Romantics. Goethe, it is true, realized more than Heine the intense difficulty of the task, and so arrived at conclusions differing from those of Heine, whose approach was often altogether too facile. Nor must it be overlooked that Goethe's individualism and concrete view of life proceeded from the broad view and conscious will which he was able to exercise, whereas Heine had been cramped into his isolation by an unfriendly fate and hence was forced into his individualism and concrete view of life. He had

to endure them passively, being without any prop or stay, being
without any reserves as he was. . . . It is extraordinary, indeed
little short of a miracle, in view of Heine's situation, of the state
of the Jewish community at the time, that his soul remained so
largely unsullied. Heine's life was hard, and yet there were times
when he was able to display that surplus energy without which it
is impossible to write even a line of fine verse. We might hazard
the somewhat adventurous question: ' Was Goethe's life easier ? '
The parallel cannot be drawn; we are on impenetrable ground. For
Goethe, too, had his terrible temptations, had the snare in his soul.
Perhaps this at least may be said, though: the good and the
beautiful, hard as it may have been for him—as for everyone—to
seize, at any rate was *presented* to him from the outset in a purer,
more gracious form than it was to Heine.

It is strange, and was to have a momentous effect on the course
of his life, that Heine never realised that his innate disposition to
the concrete, to ' this-sidedness,' his dislike of ' fleeing the world '
and of the condemnation of the flesh, were something Jewish. Such
they are, not quite in this simple form, but in the form of the
' miracle of this side ' as I have described it in my book, *Heidentum,
Christentum, Judentum.* Heine, on the other hand, was led by his
inadequate knowledge of the Jewish sources to believe that Judaism
made a principle of asceticism, of ' torture,' of anti-sensualism. He
does not differentiate in this respect between the Jewish and the
Christian attitudes. Both fuse for him into the ' Nazarenism ' he
fought against. Hence arose the contradiction that the spirit of
Judaism worked within him, in his personal situation, in his life,
and in his general intellectual outlook, in part hindering, in part
helping him, what time in his definitions of Judaism he looked for
this spirit in the wrong place. Only in the last years of his life,
through his repeated readings of the Old Testament, did this
misunderstanding clear up.

The struggle against the ascendancy of Reason, against the fixed
arrangements imposed by the seriousness of life, leads to Romantic
irony. On the form of a work of art this has the effect of breaking
it up haphazard into its parts, playing skittles with them, arbitrarily
mixing them up and deliberately letting them run riot, misnumbering
chapters as in Immermann's *Münchhausen.* It is responsible for the
rambling nature of much of Heine's prose. And the causerie of

journalism is the respectable late offspring of a union contracted between fantasy and negation of the world.

In so far as the content of a work is concerned, irony and ironic wit denote the rejection of any kind of ' plain ' view of life, of any facile panoramic view, and of any view the significance of the individual features of which can be understood. ' It is the sense of the infinity of the whole shattering the conclusiveness of everything that is finite and individual. *Vis-à-vis* the infinity of the whole, the limited transient individual is unimportant ' (Margarete Susman, *Frauen der Romantik*). It is related to the irony of Socrates and Plato, the ' double star, which the most powerful instruments will not entirely separate ' (Emerson).

The instructive third and seventh chapters in Friedländer's book on Plato deal particularly with Socratic irony. They show that Socrates' assumption of ignorance was made necessary by the incommunicable mysteries of life in which he shared, the mysteries of the truly good and beautiful which have their being in the ' super-celestial sphere,' in the world of ideas, not in the world of prosaic reality. ' It is the incommunicability of the highest Platonic ideas that is symbolized by the irony of Socratic ignorance.' What Socrates could not say, because it was no longer one of the things that could be said, he lived ; he died for it, he taught it his pupil by his life and death, not in mere words. And it was purely a happy chance that Plato did not die, too, when he went over from study to action in Sicily.

Irony, then, becomes the natural accompaniment of the play of ideas, of the daimon, of Eros, of the true political deeds, of death. In the words of Schlegel (quoted by Friedländer): ' Irony contains and excites a feeling of the insoluble conflict of the Absolute and the Conditional, of the impossibility and the necessity of a complete communication.' From which it is clear that while Romantic irony contents itself with stating opposites and the necessity for them—it can do no more than pose the *complexio oppositorum*—Socrates' irony (and Kierkegaard's), because of the power of paradox, moves beyond this into the certainty of recognition and faith.

How do Heine's irony and wit, which are without doubt among the chief characteristics of his writing, stand in relation to these exalted levels of non-prosaic reality ? One's first reaction is to say that they are diametrically opposed. The Romantics used irony to

switch from the level of everyday reality on to a dream level.
Socratic irony shows us that even the dream is nothing but a
variegated cloud bank lowering in front of a new, blissful mainland ; that behind that which has no power to bind lies that which
is truly certain and has the greatest possible power to bind. Heine's
wit, on the other hand, rudely shatters the dream and switches back
to everyday reality. As, for example, in the poem *Seegespenst*
(' Sea vision '), where the poet, perched precariously on the edge of
the ship and looking down into the depths of the sea, which in
his reverie he peoples with the inhabitants of a sunken legendary
city, is rudely awakened by the captain with a : ' Doctor, have
you taken leave of your senses ? ' The poet's wit shakes him out
of his reverie, gives him back the ground under his feet.

Heine's irony has this in common with that of the Romantics :
both shatter the mood which they have previously created. The
only difference is that the Romantics jolt the reader out of the
world of everyday reality into a higher world, whereas Heine does
the reverse. The irony of Socrates differs from both ; the mood is
not broken but uniform, maintained. It is the mood of the eternal
question to which there can never be any adequate reply—the
imperfectible perception that needs an interlocutor, the reader, to
become living reality. The reader must co-operate actively, Plato's
dialogues insist. Thus Plato draws the reader separated from him
by millennia into everlasting converse. Irony provokes a dialogue
between author and reader, shakes the latter out of his comfortable
groove. Only a sentimental commentator like Schleiermacher can
see in this ' a hindrance to smoothness of exposition which only
serves to puzzle us.' In reality this kind of exposition it is which
is indispensable, for it deals with life at its most concrete, which
just cannot be resolved in terms of abstract logic.

As far as Heine is concerned, though, does Goethe's rule,
' humorous, therefore second-rate,' apply ? Heine himself had his
own views on the matter. In *The City of Lucca* he says :

> I was irritated by the witty Englishwoman's equally
> persistent habit of making a joke of everything. Perhaps I was
> annoyed by it all the more as it was a habit of which I felt
> by no means innocent myself, nor did I think it was a habit
> which was in any way commendable. It cannot be denied that
> the habit of joking about everything, finding delight in the

contrariness of things, has something malicious about it; whereas seriousness is more akin to the better feelings—virtue, love of liberty and love itself are very serious things. At the same time, there are people in whose hearts jest and earnest, evil and holiness, glowing passion and coldness are so strangely mixed that it becomes difficult to pass judgment about it.

This passage reveals the whole dialectic of Heine's character. He cannot be understood unless his peculiar kind of wit and irony are understood. They are at the centre of his personality and of his art.

His wit is not uniform. Several strata can be distinguished, corresponding to periods in his life. With increasing age the wit becomes finer. Primarily it serves for protection. Persecuted, frequently battered by adversity, always living on the edge of stable society, Heine used his wit as a defence mechanism of the most primitive kind. He was poor, was a Jew, was unhappy in love, was mistrustful, was proud, ambitious, and sensitive, and he saw nothing wrong in attempting to gratify the pleasures he so keenly enjoyed; hence he was marked out for suffering on all counts.

He is frequently reproached with not having taken this, that, or the other seriously. But he would have gone mad had he taken them seriously! To a discerning mind it is clear that irony is always the signal of an insuperable reality lurking ahead; were the signaller to meet the reality head-on he would inevitably succumb to it, he would be going against his own signal, so to speak; but he saves himself by leaping from seriousness to irony. Most of those who disapprove of irony in general have no conception of the strength of will required to leap aside in this way, instead of holding out one's head, like a bird hypnotized by a snake, for reality to swallow. Of course, the leap aside must be taken at the very last moment, when there is absolutely no other way out. Irony must be the signal of a genuinely impossible situation, not merely of a situation asserted or imagined to be impossible. For Heine the Jewish question was very often, practically always, the impossible situation that lurked ahead. In the last years of his German period the situation became one of despair of ever being able to find a place in German society, of ever being able to exercise a profession. To this extent he had no choice between being ironical

or unironical ; he had to have recourse to irony or else suffocate.
Socrates' irony is of a different kind, metaphysical. He uses it when
faced with *his* impossible situation, when the unsayable (*Arrheton*)
has to be said. As employed by Socrates, it then seems to become
part of his way of living, his habitual style of speech.

So the view taken of Heine's irony will always be linked with
the view taken of the Jewish situation in his day. Was this situation
a genuinely impossible one ? To me it seems that it would be an
impossible situation even in our own day, did not Zionism point
a way to a solution. But for Heine's generation and the succeeding
ones even this narrow way was not available.

It is not my intention in this book to present Heine as one who
wore the white flower of a blameless life—I would be unable to
do so even if I wanted to. Instead of lengthy special pleading, I
would refer the reader to the words of Rahel Varnhagen which
I have placed at the head of this chapter.

Frequently in Heine's verse the tension is so palpable as to give
the impression that he was forced to choose between irony and
suicide. In such cases irony is seen to be the symptom of the
impossible situation, of the misery that but for this irony could
not have been endured. At other times he just lets his irony run
away with him, but perhaps here, too, he had no alternative ; it
was essential for him to relax from the continual struggles in which
he was involved, to recuperate ; and to do this there were times
when he had to be free and easy, shameless, and insolent, even.
Heine's sybaritic talk of food, *bonnes bouches* and champagne,
Mæcenases, money—his exposure to public gaze of what would
have been better concealed—his obvious delight in painfully cynical
sincerity: what lay behind it all ? Not, in spite of everything,
contempt for goodness and fullness of life as we find it in, say,
Céline ; not, in spite of everything, a throwing-in of the towel, a
determination henceforth to wallow in mud, but often enough a
love of his fellow-creatures which reveals itself precisely in those
utterances which seem the most materialistic. ' Im hungrigen Magen
Eingang finden/Nur Suppenlogik mit Knödelgründen/Nur Argu-
mente von Rinderbraten, etc.'—Let us gain entry to the hungry
stomach, let us have soup-logic and dumpling-reasoning only,
roast-beef arguments only. All that is required is to abolish the
hungry stomach ; immediately the poet will be delighted to adopt

more elegant language! The conditions then existing, though, were
obviously a red rag to him, and he positively enjoyed incurring
disapproval by exposing them. Added to which was his innate love
of leg-pulling. On his Harz journey he calls himself Herr Peregrinus,
who is 'on a recruiting voyage for the Turkish Emperor.' By
chance he met his match in another traveller named Karl Dörne,
who introduces himself to Heine as a tailor's journeyman and in
this form ('a queer mixture of caprice and melancholy such as
can be found among the mass of the people') made his bow in
the *Harzreise* and to posterity. Dörne gave a friendly account of
this *quid pro quo* in an issue of the *Gesellschafter*.

Another instance of Heine's love of 'leading people on,' and
which at the same time shows how he liked to pretend to be worse
than he was, is related by Peter Lyser, who visited the poet in
Wandsbeck in 1830. The following conversation took place: 'But
Heine, how can you stick here in this cold, dark hole in such
glorious weather? That's no way to enjoy a spring morning in
the country, least of all in the place where honest Claudius sang
his spring songs.' 'Claudius, who's he?' 'Asmus, the *Wands-
becker Bote*!' 'Don't know him!' 'Of course not, you don't
know Schiller's poems either, do you?' 'No, I don't, I've never
read them!' The conversation turned to other matters, to the
subject of Heine's imitators. Then:

> Soon we were out in the exhilarating sunshine. To my
> surprise Heine took the path leading to the churchyard, where
> he passed a few words with the sexton and then strolled with
> me between the rows of graves. Suddenly he stopped, took my
> hand with a smile and pointed to a grave surmounted by a
> simple tombstone. It was the grave of the *Wandsbecker Bote*,
> Matthias Claudius, who wrote under the name of Asmus.
> Surprised and touched by this revelation of tender feeling on
> my friend's part, I looked at him. He smiled, and a tear
> glistened in his eye. And the same Heine, who a few minutes
> before had wanted to tease me by pretending never to have
> heard of old Claudius, now quoted his words:

> > —Sie haben
> > Einen guten Mann begraben
> > Und mir war er mehr.

They've buried a good man, and to me he was more than that.

Heine's portrayal of himself in an unfavourable light was more often than not, then, a mask for his sensitive pride. But just as he often displayed himself to disadvantage, so he could reveal a charming side to his character—he could be gay, full of youthful and wholly delightful high spirits ; as he is in a poem, for instance, the mere march-rhythm of which is so enchanting: Schlage die Trommel und fürchte dich nicht ('Beat the drum and be not afraid '), and ending: Das ist die Hegelsche Philosophie/Das ist der Bücher tiefster Sinn,/Ich hab sie begriffen, weil ich gescheit,/Und weil ich ein guter Tambour bin—This is the Hegelian philosophy, this is the profoundest wisdom to be found in books ; I have grasped it because I am clever and because I am a good drummer. Is not the superb assurance of the verses delightfully youthful ? 'Because I am clever'—this last, as it were yodelling verse, could only come from the lips of a strong and handsome lad.

There are other passages, though, in which Heine's licentiousness and irony conceal his fear of giving full play to his emotions. He is not in a strong enough position, internally or externally, to do so. (An extreme contrast: Novalis, who abandons himself to his emotion completely and gives himself up to death almost wantonly, albeit in serene consciousness of his strength.) And again there are moments when beneath the surface gaiety lies a tender melancholy. I love you, Mathilde—he is too shy to say so (though elsewhere he does say it)—he indulges in witticisms from the other side, as it were, while his wife stands at his graveside: ' Leider wohn ich viel zu hoch,/Und ich habe meiner Süssen/Keinen Stuhl hier anzubieten —Unfortunately I live too high up and I haven't a chair to give my sweetest one. And then: ' Süsses, dickes Kind, du darfst/Nicht zu Fuss nach Hause gehen ;/An dem Barrière-Gitter/Siehst du die Fiaker stehen '/Sweet, plump child, you must not walk home, take a *fiacre* at the gate. This poem, that begins on a solemn note (' Keine Messe wird man singen '—No mass will be said), with its melodious-ness, its change of mood, its glance turned towards eternity and Paris, towards a great love and the melancholy realities of day-to-day existence, towards destruction and resignation, can be counted amongst the finest, most human in the German language.

The attitude of Heine's contemporaries to his wit was ambi-valent ; often it made a thoroughly bad impression on them. People began to echo Rahel's ' Open the windows ! ' This was somewhat

Grillparzer's reaction. Gentlemanly, reserved, crystal-pure, Grillparzer was once a luncheon guest with Heine at Baron Rothschild's in Paris.

> I found Heine as unlikeable when lunching with him at Rothschild's as I had found him likeable a few days previously when I had had an enjoyable *tête-à-tête* with him. It was evident that his hosts were afraid of him, and he exploited their fear in order to make fun of them in secret on every possible occasion. But no one ought to dine with people to whom they are not well disposed, and if one finds people contemptible one ought not to dine with them. Our relationship ceased accordingly from that moment.

Occasionally Heine would practise his wit as if it were a kind of sport, as on an occasion when Hebbel brought a Swedish professor to visit him.

> Heine was in the best of moods and thought in all innocence that Hebbel had brought him a sacrifice whom he (Heine) could comfortably slaughter. Heine immediately loosed a few shafts of his wit at the harmless professor. Hebbel, however, did not like this at all and he found ways and means of diverting Heine from his beloved satirical path. The result of the visit was that the Swedish professor kept as far as he could from Heine but clung all the more intimately and trustfully to Hebbel.

A similar scene was enacted in George Sand's salon, where Heine once made an onslaught on Lamennais, a priest who was friendly with Börne. Laube relates:

> There was a spiritual friendship between Lamennais and George Sand which no one was less fitted to appreciate than Heine. On this occasion, as ill-luck would have it, Heine was in brilliant but merciless form. The hostess sensed the danger and tried to limit the conversation to small talk. Heine, however, persisted in trying to discuss general principles, and fastened relentlessly on to the mild priest, who amiably tried to change the subject. It was quite clear he was being cheeky and trying to chaff Lamennais; what the French call *railler*. He always had a strong antipathy to the idea ' priest.' To increase my enjoyment he whispered in my ear: ' This sentimental priest was once in the running for the papacy; just listen ! ' and he began to lay about him with increasingly pointed questions, *aperçus* and such keen witticisms that the company laughed with him. . . . Though she forced a sweet-

sour smile at Heine's quaintly comic remarks, La Sand was dreadfully embarrassed and begged him repeatedly with her eyes to leave off ! Lamennais, too, forced a smile and took everything that the *enfant terrible* said in good part. Never have I seen Heine so powerful in social intercourse. His French— which, by the way, he carefully cultivated—was often harsh and halting, but this time it flowed from his lips in a torrent, and the most striking phrases came as fluently from his lips as they would have done from those of a Frenchman of high ability ; he ruled at this levee like an emperor of the intellect.

It must not be thought that Heine indulged in his witticisms for his own satisfaction or that of the company in which he found himself. They were an expression of his nature, they arose from a daimon within him which he was unable to master. Satirical wit is, after all, inborn deep within the Jewish make-up ; it can be found in the Bible and Talmud (cf. Heinrich Gross, *Die Satire in der jüdischen Literatur,* Augsburg, 1908). In a way it constitutes our anonymous folk-tradition, our folk-song. David Friedländer, whose name for praise and for blame I have found myself mentioning so often in this book, says in the forgotten *Zeitschrift für die Wissenschaft des Judentums* to which I have previously referred (1822, p. 193) that ' the play on words is regarded differently by Oriental and Occidental. The latter regards it simply as a display of wit, capable of affording passing entertainment and delight but which when overdone infringes the bounds of good taste. For the former it is often an indispensable necessity and is partly attributable to the structure of his language.'

Heine's wit likewise springs from profound spiritual depths : subjectively it is irresistible and organic (the criticism of polemics expressed in Chapter IV applies only to their *objective* value). As a wit Heine, far from calculating what effect his sallies would have, was unwise, impetuous, and created enmities for himself in the most unpractical fashion. Something of this lack of wisdom and of reflection comes out in his whole *œuvre*. Heine insulted people and then was astonished to find that they were furious with him. He hadn't meant to hurt that much ! I once knew a successful author— Theodor Lessing ; he died all too soon, alas—who both in writing and speaking was similarly unable to avoid ' digging ' at all and sundry. He honestly believed, though, that he had said nothing but good about the persons concerned and that he had referred to them

in the kindest terms imaginable. Indeed, he expected them to thank
him for his references to them. In this respect he admittedly went
one better—or worse—than Heine. The point is, at the bottom of
this sort of behaviour there is something more than mere gaucherie
and lack of diplomacy. It is only himself whom the satirist actually
sees as a real living being ; he is inclined to doubt the reality of the
others. It is a kind of mania leading in its extreme form to solipsism,
to a pathological conviction that all people except the ' self ' are but
' passing shadows on the wall.' It is impossible not to recognise in
these cases a culpable overemphasis of the ego.

Wit and irony then may have two faces, looking in fact in
opposite directions. One is the face of someone who doesn't take
the world seriously enough ; the other is the face of someone who
takes it so seriously, experiences so deeply its inner contradiction,
its mystery that cannot be put into words, that he is no longer able
to express himself in ordinary speech ; he is forced to use extraordinary means of expression. The great irony of the Romantics, as
well as of Socrates, is of this kind. As long as wit indicates nothing
more than that its possessor regards his own ego as something so
colossal that the whole world fades into nothingness by comparison
—it is sheer vanity. Wit always has an element of the incommen-
surable in it. But on the higher level of wit this incommensurability
will show itself in the ego's acknowledging its powerlessness
vis-à-vis the world, its inability to bridge the gulf between the world
and itself by ordinary means. On the lower level of wit, however,
it is the ego which is incomparably great, and vis-à-vis which the
world becomes unreal.

Gradually Heine's wit passed on to the higher level. The mystery
that could not be put into words, but which nevertheless he felt
called on to express (from about the time he fled to Paris onwards),
is the political mean between extremes, between Jacobins and Con-
servatives. In his letters about the ' citizen monarchy ' he tackled
this problem sincerely. It was granted him to sense this mean, to
live it ; not to formulate it. Since, however, once you use words you
must formulate, Heine's wit takes on ever and more sublime forms
in expressing that which cannot be put into words. Especially is this
so in his book on Börne. In the end his wit assumes a religious
quality, like Clemens Brentano's, Kierkegaard's. A heavy heart
wears a cheerful countenance. The garment eventually fitted the

body, Heine's genius for wit found its proper outlet and became
an existentialist philosophizing. Already in his cry to a helping,
personal God Heine's wit had assumed, so to speak, a metaphysical
form. In the epilogue to *Romanzero* the transition had been
completed. Here, before the statue of Venus, Heine's wit enters
the religious sphere. ' I have renounced nothing,' we read,

> not even my old pagan gods, from whom I have turned away,
> I admit, but parting from them in love and friendship. It was
> in May, 1848, on the day when I went out for the last time, that
> I took my leave of the charming idols I had worshipped in the
> days of my happiness. It was with an effort that I managed to
> drag myself to the Louvre, and I almost collapsed on entering
> the sublime hall where the most blessed goddess of beauty,
> our dear Lady of Milo, stands on her pedestal. A long time
> I lay at her feet, and I wept so bitterly that a stone would have
> taken pity. The goddess, too, looked down on me compas-
> sionately, but cheerlessly withal, as if to say : ' Don't you see
> I have no arms and cannot help ? '

Is the right label for Heine ' Romantic ' ? Does his personal
kind of irony and wit come within the category of Romantic irony ?
We have sought to answer these questions neither with ' Yes ' nor
' No,' but by illustrating the complexity of the factors involved. In
doing so we have broached another question : that of Heine's
relationship to German culture. Allied to this question is the consideration of the extent to which Heine's genius was a universal
one or limited by racial factors. We shall have to learn to appreciate
both sets of qualities in human beings, those determined by race
and those common to all mankind, universal. The common factors
include the lowest region of all, the basic drives of all human
activity ; of life, birth, death—the purely animal factors, in a word.
We need not consider these further here. They also include, though,
the very highest functions of the soul, expressed in form, truth,
ethics and religion. Between these two ' universal ' zones lies an
extensive territory in which racially determined and universal
factors are considerably intertwined. An analogy may serve to
illustrate how what is highest in man grows organically from this
intermediate region in which universal and national factors inter-
mingle; how, indeed, man could not reach his highest stature but
for the existence of this richly patterned middle territory, these

summa constituting withal a sovereign order of uniform, universal values obeying their own laws.

During the course of a fairly lengthy stay in the Southern Carnic Alps I climbed one day to a height that commanded a magnificent view. It struck me very forcibly that from this height not only could I see the peaks of the Carnic Alps that had become so familiar to me from my stay in the region, the peaks that soared out of the landscape and joined with it to constitute a system of mountain heights and valleys and torrents ; but that the great Alps themselves with the Gross Glockner chain were also visible to me. In the pure mountain air the thought crossed my mind : *the peaks of the mountains see each other*. To themselves they lie cheek by jowl : what though from the valley below only one or other of the glacier masses is visible ? It is only here above that their true relationship becomes apparent. Each of these peaks belongs to its own valley-system, would not be complete without the lesser heights surrounding it, resembles and is serviceable to them in structure, vegetation, etc. Yet : the peaks of the mountains see each other, they belong to each other ; they are, as it were, a world in themselves, assigned to each other and enjoying eternal uninterrupted communication with each other.

Or another analogy to illustrate the same idea : every tree is rooted in its own earth, in the national soil that nourishes it—but the same universal wind and rain blows through the tops of *all* the trees, and it is the same sun that sends the rich sap coursing into exquisite leaf.

I had already written in this strain in my monograph (1925) on Leos Janácek. I defended him against his compatriots who criticised him for being too folklorist, insufficiently cosmopolitan. I wrote : ' The folk-song is full of unbroken, unsophisticated vitality. Of course, we no longer see the " folk " with the eyes of Rousseau, who saw in it the archetype of innocence, of purity in the ethical sense ; just as Professor Freud's psycho-analytical researches have made it no longer possible for us to regard the child as " innocent " (in the ethical sense). But there is another sense to " innocence " ; that of " non-hypocrisy," of undisguised vitality. In this sense the " folk," the child, are innocent ; in this sense no art can dispense with innocence. Indeed, without this warm feeling of love for the innocence of vitality (and every form of academicism is diametrically opposed to this feeling of love) there can be no understanding of art.

'The whole music of Western Europe is inconceivable without the ground note of the folk-music of the various individual nations: German folk-song and German hymn course no less strongly in Bach's blood than do Chopin's native mazurkas in his. In Berlioz there is a queer mixture of French romance and Italian song ; in Schumann, Wagner, Mozart, Verdi, Debussy the national character of their music is unmistakable. Mahler, the Jew, could have wished to avoid hearing the excessive seconds of Eastern European Jewish folk-song that mysteriously surrounded him ; he sought a home in German and Czech melodies, but eventually came to rest musically in his ancestral Asiatic homeland, the notes of which he struck in his *Song of the Earth.*

That in all great artists this national basis is merely the foundation—admittedly indispensable—on which each one erects with consummate skill a heaven-soaring edifice allying itself with all the creative powers of the universe—so much everyone takes for granted. What is of absolutely equal importance, however, is less generally realized ; namely that a life-giving stream must be pumped up, through an exceedingly fine system of capillary tubing, from the very bottom of the foundation, from the blood-spring of vitality, into the uppermost parts of the building, those furthest removed from the ground of nature. There is no abstract, universal quality in an artist that is not permeated by what is most concrete and vital within him. Not until these three factors synthesize can there be an artist: the depth of his blood-spring, the loftiness of his world-surveying glance, and the interpenetration by the dark elemental forces of nature of an edifice that looks out over a sunlit universe. There will always be a school of art criticism, however, sympathizing only with the sunlit, rational side of the artist's nature. This school will be unable to do justice to the dark, instinctive side of the artist and to the interpenetration of his cultural and instinctive qualities.

All this was written at a time when there was need of defending the valleys against the summits ; present-day tactics call for the reverse procedure. Those of us, however, who are concerned not with tactics but with the whole truth will always strive to assert the vital importance of *both* elements in the make-up of the artist, the deep-lying roots and the free universal topmost boughs. This is the system of thought I have called ' national humanism.' Within such a system the right approach to any critical evaluation of a personality would consist in neither under- nor over-estimating the qualities determined by race *vis-à-vis* those qualities which are common to all mankind. Where is the boundary between the two sets of qualities to be drawn ? To resolve this problem is as difficult as to determine where the qualities characterizing a given age or century end and where within the same period of time the qualities common to all mankind begin ; after all, every age, every century has its own spirit, and yet all ages are but the history of the one human race and therefore variations on the theme of the human spirit that is common to all of them. It is clear that only a very wise, very just, and, withal, humane observer whose heart is filled with a warm love for all mankind is fitted to tackle questions of this kind.

Heine's own utterances, some of which have already been quoted, cannot by any means be taken as unequivocal indications of the values he assigned to the German, Jewish and universal-human elements in his make-up. When expounding German philosophy and the characteristics of German literature to French audiences he usually says ' You French,' and ' We Germans.' Nevertheless, passages such as the following, in connection with the theological controversies in German universities (*From Luther to Kant,* in *History of Religion and Philosophy in Germany*) engender a suspicion that the identification is not as thorough-going as it seems :

> You French have no idea of the hatred that is unleashed on such occasions. The fact is, the Germans are altogether more vindictive than the Romance peoples, the reason being that they are idealists in their hatred too. Unlike you, we don't hate for trivialities : offended vanity, say ; an epigram ; an unexchanged visiting card. We hate our enemies for what is deepest in them, for what makes them essentially what they are : we hate them for what they think. You French are frivolous and superficial in love and in hate. We Germans hate thoroughly, permanently ; as we are too honest, and indeed too clumsy, to avenge our- selves by speedy double-dealing we hate to the last breath in our bodies. I know this famous German calmness, Monsieur, said a young lady once, looking at me sceptically and with disquiet in her wide-open eyes : I know you Germans use the same word for forgive and poison. And of course she was right, *vergeben* means both.

Does Heine genuinely consider himself a German in this piece,

or is not the expression ' we Germans ' more likely to be a stylistic
device suggesting that he is in fact far outside the German camp ?
The question assumes decisive importance in the concluding passage
of the *History of Religion and Philosophy,* when Heine warns
France against disarmament:

> A young Teutomaniac once said, in a Göttingen Bierkeller,
> that the Germans ought to take revenge on the French for
> having beheaded Conradin of Hohenstaufen in Naples. You've
> certainly forgotten that a long time ago. We forget nothing,
> though. You see, if we fancy picking a quarrel with you we shall
> have no lack of weighty reasons, etc.

On the other hand, it is well known how intensely Heine clung
to his German inheritance in Paris, how unwearying he was in proclaiming his love for what was German. Alexandre Dumas said of
him: ' Si l'Allemagne ne veut pas de Heine, nous l'adoptons
volontiers, mais malheureusement Heine aime plus l'Allemagne
qu'elle ne mérite.' He refused to take out French naturalization
papers. Laube testified that in Paris society Heine

> gave a more powerful display of our Fatherland's debating
> ability than did any other German agency, and this against the
> best French talent of the time. Could anything be more heart-
> ening for a German than to take part in such contests, in which
> the French always assume their gifts of speech-making and
> *esprit* will give them the victory, and to see how a German
> fighting as a German would suddenly commence skirmishing
> on the outposts to left and to right of him and alone, all alone,
> would gradually draw the whole enemy line and engage it with
> cut and thrust and shot ; and not only engage it, but threaten
> it and, how often, drive it completely from the field ? Yes, he
> who in German had often poured such bitter scorn on German
> learning and art and morality, considering only the pedantry
> and formalism and rigidity in which they clothed themselves
> —now he spoke up for them as a much-feared gladiator against
> every challenging smile of the French, defended them as if it
> was a matter close to his heart, with that scintillating wit which
> was peculiarly his and in which even the most gifted Frenchmen
> had to concede he was really their superior. Never, perhaps,
> have German interests been so characteristically and so
> devastatingly defended as in these contests ; I say so character-
> istically, because the French even now do not suspect the
> intensity of the national spirit that emanated from this man
> whom they so liked to represent as a Frenchman by adoption.

Speaking in his *History of German Philosophy* of Fichte's pecuniary embarrassments, mentioned by Fichte in a letter to Kant, Heine says movingly:

> I cannot bring myself to insert this letter, remarkable though it is, in a French translation here. I believe my cheeks are suffused with red at the thought, and it seems to me that I would be exposing the dirty family linen to the gaze of strangers. For all my striving to acquire French worldliness, for all my philosophical cosmopolitanism, old Germany with all its *bourgeois* sentiments is lodged in my heart.

Justly famed, too, is the preface to the first volume of the *Salon*, in which Heine described how he met a group of German emigrants in France:

> Without quite knowing how, I suddenly found myself on the main Havre road, and in front of me several big, high peasant wagons were slowly rumbling by. They were packed with all kinds of pitiable boxes and crates, old-fashioned household goods, women and children. By the side of the wagons walked the men, and I received no little shock of surprise when I heard them speak—they spoke German, in the Swabian dialect. I soon saw that these people were emigrants, and when I looked at them more closely a sudden feeling stabbed me such as I had never experienced in my life before ; all the blood suddenly rushed to the region of my heart and beat against my ribs as if compelled to leave my breast, as if it had to get out with all speed, and my breath caught in my throat. Yes, it was the Fatherland itself that met my gaze ; in those wagons sat blond Germany with its earnest blue eyes, its homely, all too stolid features ; in the corners of its mouth that pitiable narrowness that once bored and irritated me so much, but which I now found poignantly moving. For though with the flushed pride of youth I had many a time and oft been ruthless in sour criticism of the abuses and petty conventional prejudices that were rife in my native land, though I had sometimes been involved in tiffs with my happy, comfortably bourgeois, spiritually slothful Fatherland—such tiffs as occur in any big family—I remembered nothing of these things when I saw the Fatherland wretched, a stranger in a strange land ; I suddenly found even its failings dear and precious, I was reconciled even to its provincial pettinesses, and I shook it by the hand, I shook the hand of these German emigrants as if it were a handshake with the Fatherland itself in token of a renewed covenant of love, and we spoke German.

I cannot quote the whole magnificent passage here, and would ask that it be read, up to the climax:

> There you have it. Germany is us. And that is why I suddenly became so depressed and ill on seeing those emigrants, the great blood streams pouring from the Fatherland's wounds and losing themselves in the African sand. There you have it; it was a bodily loss, and in my soul I felt an almost physical pain.

Utterances similar to this abound in Heine's writings. There is the passage on Johannes Tauler's sermons:

> And when his heart swelled in its greatest holiness, he had to speak German. His language is like a mountain spring that gushes forth from the hard rocks, its waters marvellously impregnated with the fragrance of plants whose existence had long been lost sight of and with the mysterious forces that reside in the mountain stones. But only in recent times did the serviceability of the German language for philosophy become obvious. In no other language could Nature have revealed her most secret work as in our dear beloved German mother-tongue. Only on the strong oak could the holy mistletoe prosper.

His letter to Christiani:

> You say in your letter that I find it so hard to rid myself completely of my Teutonism. What I have just written may tend to confirm you in your belief that I consciously strive to do so. You are mistaken, however. I know that I am one of the most completely German animals there are, I know only too well that the German element is to me what water is to fish, that I cannot escape from this element in which I live, and that—to retain the piscine analogy—I would inevitably turn into dried cod were I—to retain the aquatic analogy—to jump out of German waters. I love what is German from the bottom of my heart, more than anything else in the world. I enjoy it, and in my bosom are the archives of German emotion just as in my two books are the archives of German song. My first book is wholly German even in its externals, my love of things German was at that time unclouded; my second book is only German in its inner character, in externals it is more of an alien. It is likely that in her displeasure with things German the German garment my Muse wore this time was of rather strange cut. There were good reasons for this displeasure, and my Muse's annoyance was justifiable.

Heine's Germanophile protestations in this letter were uttered

in refutation of an imagined charge against him of ' de-Germaniza-
tion,' and in the result convey an impression of dissociation from
the German spirit. There are other occasions when to express this
dissociation seems to be Heine's chief concern; it sets the tone of
the particular piece of writing. We find ourselves involved in a
mass of contradictions. We shall probably not go far wrong in
thinking that Heine considered himself in his own subjective estimation as a poet fully integrated into German culture, in fact as one
of the pioneers in the struggle for German culture in France, but
at the same time as one who felt bound to express the severest
political criticism of German conditions (fragmentation into petty
principalities, aristocratic privilege, lack of freedom) for the sake
of the Germans themselves and of a better German future. He was
aware that the German national character was rooted in romanticism. He felt that this character was in conflict with the requirements of the age, which he would have liked to stabilize on the
French revolutionary pattern (though a very mildly revolutionary
pattern; his ideal was constitutional monarchy). He tried to resolve
the conflict by his thesis, constantly propounded and passionately
maintained, that German philosophy had been in the sphere of
thought what the French revolution had been in the sphere of action.

It is strange that the practical activities of our neighbours
the other side of the Rhine should have had their own elective
affinity with our philosophical dreams in Germany. Comparing
the history of the French revolution with that of German
philosophy one gets the impression that the French, who did
really have a lot of practical business that took up all their
energies to get on with, had asked us Germans to sleep and to
dream for them while they were at work, and that our German
philosophy is nothing but the dream of the French revolution.
Thus we broke with the established and traditional order in the
sphere of thought just as the French did in the sphere of
society ; round the standard of the Critique of Pure Reason
gathered our philosophical Jacobins who refused to let anything pass that did not conform to the Critique, Kant was our
Robespierre.

In Heine's own late theistic phase he dropped this rather violent
parallel.

Let us try, then, to appraise objectively Heine's position in the
world of German culture and German literature, taking into account

his own testimony (with necessary *caveats*), and starting from my previously elaborated premise that national and racial elements, *while accounting for much, do not account for everything.* In making such an appraisal we shall have to be constantly on our guard against the malicious attacks and sweeping generalisations alike of the Right and Left. After years of continually revising our impressions and judgments we may be able to arrive at certain Propositions, which I would summarize thus:

(1) Heine wanted to be German and was firmly convinced, at any rate in a certain layer of his consciousness, that he was. Even if it is held that he did not succeed, or only seldom succeeded, in landing on the shores of German culture, his will to do so, his longing to do so, his feeling of being German were something real and are therefore genuine. This will and longing do not of course constitute an aspect of German culture ; perhaps they are of little or no importance in the history of the German soul, although I can conceive of someone finding a repercussion of his own soul in a neighbour's not without interest. Nevertheless, this will and longing are a phase in Jewish historical development, are an organic part in the line of development of Judaism. By way of analogy I would cite Mahler's *Wunderhornlieder.* Considered purely and simply as ' German songs ' they seem irregular, indeed strange. Directly they are placed against their Jewish background, however, they convey a different impression ; their profound, unqualified longing to be seen as German appears characteristic of a certain historical situation in European Jewry. Because this longing is genuine it is a soil on which genuine art can flourish.

(2) For German art and culture achievements such as Heine's and Mahler's are at least a marginal enrichment and of marginal importance. Moreover, they are quite able to assume a central significance, given the prerequisites for universal-human, absolute art-values (Proposition 6). In any case, the culture of a great nation cannot rest on such insecure foundations that it is compelled to disapprove of and reject what are in the last analysis its own emanations (*e.g.,* Heine's and Mahler's longing to contribute to German culture). Rather, it has every reason at least to register these mixed forms and give them proper attention.

(3) Any other procedure than that suggested in (2) above could only be justified on the assumption of an unbridgeable chasm

existing between the nations. We do not believe, however, that any such chasm exists ; the races (nations) of the world have their essentially human characteristics in common and differ only in matters of secondary importance.

(4) The right attitude to German culture of a Jewish author writing in the German language is that of ' detached love ' which I have elaborated in my novel *Die Frau, die nicht enttäuscht*. A realization of the differences that lie on the surface, as it were, of German and Jewish sensibilities makes it impossible not to proceed to an examination of those profoundest spiritual depths to which no differences can penetrate. ' Detached love,' anyway, is a dialectical, self-contradictory concept. Maintain your detachment and you injure your love. Love and detachment fight against each other. However, self-contradictory and full of difficulties as it is, ' detached love ' is the only possible expression for the attitude of the Diaspora Jew towards the nation in whose midst he lives. There just is no easier way for us. All we can do is to avoid the rigid extremes of ' detachment ' and ' love ' and seek a living, midway position. Such a position cannot be defined in words, nor can it be covered by any general formula. It has to be won anew from day to day by constant creative effort, requiring the greatest tact and finger-tip delicacy of feeling. It can only be lived, not described in abstract terms. It carries the individual on a wave, it is something vibrant, passionate and withal infinitely tender—and requires of necessity that the individual be firmly anchored in Judaism. For the soul needs to be protected in its innermost depths if it is not to become weary and worn out before its time in the struggle to maintain, without nervousness and hysteria, this tremulous existence that hovers between detachment and love, if it is to be neither unsympathetic to the fate of the nation that shelters it nor to plunge all too unrestrainedly into the maelstrom of the nation's life. From this viewpoint of detached love as the only possible attitude for the Diaspora Jew has arisen a new recognition of the necessity for Zionism. I am indebted for this latter point to a review by Felix Weltsch of my previously mentioned novel (*Selbstwehr* 5.1.1934): ' Detachment can only be maintained by standing firmly on one's own ground. Detached love demands a balance of forces ; but such a balance can be achieved only by opposing to the blandishments of a foreign national culture one's own secure Jewish self.'

(5) For the reasons given in Chapters V and VI it was historically inevitable that Heine's generation could have no inkling of
any concept of balance of forces. The German Jewry that had just
achieved emancipation, still more the German Jewry that was still
in the thick of the struggle for it, was incapable of taking that
immediate step in the opposite direction—of recovering its
Jewishness—that was necessary to achieve a balance of forces. In
the optimum of Jewish national instinct that he had, Heine was
far ahead of his generation.

(6) Hitherto Jewish assimilation has been studied only in its
ethical and sociological aspects. The time has now come, it would
seem, for a thoroughgoing ' Aesthetic of Assimilation ' to be undertaken. To all intents and purposes assimilation is an historical manifestation that has now come to an end. It is accordingly possible
to study it without indulging in polemics and to give due recognition
to what was good in it. The book by Max Wiener to which I have
referred seems to me exemplary in this respect.

In pronouncing aesthetic value-judgments we must bear in mind
that we are here dealing with Jewish spirit working in an alien
material. The principle of parity between the German and Jewish
nations (Proposition 3) accordingly does not apply. The standards
to be applied to a German work of art must be the standards of
German art itself (e.g., German linguistic standards). Any work of
art coming within the purview of German culture must submit to
be judged by these standards, and if it is to lay claim to wholeness,
to aesthetic perfection, it must acknowledge their unconditional
sovereignty. Does it follow that a literary work written by a Jew in
German or a musical work composed by a Jew in the German
manner must come to grief on what is strange territory, must
inevitably be incongruous, unsuccessful ? The danger is there,
certainly. But *inevitable* failure ? No. Even when the Jewish artist's
basic—erroneous—premise is his complete absorption within the
German nation, there is still the possibility that his error may yet
be creative. Goethe, under the heading of *Bedenklichstes* (' For
Serious Consideration ') expresses in his incomparable style everything that can be said about such ' errors ':

> It happens quite frequently in life that when we have set
> our course with the utmost confidence we suddenly find our-
> selves on the wrong tack. We see that we have espoused

persons, causes ; had dreams about them which the cold light
of day has revealed for the illusions they were. Yet we are
unable to tear ourselves away from them ; some power we may
not understand holds us fast. Sometimes, however, we realize
in full consciousness that an error, no less than a true perception, may lead and spur us on to activity. And since action is
decisive everywhere, an active error may produce a worth-
while result, the repercussions of every deed that is done being
endless. So that, while a productive deed is always the best,
even destructiveness is not without its fortunate consequences.
The strangest error of all, though, concerns ourselves and our
own powers, when we embark on some worth-while business,
some honourable enterprise to which we are not equal ; when
we strive for a goal we can never reach. The more   sincere
anyone's   strivings are, the more bitter are the tortures of
Tantalus-Sisyphus that he finds to be his lot. And yet very
often, in realizing that we shall never be able to get within sight
of our original goal we find that in attempting to reach it we
have discovered some other desirable aim on our way, something suited to us, to content ourselves with which is what we
were really born for.

Applying Goethe's dictum to the special case of Heine it may
be said that Heine's error was rendered inevitable by the conditions
of the time. Hence to some extent it was legitimate, and the genuine
ardour of his desire to be German favoured the creative potenti-
alities of the error. Furthermore it must again be stressed that the
whole question depends on our opinion of the width of the gulf that
separates German and Jewish sensibilities. Differences need not
connote incompatibility, hostility ; doctrinaires who insist that there
can be no racial differences of any kind, who regard the mere
mention of the possibility of the existence of such differences as
' racialism,' as plunging humanity into eternally warring camps—
please note. The various races can help each other to develop certain
qualities they possess amongst themselves. A symbiosis is possible
which will produce works which, if not in the main national stream,
will certainly be very noteworthy and valuable. For ' the world-spirit
is more tolerant than we suppose ' (Goethe).

After all, in the world of art *foreign* themes, too, can lend
themselves to most stimulating treatment. Shakespeare did not
create English characters only ; he drew the ancient world, Italy,
Shylock the Jew. Hence it is difficult to see why a Jew could not
equally portray in their essential features an Englishman, a Roman,

or even a German; particularly if he preserves a proper detachment
from the object he loves. Failure to do so is a source of danger,
but no more; shipwreck is not inevitable. Success in art is a matter
of grace and in the final analysis holds man-made rules in defiance.
The wind bloweth where it listeth. Success is *a priori* possible by
virtue of the existence of a universal zone in which precisely the
highest human values reside, those values which constitute the
dignity of man ; truth, moral freedom, Plato's ideas. ' The peaks
of the mountains see each other.' In this highest sphere, in the very
innermost recesses of the soul, all barriers disappear, lose all
meaning, in fact. The Jewish artist handling non-Jewish material
needs to be endowed, it is true, with a double portion of grace, as
it were ; the general grace that must smile on every work of art,
and the particular grace needed to help him avoid the difficulties
and dangers of spuriousness and incompleteness that we have
described. In discussing the *Buch der Lieder* adequate stress was
laid on the sovereign independence of all mundane considerations
possessed by every complete work of art. Heine was vouchsafed
the grace to achieve such independent moments. Likewise Mahler,
whose passionate desire to be German was determined by the
conditions of his time, and was legitimate, therefore, in the same
way as was Heine's, and was similarly as full of inner danger for
him as it was for Heine. Nevertheless, quite apart from the *sine
qua non* of the universal, religious pristine oriental elements in
Mahler's music,[1] his compositions lying on the ' German frontier '
have been touched with the grace necessary to endow them with
German qualities, e.g. in the *Wunderhornlieder* or in the first
Nachtmusik of the Seventh Symphony. Here all theoretical specula-
tions are beside the point. All we are conscious of is the perfection
of the finished work.

As yet little or no attempt has been made to place Heine's work
in the Jewish literary line to which it organically belongs. His fore-
runners are to be sought in Jewish-German literature. He also has
many affinities with the older Hebrew authors in other cultural
spheres, e.g. with Abraham Gorni, the Provençal satirist (13th

---

[1] I have shown—as the first to do so—the Jewish, indeed chassidic
character of Mahler's music in *Der Jude*, i, 344.

century), quoted by Heinrich Gross in *Die Satire in der jüdischen Literatur*, with Kalonymos (c. 1300) author of a ' Touchstone ' and a Talmud parody, with the apostate Profiat Duran, who wrote a remarkable work in praise of Christianity, the satirical nature of which was not realized till long afterwards, and above all with Immanuel of Rome, who was Dante's contemporary and perhaps enjoyed friendly relations with him ; he wrote not only in Hebrew, but in Latin, in which latter tongue he wrote a sonnet on Dante's death. A satirical poem by Cino of Pistoia (a member of Dante's circle) on ' the Jew Manoello ' has come down to us. Evidently this medieval Heine had his Count Platen too. And he seems to have defended himself with Heinesque vigour against opponents of all kinds. His much censured ' frivolity,' too, no doubt flows from the same source as Heine's. Just as all his life Heine was unable to give up religious and philosophical speculation, so too Immanuel wrote a commentary on the books of the Bible. ' Love is the central point round which all the teaching of the Torah revolves,' he says in his commentary on the Song of Songs, and his erotic poems in which he praises beautiful women and very coarsely abuses ugly ones shocked the pious spirits of his day. In the 28th chapter of his masterpiece he imitates Dante's *Divine Comedy*. He describes a visit to Hell and to Paradise, where he finds the pious of all nations ('No matter what the country's name/The God who made it's just the same/The power that watches over peoples all/Is He whom God all nations call') and where he meets King David, who tells him that of all the commentators on the psalms only he, Immanuel, has given a true exegesis. (Cf. Gustav Karpeles, *Geschichte der jüdischen Literatur*.) Self-irony or exaggerated self-esteem ? Something midway between that is hard to put into words, such as we can find often enough in Heine too.

Of course there is as little question of Heine's being consciously influenced by these predecessors of his as there is, to repeat my previous analogy, of Mahler's consciously slipping into the rhythm and melodic line of chassidic tunes and marches—he was unaware of their existence, and Heine, too, knew practically nothing of his Hebrew precursors. It is simply a question of the family likeness that emerges the more we study a group of similar faces.

Heine's immediate precursors and contemporaries in the world of German letters were of course vastly inferior to him as German

writers. L. M. Büschenthal, who in 1806 dedicated a volume of
poems to the *Herr Vollrath*, reigning Imperial Count of Solms-
Rödelheim and Assenheim, slavishly took over Klopstock's and
Schiller's metre and vocabulary ; similarly the unfortunate Breslau
poet Ephraim Moses Kuh, whom we have already mentioned,
mechanically imitated Lessing's and Logau's epigrams and his own
beloved Martial, whom he translated. There are Hebrew echoes in
both poets. Kuh, for instance, has a quatrain the original of which
I cannot trace, but which I give here in his German version as an
example of his astringent style. It bears the title : *Sacharisse* (*From
the Hebrew*), and reads : ' Der Himmel wird die Harte strafen : /
Am Tage flieht mich Sacharisse ; /Und dass ich nicht im Traume sie
küsse, /Lässt sie mich in der Nacht nicht schlafen.'—'Tis heaven
will punish Zacharissa, / Who cruelly leaves me in the day-time ; /
To stop me dreaming that I kiss her/She keeps me sleepless in the
night-time. The collection of Kuh's verse published in 1792 contains
a poem entitled *Thoughts inspired by certain misfortunes* which
strangely foreshadows a famous poem of Heine's :

> Der starke Atlas nahm die Welt auf sich,
> Und eine Welt voll Gram ertrage ich ;
> Doch, hoher Zeus ! dir sey's gedankt,
> Nie hab' ich unter ihr gewankt.

> A world did mighty Atlas learn to bear,
> I too am burdened with a world of care ;
> But thanks to Zeus be now bestowed,
> I've never faltered 'neath its load.

Büschental, too, on those occasions when he can bring himself to
leave the ' bardic grove,' is capable of a personal expression of a
genuine emotion. He sings of Schiller's death, Schiller's philosophy
of resignation, writes a poem *Leichen-phantasie* (' corpse-phantasy '),
much mythological verse, *Presentiment—to Laura*, the fine epigram
To the dead Laura : ' Heavenly Laura, you lived—and were my
finest thought ; you died and are—Laura, now my own.' An ode
to Napoleon has been preserved, as well ; also a ' Collection of
humorous anecdotes as a contribution to a characterization of the
Jewish Nation,' and a tragedy, *Der Siegelring des Salomo*
(' Solomon's Signet '). His writings should be rescued from oblivion,
as should those of Michael Beer and I. F. Koreff. The latter was
one of E. T. A. Hoffmann's circle. He wrote an opera libretto for

Spontini, and another, *Aucassin and Nicolette,* for which Heine thanked him with a sonnet. In spite of his baptism, and although he was a University professor and Hardenberg's personal physician, anti-Semitic attacks eventually drove him to emigrate to Paris as Heine did. He was well received by the French literary world and Paris society. Heine used to visit him in his house. Attention has been drawn to another contemporary figure of the same spiritual stamp, Daniel Lessmann—also an émigré—by Hermann Conradi and, recently, Willy Haas (*Die Welt im Wort,* 26 October '33).

Heine's spiritual affinities with his German-Jewish precursors and contemporaries are seen more clearly, however, if we go back a few centuries in German literature and light on the Minnesinger Süsskind von Trimberg. His songs come immediately next to Brother Werner's and the Knight of Burenberg's in the Manesse MS. He is called *Suesskint, der Jude von Trimperg* in the original, and the brightly coloured picture in the MS shows him in conversation with two nobles and a cleric. He wears the conical Jew's hat and has a long beard. In her edition of the poems (Verlag Fritz Gurlitt) Frau Dr. B. Badt observes pertinently that Süsskind's world-view differs fundamentally from that of his Christian contemporaries. There are recognizable links in his poems with the Jewish conception of God, with ancient Jewish literature, e.g. the Proverbs of Solomon. Moreover, his songs are characterized by the longing for social justice that permeates the whole of Jewish literature from Moses and the prophets onwards.

That all these traits are repeated in Heine can be seen at a first glance. In practically every one of the twelve poems of Süsskind's that have been preserved we can easily find a thread leading to the essential Heine. The extraordinary likeness of the two poets, which six intervening centuries have not been able to obscure, can be illustrated by a few stanzas of Süsskind's, done into Modern German verse by the young lyric poet Heinz Politzer:

> Wer edel ist und wahr, den werd' ich adlig nennen.
> Lasst ihr den Adelswisch, den Zettel frisch
>   verbrennen.
> Hat Reichtum Mehl: Armut die Asche hat.
> Bedenk dies Wort, o Weiser, hör den Rat,
> Verlach des Armen Spottbild nicht, bleib ihm als
> Freund verbunden.

I call him who is gentle and true the nobleman. He may
burn his patent of nobility, it is a scrap of paper. The rich
man has his store of flour, the poor man has his ashes.
Think on this, ye wise ones, hearken to my counsel; jest not
at the poor man's sorry state, attach yourself to him as his
friend.

XI. Ich fuhr mein' Tag der Narren Fahrt
     Mit meiner Kunst fürwahr.
     Da mir die Herrn den Preis nicht geben,
     Werd ich die Höfe fliehn.
     Ich will, dass mich ein langer Bart
     Umweh aus grauem Haar.
     So wie die alten Juden leben,
     Will ich den Weg weit ziehen
     Und auch mein Mantel flattert lang
     Tief unter meinem Hut,
     Demutvoll wandre ich meinen Gang,
     Nie sing ich mehr den höfischen Gesang,
     Da mich die Herren wegstiessen von dem Gut.

In wandering with my art from place to place I have led a
life of folly, forsooth. Since the lords will not give me my
guerdon I will flee their courtyards. I will grow myself a long
flowing grey beard. I will wander far away and live as do old
Jews. My cloak, too, I will trail about me deep beneath my
hat; humbly will I travel on my way, nevermore will I sing
the courtly lay, for that the lords have driven me from their
gates.

XII. Ein Wolf voll Jammer einstmals sprach:

     Wo soll ich mich verstecken,
     Der ich, weil Fressen nötig ist,
     Geächtet schleich von allen,
     Doch bin ich so, dazu gemacht,
     Die Schuld dran ist nicht mein.

     So mancher Mann schlägt seinen Wanst
     Mit Hass voll und Verbrechen,
     Vor aller Welt rafft er sein Glück
     Und sündigt ohne Massen.
     Er sündigt ärger, als wenn ich
     Nehme ein Gänselein.

Der ich nie rotes Gold erhielt,
Mein Mahl damit zu zahlen,
Ich raub des Leibes Notdurft nur, vor Hunger wild.
Der Sünder stiftet kalten Bluts
Viel ärgern Schaden an als ich
Und will die Unschuld heissen.

A wolf once raised its voice in lamentation:
'Where shall I hide myself, seeing that as an outlaw I have
to creep away from everybody, and all because I have to eat ?

'Many a man who is full of hatred and crime drums on
his belly, displays his fortune to the whole world, and sins
without limit. He sins more than I do when I snatch a gosling.

'I have never received red gold to pay for my meal. I rob
only to satisfy my bodily necessities when I am wild with
hunger. The sinner cold-bloodedly does far more harm than
I, and wishes to appear innocent.'

The concluding lines of the 'Samson' chapters in the Book
of Judges have always moved me strangely. 'Then his brethren
and all the house of his father came down, and took him, and
brought him up, and buried him between Zorah and Eshtaol in
the burying place of Manoah his father. And he judged Israel
twenty years.'

These last words are remarkable in that they inform us of a
judicial activity of Samson's which had nowhere been previously
mentioned (except for an identical line in the preceding chapter).
For this reason the line has been held to be an interpolation. Even
if this were so it would still make the whole matter no less
remarkable ; it would merely show that the adoption and dissemination of the tradition in precisely this form accorded with the
sentiment of the nation. The 'Samson' chapters tell us of the
hero's wanderings, of his riddles and combats, of his adventures
with dangerous enemies and even more dangerous mistresses, but
there is no mention that Samson led, organized, ruled the nation.
He is a lone wolf whose actions are unpredictable and who takes
no heed of their consequences ; he is bold and strong and roams
as he pleases in enemy territory with no thought for his own folk:
even before his death he prays to be avenged on the Philistines
for his 'two eyes,' not for his people. He thinks only of himself

and of what he must do in the foreigner's country. On his death, however, his destiny takes on a different appearance: he is solemnly brought home and buried in the family grave. It becomes evident that the life even of this vagabond, whether he was aware of it or not, was a life in the service of his people and that his was the office of a judge in Israel.

This seems to me to be symbolical of the life of so many Jewish artists.

They live and practise their art in alien cultural spheres. They become entangled in controversy, are despised and praised too, sometimes they are excessively spoilt. But soon after their death comes a change. It is as if the nations, smitten with a peculiar kind of remorse, seek to cancel a certain over-estimation in which they held the artists when they were alive by an equally unjust lack of appreciation and neglect, even hostility, after their death. There is an extraordinary transition from what was frequently an all too noisy fame enjoyed by Jewish artists when alive to complete oblivion on their death. The classic example is Meyerbeer. Perhaps his success was noisily exaggerated in his lifetime ; today, however, he is the victim of an equally flagrant injustice. Following Wagner, who learnt so much from him, people turn a deaf ear to the genuine musical values in Meyerbeer's compositions, to the glorious arias of *L'Africana ;* his genuine powers of invention are represented as mere striving after effect. Other examples (not quite so striking) : Offenbach, Mahler. On a lower level : Berthold Auerbach, whose village tales were once so widely read but have now simply vanished into thin air, are no longer there. Or Börne's forgotten polemical writings.

And so the fame of these artists is subject to a strange decrease and decay amongst the nations to which they seemed to belong. Meanwhile, however, there has quietly developed within the Jewish community, frequently on the express initiative of a Jewish personality (Karl Kraus, Offenbach renaissance), a profound, loving devotion to the Jewish artist, who himself had little or no connection with the Jewish community. It becomes evident that he was always dear and of importance to this community, that in it, even though separated from it, he had exercised a judge's office. And so the brethren come down and bring the dead man ' in his father's burying place.' The dead man lies in his place. Gradually, undis-

torted, his work is now placed before the outside world too;
undistorted, because without extravagant praise, and with blame
given in its due proportions only. His work is referred to its natural,
proper elements, interpreted, and hence understood, in the context
of the true conditions which inspired it, just as we comprehend, say,
the Greek authors in the context of their Greek elements and can
comprehend their universal significance *precisely for this reason*.

Ch. N. Bialik expresses a similar idea, though with a different
purpose in mind, in his remarkable *Essays* (Jüdischer Verlag,
Berlin, 1925). He speaks of the ' phenomenon of a literary harvesting
which is known in the history of our literature as *chatima*
(conclusion).' There was a threefold repetition of this phenomenon
in classical times, and it determined which writings were to be
admitted to the canon. Bialik believes the time has come for a
fresh harvesting to be undertaken.

> We wish to cast a great wide net over the whole sea of
> human literature and gather in all the sparkling drops of Jewish
> spiritual creativity. That will be a memorable day, a day of
> redemption and liberation for the Jewish soul, which will have
> returned to its *fons et origo*, to its inheritance, to its bundle of
> life. Think of Philo, of Spinoza, think of the whole host of
> Jewish philosophers and seers in Greek, Arabic, and Spanish
> which have come to light from the dust of the libraries and
> *genizot*. Think of Heine. . . .

An attempt at ' bringing Heine home ' has been made by Heinz
Politzer, too, in an article in *Selbstwehr*, 23.3.1934, in which he
raises questions of linguistic criticism. ' Is Heine's extraordinary
addiction to impure rhyme really nothing but the mark of a
careless, slipshod style ? ' he asks.

> Is it nothing but a protest, as cheap as it is vulgar, against
> the severe, frigid forms of classicism ? Was he really no better
> than his pinchbeck successors who in their arrogance presumed
> to destroy beauty by cynically writing verses that didn't scan,
> and the world of pure purposeless literature by indolently
> shrugging their shoulders in melancholy indifference ? Is not
> rather the lulling, lilting, rocking motion that characterizes
> Heine's verse something that derives from an orgiastic impetus
> coming from the East ? A suggestion of the East that may have
> evoked such an inward response from the creator of
> *Zarathustra* ? Does Heine's verse really need the support of

strictly conceived rhyme to enable the soul of the reader—
though who can read Heine's verse with the eyes alone ?—to
enable the soul of the self-listening reciter to soar aloft in
rapturous freedom ? Are these seemingly light tones ; more, are
these flat metaphors and smooth images, light, flat, and smooth
only in their German environment ? Have they not indeed a
heady quality which gives a deeper tone to their ting-a-linging ?
Are these popular songs folk-songs, though folk-songs of the
German nation is just what they are not ? Did Heine in truth
succeed, where Platen and Rückert with all their Persian love
poems and Brahmanic aphorisms failed, in grafting an oriental
note, sensuous for all its tenderness, on to the primmer tones
of the German language ?

I might add that linguistic analysis of Heine's writings would in
all probability support the suggestions made in the foregoing quotation as well as the suggestions I have already made in this book
regarding racial influences on Heine's style. Thus the characteristic
rhythm of Heine's prose often seems to me to gain great impres-
siveness through frequent repetition of ' and,' faintly recalling the
use of the narrative *Waw* in Biblical Hebrew prose. The introduction
of alien linguistic usages of this kind into German is no more to be
classed as a ' fault ' than is the colouring of a good deal of German
historical prose by Latinities from Tacitus. The final verdict rests,
of course, as stated in Proposition 6, with German linguistic usage,
and not with the foreign usage. At the same time the foreign element
may act analogously to a chemical stimulant in developing possibilities that were dormant in the German language in accordance
with the German language's own genius ; without introducing new
idioms into the language from outside it may reveal those that
already existed within it. It is hard to know where to draw the line.

I would characterize as linguistic errors Heine's all-too-frequent
elision of the final -e, his adoption, particularly in his later prose,
of unusual foreign words not in keeping with the character of the
German language, his systematic omission of the auxiliary, and his
characteristic placing of the direct object after, instead of between,
composite verbal forms. Often this is done for the sake of the rhyme
—with disastrous results. There are numerous verses in Heine which
lead one to speak of an absolute blindness for word-order in their
writer. Example : ' Die edelsten Grazien haben gestimmt/Die Saiten
meiner Leier.—The gentlest Graces have tuned the strings of my

lyre.' Unhappily similar instances abound, so that it seems little
short of a miracle that perfect verse-formations can exist side by side
with them. The wind bloweth . . .

I am inclined to censure less severely Heine's many impure
rhymes, or even his outrageously violent burlesque rhymes. Heine
even rhymes *Preussisch* with *Beichaise, Romantik* with *Uhland,
Tieck.* But in their context these are expressions of child-like
exuberance, reflected in a feeling of linguistic mastery that can
afford to write humorously and *en pantoufles.* Or, as perhaps a severe
critic would maintain, do such rhymes betray a foreigner's crimina'
indifference in the use of a language not his own ? Just look at this .

> Und wo die Freunde verfaulen,
> Das ist ganz einerlei,
> Ob unter Marmorsaulen
> Oder im Rasen frei...

It is all one where our friends rot in their graves, whether
beneath marble pillars or in the open sward ...

Marmorsaulen ?[1] Dear, dear ! But it so happens that these
verses are not by Heine at all, but by Goethe (*Zahme Xenien V, 17*).
And things are not as simple as the severe critic would so very much
like them to be.

---

[1] The correct form is *Marmorsäulen.*

IX

Between Germany and Paris

On 28 June, 1825, shortly before he took his degree at the University at Göttingen, Heine became a convert to the Protestant religion.

It might be supposed that the situation leading to his conversion was a highly complicated one ; that this action, like so much in his life, was shot through with contradictions, since it was just at this period that Heine had reached one of the high-tides of his Jewish consciousness.

Strangely enough, however, Heine thought of his baptism, in contrast to all the other experiences of his life, as something quite simple, involving no contradictions of any kind. It was a simple matter of expediency. Not one iota of conviction did be bring to his profession of Christianity. He went to the font because as a Jew he stood no chance of getting a post in the Germany of those days. And Heine did not wish to make his living by the exercise of his poetic gifts. In this highest region of his soul he wanted to be free. But his dependence on his rich uncle he found unendurable, too ; hence he considered it essential to be able to practise some occupation which would provide him with his daily bread and butter. Viewed in this light his baptism was simply a ' ticket of admission to European culture.' Had the law permitted the stealing of silver spoons he wouldn't have been baptized, he wrote to Moser. He was guided only by material necessity. And in a letter written to the same bosom friend two years earlier, when the question of baptism was first mooted (' None of the family are against it, except me '), he complains : ' I well understand the Psalmist's words : " Lord God, give me my daily bread, that I may not profane thy name." '

It is interesting to note that Heine's precursor, Ephraim Moses Kuh, regarded baptism in a very similar light. In his epigrammatic poem, *The Polish Jew who became a Christian,* he says : 'Ein grosse Kurfürst, dem kein Mangel droht/Verläugnet die Religion/Um einen neuen Titel, einen neuen Thron : /Und mich—mir fehlen Dach und Brodt/Mich tadelt ihr mit bitterm Hohn '—A great prince who wants for nothing will deny his religion for the sake of a new title, a new religion, and yet you heap bitter scorn on me, who lack roof and bread.

The only justification for baptism was the necessity to earn one's daily bread ! As late as 1846 Heine wrote in this strain about Felix Mendelssohn : ' I dislike his Christianizing. I can't forgive the manner in which this *man of independent means* serves the religiously minded with his great, his enormous talent.'

Heine believed firmly that a formal change of faith could be justified only as a concession to the Jew's environment and on grounds of occupational necessity. He would allow no other reasons. There could be no question whatever of any inner conversion, of any spiritual change towards Christianity. Indeed, such a process would be unbecoming in anyone having pretensions to philosophy, in a disciple of the New Age of Kant and Hegel. Obdurately he maintained that baptism was ' an act of no importance,' not even of symbolical importance. He castigated his former co-worker in the *Verein,* Gans, because the latter, it was asserted, professed the views to which baptism committed him.

Regarded as anything other than a pure matter of form, baptism aroused Heine's fury. He had not the slightest understanding for genuine conversions such as were then of everyday occurrence in the circles of Rahel Levin, Henriette Herz, the Mendelssohns, and the Veits. It was this intransigent attitude towards real Christianity that enabled him to don the cloak of pseudo-Christianity so easily, and led him to a quite unpardonable over-simplification of the situation. He failed to realize that outward secession from the Jewish community, the Jewish *societas,* has more than formal significance. He failed to realize that such a secession means the severing of the only quasi-political bond that keeps Jewry together in the Diaspora. The mental reservation 'I shall still remain a Jew' is not sufficient. The temptation to deny the inner attachment is too great, once the outer link is broken.

To Heine's credit it must be said that he did not often give way to this temptation. He referred openly to his Judaism. Yet he was highly indignant if someone else did so on occasions which did not suit Heine himself. It almost looks as if he acted on the (tacit) principle: I decide *when* I'm a Jew, in much the same way that Lueger, the Mayor of Vienna, who was anti-Semitic in his political capacity but liked to mix with Jews in his private capacity, said: I decide *who's* a Jew. But the whole point is that the 'who' and the 'when' are determined not by human caprice but once and for all by the creative forces of nature herself. How completely Heine misses this point, e.g., in the autobiography he wrote in 1835 at Philarète Chasles's request: 'For a long time now badly informed or badly disposed people have spread the rumour that I have donned the Saint-Simonian robe; others honour me with Judaism.' So in this instance the Judaism to which he proudly declared his allegiance in so many passages in his writings and throughout his life had become a mere rumour, or practically such. Nor did he tell his Mathilde exactly where he stood with regard to his Jewishness. The Jew-turned-Protestant had his marriage to her solemnized in the Church of St. Sulpice according to Catholic rites because 'without such a ceremony my wife, who comes of a strict Catholic family, would not have regarded herself as properly married in the sight of God.' Poor tortured man!

It will help us to understand Heine's baptism (for we are not concerned to justify it, merely to understand it as far as possible) if we also bear in mind that as a baptized Jew Heine believed he would be better able 'to fight for the rights of his unhappy fellow-Jews' (letter to Moser, September, 1823). Moreover, to the man who 'despised all official religions' the dogmatic content of the Jewish religion meant as little as did the dogmas of Christianity. Not until the last stage of his life did he attain religious faith, when he became a Deist and endorsed the specifically Jewish form of religious faith: the Law and the rebuilding of the nation by Moses.

Later he sought spiritual bridges to the substance of that Christianity the form of which he had originally assumed under compulsion and unwillingly. In doing so he never passed beyond the peripheral regions of the Christian religion, but he was now manifestly sincere in his search for spiritual values, whereas in his youth only his violent antipathy to Christianity, often crudely expressed, asserted itself. In his portrayal of Luther he mentions the 'spiritual freedom' of Protestantism (his conception of Luther as a forerunner of Kant is strange !), after praising the virtues of the Protestant clergy. 'You have to walk through North Germany as a poor student to see how much virtue, and, let me add a noble epithet, how much evangelical virtue can often be found in unpretentious vicarages.' Thus writes Heine the alleged cynic ! The whole passage should be read in the *History of Religion and Philosophy in Germany*. On the other hand, Heine condemned the theological controversies raging in the Berliner *Evangelische Zeitung*. He says he prefers even the 'Annals of Papism.'

Still later, in his *Confessions,* he had kind words for Catholicism ; not just the Catholic *ambiance* of his Rhineland youth, but the 'consistency of Roman Catholic doctrine,' which he 'admired as a thinker, as a metaphysician.' And he gives high praise to the Protestants for their dissemination of the Bible. In doing so they had founded 'the great realm of the spirit, the realm of religious feeling, of love of neighbour, of purity and true morality. These things cannot be taught by means of dogmatic concepts and formulas, but through stories and examples such as are contained in the Bible, the beautiful, holy educational book for children both little and big.'

Hence, says Heine, in disseminating the Old and New Testament the Protestants propagate a kind of 'Palestinism.' They impress the Scandinavian, Anglo-Saxon, indeed all the Germanic and Celtic peoples with the stamp of the 'morality, thought and tenderness of feeling' of life in Palestine. And there follows the passage in which Heine comes closest to Zionism. In it he recognizes the national as well as the universal characteristics of the Jewish religion. In the United States the Old Testament life had been 'pedantically aped' but the whole effect was 'that of a daguerreotype. The outlines are painfully accurate, but everything is grey in grey, and the colour, the melting sunshine of the Promised Land is missing.' But after this highly topical sentence Heine fails to follow up his theme. He continues imprecisely and rather too easily picking up the lost

thread : ' But the time will come when this caricature will vanish.
That which is real, everlasting and true, the morality of ancient
Judaism, will flourish and be as pleasing to God in those other
countries as it once was by the Jordan and on the mountains of
Lebanon. You don't need palm-trees and camels to be good ; it is
better to be good than beautiful.'

And so three religions passed as it were in review before the
older, mellower Heine standing, or rather lying, on the edge of the
grave, and mingled with his general Deism. At the time of his
baptism, however, he felt nothing but the harshest discords within
him. A few days after his baptism he wrote to Moser, without
mentioning the event, that he was working on the *Rabbi von
Bacharach,* in the awareness that ' writing it is a useful deed,
pleasing to God. But I must break off here, as this is a subject
which may easily tempt me to vaunt my own spiritual greatness.'
A few weeks later he tells his greatly beloved sister what has
happened in the remarkable words : ' Give my best wishes to Moritz
(her husband), and if you are certain he is not a chatterbox tell him
I am now not only *Dr. Juris,* but —— as well. It rained yesterday,
as it did six weeks ago.'

In the letters to Moser that follow, the note of self-accusation,
of troubled conscience becomes stronger. ' I should be very sorry
if you could regard my own baptism in any favourable light.' ' There
was a great deal more warmth amongst us in those days. If I'm not
mistaken, Gans had not yet been baptized and wrote long speeches
for the *Verein* and adopted as his motto : *Victrix causa Diis placuit,
sed victa Catoni.'*

I remember the psalm *By the Waters of Babylon* was your
forte in those days, and you recited it so beautifully, so gloriously,
so movingly, that I could weep over it even now, and not
merely over the psalm. You had some good ideas on Judaism
in those days, on the vileness of the Christian proselyters and
on the vileness of those Jews who go to the font not simply
to eliminate difficulties but in order to wangle something for
themselves. When you get the chance you should put these
and similar ideas you had in writing. You are independent
enough not to have to worry about Gans in doing so ; as far as
I'm concerned you don't have to worry at all.

Often I get up at night and look in the mirror and soundly
berate myself. I am disliked now both by Christian and Jew.

I bitterly regret having been baptized. I don't see that things have gone better for me in any way since then ; on the contrary, I've experienced nothing but misfortune. However, I will say no more ; you are too ' enlightened ' not to smile at all this.

In the *Reisebilder* he expresses himself more offensively against Christianity than ever he had done before. Frequently one gets the impression that he regarded his baptism as an act of violence, a personal injury that Christianity had inflicted on him. At all events, after it had taken place his fine, youthful open-mindedness towards certain Christian manifestations became a thing of the past.

The ceremony took place in the Prussian township of Heiligenstadt, near Göttingen. It was conducted by Pastor G. Chr. Grimm in the presence of Pastor Bonitz. Heine, till then Harry, received the names of Christian Johann Heinrich. About midday the baptismal act was over, and the three participants withdrew into the sitting-room of a neighbouring house. More than fifty years later an article, *The Baptism of the German Aristophanes,* based on the Pastor's account, was published in which the scene was described as follows :

After midday the gentlemen retired to the sitting-room. The host introduced the stranger as Law Student Heinrich Heine, involuntarily emphasizing the first name, which caused friend Bonitz to look up quickly with a smile. Lunch proceeded quietly ; a desultory conversation was conducted practically by the host and Bonitz alone. Heine joined in no more than was necessary to avoid appearing impolite. His features bore the mark of deep inner turmoil and in his dark eyes it could be seen that his thoughts were elsewhere. The two clergymen were in like case. Both known as witty conversationalists in their circles, today their minds were manifestly not on the subjects of conversation. Often they cast searching glances at the young man, and yet of a peculiar gentleness and joyousness. Heine left soon after the meal. His leave-taking of Pastor Grimm was particularly cordial and warm. When he was already at the door he turned round again and repeatedly shook him by the hand. His eyes were wet with tears.

These tears, Heine's turmoil in general, were certainly due to quite other causes than those assumed by the good honest clergyman. He had examined Heine in matters of religion for an hour before his baptism, and had praised his knowledge of Christian doctrine. The pastor was satisfied that Heine's change of faith was due to an ' urgent inner necessity.'

Heine's last years in Germany were marked by a whole series of attempts to find a post which would enable him to settle down in the Fatherland. All his attempts failed. In just the same way Herr K., the foreign surveyor who is the hero of Kafka's novel *The Castle*, struggles in vain for the right to the normal activity of a citizen, a matter which assumes a life-and-death importance for him as a symbol of integration into society.

Heine purposed being a lawyer in Hamburg, then he wanted to settle with Varnhagen's help as a *Privatdozent* in Berlin. When nothing came of this he tried for a professorship at Munich University, placing great hopes on the influence of the Minister of the Interior, Eduard von Schenk. In the end he would have been satisfied with a post as Syndic to the Town Council in Hamburg. . . . Everything went awry. And the ban on his *Reisebilder*, limited at first to certain German States (a general ban imposed by the Federal Council on all Heine's writings did not come till later), restricted his income as an author. Quite apart from his lack of means, which would not have permitted him a life of leisure anyway, and for all his contemplative-dreamy disposition, he hated continued inactivity, non-productiveness as such. He wrote once to the friend of his Bonn University days, Karl Simrock, condemning a mutual friend: ' But the devil take his aimless goings-on! To me at any rate it seems that any person of spirit would prefer to do something bad than to do something pointless.' And he wrote in a letter to Moser: ' I feel very strongly that the time has come for me to take my leave of the German Fatherland. It is not so much footlooseness as my personal difficulties (e.g. my ineffaceable Jewishness) which are driving me from here.' These two extracts from his letters span a whole world of troubles, of energetically conducted endeavours that petered out into nothingness.

As far back as 1823 Heine had written from Lüneburg to Wohlwill, with a presentiment of what the future might hold in store for him, that he planned to go to Paris and ' get a footing in the diplomatic world.' After he took his degree the question of a career became more acute. Momentarily the huge success of *Buch der Lieder* and *Reisebilder* diverted his attention from the problem, only for him to be confronted with it again in all its urgency.

There is something deeply tragic about the way in which Heine's hopeless attempts to find some kind of post were turned down one after the other with a rigid monotony that seemed to say: No admittance ! Of course, other poets also have had to experience considerable difficulties in establishing themselves in a career ; but few have met with such an unqualified ' No ' from fate as did Heine. The tranquil security afforded by the professional ' cover ' which is theirs by virtue of their nationality is of great value precisely to those many authors who cannot endure any restrictions on their intellectual freedom. It provides them with a firm, eminently res-pectable container for the hopes and ambitions that are constantly seething in their souls. The professional ' cover ' enjoyed by Novalis, for example, who roamed fancy free in the realm of the spirit, who was all spirit, is not simply an unimportant detail in his biography. It is of importance to know that in the corporeal world here below he was the son of an aristocratic manager of an Electoral Saxon salt-mine, that on graduating in the usual way from the Mining Academy he obtained a managerial post in the mine, and was able to compete with a fair chance of success for the prefecture of Thuringia. Without coming to grief through being turned in on itself, his sombre, limitless, sweet-intoxicated ego could mature and fully develop against this contrasting outer destiny of simplicity, goodness and clear definition. Similarly we must not lose sight of Mörike's post of pastor, of the professorships held by Schiller, A. W. Schlegel, Uhland, Rückert and Grimm, of the high state appointments held by Goethe, Friedrich Schlegel and Tieck. Bürger exercised authority, though with sighs and curses, as a magistrate in Altengleichen. Even the stupendous Kleist, whose thought was so unfathomably deep, who later fell on evil days, for whom ' there was no help on earth '—even Kleist found an official post of sorts for a time in Königsberg ; Chamisso became Deputy Director of the Botanical Gardens in Schöneberg, Eichendorff a Prussian governmental official (Lord Lieutenant of East Prussia), Zacharias Werner a canon in Poland, his no less fantastical fellow countryman, E. T. A. Hoffmann, not merely musical director of theatres but eventually, extraordinarily enough, a well-paid Appeal Judge in Berlin with a salary of a thousand thalers. Immermann was a judge, later a theatre manager, Grillparzer a court archivist who eventually even became a member of the Austrian House of Lords. All were no doubt insufficiently appreciated in their lifetimes and had reason to be embittered against their contemporaries. Still, they could hardly feel themselves to be absolutely rejected and hated by their contemporaries ; they could not feel as alien as Heine, for whom there was no place anywhere in his native land. It so happens, moreover, that we seldom recognize those who share our fate, or if we do, we fail to appreciate them at their true worth. Among the German poets of the day who were likewise without a homeland (besides Kleist and Grabbe, whose importance Heine realized) there were Hölderlin, that lofty spirit, whom I can find nowhere mentioned by Heine and, indeed, Count Platen, whom Heine misrepresented no less than Platen misrepresented and shamelessly attacked Heine himself.

During his stay in England Heine had seen a huge East Indiaman which had just berthed. He went on board and was surrounded by the Hindu crew. Their exotic colourful garments, their inscrutable mien, the strange way in which they moved about, made him feel ' as if he had enough of muffled Western life, as if he were tired of Europe.' The glimpse of the bright and gay life of the East was ' balm to his soul.' ' My heart was refreshed by a few drops, at any rate, of that draught for which I had so often thirsted in dreary Hanoverian and Royal Prussian winters' nights.' Although these words express the fashionable sentiment of the time as well as poetic nostalgia in general, the mood of dissatisfaction they reveal with Germany is unmistakable. It is a mood, admittedly, that has the usual Heinesque complications. In the same account of his English experiences he describes very finely how, the minute the German coast disappeared from sight, he felt ' a curious retrospective affection for the Teutonic nightcaps and the forests of periwigs ' that had aroused his distaste only a short while before when he took his leave of them. ' After losing sight of the Fatherland I found it in my heart again.' Subsequently, in Paris, this was to become a *motif* re-echoed with ever greater intensity.

In 1827, after the first great literary triumphs, it seemed as if Heine's fortunes had taken a turn for the better. Cotta, who had published Goethe and Schiller, invited him to take over the editorship of the *Politische Annalen* in Munich. Heine travelled in comfort from Hamburg. He broke his journey at Cassel, where Ludwig Emil Grimm drew his portrait (it is inscribed with the verses : 'Verdrossnen Sinn im kalten Herzen hegend/Schau ich verdriesslich in die kalte Welt'—With moody thoughts in my cold heart I look moodily out on to the cold world. He also stayed at Frankfurt, where he spent three days with Börne, and at Stuttgart. Here he made what was at first a very pleasant friendship with Wolfgang Menzel (the ' Informer,' later his bitterest adversary).

Heine stayed in Munich from the end of November, 1827, to July, 1828. He took his editorial duties lightly, leaving most of the work to his co-editor, L. Lindner. He himself contributed only a few articles (e.g. the *Englische Fragmente*) to Cotta's *Annalen*. Occasionally he would invite a friend to contribute something ' forceful ; not deliriously demagogic, but gravely exhortatory ; calculated to arouse independent thought or promote the cause of liberty.' He concentrated his energies on securing an academic post. It was not long before he felt himself to be ' surrounded by enemies and intriguing priests' (Letter to Detmold). Döllinger and Massmann (the latter afterwards became one of the chief targets of Heine's satire) were against him, and Schenk, the Bavarian Minister and poet, seems to have supported him but feebly.

He mixed freely in aristocratic and artistic society. But he told the footman of a princess, who brought him an invitation to take coffee at the palace immediately, as the princess had guests there : ' Convey my profound respects to Her Royal Highness and be so good as to tell her that I am accustomed to take my coffee where I have lunched.' A letter to Moser is similarly forthright :

> People think I shall tone down my attacks on the nobility now, as I'm at home with the aristocrats and in love with the most lovable aristocratic ladies—and am loved by them. But they are mistaken. My love for equality, my hatred of nobility and clergy, were never stronger than now, it has become almost an obsession with me. But if you want to do things, you've just got to be obsessed.

His health was poor; he found the Munich climate trying. The news of Therese's engagement plunged him into a scarcely concealed abyss of despair. A drop in the circulation of the *Annalen* led Cotta to suspend publication for six months, and Heine started on his long-planned Italian journey. Cotta wanted to re-engage him on his return, but the negotiations broke down and were not resumed till much later, from Paris. Nor did the announcement, which he had been hoping to hear all through his Italian journey, of his appointment as a professor materialize. He complains in letters to Schenk and Cotta.

Apart from these vocational worries, the Italian journey was one of the happiest periods in Heine's life. He writes from Bagni di Lucca ' where I am now bathing, gossiping with beautiful women, scrambling up the Apennines, and perpetrating innumerable follies.' The whole of Heine's travel-book *Italy* is written in this happy mood. If anything could palliate the attack on Platen in the last chapter of *The Baths of Lucca* it would be the joyful radiant high spirits of these few weeks of happiness. Their brilliance seems to shine even over the vicious Platen pamphleteering.

The two caricatures of assimilated Jewry in *The Baths of Lucca* are genuine creations, as has already been indicated. Baron Gumpelino is a snob who wallows in false sentiment. Hirsch-Hyazinth, his footman, is a simple soul quite incapable of forming any kind of judgment, but for all that miles and away better than his master. Though he is miseducated, he is honest. Once, when he was a lottery agent in Hamburg he had paid a client 50,000 marks in cash, even though the client had merely tipped, without actually drawing, the winning number. As the good Hirsch tells the story the comedy advances into a tale of legendary proportions. The hero, moved by the honesty he has ' committed,' describes how at the Last Judgment God will praise him in the presence of ' sun, moon, and stars,' and ' will straight away work out in his head ' that after deducting all his bad deeds there ' will still be a credit balance ' due to him out of the ' 50,000 marks for honesty.' What a blend of cosmic and commercial conceptions !

Heine is equally felicitous in Marquese Gumpelino's monologues. He pins down the Marquese, with his hyperboles and pleonasms, with such sureness of touch that it is hardly necessary for the author to comment at all. Listen to the Marquese (you recognise him immediately) :

Ja, Herr Doktor, were I to lose my money, which God forbid, I should still be a great connoisseur. Blindfold me in the gallery at Florence and I'll tell you the name of the artist who painted every picture you put me in front of, or at any rate, the school he belonged to . . . I know every actress in Germany, and her poets I know by heart. And as for Nature . . . ! Italy beats everything. How do you like the scenery here ? Have you seen anything like it ?

In the same style Hirsch, who emulates his master in everything, says : ' Are you here on pleasure too ? ' And he thinks nostalgically of his native Hamburg, where there was no need ' to climb so many dangerous mountains,' and ' to endure so much awful heat (*Hitzwärme*).' These word couplets (for example *Poesiegedicht*, too) are just in the very style of the two heroes ; how much uncertainty, how much labouring to do the right things at all costs, how much of the typically Jewish ' too much ' is revealed in their very mode of speech. And since it pillories a whole class of people, a manifestation of the age, and not an individual in his private capacity, the satire has an exhilarating quality—even though in Hamburg people could point to the originals, a Herr Gumpel and an Isak Rocamora, and even though uncle Salomon, of whom the banker Gumpel was a competitor, was on this occasion well pleased with his nephew's literary activities.

The satire on Platen, however (together with Platen's previous attack on Heine), are examples of how completely pointless and futile a literary polemic can be. Neither participant derived anything but grief from it. It failed to achieve, *could* not have achieved, the slightest practical result. This because each side was abusive but wide of the mark ; each warrior was fighting an imaginary opponent. Otokar Fischer summed it up very well in his Heine biography : ' Platen strikes out at a pseudo-Heine and Heine fights a phantom Platen rather than Platen himself.' The whole affair was a wretched senseless misadventure.

The historical facts, briefly, are these : In 1826 Heine had asked a few friends for contributions to the second volume of *Reisebilder*. At the time he wanted to bring out the *Reisebilder* regularly and make them a platform for the discussion of political and cultural questions. He always derived keen pleasure from extending his field of activity. As early as the *Nordsee* poems he had said : ' They show that I am not restricted to lyrical, mordant two-stanza poems.' Now he saw prospects of a new, broader horizon opening out before him : the formation of a school of like-minded poets. But only one answered the call. Immermann sent 36 epigrams, which Heine appended to his *Norderney* essay as 'coming from the pen of my esteemed co-worker.' Heine pointed out that he had marked with an asterisk those epigrams with which he could not associate himself. Among the epigrams not thus marked were five couplets under the heading: *Eastern Poets.* One of them alluded to Goethe and his imitators. 'Aged bard, thou call'st to mind the pied piper of Hamelin ; thou pipest towards East and all the dear little songsters follow thee.' And the last reads : 'These poor poets eat too freely of the fruit they steal from the garden groves of Shiraz, and then they vomit *Ghaselen'* (Platen's poems in the Persian style). This, then, was the harmless *casus belli* that led to all the scandal.

But Platen, sensitive, lonely, jealous of every successful author in Germany as he was—he considered them and the German-reading public his inferiors—Platen breathed immediate revenge. How could the 'Jew Heine' have the hardihood (he broods in a letter to Count Fugger) to 'treat so unmercifully someone who is patently greater than he, who can crush him ?' He feels he has a moral mission to purify German literary taste. He had already published an 'Aristophanic comedy,' *Die Verhängnisvolle Gabel,* directed against the drama-of-destiny playwrights. In the autumn of 1827 he was working in Sorrento on a new literary satire, the *Romantic Œdipus,* this time attacking Romanticism. In so doing he showed himself estranged from reality, for he himself had much in common with Romanticism, for all that he believed himself to be so far removed from it. One has only to think, for example, of his glorious, death-intoxicated poem, *Tristan: Wer die Schönheit angeschaut mit Augen.* In so far as he was at odds with the Romantic movement he was in complete alignment with Immermann and Heine themselves, for the reason that he, too, shared the humanism which Immermann and Heine had inherited from Goethe. In this trio of poets—Immermann, Heine, and Platen—humanism had developed into a conception of a mankind that, without neglecting the national elements in its heritage, was free, united and steadily marching towards progress. For all the more obvious features of Hellenic love of beauty and classicism of form that mark his poetry, Count Platen was one of those politically-liberal, anti-servile German poets who hated bondage in every shape and form. Platen, Heine, and Immermann, then, who were soon to present the world with the spectacle of a group of combatants locked in mortal conflict, had in fact, and unbeknown to themselves, spiritual affinities with one another. All three were border-line Romantics, all three were anti-reactionary.

Platen had arbitrarily made Immermann (disguised with feeble humour as 'Nimmermann') the chief character in his *Romantic Œdipus*. Quite unjustifiably he considered him the representative poet of German Romanticism. It must be held against Platen, indeed, that he took very little pains to acquaint himself with the subject of his satire—as is quite usual with polemicists in general. From Italy Platen wrote to Fugger, his best friend, asking him to tell him something of Immermann's *Andreas Hofer*; he had no desire to get to know the play in its entirety, just a few humorous excerpts, 'something of the plot, and the more strikingly nonsensical parts.' 'I've made him (*i.e.,* Immermann) a hyper-Romanticist in my new comedy, but all I've read of him is *Cardenio und Zelinde*.'

Platen, constantly travelling up and down Italy as he was, probably knew even less of Heine's writings than he did of Immermann's ; all the same, Heine was to 'have his salvo' fired at him. Fugger defended Heine in a letter. Platen's reply:

> It is beyond doubt that the epigrams are directed at Rückert and myself ; we are the 'little songsters.' Immermann's authorship of the epigrams is pardonable ; that Heine should have accepted them, endorsed them, and lampooned me through a third party is unpardonable and, incidentally, a typically Jewish manœuvre. Moreover, I understand the *Reisebilder* is a very popular book, so that he has told all Germany my poems are less than dirt (*etwas Gespieenes*). It seems to me I treated him far more gently than he me. If he has wit and talent, all the better for him. In any case, what someone who calls a botcher like Immermann his 'esteemed co-worker' thinks of me, and the way he judges me, is a matter of complete indifference. The fact that he is or was a Jew is no moral failing, though it is a comic ingredient in the whole situation. Discriminating critics will be able to judge whether I haven't used this ingredient with Aristophanic subtlety.

Platen had previously expressed the remarkable view, in writing of the *Verhängnisvolle Gabel*, that it was only epigrams which could be offensive, because they consisted exclusively of the offensive matter. 'In comedy, however, such mild outbursts as occur seem trifles. Even those affected by them will be carried away

by the charm of their form and will incline to forgiveness.' Strange
the illusionary theories by which even eminent people will judge
their own errors and transgressions more leniently than those of
their fellow-men. Their own excesses are classed as venial short-
comings or mere humorous sallies of 'Aristophanic subtlety';
other people's failings immediately become the grossest of crimes.
In political affairs, too, much of the havoc that has been loosed on
the world arises from this false perspective condemned by Jesus in
his parable of the mote and the beam.

Let us consider these 'trifles' and the charm of their form by
which Heine, the injured party, was to be 'carried away.' Let us
be quite clear, at the same time, that the analogy with Aristophanes
will not hold for modern times. As I have indicated earlier on, we
are no longer able to conjure up the mood of the Dionysian assem-
blies at which, apparently, nobody bore a grudge against anybody
else. In all fairness let us bear in mind also that Tieck had made
satirical comedy fashionable, that in the *Hyperboräischer Esel*
Kotzebue had attacked Schlegel and that Kotzebue was attacked in
his turn by Brentano, and so on. It was quite usual, therefore, for
literary men to indulge in mutual excoriation.

In the *Romantic Œdipus* Heine is called the 'Pindar of the
little tribe of Benjamin,' the 'Seed of Abraham.' Nimmermann dies
and calls 'Friend Hein' (death) to his side. 'You're mistaken, he's
not calling friend Hein, he's just entreating the glorious Petrarch
of the Feast of Tabernacles.' All extraordinarily unfunny; it is little
short of astonishing that a poet of refinement could indulge in such
pleasantries. 'Pride of the synagogue, who do you think you are?'
is another witticism. And again: 'It is your bosom friend, the most
shameless of all the mortal race of men.' Nimmermann replies:
'I am his friend, but I don't want to be his darling; his kisses
smell too much of garlic.'

All the same, Platen believed he had treated Heine 'far more
gently' than Heine had treated him. And all Heine had done had
been to print an epigram of Immermann's aimed at all *Ghaselen*
poets, without mentioning Platen's name. No doubt Platen, who
was living unappreciated, longing for some sign of affection in
Italy—he had made up his mind at the time never to return to
Germany—no doubt Platen was over-sensitive. But Heine had been
touched on his sorest point, too, the Judaism he had only just

renounced. And so Jewish destiny again decided the course Heine's life was to take. In all likelihood the whole distasteful polemic that now ensued and was destined to have such disastrous effects on Heine's contemporary and posthumous reputation would never have taken place had Platen attacked Heine at any other point than his Jewishness.

Heine tried to justify his attack as concerned with a question of principle. He wanted to expose Platen as the enemy of equality and the people, as an aristocrat and supporter of the clerical party— so he tried to persuade himself afterwards. He wrote to Varnhagen in 1830 that he ' *had* to make an example.' And:

> Of course, everybody thinks he's fighting his own particular battle when in fact he's merely fighting the public battle. I say this, because I lay no claim to a citizen's crown in my handling of the Platen affair ; I was fighting first and foremost for myself. But the reasons that led me to fight are to be sought in the general conflict. When the clericals in Munich first attacked me and brought up my Jewishness, I laughed—I thought they were plain silly. But when I scented a conspiracy, when I saw how the absurd ghost of my past gradually became a vampyre, when I saw through the intention of Platen's satire, when the book-sellers told me that similar poisonous productions were crawling about in manuscript—then I girded up my loins and hit out as hard and fast as I could. Robert, Gans, Michael Beer, and others, whenever they have been attacked as I have been, have always suffered in Christian fashion, have maintained a wise silence—I'm different, and it's good that it is so. It's good for the wicked to hit for once upon the right man who will carry out ruthless and pitiless retribution for himself and others.

All this would be very fair but for one thing: it is untrue from beginning to end. Platen took no part in the activities of the Munich clericals, although Ignaz Döllinger and he had been friends as young men ; he sided with the Liberal party of Ludwig I. It was the Liberal party to which he owed his ridiculously small pension of 500 gulden a year, which seemed to him to be more suitable ' as an encouragement to a beginner than as a recognition of a poet,' and of which he says the King ought to be a little ashamed of this ' clerk's pension ' (Max Koch, *Platens Leben und Schaffen,* I, 895). He enjoyed more of the literary-minded King's favour than did Heine, but was in no way to blame for the latter's failure to secure a University professorship at Munich.

Nor, in spite of occasional anti-Jewish outbursts, was Platen anti-Semitic. Had he been, he would hardly have let the Jew Schmuhl appear as chorus in the *Verhängnisvolle Gabel* and speak, representing the author, the sublime lines he does, as for instance: ' Und des Himmels Lampen löschen mit dem letzten Dichter aus '— And the lamps of heaven are extinguished when the last poet dies. The digs at Heine's Jewish origin are admittedly in poor taste ; still, it should not be overlooked that Börne's *Letters from Paris* later became Platen's favourite reading and that he wrote the following epigram on Lessing's *Nathan*:

> Deutsche Tragödien hab' ich in Masse gelesen, die beste
> Schien mir diese, wiewohl ohne Gespenster und Spuk:
> Hier ist alles, Charakter und Geist und der edelsten Menschheit
> Bild, und die Götter vergehn vor dem alleinigen Gott.

I have read innumerable German tragedies, this seemed to me the best, even though it has no ghosts or spooks. Everything is here: character and intellect and a portrayal of noblest humanity, and the gods disappear in the presence of the one God.

Heine's attack on Platen's politics is a classic example of polemical misunderstanding. Platen was not a whit reactionary ; among contemporary poets he was one of those whose political convictions were closest to Heine's. The similarity in their personal vicissitudes is striking, too. Both lived in voluntary exile outside Germany for many years, violently criticizing the German, and particularly the North German, way of life ; both revisited Germany for short intervals only, and then returned into exile, where they died ; the one in Paris, the other in Syracuse. Both wrote political ' Poems for the Times ' and throughout their lives waged a battle with the censorship, particularly Metternich's and the Prussian censorship. Platen's letters to his publishers in which he complains of the way in which his work has been mutilated by the censorship read exactly like Heine's letters to Campe on the same subject.

Really, of course, the two ought to have been friends, if only as opponents of the reactionary wing of German Romanticism. In spite of their differing æsthetic temperaments they ought to have been brought together by the actual tasks of the day. Compare, for example, Platen's eulogy of 'golden freedom' (in the *Verhängnisvolle Gabel*) ; in the same work Metternich, on the other hand, is declared to be a 'mortal being.' The poem *To a Die-hard* begins : ' You praise the days when your caste enjoyed tranquil happiness ? ' and goes on :

> You say the ruler's sceptre should command unlimited obedience, as if he were a man aiming his gun at wild animals ? You want to circumscribe speech, incarcerate the written and the spoken word ? In vain! Each glowing thought blazes a Bacchantic, immortal trail for itself.

The *Polenlieder* (' Polish Songs ') were even more outspoken. In the preface to a posthumous publication in 1849 the editors declare these poems to be ' the most glorious, the manliest, the most ardent song of freedom that ever sprang from a German poet's breast.' Platen's *Correspondence between a Berliner and a German* is in the same strain. There are whole passages in it which in their highly ironical tone might have been written by Heine. The theme of the correspondence is ' the Berliner's unconquerable enthusiasm for the Muscovites and the Tamerlanean principle.' ' They have misread my soul very badly,' writes Platen's Berliner to the German, ' if they think to offend me by calling me a servant. I am, thank God, the King's most submissive servant. . . . Nothing caused such displeasure here as the session in the French Chamber of Deputies at which certain speakers declared they were citizens of the State, but not subjects. Even the moderates were taken aback ; they were afraid our claim to the title of subjects would be disputed. People ran up and down the streets exclaiming : " We are subjects! We are subjects!" ' The ' epilogue ' attacking the ' murderous censor ' is equally outspoken. The poem's reckless concluding stanzas are barely quotable.

A particularly grotesque side to the tragic misunderstanding between Heine and Platen was that the latter, whom Heine castigated as a venal obscurantist, was provoked to his assault on Heine by his belief in Heine's venality. Platen's friend Rumohr, to whom Heine spoke in Florence, and who gave Heine the first intimation of Platen's contemplated attack, subsequently told Platen that Heine had told him (Rumohr) that ' if the princes would pay him, he'd write for the princes ; as long as they didn't

pay him, he'd write against them.' Rumohr's meddlesome gossiping
fanned the flames of Platen's ire. It is quite certain that the remark
about the princes had little more truth to it than Heine's leg-pulling
assertion in Wandsbeck that he had never read anything by
Claudius. His habit of ' shocking,' ' stunning ' people with his talk,
however, this time had the most unhappy results ; on this occasion,
moreover, he was unable to furnish such an unequivocal disavowal
as he had been able to do before, when he had quoted from Claudius.
At the same time, there was no doubt a grain of truth in Heine's
rodomontade. It might indeed be worth investigating whether such
facetious remarks are not frequently a façade erected by an uneasy
conscience (particularly in Heine is this often the case). There is
a compulsion to blurt something out. We find ourselves unable to
' bottle up ' what is so painfully uppermost in our minds, so we
' come out with it.' In doing so we exaggerate, and are thereby
enabled immediately to withdraw the confession we have just made
and declare it to be completely untrue.

It was not true, of course, that Heine was being ' paid ' by any
prince. We gather from a letter to Cotta, however, that he did
want to make the best possible impression on the King, on whom
the Munich professorship depended. In this connection it should
be borne in mind that the King of Bavaria was at that time a
pillar of Liberalism, of cultural and political progress ; in fact,
the antipode of Prussia. Heine would not have had to compromise
his intellectual integrity, therefore, in accepting the professorship.
This is quite evident from everything he wrote in Cotta's paper
immediately before starting on his Italian journey ; from the
English Fragments, with their encomium on Canning, ' the bold
bourgeois minister who sought to curb the power of the oligarchs,'
as well as from his criticism of Michael Beer's drama, *Struensee,*
which was performed at the Munich National Theatre towards the
end of March, 1828. The chief weight of this lengthy review is
brought to bear on the play's political significance. In it Heine
speaks of the ' noble indignation aroused by the inequality of the
classes,' and of ' every kind of privilege that is detrimental to whole
classes of people.' He praises the god who is greater than Apollo
and all the other gods on Olympus, the god of freedom. This
publication alone would be sufficient to refute the charge of
opportunism that is often brought against Heine in his Munich

period. Heine was much more an ebullient genius ruined by his own naïveté than a coolly calculating careerist.

All Heine's ebullience, however, and all his brilliant wit, cannot justify his attack on Platen. In it he does not confine himself to objective criticism of Platen's writings, but derides the Count's disastrous homosexual tendencies in language unbefitting civilized discussion. It may be that a suppressed homosexual urge of Heine's was partly responsible for the violence of his attack on Platen—a possibility I suggested when discussing Heine's ardent friendship with Christian Sethe.

It is not only the fact that Heine intersperses his literary criticism with the crudest attacks on Platen's private life that is so discreditable (Platen, too, did not discuss Heine's writings, but indulged in personalities at his expense). It is, above all, the *Tartuferie* of his attack and the way in which he summarily deals with the most intimate and highly delicate matters that is so offensive. In spite of his parade of open-mindedness on the subject, a certain priggishness to which he always tended in secret is indeed observable in Heine's love life and in the views he held on the nature of love. It appears at its worst again in his attack on Börne. Even this priggishness, though, is connected with a better side of his nature in which he revealed something of the depths of Jewish character and tradition ; namely, the discipline and modesty that is a special quality of the Jewish race in sexual matters. Heine himself drew attention to this quality in his appreciation of Jessica (*Shakespeare's Maidens and Women*):

> The chastity of the Jews is perhaps due to the opposition in which they always stood to the oriental cult of sensuality and voluptuousness which at one time rankly luxuriated among their Egyptian, Phœnician, Assyrian, and Babylonian neighbours, an opposition which, with continual modifications, has survived to this day. The Jews are a chaste, continent, I would say, abstract people, and in their moral purity they come closest to the Germanic races.

There are two comments to make on this: that when this strict traditional Jewish discipline is loosened it frequently gives way to prudery (even more frequently it gives way to its exact opposite, complete sexual licence, unless a new sense of Jewish national consciousness is able to make the Jew realize his responsibilities);

and that, as it happens, Count Platen by all accounts kept his tendencies under control in a truly heroic manner, so that here, too, Heine's attack was futile.

Among Platen's posthumous papers epigrams were found even coarser and more obtuse than anything the two men had published before. But Platen had the good taste to keep these verses locked up in his desk, and he never replied to Heine's attack in any way.

It is something in Heine's favour, perhaps, that he later appraised Platen more justly. He deleted the chapter on Platen from the French edition of the *Reisebilder*. It appears from one or two remarks in his letters that he wanted to eliminate it from the German edition, but in all probability refrained from doing so to avoid incurring the charge that he had not the courage of his convictions. At any rate, in the *Romantische Schule* he accords Platen the distinction of being (with Schlegel) 'Germany's greatest prosodist.' Could Heine the lyric poet really be insensitive to the inexpressible enchantment of Platen's verse ? Even the poems he quotes derisively in his attack outshine in their flawless beauty the whole murky invective.

In his later years Heine regretted the whole affair. It is certain this had nothing to do with the nasty impression it created on friend and foe at the time. The whole controversy had long since become academic by the time Heine's more indulgent attitude to Platen became known. Heine evidently felt in retrospect the need to achieve justice between his dead opponent and himself. In *Romanzero* the poem *Plateniden* is much more restrained in tone and only censures Platen's vaingloriousness. ' Platen had learnt the art of poetical cookery from A to Z—all he lacked was a joint and a stove,' said Heine (still wrongly) to Alfred Meissner in 1847. He showed he had at this stage reached a proper view by going on to say: ' But that doesn't mean he deserved the attacks I made on him. I wish I had never given the offending chapters in the *Baths of Lucca* to the world.' Another visitor relates that in the same year Heine, after lauding Immermann, suddenly came to speak of Platen. ' The whirligig of time! Of a sudden he did full justice to this noble spirit and heartily regretted attacking a man who had cultivated the noblest trends in poetry and whose continuously increasing powers he said he had underestimated.'

There is no record of Platen having expressed in the years

remaining to him (they were in any case short, he died in 1835)
a single word showing any desire to atone for the wrong he had
done Heine or giving any indication that he had reached a better
understanding of him. And that perhaps is the only point in which
his opponent has really been able to claim the victory over him.

It needs some effort to recall that the background to the attack
on Platen was the joyous abandon of Heine's Italian journey.
Heine possessed the admirable quality of being able to give himself
over completely to these isolated periods of happiness in his life.
His native resilience enabled him to forget his previous worries
and to gain from the joyous present new courage with which to
meet the troublous times that lay ahead. It was as well for one
of his pugnacious and at the same time sensitive disposition that
this *carpe diem* faculty was his. It saved him from premature
collapse.

The happiness of this period of Southern travel is reflected in
the associations that come tumbling after one, another, in the
numerous felicitous images and tropes, never forced, with which
the prose of his Italian travel-book is studded. Without indulging
in much preliminary study he went to Italy prepared to absorb all
the country had to offer. He found a land romantic but teeming
with vitality, and populated by English miladies and black-eyed
ballet dancers. He loved and was loved, but here, too, the
'cynical' poet has given us no names. We know less about his
amorous adventures than we do about those of many finely
sensitive authors who practise a studied reticence. In the midst of
all this rapturous bliss in Florence he was filled with forebodings
about his father. He abandoned his plan of continuing his journey
to Rome and returned to Germany. Samson Heine had died of a
stroke in Hamburg on 2nd December, 1828. His son stood by his
grave in the Jewish cemetery at Altona.

In a letter to Friederike Robert written six months later from
Potsdam, whither he had gone from Hamburg to finish the third
volume of the *Reisebilder,* which he had begun in Bagni di Lucca,
Heine described the sudden change that had taken place in his
situation. He had 'nothing left in him'; he wanted to die.

Ah, ill and miserable as I am, I am now depicting—it seems
a joke directed against myself—the most brilliant period in

my life. It was a time when I ran exulting from one peak of
the Apennines to the other, when the ichor of youth and
amorous bliss filled my veins, and I dreamt great wild dreams
in which my fame spread the whole world over to the farthest
islands, and old sea-salts would tell of my deeds seated by
their fires in the evening. How tame I have become now since
the death of my father! Now I wish for nothing better than to
be an old tabby sitting by a warm fire in some such far-flung
island and to listen to others reciting tales of famous deeds.

He discusses his father's death with Christiani and says:

> Yes, yes, they talk about seeing him again in transfigured
form. What use is that to me? I know him in his old brown
frock-coat, and that's how I want to see him again. That's how
he sat at the table, salt-cellar and pepper-pot in front of him,
one on the right and the other on the left, and if the pepper-
pot happened to be on the right and the salt-cellar on the left,
he turned them round again. I know him in his brown frock-
coat, and that's how I want to see him again.

The drawing for which Heine sat to Franz Kugler shows him
with dreamy, melancholy features. He is looking blankly ahead.
There is a nervous downward twitch in one corner of the mouth.
The narrow head with its mass of hair rests in his right hand, his
left hand lies loosely on his knees. The high turned-up stiff collar
of the ' Biedermeier ' jacket emphasises the spirituality of the oval,
beardless face. In the left-hand margin Heine wrote the words:
' This is how I looked this morning, 6th April, 1829.—H. Heine.'
This portrait and a later one from his Paris period showing him
with bowed head, closed eyelids, small imperial beard have
contributed most to the popular visual image of Heine.

The third volume of *Reisebilder* appeared early in 1830. It was
immediately banned in Prussia. Heine, who had gained a wide
reputation as a lyric poet, was now also known through his two
previous *Reisebilder* volumes as a champion of Liberalism in
politics. In some of the German States every word he wrote was
rigorously examined for subversive tendencies. Moreover, the
Platen affair had had disastrous repercussions. Varnhagen was the
only one of his friends to defend him. Immermann was silent.
Some, like Michael Beer and Fritz Veit, refused to have anything
more to do with him. Hardest of all to bear was the loss of his
devoted friend Moser.

However, a small group of friends had gathered round the sorely tried poet in Hamburg: August Lewald the producer; Lyser the artist; Merckel, a young business man and friend of the arts; Töpfer, a writer of comedies; above all, Ludolf Wienbarg, who later became one of the leaders of 'Young Germany.' Light-hearted conversation, amateur theatricals, flirtations, visits to the theatre were the order of the day. Only the demonic eruption of Paganini shattered the calm of this provincial idyll.

Wienbarg has given us a graphic description of Heine's appearance at this time. Before he got to know him in person he had pictured him from his writings as a combination of Faust and Mephistopheles. ' Accordingly, when I first met him I had expected to find a bursting, dynamic, life-and-soul-of-the-party personage; the sensitive features, distinguished appearance, quiet and friendly bearing I actually saw came as no little surprise.' On another occasion he described him thus: 'Although he had been comfortably installed for some months in a respectable Hamburg dwelling, he gave me the impression of having just got out of the stage-coach and having spent a rough night at an inn.' There was something of the Wandering Jew about him. He could not settle down. Germany was not destined to keep him much longer.

Heine spent the summer of 1830 in Heligoland. ' Women are the bane of my existence here,' he writes to Immermann. ' I believe if I went to Nova Zembla I should be plagued by female singers and dancers. Regarding the former, barely do I succeed in getting rid of one when another attaches herself to me.'

He tired of the guerrilla warfare of politics and longed to get back to poetry. In the Heligoland chapters of his book on Börne, which are among his prose masterpieces, he described what was later to be an often-recurring mood:

> What an irony of fate that I, who would like nothing better than to luxuriate in a life of serene meditation, have been called upon to shake my poor fellow-Germans out of their comfortable existence and goad them into activity! I, who would like best of all to watch the passing clouds, to weave word-spells in rhyme, to listen to the secrets of the elemental spirits and to lose myself in the magic world of old legends. . . . I had to edit political annals, publicize the needs of the time, instigate revolutionary demands, arouse passions, pinch the poor

German Michel's nose all the time so as to get him to wake
from his health-giving giant's sleep. . . .

The cause of progress was at a lower ebb than ever. Even in
France, the Promised Land of the Revolution, the Jesuits were in
power; the ' great retreat continues.' Italy was enslaved by Austria.
And America seemed to the poet to be a ' huge prison of liberty,'
where ' the most repulsive tyrant of all, the mob, exercises its
brutal dominion.'

Heine was never a democrat of the extreme egalitarian kind,
still less a Communist. What fascinated him was the romantic side
of revolution, the heroic self-sacrifice of the popular leaders, the
supra-individual valour attained by the revolutionary group through
the willing submersion of the individual within it—also the negative
side: the abolition of unjust privilege. He had little idea of what
to do once the positive aims of the revolution were achieved. He
failed to take into account the possible results of the revolution.
It is this that makes it so difficult to find any element of consistency
in his politics.

He found relief from the general political stagnation in reading.
He re-read the Old Testament, delighted in the fragrance of the
' tenderest feelings of morality,' skimmed the pages of Byron and
Plutarch, shuddered at the death of his beloved Greek gods, heard
the cry in the old saga: ' Great Pan is dead!'

He also read Mignet's history of the Revolution. Afterwards
it seemed to him that all his studies in Heligoland referred to the
great events the news of which overtook him on the island. ' Just
as there are birds,' he wrote to Varnhagen,

> who know in advance that some physical revolution like
> thunderstorm, earthquake, or flood is about to ensue, so there
> are people in whose minds social revolutions are heralded in
> advance. It induces a general atrophy and has a strangely
> enervating effect on them. So I account for my condition this
> year till the end of July. I was vigorous and healthy and yet
> I could do nothing but study revolutionary history day and
> night. For two months I bathed in Heligoland. When the news
> of the great week reached me there it seemed to me to be
> something obvious, as if it were merely a continuation of my
> studies.

It was the Paris July revolution, the ' great week ' whose echo
had reached the island.

The thick bundle of newspapers with their heart-warming, red-hot news from the mainland. . . . They were rays of sunshine wrapped up in printed paper and they set my heart aflame in a fierce conflagration. I felt I could set the ocean alight right up to the North Pole with the flares of the enthusiasm and the wild joy that blazed within me.

On the 25th July the Bourbon King Charles X and his clericalist Minister, Polignac, had by their 'July ordinances' brought off a long-prepared *coup* against the young constitutional life of France. The Chamber was dissolved, freedom of the press suspended, the suffrage restricted. The next day the population of Paris came out on the barricades; on the 28th and 29th the army went over to the revolutionaries. On the 30th Louis Philippe of the House of Orleans, which from the Palais Royal had been in the van of the original Revolution, entered Paris on the invitation of Thiers and other Parliamentarians. The aged Lafayette appeared with him on the balcony of the Hôtel de Ville, the revolutionary tricolour replaced once more the banner of white lilies, the 'citizen monarchy' was inaugurated.

Heine rejoiced :

Lafayette, the tricolour, the Marseillaise. I feel intoxicated. Daring hopes surge passionately within me. . . . My longing for peace and quiet has gone. I know once more what I ought, what I *must* do. . . . I am the son of the Revolution and grasp once more the charmed weapons on which my mother once pronounced her enchanted blessing. . . . Flowers, flowers! I want to garland my brow for the death struggle. And the lyre as well, give me my lyre, that I may sing a battle song. . . . . Words like flaming stars that shoot down from on high and burn the palaces and light up the cottages.

This antithesis was to re-echo shortly afterwards in Georg Büchner's 'Peace to the cottages, war on the palaces!' Heine's great experience in those days was his sense of kinship with the common people.

Even the poor Heligolanders rejoice, although they only understand what has happened instinctively. The fisherman who took me over yesterday to the little sandy island from which I bathe greeted me laughingly with the words : 'The poor people have conquered.' Yes, perhaps the common people understand better with their instinct what is happening than

we do with all our intellectual resources. I remember once
Frau von Varnhagen telling me how before the outcome of
the Battle of Leipzig was known her maid suddenly rushed
into her room with a startled cry: 'The nobles have won!'
This time it is the poor people who have wrested the victory.

Heine was particularly impressed by the fact that there had
been 'no excesses' in the July days.

The Parisians have given us such a splendid example of
mercy. Of a truth, you deserve to be free, you French, for you
carry freedom in your hearts. Therein you differ from your
poor fathers who rose from centuries of bondage and after all
their heroic deeds carried out those insane atrocities which
forced the spirit of mankind to cover her eyes. This time the
people's hands became bloodstained only in the course of
justified self-defensive actions, not after the battle was over.
The people themselves bound up the wounds of their enemies,
and when the deed was done went quietly about their daily
business again without asking so much as a tip for the great
work they had done!

Heine's literary contribution to the year of revolution consisted
of the *Supplements to the Travel Pictures*. They contained *The City
of Lucca* and the *English Fragments* with the addition of a new
chapter, *The Liberation*.

Freedom is a new religion (we read in *The Liberation*),
the religion of our times. Although Christ is not the God of
this religion, he is one of its high priests, and his name fills the
hearts of the disciples with bliss. It is the French, however,
who are the Chosen People of the new religion, the first
gospels and dogmas were recorded in their language.

This utterance reveals the influence on Heine of the new
doctrine of Saint-Simonism, a creed which sought to synthesize
socialist ideas and the religious framework of a 'New
Christianity.' In the light of Saint-Simonism Heine saw Jesus as
one who was 'born a Dauphin of heaven but who nevertheless
was a good democrat. One who disliked the pomp and ceremony
of courts because he was not the god of an aristocracy of tonsured
scribes and braided generals and because he was a humble god of
the people, a citizen god, *un bon dieu citoyen*.'
With these ideas fresh in his mind Heine met Buchez, a disciple

of Saint-Simon and a theoretician of the modern co-operative movement. Later the two men argued furiously in Alfred de Vigny's salon in Paris: Buchez wanted to achieve for his own moderate form of Saint-Simonism a world-embracing organization modelled on that of Roman Catholicism, which indeed he would have liked to reform along his own lines ; Heine, however, for some years afterwards inclined more and more emphatically to a joyous, Hellenizing paganism that accorded more with the views of another of Saint-Simon's disciples, ' Père ' Enfantin, the champion of ' free woman.' Subsequently Heine quickly parted company from the sexual extravagances of Enfantin and his supporters. He jibbed as much at ' collective ownership of women ' as previously his deep-rooted family instincts had caused him to denounce Platen's homoeroticism with an excessive degree of fierce holier-than-thou moral indignation. For his paganism he later sought new paths before dismissing it with a melancholy smile and returning to the God of his fathers.

Heine's pæan of a new Saint-Simonian Christianity in *The City of Lucca* forms a brightly coloured background to his attacks on church and nobility.

The fact that he concentrated his attack exclusively on these two classes of society is probably due to his more youthful memories (the Hanoverian Junkers in Göttingen, etc.!), but the events of the day also played their part. The reactionary régime of the Bourbons which had been overthrown in 1830 derived its chief support, just as did the restoration régimes of the Metternich era, from these ' privileged ' classes. It was against them accordingly that Heine primarily directed his attacks. But he was not blind to the profound changes that were being brought about by industrialization and large-scale capitalism. Thus he writes to Varnhagen:

> I am well aware that the revolution embraces all social classes and that the nobility and the clergy are not its only enemies. But for greater effect I have concentrated my fire on these two classes as being the sole forces joined in alliance against the revolution. Personally I hate the *aristocratie bourgeoise* much more. If my book contributes to the emancipation of people's minds in matters of religion in Germany, where they are religious to the core, I shall be very pleased, and will endure with equanimity the inevitable howls of the pious.

For the time being, then, Heine left the capitalists alone. He even professed to find a progressive-revolutionary element in the activities of the Rothschilds, in contrast to Börne, who hated and attacked them. Later, indeed, he modified his views. He came to perceive the *juste milieu* and what he called the *juste millionnaire*. ' Not for themselves have the people bled and fought, from time immemorial not for themselves, but for others. In July, 1830, they won a victory for a *bourgeoisie* that was as worthless as the aristocracy it replaced.' These words were the sad echo of ' nine years after.' Even so, the fact remains that Heine's assaults were first and foremost launched against church and nobility, in the tradition, still, of the great revolution of 1789.

In *The City of Lucca* Heine blames the ancient Egyptians and their pupils, the Jews, for having made the Church an intellectual strait-jacket, a receptacle for containing an official religion. *En passant,* he calls the Jews the ' people who started all the trouble ' (*Urübelvolk*). Among the Greeks there was no such enforcement of the official religion. (But what about the trial of Socrates ?) It was the Jews who first introduced State religion, ' dealing in souls,' making converts and ' all those sacred outrages ' which ' had cost the human race so much blood and tears.' Highly questionable as is this Heinesque version of history, we may more readily assent to Heine's general view of religion. He honours ' the inner sanctity of every religion,' but castigates its association with the State power, the secular control of the State and its bayonets. In modern terminology Heine is in favour of the separation of Church and State ; he is not opposed to religion as such.

Heine would like to be loyal to the throne; ' his deepest convictions ' lead him ' to support the idea of kinghood, the monarchical principle.' With all the more vigour he rejected the nobility who, together with the clergy, placed themselves between king and people. This viewpoint, which Heine had already expressed in 1830 in *The City of Lucca,* is his best defence to the charge that he only supported the citizen monarchy because of the pension he received from the Thiers ministry from 1836. In 1831, too, he had expounded the same thesis in an introduction to a book, *Kahldorf on Aristocracy,* in which he advocated ' a citizen-king without court etiquette, without aristocratic hirelings, without courtesans, without match-makers, without *pourboires* of diamonds and similar flummeries.' And again in 1832 he pointed out more specifically and with considerable insight, in one of his Paris articles (the intermediate note to the ninth article), that the effect of a written constitution would be nullified as long as the kings had an entourage of nobles. ' Once we belonged to the kings, now they belong to us. Accordingly we must educate them ourselves and not leave them any longer to the tender mercies of those high-born princely tutors who educate them in the service of their own caste and cripple them body and soul. Nothing exposes the people to greater peril than the way in which crown princes are surrounded from their infancy by these court Junkers.' Heine attacked the nobility on the one side just as, on the other, he was opposed, as a constitutional monarchist, a man of the centre all his life, to radical Jacobinism, to the Republic. Fundamentally, he found the citizen-monarchy by far the most congenial political form. For this reason he considered himself entitled later on to accept from it a pension which could not effect any change in his views. When he disagreed with the Thiers ministry, e.g. in the Damascus affair, he did not mince his words, regardless of the possible forfeiture of his pension. In this matter of the pension, which has been the subject of so much misunderstanding, Heine again showed himself to be a man of consistent courage in the most trying circumstances.

The July revolution reverberated and was imitated in Belgium, Poland, Italy, and Switzerland. In Germany, too, the people rose. But the unpopular Duke of Brunswick was the only prince to lose his throne. And in Southern Germany there were a few Liberal amendments to the constitution. These things apart, in Germany the clamour for freedom simply resulted in the government adopting a more reactionary policy. In his epilogue to the *Travel Pictures* Heine declared that invisible but even thicker prison walls were closing in on the German people. He and those who thought like him were generals without an army. Seven Göttingen professors, among them the brothers Grimm and Gervinus, protested at the violation of the constitution. Fritz Reuter went to prison, started on his ' period of incarceration.' Uhland and Rotteck were relieved of their Chairs. As Heine said, ' a new, dismal, depressing period ' had started. He compared himself with Kunz von der Rosen, Maximilian's court jester, who had rescued the emperor from his imprisonment. 'Oh, my German Fatherland! My dear German people! I am your Kunz von der Rosen.' And the emperor speaks to his rescuer, the jester—he cannot believe that his jester can free him: 'Kunz von der Rosen, my jester, what will you do if I regain my freedom? '—' I will sew new bells on my cap.'—'And how shall I reward your loyalty? '—' Oh, dear Sire, let me not be killed.'

Heine arrived in Paris at the beginning of May, 1831. He had started on his journey from Hamburg in mid-April, stopping for a few days at Hanover, Cassel, Frankfurt, and Heidelberg *en route*. He travelled in comfort ; he was not fleeing, nor was he going into forced exile. No sudden catastrophe, no one reason that could be pinned down, had led him to his momentous decision. It was just that he had begun to feel that in Germany it was gradually becoming more difficult for him to breathe, that in Germany there was no opportunity anywhere for him to do the work he wanted to do.

His last letters from Germany to Varnhagen are full of new plans for acquiring ' resources ' of one kind or another. He had fallen out with his uncle once more, then patched matters up ' so that in the event of a sudden blow I can at least have some protection.' 'But I am keeping this purely for a desperate emergency,' the letter goes on,

> and I shall do all I can to get a steady post at all costs. I can't do anything otherwise. If I can't get such a post very shortly in Germany I shall go to Paris, where, unfortunately, I should have to take on a rôle which would spell the ruin of all my belletristic and poetical talents, and where the seal would be placed on my break with Germany's rulers. Meanwhile, I'm not taking any steps until I hear from you whether there isn't a chance of my being able to get something in Berlin—or Vienna(!). I shall leave no stone unturned and shall take desperate decisions only in a desperate situation.

At the beginning of April he dreamed every night he was packing his bags and leaving for Paris ' to breathe fresh air, to dedicate myself wholly to the sacred emotions of my new religion and perhaps to be finally ordained as its priest.'

He never dreamt he would have to spend all the rest of his life as an émigré. He had intended his stay in Paris to be of short duration. In point of fact it was to last twenty-five years, broken only by two brief visits to his mother in Hamburg. But he had an accurate presentiment of what was to come when he wrote that his rôle in Paris would involve him more and more in politics and bring him into ever sharper conflict with the German rulers. Looking back, he speaks (again in a letter to Varnhagen, in 1833) of the ' most painful emotions ' he experienced when leaving Germany. ' And yet duty and prudence alike counselled departure. I had the choice between laying down my arms completely and life-long combat. I chose the latter, and certainly not lightly. That I did take up arms, however, was forced on me by the way in which I found myself scorned, by the insolence of those who arrogantly claimed a superiority of birth—in my cradle were my marching orders for the rest of my life.'

X

Paris

' IF ANYONE asks you how I'm getting on here, tell them:
" Like a fish in water " ; or, rather, tell them that when one fish
asks another fish how he's getting on, the reply is: " Like Heine
in Paris." '

Practically all Heine's letters and recorded utterances during
his early Paris period are in this strain, until sickness and financial
difficulties cast their dark shadows. ' Things have put me on top
of the world, on top of the world, in Paris,' he triumphed. He
felt himself blissfully being sucked under ' in the maelstrom of
events, in the waves of the day, in the seething revolution.' He
was ' all phosphorus now.' ' And while I'm drowning in a sea
of human beings I'm also being consumed by the fire of my own
nature.' He was homesick, it is true. ' I'm painfully parodying
Danton. It's painful walking in the Luxembourg and dragging a
piece of Hamburg or a piece of Prussia or Bavaria on the soles
of your shoes with you wherever you go.' All the same, he sums
up: ' I can't be worse off here than in my own country, where
there is nothing for me but struggling and poverty, where I can't
sleep safely, and where all the springs of life are poisoned for me.'
His position is ' outwardly brilliant.' He is ' practically crushed by
the extraordinary honours ' lavished on him. True, his ' colossal
reputation ' is not without its drawbacks ; he is annoyed,
embarrassed, fatigued by it. But all in all he feels relaxed, free,
secure, happy.

Even in the terrible last years of his illness his eye would light up and his voice take on a more cheerful note when he spoke of his break-through to Paris. It had the same revitalizing effect on him as the flight to Italy had on Goethe. ' I had done and suffered much, and by the time the sun of the July revolution burst forth in France I was feeling very tired and needed to recuperate,' he wrote in the *Confessions*. His description of his crossing of the Rhine is full of high spirits. Father Rhine, they told him, was sitting at the bottom of the river studying French grammar: *J'aime, tu aimes, il aime, nous aimons.* In the distance the Strasbourg Minster shook its head as once old faithful Eckart did when he saw the young wight heading for the Venusberg. Admittedly, when he reached Paris he found that the inscriptions of ' Liberty, Equality, Fraternity' had once again been erased from the street corners. There follows shortly afterwards a very sober criticism of Louis Philippe, the citizen king, and his system. Eschewing phrase-making, Heine examines with penetrating insight the king's personal characteristics.

For the moment, however, he had eyes and ears only for the gaiety and friendliness of the Parisians. They restored his good temper, so sorely tried by German rudeness and surliness.

For the first time I heard loud Gallic laughter. We don't know what it is in Germany. It is good-tempered and mocking at the same time, like the delightful noble French wines or a chapter of Rabelais. Nothing is more infectious than such gaiety, and I began to laugh with a real heartiness that I had never been able to achieve in the home country.

He plunged enthusiastically into the round of dance-hall visiting. His description of the Grande Chaumière is a masterpiece of good-humoured reporting and feminine psychology. Oh, the unforgettable little Fifine, so appetizing and so full of appetite, who, to use her own expression, ' identifies herself with an orange' (i.e., eats it up with enjoyment). ' Just imagine, I've had no education,' she says, ' all the natural history I know I've taught myself.' Then comes the brilliant sketch of a can-can dancer, followed by that of Victor Bohain, whose verve and skill had enabled him to found a periodical, *L'Europe Littéraire*. This was the paper in which Heine made his bow to the French public with his essays on the ' Romantic School,' shortly after the French translation of his

Harz Journey in the *Revue des Deux Mondes* had scored a great success.

Heine sees Victor Bohain—he had also founded the *Figaro*—as a second Vulcan stumping with his wooden leg round the table and pouring out champagne for his guests. A cheerful *entrepreneur.* He presented the shareholders of *L'Europe Littéraire* with an expense account of a hundred thousand francs. Many years later Heine came across him in a provincial town. With great eloquence he was telling a local burgess how he could put him in the way of picking up a million.

How well we know him, this resourceful latter-day merchant adventurer who flourished in the golden age of capitalism! He is none other than M. Arnoux, the celebrated founder of *L'art industriel* in the book of books: I mean Flaubert's *Education Sentimentale.* This is in fact the book which will best help us to get the feel of the age in which Heine lived in Paris. (Next to Plato's and Goethe's writings and the Old Testament it is the book I have most greatly admired and loved.)

As we read the well-loved paragraphs of the 'Education' again and again we feel, almost, that our reading of other books has been nothing but a pointless waste of time. Whereas we read the book before, though, for its impassioned writing, its genuine ardour and deep melancholy, we may now concentrate on the many admirable political reflections it contains. Here we may view the portrait of the age itself: its dissatisfactions and its spurious satisfactions, its luxury and its romanticism, and the impending battle-cries of the masses looming darkly on the horizon. Here we may see the symbol of the *bourgeois* monarchy and its admirable utilitarian maxims, the well-known lithograph depicting the whole royal family engaged in the most edifying occupations: Louis Phillipe holding a copy of the Code in his hands, the queen a prayer-book, the princesses embroidering, the Duke of Nemours girding on his sword ; Monsieur de Joinville showing his younger brothers a map ; in the background a double bed. This picture, called 'A Good Family,' was the delight of the *bourgeois,* the despair of the revolutionaries. Here, too, we may meet the Socialist theoretician, M. Sénécal, who annotates Rousseau's *Social Contract,* who devours the *Revue Indépendente,* as well as studying the works of Mably, Moselly, Fourier, Saint-Simon, Comte, Cabet,

Louis Blanc, the 'whole pack of Socialist writers' (says Flaubert, and Heine, for all his aversion to the privileged classes, says much the same thing) 'who want to reduce mankind to the level of a barracks, to entertain them in brothels, and condition them to counting-houses. Out of a hotch-potch of this kind he had rigged up his ideal of a virtuous democracy, in the double aspect of a small country estate and a large spinning-mill, a kind of American Sparta where the individual exists only to serve society, which is much more all-mighty, absolute, infallible, and divine than all your Grand Lamas and Nebuchadnezzars.'

As a counterpoise to M. Sénécal, and no more congenial, is the room which serves as study to Dambreuse the banker. The mirror on the wall is flanked by the portrait of the King on one side and of a general on the other. There are two huge safes in the room. Dambreuse could stand for Rothschild. We may imagine Heine being received in Dambreuse's counting-house ; he would frequent, too, Mme. Dambreuse's luxurious and voluble salon. Then he would be off to join the artists and Bohemians enjoying Arnoux's hospitality, then he would mingle with students and grisettes, go to dances, meetings, talk politics with the ambitious M. Deslauriers. Perhaps, before hurrying off to write his reports on the art exhibitions, he would listen to M. Pellerin expounding every conceivable theory of painting, and perhaps he would also meet— let us hope he did—the simple-hearted clerk who reduced all the impassioned and rhapsodizing Don Juans to silence by declaring, when they asked him *his* view: 'I—I would always love the same one!' 'It was said in such a way that a momentary silence ensued ; some were startled by such candour, to others perhaps it revealed the secret longing of their own souls.' Among these latter would have been Heine. Forcing back his tears on such an occasion, he would have thought of his Germany. In Paris Germany assumed an increasingly idealized form for him, although he steadfastly continued to recognize and denounce the failings of its rulers. In Paris, and not before, did he acquire the proper detached affection for, and affectionate detachment from, the German people and the German character.

He was the Paris correspondent of Cotta's *Morgenblatt* and *Allgemeine Zeitung*. These two papers, published in Augsburg, had a dominating influence in the Liberal circles of Germany and,

indeed, of Europe. He wrote his reports on ' French Painters ' for
the *Morgenblatt*. At the same time he acted as the intermediary of
German Romanticism, German philosophy, and German religious
formularies to the French public. In these fruitful years he
rendered valuable service to both sides through his endeavours to
promote mutual understanding between the two nations. Nothing
of the kind had been attempted since Madame de Staël's
De L'Allemagne ; Heine was the first to take up the thread. He
always took his mission as a conciliator very seriously. ' The great
task to which I dedicated my life was the bringing about of a
cordial understanding between Germany and France,' he solemnly
declared in his testament. Did Heine succeed in his task ? Let us
answer this question with a maxim of Goethe's : ' The man of
action strives to do what is right ; whether what is right is done
need not worry him.' In any case, Heine has left ample scope for
those men of good will who wish to continue his work in this field.

The political background of the era comes through clearly in
Heine's articles on the Paris art exhibitions. It is this which gives
them a permanent value transcending their significance as feuilletons
and converts them into source-material for the historian. Heine
was aware of the political function he exercised in these articles ;
on the other hand his artistic judgment, which couples Delacroix
and Horace Vernet as of *equal* worth, does not concern us unduly.
The paintings are practically all considered with reference to their
subject-matter ; Delacroix's magnificent picture of revolution is no
exception. An artist who paints ' Cromwell by the body of Charles
I ' enables Heine to launch into a disquisition on regicide and
popular revolt. In the process many ideas of significance emerge,
but none concerned with painting. Occasionally we do get important
glimpses of Heine's own views on the nature of art ; the expression
of these views furnished the few bright spots in his Platen polemic,
too. In both works Heine's enthusiasm for the touch of nature
asserts itself, for the essential simplicity and uniqueness of genius.
No rules ! But no mere copying of nature either ! ' In art I am a
supernaturalist '—the cry of all great artists !

Suddenly the tranquillity of the exhibition halls is shattered by
the agonized cry of the demonstrating crowds : ' Warsaw has fallen !
Our front-line has fallen ! Down with the ministers ! War on the
Russians ! Death to Prussia ! '

Embittered though he was by the anti-Liberal turn of policy of which the Polish insurgents were the victims, Heine remained a supporter of the principles of constitutional monarchy. In his article on the exhibition of 1833 he wrote that these principles were the 'last guarantee of our society' and rejected the republican idea, particularly for Germany.

He attacked the German demagogues (that is, Börne's circle and those émigrés who were even more to the left than Börne) for 'blindly aping the French in urging a German republic.' We must remember this in our general appraisal of Heine; too often his constitutional monarchism is either blandly passed over or put down, quite absurdly, as opportunism. Heine was never an opportunist in matters of political principle. He always consistently favoured a constitutional monarchy, which for him was the *juste milieu*. All he can be blamed for is the excessively formalistic nature of his approach to the question. This is quite a different matter, however, from the charges of trimming, vacillation, and insincerity levelled at him by many of his contemporaries and nearly all his biographers. It is obvious that a sincere person—a sincere person most of all— can only find the middle path through constant experimental groping and clear-eyed endeavour. With the self-seeking of which Heine has been accused—unjustly, in my opinion—this groping and endeavour has no point of contact at all. Heine's politics will be condemned outright only by those who believe that salvation for mankind is to be found in rigid extremes, and not in some midway, admittedly flexible, not mathematically ascertainable position. Those who strive to pursue the golden mean themselves will have nothing but the most heartfelt sympathy for Heine in his efforts— which in the final analysis were unsuccessful—to achieve this golden mean himself.

As a good man of the centre Heine finely concludes his political report on the art exhibition of 1833 with the words: 'I am proud of once having had the courage to resist all attempts at cajoling or tricking or bullying me into unreason and error. He who does not go as far as his heart urges, and reason permits, is a poltroon; he who goes farther than he wanted to go is a slave.'

Besides his articles on the Paris art exhibitions Heine also wrote a series of articles under the heading of *The French Stage* and

Letters on Music. These latter are too little read. There are some
remarkable sentiments in them, well worth taking to heart. There
is his surprising reference, for example—surprising in the Heine
stereotype of the literary histories—to the symptoms of moral
decline in the French comedy and, indeed, in the French attitude
to sex itself. He denounces the perilous, murderous trade of
prostitution and

> then the laughter sticks in my throat and were I not afraid of
> being thought a fool by the most educated public in the world
> I would not hold back my tears. You see, my dear friend,
> that's the exile's secret curse: he can never really feel at home
> in foreign parts. The thoughts and feelings we bring with us
> from our own native land isolate us all the time from a people
> who feel and think quite differently from us. We are always
> jibbing at moral or rather immoral manifestations to which the
> natives have long since become reconciled ; indeed custom has
> rendered them insensible to their very existence, just as it has
> to the country's natural phenomena.

Heine undoubtedly speaks in this as a German, but it seems clear
to me that his Jewish feeling is at work, too.

Heine's criticism of Victor Hugo, of the French poets in general,
is scathing. Unlike the Germans, the French never dream, they are
always wide awake in the conduct of their daily business, which is
politics ; such is the constantly recurring antithesis. The materialist
philosophy and education of the French deprives their poets of
' naïveté, feeling, the insight gained from observation and self-
identification with the person or thing observed. All they are capable
of is reflection, passion and sentimentality.' It may come as a
surprise to find ' sentimentality ' quoted in this context. Heine's
explanation goes deep:

> Sentimentality is a product of materialism. In the soul of
> the materialist, you see, there is a glimmering consciousness
> of the fact that everything in the world is not matter, after all.
> Sentimentality is matter in despair because it can never be
> self-sufficient, and in its yearning for something better finding
> an outlet in vague emotionalism. I have in fact found that it
> was always the sentimental authors who in the privacy of their
> own homes, or when wine had loosened their tongue, were most
> prone to display their materialism in language that left nothing
> to the imagination.

We may well ask : who knows *this* Heine ? It is not only Heine's psychology that calls forth my admiration in aperçus like this ; I see in them the shape of the religious faith and the existentialist philosophizing to which he was to be impelled in his last years. Heine—the anti-Hegelian, the forerunner of Kierkegaard ! It was not just his illness that brought about his conversion ; already we can see indications of it when he was in the plenitude of his powers ; in a piece of dramatic criticism he wrote then he expressed the yearning of the soul to anchor itself in solid values outside the realm of matter.

Heine never broke faith with the irrational powers of the soul. Although he had always proudly proclaimed the rights of Reason, of Enlightenment, of Progress, it was precisely here in France that he became aware of the reverse side of these nobles forces: their estrangement from nature. The very language of France reflected this estrangement:

it has been so finely filtered that every coarse expression, every imprecise locution, everything that is obscure and mean, but also all the fragrance, all the healing forces growing wild in nature, all those secret enchantments that run in and out of the untamed word have been irretrievably lost to it. The French language, and hence French declamation, too, like the nation itself, is concerned only with the day, the present ; the twilight realm of recollection and presentiment is closed to it. It flourishes in the light of the sun ; it is from this source that it derives its beautiful clarity and warmth ; night with its pale moon and mysterious stars, its sweet dreams and eerie phantoms, is strange and inhospitable to it.

It would be hard to find the fundamental Romantic-Irrational position more powerfully and finely expressed.

Nor were Heine's continued attacks (often wrung from him against his will) on the gods of astuteness and utilitarianism, on the era of railways and capitalism, merely the vapourings of an æsthetic trifler. Behind the Romantic veil was the proclamation of the living soul's right to mystery, greatness, infinity, incomprehensibility. Precisely for this reason the citizen monarchy with its pronounced levelling tendencies was a bitter pill for Heine to swallow.

But was not Heine the poet *par excellence* of fraternity, equality? The question is full of pitfalls. Heine had a strong dislike of equality in the literal sense ; in fact, it disgusted him. The passages in his book on Börne in which he dissociates himself from his Left-wing radical German compatriots in Paris is full of expressions of distaste called forth by egalitarian pretensions: 'A misshapen, bandy-legged cobbler appeared and said that all men were equal. I was not a little annoyed at such impertinence.' 'I cannot stand the reek of tobacco . . . I am speaking not figuratively but quite literally, when I say that if the people were to shake my hand I would wash it afterwards . . . you have to have seen the people with your own eyes when the revolution is really on, you have to have smelt it with your own nose. You have to hear with your own ears how this sovereign king-rat talks. . . .'

Is this Heine the hater of aristocracy talking? In one corner of his soul, and not a small one, is he not himself an aristocrat through and through? At all events Heine did not share the attitude which Kurt Hiller found to be common to so many politicians and which he aptly named 'inverse Byzantinism.' Heine never evinced any respect for the common man. At the same time, he had just as little respect for capitalists, those ' busy knights-errant of money ' (*The French Stage*, Fourth Letter). He accuses them of ' diminishing everything great and utterly destroying what is heroic ; narrow, calculating, shopkeeping minds.' ' Before long every heroic idea and feeling in this part of the world will become, I won't say a thing of the past, but at any rate something ridiculous. I am the last to wish for a return to the old régime of a privileged aristocracy . . . but the new régime that has replaced the old is far worse.' It is the friend of the Rothschilds who writes thus. It is being less than just to Heine to accuse him of trimming, of wanting to run with the hares and hunt with the hounds. How much easier could he have made things for himself by fighting definitely for one side or the other. In that case his powerful pen would have gained him at least one grateful and assured following. It was just this, however, that his *deep intellectual sincerity,* which eschewed phrases and insisted on ultimate values, would not permit him to do.

Even heroism, to which he assigns such decisive value in the fourth letter, is but a mask for what is really metaphysical, imperishable, unanalysable in the soul. Immediately afterwards, in the fifth letter, in discussing the Bonapartist intrigues, he merci-lessly ' debunks ' it : ' Were the days of the Empire really the golden age that these Bonapartists, small and great, from the war-disabled Ricou to the Duchess of Abrantès, love to tell us they were ? I think not. The fields were uncultivated and men were led to the slaughter. Everywhere the tears of mothers and desolated homes.'

His creed, then, was epitomized in the words : ' The world must be governed not by petty accountancy, not by highly-taxed calculating ability, but by genius, beauty, love and strength.' All his life Heine groped his way between the opposing values of Rational and Irrational ; desperately—it is not too much to say—did he move his men from one square on the chessboard of life to another.. He failed to get his men on to the right squares. These squares, I have suggested in my ' double track theory ' (in my novel, *Stefan Rott*), are to be found in the realm of social intercourse for the Rational ; in the sphere of the ego, of the lonely relationship of the individual to the Absolute, for the Irrational (' noble misfortune '). Heine never succeeded in distinguishing between the two concepts. That, although true insight was denied him, he was unable to be at ease with perceptions that were false ; that his conscience was too sensitive, his intellect too fine to allow him to settle down comfortably at any of the extremes from which it would have been so easy to sound a fanfaronade : this, more than anything else, redounds to his glory !

It is typical of the perverse manner in which these vitally important problems affecting mankind are rigidly judged in accordance with the party line that Heine's early Paris writings have failed to be acknowledged as important contributions to the solution of these problems, or at any rate to their clearer definition. They have been dismissed as ' feuilletonistic.' In all probability this is simply because they were originally contributed to periodicals, and because the title of *Salon* under which Heine issued them in volume form was not a particularly happy inspiration.

The care with which Heine strives to seize on what is of permanent importance in the events that are rapidly unfolding themselves before his eyes is wholly admirable, as is also the way in which he seeks to do justice to the personality of the King, to weigh up the pros and cons of his system and to distinguish it from the monarchical system in general. Heine does not make things easy for himself, he does not simplify. In this respect he reveals his true love of mankind and of life. *Simplification* is the sign by which the

foes of mankind and of life recognize each other! Not, indeed, that
what I might call the negative of simplification should be employed
either: the trick of representing what is in fact quite simple as so
complicated that all generalization, all responsibility is evaded.
Heine does not hesitate to make round assertions wherever possible.
In the *Citizen Monarchy* (*Französische Zustände*, IX), for instance,
he describes the republicanism of the French as ' mistrust ' ·of
authority, but declares that belief in authority, royalism out of
conviction, is a characteristic of the Germans. Intuition joins with
prudence and carefulness, in his reporting of the arts as elsewhere.
There is room here only to refer the musicologist to his eerie description of Spontini and to his appraisal, in which he was far in
advance of his time, of Berlioz—' a colossal nightingale, a songster
of eagle's dimensions such as no doubt existed in primeval times.'
The same qualities are marked in Heine's political reports: *The
Citizen Monarchy, 1832* and *The Parliamentary Period of the
Citizen Monarchy.*

This is not the case in the two great surveys which have been
repeatedly mentioned in this book: *Concerning the History of
Religion and Philosophy in Germany* and *The Romantic School.*
These two books were first published in French. Their German
publication followed in the face of censorship difficulties. Their
value does not lie in the objective soundness of what Heine has to
tell us about German evolution from early times to Luther, Kant
and Hegel; about Lessing, ' the literary Arminius who liberated
our theatre from its foreign domination '; about Goethe and his
leadership of the ' art-for-art's-sake ' school ; about the effect of the
irruption of the Middle Ages on German life ; about the political
resistance to the forces of the Reformation ; about Romanticists
and ' Young Germany.' Heine's presentation of German, indeed of
universal theology and philosophy, as a preparation for atheism,
as a mortal blow inflicted on the Egyptian-Jewish Jehovah, is, to
say the least, tendentious. Even Luther is made to appear as a link
in this liberating chain and as a pioneer in the struggle for freedom
of thought.

This one-sidedness, with all its many errors, is due to the
temporary influence exerted by Saint-Simonian doctrines on Heine.
They caused him to depict Spinoza as a kind of anticipation of the
harmony between the physical and the spiritual worlds proclaimed

by Saint-Simon's disciples, from which it was but a short step to the ' emancipation of the flesh ' proclaimed by Enfantin. Heine's early adoption of Saint-Simonian ideas prepared the way for him eventually to overcome them—for the radical recanting in his *Confessions* and in the remarkable preface to the second edition (1852) of the *Religion and Philosophy*, as well as in the epilogue to *Romanzero*. Thus Heine's two great theoretical works are well worth reading as a self-portrait of a thinker wrestling with himself and developing in the process. This is not by any means to deny that they also contain some profound insights into, and brilliantly accurate descriptions of, the trends, movements and personalities they describe.

Heine's steady progress with these arduous labours of political and philosophical exposition in his early Paris period was accompanied by increased firmness, vigour and self-assurance in his social life. His disciple Laube is unable to conceal his astonishment at Heine's popularity in Paris. ' All doors, even those usually most firmly closed, opened to him, and the George Sands, Balzacs, de Vignys, Victor Hugos, Janins and all the rest of them treated him as their peer.' Quite different from the Berlin salons where he had been so cruelly ridiculed and lectured at by such well-meaning persons. Other leaders of the Paris intellectual world with whom he came into contact were Mignet the historian, Eugène Sue the novelist, Musset, Chopin, Liszt, Béranger, Théophile Gautier, Victor Cousin the philosopher ; the Saint-Simonians ; Gérard de Nerval, who translated him and dedicated an enthusiastic essay to him, and Berlioz. Berlioz took Heine as a witness for his wedding to the Irish actress Smithson with whom he was infatuated. Later—' always original,' said Heine—Berlioz visited the poet on his last bed of pain.

Many found the slight German accent with which he spoke French an additional attraction. When he was in form he spoke freely and with brilliant wit in what was a foreign language to him. Society ladies begged their friends to bring him with them, says Philarète Chasles.

Heine was a very handsome fellow, quite smart for a man who had to work for his living ; but the forms and ceremonies of Western European social intercourse seemed to him so much false flummery and nauseated him. He didn't actually withdraw into his own house like a snail in its shell, but all the same he couldn't stand the noise of the salons. Consequently he turned down invitations, rather curtly. This made people all the more anxious to meet him. Achille Deveria, who usually took only women as sitters, had painted him.

The warm atmosphere of liking and respect which he enjoyed in Paris—so unlike the atmosphere of his German environment— steadied his nerves. He began to recuperate physically, too.

' I saw Heine frequently in his best years ' (wrote Théophile Gautier), he was a fellow like a god, mischievous as the devil, but good-natured with it all, whatever people say to the contrary. I was little concerned whether he regarded me as a friend or a supporter, so long as I could listen to his sparkling conversation ; for extravagantly as he expended his wealth and health, his expenditure of *esprit* was more lavish still. He spoke French very well, but for the sake of humorous effect would every now and then utter one of his sarcastic pronouncements with a typical German accent. Had it been imitated it could have developed into those curious onomatopœic utterances of Baron de Nucinger's in Balzac's *Comédie Humaine*. The effect was irresistibly comic : Aristophanes and Eulenspiegel in the same person.

He could be found with Richard Wagner and Laube in Brocci's restaurant opposite the Opera. So lively and brilliant was their con- versation that everyone at the neighbouring tables would listen to it. Wagner thought a good deal of Heine's judgment at the time. Even in his autobiography, written later, he notes complacently a com- pliment Heine paid him—Heine had read Wagner's long short story, *Un musicien étranger à Paris*, and said of it : ' Hoffmann couldn't have written anything like that.'

Gradually it became a matter of course for all German writers of note arriving in Paris to call on him. In his apartment with ' the smallest possible rooms ' Grillparzer found him with two grisettes, one of whom he introduced as his *petite*. ' He himself, though, looked the very personification of *joie de vivre* and, with his thick neck, of vital energy.' And Grillparzer was delighted, in the course of the technical conversation which immediately followed, ' to have the unusual experience of talking with a German man of letters who was endowed with common sense.' ' He would have nothing to do with ultra-Liberalism.'

On Hebbel he made 'an unexpectedly good impression.'

His figure is indeed somewhat rotund, but he is definitely not fat. His features, with their small sharp eyes, inspire confidence. Both mien and speech proclaim the poet ; a profound, true poet ; not one who takes a header into the sea on the chance of picking up a few pearls, but one who dwells at the bottom of ocean's depths with fairies and mermaids and has all their wealth in his command. His observations on Grabbe, Kleist, Immermann, etc., always hit the nail right on the head. I believe him to be a remorseless enemy of all that is mediocre, even of the mediocrity of the true poet if he fails in his purpose ; but he respects strength.

Characteristically enough, it was precisely the truly great among his visitors who were struck by his greatness and his frankness ; whereas the nonentities suspected all kinds of hidden motives and ugly, sordid intrigues. We all tend to see ourselves in others !

Among the Germans with whom Heine came into contact were also a number of Metternich's spies. Their reports only came to light in 1912, when Karl Glossy issued *Secret Reports on the Literary World of the pre-March (1848) Revolution*. Gentlemen who were paid for the purpose struck up Heine's acquaintance in Heideloff and Campe's German bookshop in Paris and in reading rooms which Heine regularly visited to see from the German newspapers what was going on in his native land. He would get into conversation, thereby furnishing the agents with material with which to denounce him to the Austrian Government.

It is hardly surprising that this constant shadowing affected the sensitive poet's nerves. Moreover, he was on bad terms with the German émigrés in Paris. 'All Germans in Paris,' declared one of Metternich's worthy spies, 'even the majority of the refugees and littérateurs who to all outward appearance keep together, tear each other to pieces behind one another's backs and lead a cat-and-dog life.' The causes of these dissensions were partly personal, partly party-political and partly inherent in the special material and moral difficulties confronting people uprooted from their natural soil. Heine himself, in his *Memoir* on Ludwig Marcus, had anxiously speculated on 'why so many Germans who have come over to France have fallen into insanity.'

The number who suffer, with more or less lucid intervals, from this dark malady is very great. One is tempted to say that insanity is the national malady of Germans in France. In all likelihood we bring the germ of the malady with us when we cross the Rhine, and what in Germany would have remained a mere stunted plant of foolishness throughout a lifetime, quickly grows in the hot climate and burning asphalt pavements of society here into rank madness. Or does the mere fact of leaving the Fatherland to ascend and descend ' the hard steps ' of a foreign country and to moisten with one's tears the still harder bread of exile betoken in itself a high degree of insanity ? In any case it would be wrong to think that those who lose their way here in the abysses of insanity are violent eccentrics ; still less, devotees of idleness and riotous living— no, it has always been the most honourable minds, the most industrious and abstemious personages who have chiefly been struck down by this disaster.

Heine himself found his exile hard to bear. At first, it is true, it had been voluntary. Later, however, under the pressure of German bans on his books and of German police measures it had assumed an increasingly compulsory character, though with remissions to the very end (he was unmolested on his two visits to Hamburg in 1843 and 1844, but forbidden entry to Prussia). In his book on Börne he speaks of the hardships of his exile:

> More than six moons have passed since I last heard a German sound, and everything I write and think has to clothe itself laboriously in foreign expressions. . . . No doubt you have some idea of what bodily exile means, but only a German poet condemned to speak and write French the whole livelong day, and even to sigh in French on his loved one's breast at night, can have any idea of what spiritual exile means ! Even my thoughts are exiled, exiled into a foreign tongue.

And he breaks out in a despairing cry:

> Happy are they who rot peacefully in the gaols of the Fatherland . . . for these gaols are a Fatherland with iron bars, and German winds blow through them, and the gaoler, if he is not absolutely mute, speaks German !

It goes without saying that Heine, even in moods of such bitterness, ought not to have idealized ' the gaols of the Fatherland.' He failed to think of the treatment meted out in these gaols ; in Butzbach, for example, to Rektor Weidig, the leader of the Hessian Liberals—he was driven to a frightful suicide. In these moods Heine distrusted everyone round him: fellow exiles, fellow paranoiacs, but also those who had come to visit him from Germany ; in short, everybody. In such moods he resembled, as Heinrich Laube says,

a beast of prey always on the watch. It was in this that he most clearly revealed his descent from a persecuted race. When I urged calmness on him he replied, half fiercely, half humorously : ' How can I slough off my hide, which comes from Palestine and has been tanned by Christians for eighteen centuries. The baptismal waters of Langensalza have not made things any better, and the expression " Eternal Jew " has a thousandfold significance.'

Heine's mistrust was not without good reason, as has been stated. Heine had not joined the radical German émigrés ; hence he was attacked not only from Germany, by governments and police ministers, but also by the new German Jacobins in Paris. These were organized in a movement—called by Franz Mehring ' Young Artisan Communism '—consisting of a core of journeyman-artisans who had no prospect of becoming their own masters in Germany, with a sprinkling of left-*bourgeois* literati. The majority of the League's members consisted of young artisans ; not only those who were settled in Paris, but also travelling craftsmen who sooner or later returned to Germany. These were the men who had to be cultivated by the League for its contacts in Germany. A ' League of the Outlawed ' had been founded in Paris in 1834 as the first secret organization of German fugitives. Its aims, according to its Statutes as quoted by Mehring, were: Liberation and rebirth of Germany ; establishment and preservation of social and political equality, liberty, civic virtue and national unity.

Among the League's leaders were two former University tutors (*Privatdozenten*): Theodor Schuster of Göttingen and Jakob Venedey of Heidelberg. The League is described in more detail by Friedrich Brügel (*Aus den Anfängen der deutschen Sozialistischen Presse*, Vienna, 1929), who gives an earlier date for the League's establishment and particularly emphasizes the importance of Schuster, which is also stressed by Mehring. Brügel reaches the conclusion: ' Dating from the conflict between Jakob Venedey and Karl Wilhelm Theodor Schuster the German oppositional and emigrational movement was divided into two camps, a bourgeois and a Socialist camp.'

Heine came into close contact with both leaders ; when Venedey was expelled from Paris in 1835, he intervened on his behalf ; he placed the common destiny of the émigrés above internal party differences ; he gave Venedey the money he needed for travelling. After 1848 Venedey played a major rôle : Heine's poem, *Kobes I*, was directed against him. In 1841 Schuster gave evidence for Herr Strauss, who felt himself to have been libelled by Heine's book on Börne, in support of Strauss's untrue assertion that he had boxed Heine's ears in the street. Schuster had to admit, however, that he had not even been present at the alleged assault. Eventually Heine and Strauss engaged in a duel to settle their differences.

Börne associated himself closely with the ' League of the Outlawed.' He spoke at artisans' meetings, worked to get the League's organ, *Der Geächtete* (' The Outlawed '), financed, and inaugurated it with an article on Lamennais, the Catholic Socialist. If we accept Heine's testimony in his book on Börne, the latter's speeches in the Passage Saumon evoked a fanatical response. ' And as republicanism is so straightforword and is so much easier to understand than, for example, constitutional monarchy, which pre-supposes considerable knowledge for its proper comprehension, it was not long before thousands of young German artisans became Republicans and preached the new gospel.'

' Was it virtue or madness,' Heine goes on to ask, ' that led this Ludwig Börne to inhale blissfully the rankest odours and to enjoy wallowing in the plebeian mire ? ' Börne's resolute concentration on public activity seemed to Heine to be the ' terrible tragedy of a wasted life,' a plunge into the ' howling abyss,' inasmuch as for Börne ' all the flowers were faded.' Heine failed to understand Börne's simpleness and single-mindedness. He endeavoured to explain them as having been caused by personal disappointments. He failed to realize that these were qualities possessed by most practical politicians.

Even more pronounced, however, was Börne's failure to under-stand the complexity of Heine's character, which continued to oscillate in the difficult task of finding a mean between the irra-tionally poetical and the rational espousal of the people's cause. ' What did you do the first day you arrived in Paris ? ' Börne demanded of Heine, expecting to hear of some revolutionary pilgrimage. But Heine's first visit was to the *Bibliothèque Royale*, where he asked the Keeper of Manuscripts to show him the Manesse Minnesinger Codex. ' For years I had been seized with a desire to see with my own eyes the precious pages in which are preserved, among others, the poems of Walther von der Vogelweide, the greatest of German lyric poets.'

The symbolism is moving : Heine flees from Germany, and in Paris his first steps are directed towards the spot where he may venerate a monument of the German spirit. Börne, too, was ravaged by homesickness, but on hearing what Heine says about Walther von der Vogelweide ' his features assumed a peculiar expression.'

Gradually this expression turned into a grimace. Becoming very much the prosecuting counsel, Börne misrepresents Heine's perfectly consistent outlook, even hints at venality. He taxes him with his ' sybaritic nature ' and his individualism, and asserts that Heine ' overestimates the power capable of being exerted by individuals.' ' What are we, even if we are many ? Nothing but the people's heralds,' maintains Börne. He distinguishes between ' character ' and ' poet ' ; to a certain limited extent he is prepared to concede that Heine is a poet, but he will not grant him character. In *Atta Troll* Heine turned the tables with his famous ' No talent, but certainly a character.'

Once only did Börne come near to a perception of the truth. He wrote :

> If ever there was anybody who nature had decided should be an honest man, that man is Heine, and as an honest man he could have been happy. He can't be hypocritical even for five minutes, even for twenty lines ; he can't lie even for a day, even for half a page. He can't stop smiling, ridiculing, joking ; no, not if you were to crown him. Whenever he is false to himself and does lie, is hypocritical ; whenever he assumes an air of gravity when he really wants to laugh and a tone of humility when he really wants to wield the lash of satire, everybody sees through him at once, and instead of gain he reaps reproaches by his duplicity.

It never dawned on Börne that Heine avoided extremes precisely because he was so honest. And he forgets what he himself said about Heine's failure to derive any gain from his methods. A few lines later he declares that the game Heine played was ' quite lucrative.' It is always the keenly logical minds who, when they allow themselves to be swayed by passion, perpetrate the crassest logical errors !

'I believe Heine's a rogue, but I can't find any particular misdeed to fasten on to him' is the most characteristic of the many observations Börne makes about Heine in his letters to Jeanette Wohl, the friend whom he idolized. The spirit in which he pronounces on Heine in private is one of malice, envy and resentment, and shows how far, in terms of common decency, the 'virtuous' Börne is inferior to the allegedly so lax and immoral Heine. According to a third party (Eduard Beurmann), 'when Heine called on Börne for the first time he did so in humility and awe, explaining that he had paced up and down outside the house before " plucking up courage " to go in.' The first time Börne mentions Heine to Frau Wohl, on the other hand, he relies on gossiping rumour-mongers in order to denigrate his rival : 'several people have told me that Heine likes to affect a melancholy he is far from feeling. They say he is terribly vain.' Of course insincerity is always the easiest, handiest charge to bring against a poet. It is the one least capable of proof, which is why critics are so fond of it.

The two men would undoubtedly soon have parted company for impersonal reasons, in any case. At their very first meeting in Frankfurt the differences in their vision of life were clearly revealed in their opposing views of Goethe. But apart from this, Börne was personally prejudiced against Heine. In his scandal-mongering letter to his *amie* he openly goes on to admit as much :

> Heine has the reputation of being a common roué. He lives at the end of the town and frequently tells me he does so to avoid having visitors. He says he doesn't want me to visit him, either. Well yes, there is a little spite in the way I slander Heine to you. I've only just realized, what I hadn't noticed when I met him before, that he's handsome and has the sort of face women like. But take my word for it, there's nothing behind the face, nothing ; I understand these things.

In one of his next letters the jealous Börne continues his extraordinary campaign of slander :

> Heine came to see me this morning. He asked after you and said you were a very charming woman. It's funny about Heine and me. I find my first impression of him increasingly confirmed. He seems to me to be lacking a heart and his conver-

sation itself to be lacking wit. Apparently his wit is in his pen
only. He can't make a single sensible remark himself and
can't get a singe sensible remark out of me. He affects hatred
and scorn of mankind. He is very sensitive to open criticism
of his writings. He himself told me he preferred to go about
with nonentities. He's very resentful and dispirited. It was quite
obvious he was only waiting for the minute he could get away
from me. I was glad to see him go, too, for he'd bored me.

Slander, say I. In Börne's first letter quoted by me he had
admitted Heine's conversational pyrotechnics. ' But he likes to
repeat his witticisms and laughs at them himself.' Of course it is
just this out-of-the-run ingenuousness which is one of Heine's most
endearing traits and justifies us in thinking, perhaps, that his gibes,
both in speech and writing, were not always seriously intended but
often the outcome of sheer light-heartedness. ' In his goodness of
heart he was essentially some quite ordinary person,' wrote Laube,
' but he had a spiteful tongue.' But Börne took Heine quite literally.
When Heine said once, laying on the badinage with a trowel, that
Metternich could buy him only in one way, by giving him all the
girls in Paris—Börne just couldn't realize that Heine was indulging
in irony at his own expense. In a fit of puritanical self-righteousness
he exclaims indignantly to his adored Frau Wohl : ' I say " girls,"
but Heine used an expression of the utmost coarseness.'

These letters of Börne's show their writer in a very bad light.
There is something pathological about them.

I come back to Heine, but you mustn't think it gives me
pleasure to speak ill of him, not at all. But he interests me as
an author and therefore also as a human being. I'm collecting
everything I hear others say about him and that I myself
observe in him. As I find it boring having to enter up Heine's
account just for myself alone I'm writing down in my letters
to you everything about him as it comes to light. A weak
character like Heine—and the weakness of his character was
quite obvious to me from his writings alone—is bound to
degenerate completely in Paris. I can see he's on the downward
path and shall follow his track as a matter of historical and
anthropological interest.

And again :
His libertinism is of a kind I have never come across before,
either in life or books, and I just can't find any psychological

explanation for it. Ordinary sensuality one meets with quite
frequently, but it is rare for a young man to speak openly of his
debaucheries as if they were something fine . . . Heine, though,
runs after common street-girls night and day, and never stops
talking about this sordid pursuit, from which he derives
aesthetic pleasure. The other day, after we'd just had supper, he
said he was going to the Passage des Panoramas. ' What for ? '
' I want to see whether any of the girls I know has a new dress
on.' And Heine is now thirty!

Börne, the fanatic! As such he could not possibly understand
Heine's boyish high spirits, engaging though they are to us, and
though, with the great example of Plato before us, we do not find
them incompatible with true seriousness.

All the same, the gibes against Heine in which Börne indulged
in his letters rather exceed the bounds of the strong sense of justice
and the severe moral code for which he was famous, and which,
incidentally, Heine fully acknowledged in his book on Börne. Nor
can anything be said for the following statement : ' Poor Heine
is being chemically decomposed by me, and he hasn't the faintest
suspicion that I'm continually experimenting with him in secret.'

So much may serve as a specimen of the animosity Heine could
expect from the radical émigrés. It is understandable, therefore, that
he did not want to have too much to do with the ' Terrorists.' For
a time he would sign all political resolutions put before him. But
once, when he was asked to protest against the Pope and his
political activities in the Romagna, he felt he'd had enough, and
he asked irritably what the Pope had to do with the ' Terrorists.'

Increasingly he separated himself from the radical émigrés.

He keeps the exiled Germans at a distance (relates a contemporary), for which, in view of the petulance and stupidity
of very many of them, he can hardly be blamed. On the other
hand, he shows them much kindness in the right sort of way,
without his left hand knowing what his right is doing. He never
told me anything about it, either, I learnt of his generosity from
one of those unfortunate people whose muddled thinking and
rashness had led them into misery, and whom Heine had
magnanimously helped with appreciable sums on various
occasions.

He would give away clothes, and when he once acted as a

guarantor was himself plunged into debt. He was nothing if not
kind-hearted. 'He helped me in everything like a brother,' says
Heinrich Laube. 'He was always anxious to please and oblige.
People don't credit him with kindness of heart. They are quite
wrong! In fact he is more soft-hearted than anything. He has often
apologized for it himself and called himself a " silly old woman "
for it. But while he apologized he continued to give.' Gérard de
Nerval's testimony is similar : ' Helping friends in need was a fixed
principle with him which he practised with such generosity that
he never worried about the sums of money he lent being returned.'
It was not till after he had some extremely unfortunate experiences
with the spies and sensationalist newspaper correspondents who
surrounded him that he became cold and reserved in his attitude to
foreigners, especially Germans, whom he subsequently allowed into
his house only with considerable reluctance.

His helpfulness was not confined to money matters. During the
terrible cholera epidemic, of whose terrors he gives such a horrifying
description in *Französische Zustände* ('The French Scene'), he stuck
it out in Paris so that he could look after his cousin Karl. He pulled
him through, then wrote to Varnhagen : ' It wasn't really pluck that
stopped me fleeing from Paris. To be honest, I was too lazy to do
so.' Typically Heinesque self-deprecation. This self-mockery covers
a profound metaphysical faith in the triumph of truth. ' The truth
will come to light without me. It doesn't need my explanations ; in
fact, it will emerge in spite of my transparent irony, because truth
possesses the power of the perfectly real. It's unsporting of me to
give truth any assistance in breaking through. It must come of
itself, gaining thereby in dignity, and increasing in worth. . . .' But
Heine miscalculated in his biographers. They take his ' lazy ' and
similar utterances at their face value. Either they really are naïve
or they pretend to be so.

All these examples—which could be multiplied—of Heine's
philanthropy would avail him nothing, of course, against the charge
of political jobbery, could it be proved that the mean which he
sought and pursued so laboriously did not spring from genuine
conviction. But it is precisely this proof which is lacking ; in fact
we can prove pretty conclusively the opposite thesis.

The decisive period of Heine's life in this connexion is from
1836 to 1848. Secret documents published after the Revolution of

1848 showed that during this period Heine was one of those who
had received a yearly subvention from the French Government.
Heine himself described this pension—4,600 francs (about £200) a
year—as the generous alms bestowed by the French nation on a
few thousand foreigners who had sought asylum in France after
having compromised themselves in the cause of liberty in their
native lands. And in fact, on the list of those receiving subventions
were the names of numerous respected honest revolutionaries and
revolutionary writers. Moreover, it was in 1836 that the German
Federal Council had banned the writings of 'Young Germany,'
including Heine's works. In doing so they robbed Heine of his chief
source of income and incurred the responsibility for exposing him to
an uncertain future and to pecuniary distress. And finally : ' It is a
matter of certainty that Heine's judgments on France and on French
conditions were not influenced by his subvention.' The author of
this pronouncement is Houben, whose judgment is strictly objective,
or if anything slightly tinged with antipathy, but is in this case
buttressed with all the details procurable. He continues : ' I cannot
regard it (the pension) in any different light from the 6,000 thalers
a year pension which Frederick the Great paid Voltaire.'

In spite of which Heine's acceptance of the pension constitutes
a blemish on his life, even taking into account that life with a wife
whom he loved beyond all else, but whose extravagances were
wholly unreasonable, added to his publisher's tight-fistedness, his rich
uncle's unreliability, and the German ban on his books had reduced
him to the most desperate straits. An independent reporter should
avoid even the appearance of compromising his independence by
the acceptance of gifts. In happier times no one was more finely
sensitive on this score than Heine. August Lewald, who was able
to observe in 1832 how Heine disdained danger in voicing his
opinions, wrote:

> He fled from all contacts with vileness . . . I myself saw him
> reject offers from booksellers whom he did not consider
> reputable. At the time when he was writing *The French Scene*
> a Paris bookseller offered him a large sum for the rights. He was
> reproached in my hearing for not taking the money that was
> waiting for him, but he steadfastly rejected all offers of the
> kind. ' One has to be on one's guard against associations of
> that kind,' he said to me, ' they bring no honour.'

As far as the French Government, the bourgeois monarchy, was concerned, however, Heine would certainly have been able to assure himself that his conduct was in no way blameworthy, since he had always been broadly in sympathy with the Government. This is the salient point ! Had he not come to Paris because the bourgeois monarchy approximated most closely to his ideal ? Long before 1836, in his reports from Paris, he had accepted in its fundamentals Louis Philippe's system, though constantly warning against the dangers of dilution and deviation. And as late as 1853 he wrote in his *Confessions*: ' Louis Philippe was a great and noble king. He had all the respectable virtues of a bourgeois, and not one of the vices of a grand seigneur. He was a model king, a Marcus Aurelius in a modern wig, a crowned sage, an honest man.' He had written in the same strain, rather more frigidly, if anything, during the crucial years between 1836 and 1848 when he was in receipt of the pension. And if there were things on which he did not see eye to eye with the Government during this period he did not hesitate to attack it violently. Thus he denounced Thiers, not only in the Damascus affair, but also in 1840 when Thiers was advocating war with England. Heine bluntly told the biographer of Napoleon that it was perhaps his misfortune to have described Napoleon's life only up to the Consulate—the period of conquests, that is—and not to have lived in spirit through the Russian campaign and the great retreat. ' Had M. Thiers reached Waterloo in his book perhaps his martial ardour would have cooled down somewhat.' It will be seen that the pension Heine received could not muzzle him, even in a moment of such decisive importance for the Ministry. Shortly afterwards Thiers did in fact fall on the armament issue.

It is clear, then, that Heine supported the bourgeois monarchy out of conviction, but for no other reason. A monarchy with a citizen at its head—this, in principle, seemed to him to indicate the path of justice. The Bourbon rule of aristocrats and Jesuits had at last been decisively defeated. The monarchy was the Revolution continued. The veteran Lafayette himself, pioneer fighter for American liberty, the hero of 1789, had welcomed King Louis Philippe as ' the best republic.' Moreover, a bourgeois monarchy guaranteed stability and progress and so eliminated the destructiveness which Heine dreaded as the inevitable accompaniment of revolution. It was the mean between two extremes, between abso-

lutism and revolution ; it had a constitution, a parliament, which the
liberals in Germany were fighting vainly to obtain. Repeatedly
Heine declared : ' I am in favour of a republic ruled by monarchists,
or a monarchy ruled by republicans.' I am not claiming that the
formula is a happy one ; I don't consider Heine an outstandingly
good politician, anyway, but I do consider him to be an *honest*
politician. That Heine avoided extremes out of conviction and
profound instinct ; that he laboured honestly and consistently constantly to re-establish his middle-of-the-road position, giving it new
vitality under the impact of new problems and considering only
the cause of humanity, not his own personal advantage : this is the
thesis I venture to maintain against numerous assertions to the
contrary.

The privileges of nobility and clergy, which seemed to him to
constitute the chief impediments in the path of justice, had been
eliminated. But the haute bourgeoisie had arisen in their place. He
saw clearly the risk of the king becoming a tool of a ' small coterie
of people with money.' In that case the *juste-milieu* would be a
caricature ; it would be a ' mean ' only in *name* ; in practice it
would enthrone a new privileged class. Heine does not tire of
warning the King and his Ministers against this new swing to the
Right ; he reminds them of the revolutionary origin of the system ;
his opinion of the King varies according to whether he finds him
true to this origin or yielding to new plutocratic influences (this
applies to foreign policy, too ; the Polish revolt, for example).
Plutocracy is not merely unjust ; it is ugly (' unheroic ') ; by contrast
he declares, in one of the few passages which eye the future positively rather than polemically, that the accredited rulers of the
world are (as previously quoted) ' genius, beauty, love, and strength.'

A further ideal of Heine's should be added to this list: justice,
which he loved passionately. But justice is not equality. Heine
sharply dissociated himself from Proudhon, whose style he admired,
but thought a demon, not a human being, his blue spectacles notwithstanding. He dissociated himself sharply from Louis Blanc, too.

> Who wants to introduce general kitchen equality into the
> State, and have the same Spartan black soup cooked for all of
> us and, what is more terrifying, wants the giant to have the
> same portion enjoyed by brother pygmy. No thanks, latter-day
> Lycurgus ! It's true we're all brothers, but I'm the big brother

and you're the little brothers, and I'm entitled to a bigger portion.

In Saint-Simonism, too, it was not the political side of the doctrine (the theory of property) which interested him (letter to Varnhagen, May, 1832), but the religious idea, which he conceived of as Hellénistic, as the anti-Nazarene liberation of matter from the bonds of a one-sided spirituality ; in a word, it was in Saint-Simonism as a philosophical problem that he was interested. From Marx and Lassalle, whose development as young men coincided in time with his late Paris period, he was still further removed than from these early Socialists and from Börne, the ' ultra-Liberal.' Heine wanted justice for the masses. He condemned their exploitation through the ' demoralizing factory system.' He wrote the starving Silesian weavers' poem of commination. But the idea of the masses taking their destiny into their own hands rendered him sceptical. He had a horror of the masses ; their rule would be the end of the world.

First of all we have the Radicals who prescribe a radical treatment which in the long run has only an outward effect. The most it does is to get rid of the scurf on society, but it does not eliminate the rottenness inside. Even if they could succeed in relieving for a short time suffering humanity of its most excruciating torments, it could only be at the expense of the last remnants of beauty which the patient has still retained ; he will get up from his sick-bed as an ugly Philistine, and he will have to drag himself around for the rest of his life in ugly hospital uniform, in the ash-grey garb of equality. All the gaiety that has been handed down to us, all the sweetness, all the fragrance of flowers, all the poetry will have been pumped out of life, and nothing will be left except Rumfordian utility soup.[1]

This represents Heine's fundamental attitude. Alongside every rational advance towards justice, which he approved, he applied an irrational test: the test of beauty and of the soul. In so doing, he never achieved a synthesis. ' The depressing workday philosophy of the modern Puritans is spreading over the whole of Europe like a

---

[1] A soup made of ' bones, blood, and other nourishing ingredients ' named after its inventor, Sir Benjamin Thompson, Count von Rumford (1753-1814).

grey twilight that precurses a bleak winter.' He is terrified of the dominance, in a republic, ' of an envious egalitarianism which always rebuffs outstanding personalities ; renders their emergence impossible, in fact,' and in periods of crisis 'hands over the reins of government to none but comrade tanners and pork-butchers.' Such republics must collapse ' immediately they are joined in decisive battle with energetic oligarches and autocracies represented by men of exceptional calibre.' How Heine reconciles this view with the admiration that crops up elsewhere in his writings for the men of the Convention must remain one of the unresolved contradictions in his personality.

' Everything for justice, everything for the exploited proletariat, but nothing through the agency of the proletariat ' might well sum up (not in his own words) Heine's politico-social formula. True, he avers with great self-satisfaction, in the introduction to *Lutetia* (1854), that quite early in his writings he had ' often referred in explicit terms to the demons lying dormant in the lower classes of society.' And somewhat ungraciously he points out :

> In those days people saw these monsters, to whom the future belongs, only through a microscope. Seen thus, they really did look like performing fleas, but I showed them to the public in their true life-size, when they looked more like the most terrifying crocodiles ever to have emerged from their native mud than anything else.

He indulges in purple patches, as when he writes of

> The huge workshops where metals are processed by defiant half-naked figures singing as they work and beating time with their great iron hammers resounding on the anvils. The effect of such an accompaniment is spectacular, as are the lighting effects of the angry sparks leaping from the forge.

He was never quite happy about the mighty proletarian forces which were beginning to appear on the world stage. He was unable to assign any historical rôle to them ; he thought the proletariat should be the object, not the author of politics. ' These are questions neither of forms nor persons, neither of introducing a republic nor of limiting a monarchy, but of providing for the material welfare of the people,' he wrote to Laube in 1833. This reflection led him to observe, not indeed that the people should be given power, but

that the prevailing philosophy of spirituality should give way to
one that sanctified matter equally with spirit, to Saint-Simonism.
It is evident that he thought in terms of a revolution from above.

Similarly in a letter to Laube in 1835 it was the religious, not
the political question which was in the foreground of his consciousness. The struggle was for the ' first principles of life, for the idea of
life itself.' Forms of government were only means in the service of
this idea, ?nd here concessions could be made. Opportunistic as
this might sound, it embodied what always remained in fact Heine's
great passion: ' the idea of life itself!' One thing he saw clearly:
both extreme poles were to be rejected : both the nobility and the
haute bourgeoisie with their unjust privileges, and a plebeian society
in which the collective was the measure of all things and in which
all the mysteries of individuality were remorselessly levelled out.
Between these extremes lay a wide field for endeavour. But where,
in this wide field, was the right compromise to be found ? ' Alas, it
will be many years before we find out the great cure '—thus Heine
wearily concludes his book on Börne. Wearily, not resignedly. His
search goes on.

In one of Heine's short essays that have received too little
attention (*Verschiedenartige Geschichtsauffassung*—' Ways of
Interpreting History ') the rejection of extremes, the search for a
middle path is expressed sharply and categorically. In this essay
Heine condemns (a) the ' elegiac indifferentism of historians and
poets,' the tragic vision of life of the Romantics which, because it
asserted that in the eternally revolving cycle of life all attempts at
progress were futile was ' encouraged by a Government of North
Germany whose character we know well enough,' (b) the
' enthusings of the Utopians,' which were based entirely on rational
premises and aspired ' finally ' to ennoble and make happy all
mankind. To these two extremes Heine opposed Saint-Just's much
more modest claim : ' *Le pain est le droit du peuple.*'

So it was not dominion which was the people's right—but the
satisfaction of their minimal needs ! Food, shelter, clothing: the
aims laid down by Popper-Lynkeus for his ' army of breadwinners.'

' We must not be led astray by the enthusings of the Utopians
into neglecting our immediate interests and into jeopardizing the
human right for which we must chiefly struggle, the right to live,'

says Heine, thereby forfeiting the honour of being claimed by one of the powerful political parties of today as its progenitor. But the line connecting him to Popper-Lynkeus becomes clearly evident, even to the actual words used. And equally evident is the line that connects him to Goethe's verdict in the *Maxims and Reflections*: ' Pure, balanced striving for goodness and justice is very rare ; usually we get either obstructive pedantry or over-hasty boldness.'

What makes Heine's case infinitely complex is that not only did he seek the mean in politics, he often sought this mean with but mediocre energy. In his best moments Heine did indeed seek to impart to the abstract matter-of-factness of politics the corrective of the poet's irrational vision of life, and thereby to achieve a sound concrete political synthesis. But often he made no such attempt and wearied of politics altogether, clinging only to poetry. At such moments the two worlds fall asunder like the light and the darkness in Goethe's great symbolic love-poem[1] : the ' pure balanced striving ' which he had set out with such high hopes to attain, the morning redness, gives way to darkness again ; politics is simply duty, the natural activity of man is poetry. ' By temperament I tend to a certain *dolce far niente,*' Heine will write at such moments, ' and I would like best of all to lie down in the flower-decked meadows and watch with delight the clouds moving quietly overhead in the bright sky. Chance willed it, however, that I was often to be awakened from my comfortable reverie by people violently jabbing me in the ribs. The result was, *nolens volens* I had to join in the sorrows and struggles of mankind, but I can say that when I did join in I did so in all honesty.' Heine is even more explicit in a letter to his mother: ' God knows I wouldn't be a trouble-maker if I weren't always forced to be.'

Some biographers have expressed the view that Heine's purely poetical talent was marred by his political activities. Ludwig Marcuse, on the other hand, in a book on Heine which is rich in first-rate *aperçus,* tends to think that Heine's sound political sense was vitiated by his overpowering leanings to art, to the anti-moral, in fact ; that is, to ' unviolated existence.' Marcuse concedes that

---

[1] *Wiederfinden,* in *West-östlicher Diwan (Buch Suleika).*

mitigating circumstances may be pleaded for the artistic temperament, and is even able to quote a remark made by Karl Marx in defence of Heine. Marx had been 'most indulgent' in commenting on Heine's political weaknesses and said that poets were queer fish who had to be allowed to go their own way.

I disagree with both views: I believe that Heine ruined neither his poetical genius by political activity nor his grasp of politics by poetry; but that his significance lies in his *ceaseless struggles to fuse his poetical and political-philosophic powers, his irrational and rational urges, into a higher type of humanity,* and that this significance has not been recognized even yet. There was nothing anti-moral in this struggle of Heine's to achieve a synthesis; it affords no parallel to Nietzsche who was in fact anti-moral. Heine's struggle is an expression at once of the most refined and the most resolute morality. Of course Heine could not always stay on this high level. From time to time the overpowering tension had to be relaxed in spite of all his efforts to maintain it. When this happened, he crashed. Politics, the longing for earthly justice, was then simply a nuisance, a curse he would have liked to avoid by fleeing to some romantic dream-land. Or his flight took the opposite direction. He refused to be seduced by sweet dream-fancies, however insistent, and persuaded himself that life could be expressed in an over-simplified and unqualified political formula. But in each case his conscience soon protested. He was unable permanently to relax, permanently to simplify the problem of living. Precisely in his inability to relax, to deceive himself, lies his greatness. The tension began to be renewed, to lead him into the dangerous adventure of seeking new syntheses of antinomies.

Marcuse thinks he has discerned a time-law in Heine's life, a periodicity in his political activities. 'It became more and more characteristic of Heine to launch his sharpest attacks simultaneously with mounting pressure from his opponent; immediately he felt his personal intervention was no longer required, he lost interest.' Such a law is for heroes. The average politician is drawn from his hiding-place more by the prospect of success than by danger. I, too, think Heine was a hero. But the danger he had to meet lay within him, in his own highly personal ideological formulations. It was to these he reacted, not to external stimuli. When he felt he had gone further in any one direction than his intellectual honesty permitted he experienced a compulsion to reverse his course. Hence he zig-zagged in a perpetual endeavour to find the mean. He failed to find it. Perhaps in that era of completely unsettled early capitalism, in the midst of shifts of power of the most amazing kind, no such mean was possible. His zig-zagging arose neither from considerations of political expediency nor from the opposite: heroic defiance. It was inherent in the difficulty, at times insolubility, of the problem itself.

Be that as it may, the periodicity noted by Marcuse was certainly a fact. On arriving in Paris Heine was impressed chiefly by the difference between the French citizen monarchy, the pattern of which he approved, and Prussian absolutism. He ' couldn't stand ' republicanism, he wrote to Cotta. ' But it serves the kings right. They wouldn't listen to the Liberals, who campaigned against aristocracy and clericalism only, and now the bloodiest Jacobinism is paying them out . . . we moderates are in for it too.' He considered himself a moderate, it will .be observed. Soon he became aware of the citizen monarchy's defects, the plutocrats whom he satirized as *justes millionnaires*. Inevitably he moved to the Left, still clinging to the monarchy (he thought the cheap joke about the king's head—the ' pear '—in bad taste), still exhorting, hoping, seeking the right solution.

To the German rulers, of course, he was by now far too ' left.' Gentz, the head of Metternich's press bureau, wrote privately to Cotta. He described Heine as a ' desperate adventurer,' but did not fail to add that he found him ' tolerable as a poet; indeed, I love him as such.' Cotta terminated Heine's series of articles in the *Allgemeine Zeitung*. Heine decided to bring out the articles in an even sharper version as a book with Campe, and wrote a preface expressing the extreme of his left-wing views. He denounced the decrees of the Federal Diet which suppressed all political life in Germany after the Hambach festival of liberty. Heine was pursued by the censorship. He inveighed against Campe for making too many concessions to it and often mutilating his works to such an extent that frequently the opposite was printed of what he wrote. Heine was to have barely any respite from this unequal, nerve-destroying struggle that tore at the roots of his being, his right to free expression as an author. He was forced to express his thoughts in such a way that they could slip past lynx-eyed censors and publisher. Alternatively, he had to publish them, as he did his intransigent preface, under a French imprint. And he had to stoop to the device of combining a short political piece with quantities of ' padding ' in a single book. (Works of more than twenty printed sheets were not subject—initially—to preliminary censorship.) But his publisher imposed his own censorship, nevertheless. For understandable commercial reasons he was afraid of having his book stocks confiscated after printing. In addition, the decrees affecting Heine became more stringent from year to year. In 1836 special decrees were promulgated specifically against the ' Young Germany ' school of writers, among whom Heine was named. Their effect was punitive. This being so, perhaps the biographer of Heine will not be begrudged the pleasure of taking Heine at his word when he writes to Varnhagen that he had written the preface to save himself from being ' hanged from a lamp-post in the next insurrection ' ; in other words, through fear of the left-wing extremists, Börne and Co.'

Heine took up the cudgels for ' Young Germany,' which numbered Gutskow, Börne, Laube, Wienbarg among its members, in his satires *Über den Denunziaten* (' *The Informer* ') and *Der Schwabenspiegel* (' The Swabian Mirror '). He pokes fun at the Swabian wallflowers and ' sentimental cockchafers,' but expressly excludes the older authors like Schiller, and Uhland and Lenau, from his criticism. He does not mention Mörike. His tone becomes sharper when he comes to speak of misrepresentations and falsifications of his writings. He maintains that the complications and frequent changes of front in his writings were forced on him : ' Ah, if only people realized the strange complications to which the strategy of an author who fights for Europe's liberty is subjected ! ' He does not omit to conclude by personal abuse of Menzel, the informer. His intention was to provoke Menzel to challenge him to a duel. Menzel's criticisms of Gutzkow's *Wally* had landed the latter author in prison and eventually contributed to the severe measures taken by the Federal Diet against the books of ' Young Germany.' Heine, the political opponent of all medieval institutions, had a particular predilection for settling differences of opinion ' chivalrously.' In one of his letters he justified in detail the necessity for duelling ; this, too, is one of the many unresolved contradictions in Heine.

Heine had sided with Gutzkow and Börne, who had also joined

in the fray against Menzel. But for all his outward sympathies with
them the inner gulf between himself and the other two became more
and more clearly manifest and gave him no rest. The pendulum
now swung in the other direction. Heine's grand debate with the
abstract radicalism of the revolutionaries is contained in his
Heinrich Heine on [über] *Ludwig Börne* (with minor attacks on
Gutzkow). In contrast to the Platen controversy, we have here a
genuine conflict between two differing personalities. And even at
this date Heine's comprehensive work on Börne seems an objective
biographical appraisal, in its opening chapters full of warmth and
appreciation of its subject. With great skill Heine develops the
gradually emerging contrast, which, however, was already implicit
in their temperaments, between the two authors. It is not Heine and
Börne who confront one another, but two great world-views, the
Hellenic and the Nazarene. (On which more will be said later.) Heine
stresses in the strongest terms Börne's honesty, selflessness, his
unshakable patriotism—Börne's virtue is bounded only by itself of
necessity. . . . This is the magnificent new vista opened by Heine,
an enrichment of world literature.

None of Heine's writings was treated with such bitter injustice
in the author's lifetime as this one. It was left for Thomas Mann in
our own time to recognize this book at its true worth as being in
the forefront of Heine's writings. He writes powerfully of Heine's
' deep insight into the antinomy of spirit and art (not merely of
man and art), his question whether perhaps the harmonious blending
of the two elements, the spiritual and the Greek, might not be the
task of European civilization as a whole.' Heine's contemporaries,
including his friends, could see in his weighty examination, on a
fundamental philosophical level, of the two contrasting outlooks
nothing but a pamphlet of a personal nature. Even the ' *über* '
(' above ') in the title was deliberately misconstrued as an indication
that Heine wished in the very title of his book to assert his
superiority to Börne. Heine was condemned, also, for writing of an
opponent who had been dead now for three years—a condemnation
which would have been justified if, and only if, Heine's book had
been a personal attack and not an attempt at objectively clarifying
the issues. The dead man had enjoyed general esteem in left-wing
circles ; both his old and new supporters regarded an attack on
him as a kind of *lèse-majesté*. Heine forfeited a great deal of

sympathy, in this instance unjustly so ; whereas there had been
sound reasons for the odium he had incurred by his handling of
the Platen affair. Commercially too the book was a failure. Campe
called it Heine's 'Retreat from Moscow.'
    There was a widespread feeling that Heine had betrayed his
liberal ideas. People spoke of shameful compromising. Thus is the
deepest courage for truth rewarded on earth !

    Time showed I was right (Heine was able to say only six
years later, in his preface to *Atta Troll*), and I must gratefully
acknowledge that the various German governments have placed
me in their debt in this matter. The warrants for his arrest
which are already waiting for the poet on his homecoming
at every station from the German border onwards are con-
scientiously renewed every year, at the holy season when the
coloured lamps gleam cheerfully on the Christmas trees.
Because of these hazards of the roads I find I have almost lost
my inclination to travel in German territory. Accordingly, I
celebrate my Christmases in a strange land and I shall end
my days in a strange land, in exile, as well. Meanwhile the
stout champions of light and truth who accuse me of vacillation
and servility enjoy comfortable jobs in the service of the state
and move about the Fatherland without running any risks at
all.

    The seemingly pre-destined swinging of the Heinesque pendulum
was resumed once more, on a new level, in *Atta Troll* and in
Germany, a Winter's Tale. In *Atta Troll* Heine lays about him
against the 'politically engaged' bears, the egalitarians ('strict
equality! The highest offices in the State to be open to every donkey
alike'). *Germany, a Winter's Tale*, which was written soon afterwards, is a satire on the homeland's reactionaries. Heine aligns
himself with the revolutionaries again.
    In *Germany, a Winter's Tale*, Heine describes how, at night in
the forest, after his stage-coach has had a wheel broken, he
addresses a pack of howling wolves with burning eyes who have
come comfortably close up to the coach. 'They're serenading
me,' flashes across Heine's mind. 'They've assembled to do me
honour.' He throws himself into an appropriate posture and, with
deep emotion, begins : 'Fellow wolves!' Yes, he is still one of them,
he has not turned renegade, not become a tame Privy Councillor,
although he has sometimes thrown a sheepskin round his shoulders.

' My heart and my teeth are wolfish.' The chapter ends on a melancholy note :

> Das ist die Rede, die ich hielt
> Ganz ohne Vorbereitung ;
> Verstümmelt hat Kolb sie abgedruckt
> In der ' Allgemeinen Zeitung.'

This is the speech I delivered quite extempore ; Kolb printed
a garbled version of it in the *Allgemeine Zeitung*.

And to his mother, who puts a meal on the table for him and
asks whether his wife is a good housekeeper (' tricky questions ! ')
and whether he still goes in for politics and what party he really
belongs to, he says :

> Die Apfelsinen, lieb Mütterlein,
> Sind gut, und mit wahrem Vergnügen
> Verschlucke ich den süssen Saft
> Und ich lasse die Schalen liegen.

The oranges, mother dear, are good, and I swallow their
sweet juice with real pleasure, but I leave the peel.

Heine gave expression to his furthest swing to the Left in the
preface to the French edition, in the last year of his life, of *Lutetia*.
But even here he saw in the rise of the masses, of the ' victorious
proletariat,' the end of all beauty. Utility alone will reign. The
lilies, which toil not, neither do they spin, ' will be plucked from the
soil of society, unless indeed they can be utilized by the spindle.'
The grocer will make paper bags out of the *Book of Songs*. Heine
saw no way out of the dilemma. It did not occur to him that social
life, on the whole, could be planned rationally, leaving the individual free to confront the Absolute, free to live his life irrationally,
that is. (Admittedly even modern Socialists have not yet made this
clear distinction.) He despaired and—resigned himself to the
inevitable :

A frightful syllogism has me in its coils, and if I am unable
to refute the premise that everyone has a right to eat I am also
forced to accept all the consequences that flow from it. Just
thinking of it makes me run the risk of losing my reason. I see
all the demons of truth dancing around me in triumph, and in

the end a noble despair grips me and I cry out : ' The old society has long been judged and condemned. Let it reap its deserts ! Let the old world be demolished, where innocence perished, where self-seeking flourished like a green bay tree, where man was exploited by man ! May the whited sepulchres where false-hood and crying injustice were enthroned be utterly destroyed.'

Was this Heine's last word ? In the same year came his attach-ment to Camilla Selden, his ' passion flower '—a romantic climax on the borderland of life and death. It was in the same year that Heine said to this woman, ' La Mouche ': ' Even though the good God must be allowed the first place in creation, Shakespeare comes immediately after.'

And so the preface to Lutetia is no resting-place either ; it is not the last station on Heine's journey. All the same, it showed that Heine contained within himself elements of the man who was his opposite pole, Börne the stark Radical, and that there were times when he had to dispel these elements. Precisely for this reason the debate that is carried on in the book on Börne, the struggle between the man of compromise and the man of pure action, strikes such an incomparably powerful, authentic note.

Unhappily, even in this truly grandiose arena of conflicting world-views, there was tucked away a corner devoted to person-alities. For some time before his death Börne had been living in a ménage à trois with his friend Jeanette Wohl, who had married a young man from Frankfurt, Salomon Strauss. Heine deemed it necessary to publish these ' details of Börne's private life ' and to characterize them as ' immoral.' Quite apart from the fact that Heine's censure (as in the case of Platen) was based on false premises, on an exaggeration of the facts, the harm he did himself by this attack on Börne was, if anything, even greater. In Platen's case he could at least claim that the alleged weaknesses in his poetry were due to the poet's disposition ; this time, though, there were no objective motives for Heine's nasty insinuation, which was in no way essential to the characterization of Börne. Probably Heine simply wished to repay the charges of immorality which Börne seems to have made against him. No doubt Heine got to hear of remarks made by Börne in conversation with intimate friends of a similar tenor to those in Börne's letters which I have quoted.

So it would appear from Heine's defence, quite comical in its righteous indignation, against the charge that he knew 'every Phryne of the Paris boulevards, etc.' In this controversy both writers sank below their proper level.

Strauss appeared on the scene to avenge his wife's wounded honour. He said he had publicly boxed Heine's ears in the Rue Richelieu. The *Mainzer Zeitung* published this item of news. 'Not a word of it is true,' Heine wrote on 3rd July, 1841, from the Pyrenean resort of Cauterets (subsequently the scene of *Atta Troll*) to Gustav Kolb, the Editor of the *Allgemeine*,

> I'm really not the sort of lamb who meekly lets himself be insulted in the street, in the heart of Paris, and the individual who boasted of this accomplishment is certainly the very last wolf who would dare to do it ! The whole incident was limited to this individual coming up to me and stammering a few words in my face, trembling violently as he did so. I cut him short with a laugh and with perfect composure gave him my address, telling him I was about to leave for the Pyrenees, and that if anyone ' had anything to say to me ' it could wait no doubt till I came back.

A duel with pistols took place on 7th September. Strauss showed more courage than Heine had credited him with—so Heine himself reported to Campe. Strauss's bullet grazed Heine's hip. Heine fired in the air. In a letter to his physician, Dr. Wertheim, Heine completely vindicated Frau Strauss's honour, but she pursued him with implacable hostility nevertheless.

Two days before the duel Heine had notified Campe of another important event in his life: ' my marriage to the beautiful and pure creature who under the name of Mathilde Heine has been by my side for years, has always been honoured and considered as my wife, and whom only a few scandal-mongering Germans from the Frankfurt clique have bespattered with vile epithets.' ' My happiness was decided for me with a pistol at my breast,' he said to Caroline Jaubert, who, like the Princess Belgiojoso, was one of the brilliant women who were on terms of friendship with him.

Mathilde was not intellectual. Heine loved this beautiful woman precisely because the intellect, with all its illumination, but with all its errors and perverseness too, had never found a path in this simple, vegetative female's soul. In her peasant's gaiety and

uninhibited vigour, her absolute concentration on the one man, with
whom only feminine frippery contended for her affection, she was
the absolute reverse of the faithless cousins Amalie and Therese.
She gave Heine all the happiness and all the glowing passion that
he had been unable to find in the two 'mermaids'—all the happiness,
and all the misery, too, that is inevitable when a man of intellect
abandons himself wholly to something which cannot be conquered
with intellectual weapons ; when he abandons himself to what is
remotest from him, strangest to him, but to which the mysterious
attraction of opposites draws him: pure instinct ; the formless,
intractable elemental force, the fire in the bowels of the earth.
Comparison with Goethe's Christiane is inevitable. With both men
what started as a carefree adventure became their destiny and
decided their lives. ' Ich ging im Walde so für mich hin ' (Goethe)
—I wandered gaily through the forest. And, all in all, the happiness
that blesses the strong crowned them in their lives with the women
who were so unlike them, lives which they lived like real men, not
Strindberg weaklings. Mathilde's elemental nature, appearing
evermore perfect in so many of Heine's poems, his finest, is
nowhere expressed more clearly than in the verses which banish
the ' night-thoughts,' the agonizing recollections of distant Germany
and its growing toll of corpses:

> Gottlob ! durch meine Fenster bricht
> Französisch heitres Tageslicht ;
> Es kommt mein Weib, schön wie der Morgen,
> Und lächelt fort die deutschen Sorgen.

God be praised ! Through my window the gay French daylight
breaks. My wife comes, beautiful as the morn, and smiles away
my German cares.

Crescentia Eugenie Mirat was nineteen when Heine got to know
her in October, 1834. She was an assistant in her aunt's shoe-shop,
a lively loquacious vendeuse. She came from the country, from the
village of Vinot in the Department of Seine-et-Marne. She was an
illegitimate child, the daughter—so she said—of a grand seigneur.
Her upbringing had been neglected, and when she was fifteen she
had run away from her mother to Paris. She could neither read
nor write—Heine was the first to have her given a rudimentary
education. Once he came beaming to Laube and said : ' I've sent

my big Mathilde to a girls' boarding school out in the suburbs.
There's a ball there today; you must come along and see her
dance ! ' Laube continues: ' We did in fact go, and it was really
amusing to observe Heine's childish joy. He tripped about quite
like a fairy-tale writer, and every time he whirled past us he told
us why it was he was so happy, like a high-spirited lad gaily telling
jokes against himself.'

She never learned German, of which she knew only a few
scraps, *e.g.* ' Ich bin eine wilde Katze.' She referred to herself as
' Meine Frau.' Heine wrote to his mother that Mathilde was at his
side and had just said : ' Dis à ma mère que meine Frau est très
occupée et que meine Frau l'embrasse mille fois.' Their visitors had
to speak French. She said naïvely to Laube: ' People say my
Henry is a great poet. Isn't it funny I don't understand anything
about it ? ' And Laube observes : ' It was precisely this that Heine
found delightful, for it showed she loved him for himself, not for
his talent, his fame.' ' You see how my irresistible, highly personal
charm triumphs in spite of the German Philistines,' he laughingly
exclaimed. Once, however, despite Heine's protests, Weill translated one of the miniature poems for her. And Mathilde was
enchanted by the verses. Once at the beginning of their acquaintance Heine wrote to Lewald : ' I am still so inflamed by her rosy
cheeks, my brain is still so stupefied by the overpowering scent
of flowers that emanates from her, that I am incapable of talking
to you rationally. Have you read the *Song of Songs* of King
Solomon ? Well, read it again, and you'll find everything I could
tell you today in it.'

Heine's confidante, Caroline Jaubert, knew already in 1835
of his ' love woes,' his attachment to a ' young pretty working-
girl, Juliette Mirat.' It will be seen the first names vary. ' Mathilde '
was Heine's own later invention. In his tender letters to her he
gave her the pet-name of ' Nonotte ' or ' my poor dove.' He was
jealous. He tried to get away from her, to become involved elsewhere. ' How could he please someone else,' wrote Caroline very
justly, ' if he was always thinking of the one he wept over, his
petite ? ' So the attempted rupture ended in reconciliation and in
even firmer ties of love.

A portrait of Mathilde, painted in all probability at a later
date, shows her as a ripe, dark Southern beauty. The large sensual

lips seem to be pronouncing a cynical jest, but there is a blank
look in the dream-shadowed eyes. This contrast exercises a
peculiar charm from which the observer who makes a prolonged
study of the picture cannot escape. Her toilette is arranged with
meticulous care. The full-skirted dress is of dark silk, a lace
shawl covers her Italian-style coiffure and hangs down over her
shoulders. A beautiful, ostentatiously displayed, heavily be-ringed
hand lifts one end of the shawl and holds it gently against her
breast. The rich apparel involuntarily recalls Heine's lamenting
and good-humoured grumbling at Mathilde's extravagance. To
the end she remained what he described in his letters by a Yiddish
word as a ' Verbrengerin ' (Germ. *Verbringerin,* spendthrift).

Alexander Weill, an Alsatian short story writer and journalist
who was an habitué of the Heine household—though his welcome
was not always of the heartiest—thus describes one of the many
dwellings occupied by Heine in Paris:

> Rue des Martyrs. . . . His accommodation was exactly what
> one would have expected of a German poet. No carpets, bare
> walls, no mirrors except for some shabby gilt-framed ones that
> were a fixture in the house. A table, some chairs, a bed, no
> curtains in the bedroom. No trinkets of any kind, nowhere a
> clock. A few statuettes, an old sofa, an old-fashioned writing
> table, a few pamphlets and a pile of writing paper. There was a
> coarse woollen carpet in the drawing-room and a portrait of
> Mathilde, later Heine's wife.

Weill says of Mathilde:

> She was not of bad character by any means ; in fact, she
> was good to the point of weakness, but she was too fond of
> making scenes. In a paroxysm of rage she was capable of
> beating herself with her fists. Two minutes later her fury sub-
> sided in tears and sobs. She sobbed with equal facility at the
> death of her parrot and at the death of her mother. There were
> many such scenes, particularly when her ' blood was up.' She
> was then no longer a woman, but a child, and like a child she
> would roll on the ground, stamp her feet and rain blows on
> herself. She genuinely thought she was the unhappiest creature
> in the world, and sought to win the sympathy of those who
> were present by her screams and sighs. It was side-splittingly
> funny. And—strange, but absolutely logical in one of her tem-
> perament—when she saw eventually that no one pitied her in
> the least, that no one worried about her imaginary, exaggerated

misfortunes, she burst into laughter. And this laughter suited her admirably, effectively showing off the graceful movements of her waist and divine hips. It was impossible to be angry with her, and these matrimonial scenes ended regularly with passionate ' making it up ' interspersed with Homeric laughter. ' My wild cat ' Heine called her because of these scenes. Her sudden flaring-up and then once again the tenderness with which she ' got round ' Heine were indeed cat-like. This jumping from one extreme to the other, repulsive as it seemed, kept dullness at bay, ensured that their affection would not cool off. Heine sometimes treated her like a badly brought up girl, sometimes like a pampered pet that needed smacking to bring it round, but he loved her all the more for her waywardness.

That this ménage, which for many years, moreover, was not legitimized by marriage, should have given rise to scandalmongering of the worst kind in Germany, is understandable. Heine's union with a ' Paris grisette ' was avidly seized upon by German newspaper correspondents who continually ' plugged ' it and decked it out with piquant details. As a result, Heine soon refused to receive any German writer unless he was exceptionally well recommended. Only Weill, as an ' Alsatian,' found favour. But he, as much as anybody, enjoyed describing—not without humour—how Heine would beat his wife every Monday, how the two would roll about on the carpet yelling and screaming every time they had a row, with Mathilde, for all that she was thrice as strong as her husband, who was already a sick man, never daring to strike at him in earnest.

No understanding of this unusual marriage is possible as long as one of Heine's chief traits is not taken into account: his childlike nature. ' The marriage of two children,' Marcuse aptly entitled one of the chapters of his Heine biography. In many of the manifestations of Heine's life this childlike nature seems to be something absolutely demonic. He is a childlike demon even on his bed of sickness, with his jesting piety, his infinite need of affection and his cynical *mots*, which he just couldn't understand anybody really being offended by, he averred. ' It seemed to him to be a legitimate entertainment,' wrote Caroline Jaubert—and I consider this to be one of the profoundest and most instructive *aperçus* on Heine—

to give his irony free play with the pen which was in his hand and to flay his friends with scathing sarcasm. If you tried to arouse in him some sense of remorse for what he had done, he would listen with interest and curiosity to what you were

saying, but as if he had had nothing to do with it. Then he
would resume with enthusiasm where he had left off, and
would develop his theme in another fashion, adding a number
of comparisons he hadn't dared to print and which he now
adumbrated with radiant joy on his countenance. I fancy that
if he found himself able to say, after looking into his conscience: 'My heart knows nothing of this!' he felt himself
to be innocent. Only thus can I account for the curious fact
that he did not hesitate, when the opportunity was proffered,
to lay claim to the services of people he had offended by his
writings.

It was exactly this naïveté, this childlikeness that played such
a large part in his relation to Mathilde. 'They played together like
children,' relates Laube, 'and he taught her the names of the
Phœnician kings and warned her against the disturbing literature
of Europe, and against reading altogether, and loved her most
tenderly in completely unliterary fashion.' Laube's observations are
corroborated in, among others of Heine's writings, the *Hebrew
Melodies*, which take the form of a not-too-serious lesson he is giving
to Mathilde. ' " Dear child," I replied, " such delicious ignorance
reveals the lacunæ of French education, of the Paris boarding
schools." ' And then: ' " Take my advice, sweetheart, make up for
lost time and learn Hebrew. Forget theatres and concerts, spend a
few years on your Hebrew studies, then you will be able to read
Ibn Ezra and Gabirol in the original." ' Mathilde, however, was
more interested in a precious casket which Heine had mentioned
just before and which, in his imagination, he had destined to preserve
the poems of Judah Ha-Levi:

> Meine Frau ist nicht zufrieden
> Mit dem vorigen Kapitel,
> Ganz besonders in Bezug
> Auf das Kästchen des Darius
>
> Fast mit Bitterkeit bemerkt sie:
> Dass ein Ehemann, der wahrhaft
> Religiöse sei, das Kästchen
> Gleich zu Gelde machen würde
>
> Um damit für seine arme
> Legitime Ehegattin
> Einen Kaschemir zu kaufen,
> Dessen sie so sehr bedürfe.

My wife is not satisfied with the preceding chapter, particularly as far as the casket of Darius is concerned. Almost bitterly she says a husband who was truly religious would immediately turn the casket into money with which to buy his lawful wife the cashmere shawl she needs so much.

Here as elsewhere Heine reproduces with inimitable charm the childish make-believe in which the couple indulged. We can well understand Laube saying:

Heine always took the greatest delight in Mathilde's happy, unsophisticated nature. It was a delight he never lost. To his last breath he counted himself lucky in possessing her and he himself had the air of a simple child whenever he spoke of her or described her to others. In no other relationship have I seen him display so many little charms and graces, which in his best poems peep out at us with childlike eyes.

We can also understand Heine saying to Kolb: 'My wife was quite right when she once very brusquely told someone who praised my intelligence that it was only pretence on my part.'

Like everything else that is humorous in this world, Heine's childlikeness had its serious side as well. This childlikeness was perhaps his last refuge in the conflict he could never settle between rational and irrational talent, between social justice and aristocratic individualism; it had, accordingly, the same function that Thomas Mann assigns to the poet's irony hovering over the two disparate worlds. Not, of course, that Heine deliberately constructed this 'refuge' for himself; it was part of his nature, an unalterable trait in his complex personality, given him as if to alleviate the pangs which his penchant for plunging into philosophical-theological-political difficulties would cause him. An Englishwoman who as a child of eleven had made Heine's acquaintance in Boulogne, where she had sat next to him at the *table d'hôte*, recounted in glowing terms twenty years later their walks together and the stories he had told of fishes, sirens, mermaids, a violin and a poodle. Later Heine became godfather of 'little Alice,' the daughter of a friend—Mme. Arnaut—of Mathilde's in the girls' school she attended, and was intensely devoted to the child. His imaginative sympathy with everything that had to do with children was so pronounced that he was once able to save little Jenny Marx, Karl Marx's daughter, by

his speedy medical advice. He prepared the necessary bath himself
and put the child in it. ' The picture of Heine as a practical children's
nurse may well come as a surprise to many,' rightly concludes the
reporter of this incident.

That Mathilde's unreasonableness and perennial need of money
were a source of great worry to the poet, that they provoked him
to many a questionable action which he would not have undertaken
had he had only himself to consider—this has been stressed often
enough and by many people. In this sense Mathilde must be held
responsible for Heine's bitter quarrels with Uncle Salomon's family
(his uncle had left him a small sum, but no income) and for his
campaign against his cousin Karl, whom he had rescued from
cholera.

Heine's journeys to Hamburg, his negotiations with Campe
there, and afterwards from Paris, were motivated not least by his
anxiety to see his wife provided for after his death. ' My wife, my
angel-sweet! Death drags me away from here,' he laments wildly
in the *Last Poems,* while in holy verses addressed to Thanatos, in
the entreaty he addresses to the angels, ' Protect Mathilde,' the
tone is one of profound pathos. In deeply moving words he thanks
her once more precisely for that quality of hers which captious
judges from their ivory towers have regarded with such misgiving :
her carefreeness (it has not occurred to them that Heine, after all,
must have known better than they in this matter). The peace that
flowed from one of her wholeness was deepest balm to him.

The poet who all his life stood in such need of women died
comforted by three women: his unwearying nurse Katharine was
a mother-substitute, Camilla Selden provided once more a phantom
loved one. In profoundly instinctive love and wisdom Mathilde
permitted her husband this last flickering, half-real felicity ; she
herself, however, remained a child to the last, a representation and
poeticizing of Heine's own childhood, the unshakeable childhood
of his heart. He bends over her protectingly, himself protected in
this feeling of protection: ' Ich war, o Lamm, als Hirt bestellt/
Zu hüten dich auf dieser Welt . . . Du bangtest nicht, hast nicht
gezittert,/Selbst wenn den höchsten Tann zersplittert/Der Wetter-
strahl—in meinem Schoss/Du schliefest still und sorgenlos '—I was
appointed, O lamb, thy shepherd to guard thee in this world . . .
thou fearedst not, didst not tremble even when lightning clave the

highest fir, didst sleep quietly and peacefully on my bosom. And
in his ' Thanatos ' poem[1] he sings in verse of great power and purity :

> Sie war mir Weib und Kind zugleich,
> Und geh ich in das Schattenreich,
> Wird Witwe sie und Waise sein !
> Ich lass in dieser Welt allein
> Das Weib, das Kind, das, trauend meinem Mute,
> Sorglos und treu an meinem Herzen ruhte.

She was both wife and child to me, and when I depart into
the realm of shadows she will be a widow and orphan! I leave
all on her own in this world the woman, the child who, trusting
to my courage, reposed care-free and faithful by my side.

Such words are final. There is no need to reply to the Philistines
who do not stop short at doubting the existence of an emotion even
as heartfelt as this was. One could go further, however, and apply
to Heine, as he appears to us in his love for Mathilde, the saying
that has been handed down to us from antiquity about Socrates :
the wicked are not permitted even to praise him.

He could not live without Mathilde ; that is the simple truth.
He took her with him on his second trip to Hamburg. She felt strange
among her new relatives and soon returned to Paris. ' My dear
Nonotte,' Heine wrote to her immediately, ' since you have gone
I have been worried to death.' She was to stay quite, quite still in
her nest till Heine came back. There was something fiercely
patriarchal about his jealousy. One night, during the period when
he was a physical wreck, he crawled from his mattress—he was no
longer able to walk—to the door of Mathilde's bedroom, from
whence he thought he had heard voices coming. It was nothing;
his suspicions were unfounded. Overjoyed, he fainted.

After his death, too, Mathilde loved no other man as she had
done her Henri. The Prague poet, Alfred Meissner, who was one
of Heine's intimate friends in the last years, sums up :

For Frau Mathilde Heine was not the great poet he was for
the rest of the world. He was for her, however—what the rest
of the world denied—the best, kindest-hearted, sincerest of

---

[1] *An die Engel*, No. 17 in the *Lazarus* sequence in the second book of
Romanzero.

men. With tears in her eyes she, the smiling Frenchwoman, would often tell me of certain traits in her Henri that afforded the most affecting proof of his goodness of heart. She never noted her husband's aphorisms or witticisms or brilliant inspirations, she knew nothing about them, they completely passed over her. Today (1856) she could tell you as little about him as could a child who had lived with him, but she will feel infinitely lonely, helpless and deserted, and she will live only in her memories.

' Mathilde is a Parisienne ; all Parisiennes can be seduced in five minutes,' Heine used to jest. But she lived through another generation, with her faithful friend Pauline, only for his memory, surrounded by lap-dogs and screeching parrots. Heine, jealous of the many caresses the bird received from its mistress, had once secretly poisoned her favourite parrot, Cocotte. But when he saw how upset she was, heard her cry out: ' Now I am all alone in the world,' he bought her another one within a week.

XI

' Un coin divin dans l'homme '

' It's strange that our religions should be universal in character, whereas one's religion ought of all things to be the most individual.'

Heine, in a conversation with Fanny Lewald

IN HIS SECOND YEAR in Paris (1832) Heine complained in a letter that he was unable to move two fingers of his left hand. The violent headaches which affected his ability to work and for which he sought relief in sea-bathing had made their appearance long before, in his Berlin student days. He had always been hypersensitive to noise. In Paris he began to suffer with his eyes. His left hand, soon also the whole of the left side of his body, became paralysed. He was treated by Dr. Sichel. Another doctor, Dr. Gruby, diagnosed an incipient disease of the spine. No one believed him, though. Dr. Wertheim tried his cold water treatment on the patient. A few years later Dr. Gruby was called in again, this time to save the patient. Heine greeted him with the cry: ' If only I'd listened to you ! " Gruby was unable to conceal his emotion (the Goncourts recorded in their journal) ; instead of the young, vigorous man he once knew he now found an almost blind paralytic lying on the carpet.

The treatment prescribed by Dr. Gruby restored the patient's sight and the use of his arms. Beyond that it did not prove possible to go. Heine was also able to write again. A desk was rigged up over the bedclothes and on this Heine pencilled his verses on numbered slips of paper in letters almost an inch high. Each slip of paper contained only a few lines. He recovered his sense of taste, too. He enjoyed good food, rare fruits; his appetite was good. ' Next to his doctor the most important member of the household for him was his cook,' one of his visitors felt obliged to record. His clearness of intellect had remained unimpaired the whole time. This clearness of intellect showed him the incurable nature of his disease, the inescapable presence of death.

Even in his own lifetime the experts were unable to reach any agreement on the nature of Heine's disease. Subsequently the difficulties of diagnosis have proved even greater, as the data available do not permit of any certain conclusions being drawn. Also it is difficult for us now to make anything of some of the remedies that were employed ; they seem quite fantastic. A wound in the back of the neck was kept open and injected with morphine. ' Hot cones ' were applied to the back. Dr. Rahmer's assumption of an inherited predisposition to progressive atrophy of the spinal cord seems more plausible than the rest (more plausible than tabes dorsalis or luetic infection).

In the earlier stages Heine's ailments did not confine him to his dwelling. He spent the summer of 1847 in Montmorency, where Frau Mathilde had found a pretty house with a shady garden. Alfred Meissner has a most engaging description of how Heine's friends, Alexander Weill, Heinrich Seuffert of the *Allgemeine Zeitung*, Alphonse Royer and his wife, would go down to visit the married couple every Sunday. Heine would be lying in cushioned comfort on the grass, his portfolio and pencil in hand, drafting some work or other, versifying. Every time there was a ring at the garden door Frau Mathilde would greet the newcomer with *Bon jour.* A tastefully arranged table decorated with a huge bunch of flowers stood in a large room on the ground floor. Each guest's place had a ' small arsenal of glasses ' for various wines. ' What a treat ! To sit down to table in the cool shady garden, with fragrant acacias in bloom overhead, looking into the lovely eyes of Frenchwomen, and with Heine as companion ! '

Heine was the most gracious of hosts, with an inexhaustible fund of humorous anecdote. He would describe a concert which a gathering of the composer's enemies had determined to hiss down at the end of the performance. But they failed to reckon with the

' maestro's singular genius.' The movements were so long and so
dull that the conspirators slunk off one by one. Those left behind
were fewer and fewer. In the end only the supporters' claque were
left, who were thus able to ensure the success of the piece. Or he
would describe how he called on the actress Rachel. She was not in,
but her parents were, and they left Heine in no doubt of the dignity
they felt their distinguished daughter conferred on them. It reminded
Heine of a fair-booth where a great freak of nature was being
shown, the offspring of a hare and a carp. When you went in and
paid your money you were told : ' Sorry, the freak has died, but
you're quite welcome to see its parents, the hare and the carp ! '

   The afternoon passed in laughter and merriment. In the evening
the guests would watch the *bal champêtre*. Heine in, spite of his
illness, was a joyous votary of beauty and lightheartedness, as being
' the fairest of the gods and the one who brings the most happiness.'

   Of his malady he spoke jestingly. Thus to Mme. Jaubert:' Alas,
I can now eat only on one side, weep only with one eye. Oh, ladies,
shall I be able to claim only half your hearts in future ? ' Soon,
however, the matter took a serious turn. His ' betrayal by the
family,' the parsimony of his uncle in his will, brought about a
marked relapse. He had had reason to believe that the allowance
his uncle made him would continue after his uncle's death and his
own, would provide for Mathilde; instead of which, he had been
fobbed off with a lump sum. Eventually he was successful in his
struggles with his uncle's heirs, but they cost him intense agitation.
He could not move his lips. He could not eat, talk, and, what was
hardest of all to bear, he could not kiss. Some of these symptoms
left him again, particularly under Dr. Gruby's treatment. But one
remained : he would receive visitors with a gesture that has been
described times without number : he would raise his left hand, as
if it were a lorgnette, to his eye, and would push up the atrophied
eyelid with his index finger ; at the same time he would throw back
his head to see better. He wasted away, described himself as a
' lean, one-eyed Hannibal.'

   He had hopes of a cure by German doctors, particularly by
Dieffenbach in Berlin. He asked Humboldt for a safe-conduct.
Von Bodelschwingh, Minister of Police, replied that he could expect
to be arrested the minute he set foot on Prussian soil, as he stood
accused of *lèse-majesté*. Later his yearning for Germany grew ever

more intense. ' Oh, if only I could see my Fatherland again, if only
it could be vouchsafed to me to die in Germany,' he exclaimed. An
idea he frequently hatched up in conversation with Dr. Gruby was
to have himself transported to Hamburg, to his mother, or to
Gastein, in a specially constructed ' mattress coach.' He thought of
a cure in Grafenberg, too, as his brother Gustav tells us. But
Mathilde would not feel at ease among Germans. Besides, such a
coach would cost too much. ' And really,' he added, humorously,
' the parcel isn't worth the postage.'

He went out as long as he could. To stroll through the streets
of Paris, to survey the passing scene, to go into the reading-room
in the Galerie Montpensier in the Palais Royal—these were among
his chief pleasures. A stranger who saw him enter the reading-room
has described the scene for us : people hasten to meet him, give
him their arm, lead him to a comfortable chair, immediately place
the *Augsburger Allgemeine Zeitung* before him. His one eye is
closed, the other seems immovable ; he does not follow the printed
line with it but moves the paper up and down in front of it. When
he gets up to go there is a general flutter again. Other readers see
him out, take their leave of him with a bow ; he inclines his head
gratefully. After he has gone the reading-room attendant whispers
into the stranger's ear : ' C'était Monsieur Henri Heine.'

At the beginning of January, 1848, he managed to call on Mme.
Jaubert ; he was carried on his servant's back from his coach up
to her apartment on the second floor. ' A Greek god wouldn't treat
a poet like this,' he sighed, ' but would slay him with a thunderbolt !
But to kill him off limb by limb in this wretched fashion—' A
terrible paroxysm threw him on to the sofa, one of the critical
attacks that were now becoming increasingly frequent. As soon as
he recovered he said : ' My disease is incurable. I shall lie down on
my bed and never get up. I have come here, my dear friend, to
obtain your solemn promise that you will come to see me and will
never leave me. Unless you give me your oath I shall have myself
carried in again and you will have a repetition of the distressing
scene you have just experienced ! ' Then he went on to paint a
picture of the embarrassing situation in which Mme Jaubert would
have found herself had he died on her sofa. People would have
suspected a love affair. ' What a delightful novel I would have been
the hero of ! ' Buloz, the editor of the *Revue des deux Mondes*,

would have 'ordered one of his lieutenants' to write a long short
story about it. 'No, to do me honour he would have given the job
to a captain.' Mme. Jaubert concludes her account:

> A thousand other *sottises* followed, but without his ever
> losing sight of the promise he wished to wrest from me. As I
> was extremely anxious to know him safe in his own home, I
> humoured him. Hardly had I given him the desired promise
> when he started jesting all over again. He was very good at
> getting whatever advantage he could from a misfortune, as for
> instance in claiming the 'right to be mortally ill (*droit de
> moribondage*).'

Heine went out for the last time during the revolutionary days
of February, 1848. He was caught up in a riot, took refuge in the
Louvre, where he sank down in front of the statue of Venus de
Milo. The Revolution found him weary, sceptical. He was hardly
able to credit the events in Paris having any repercussions in Vienna
and Berlin. To Campe he wrote about the 'universal anarchy,
world-mess, visible evidences of a mentally deranged divinity!
The old man will have to be locked up if this goes on.' Similarly
to his mother: 'The whole world is becoming free and bankrupt.'
He had lost his joyous hopes of 1830. He was occupied at this time,
as Meissner shows, exclusively with literary and religious questions;
he had given up politics.

> The Republic (he told Meissner) is simply a change of name,
> a revolutionary title. How could this corrupt, decadent society
> be transformed so quickly. Where could these people have been
> so carefully hiding their *bourgeois* virtues all this time? In
> Paris they are good Napoleonists, believe me—the *napoléon
> d'or* is king here.

This pessimism *vis-à-vis* his revolutionary principles is belied,
it is true, by other utterances in which he declares that the battle
that has already been joined is a just one, and in which he expressly
emphasizes that his old political opinions had been given careful
consideration, and that he would never disavow them. It is only the
personalities at the head of the good cause whom he rejects as being
too small, too much enslaved to party interests. 'All the heroes of
liberty, who had emerged after February, 1848, every single one of
them, filled him with disgust' declared one of his many visitors.
But such visitors would only be able to catch passing moods. This

reported disgust is quite incompatible, for example, with his poem, *Im Oktober, 1849*, in which he declares his sympathy with the Magyars who were in revolt against the absolutism of Vienna. (It is impossible not to be moved by the fact that there were many admirers of Heine among the Czechs, who at this time were fighting in a common front against Viennese centralism. Otokar Fischer gives a comprehensive account of the influence exerted by Heine on the Czech poets of the time. ' Our Heine,' the brilliant Bozena Nemcová called him, and recited his poems from memory. No echo of all this love penetrated into distant Paris.)

' What a disaster to experience revolutions in my condition,' lamented Heine; ' I ought to have been dead or well.' But his despondency was not caused only by his worsening malady. Even in his good times he had made a gloomy political diagnosis : ' The idyll is drawing to its close, a new blood-and-thunder piece is about to be performed ' (*Germany*, Chapter xxv). And it is in just the same spirit that he closes the poem previously mentioned on the defeat of the Hungarian heroes of freedom by Austria and her Russian ally :

> Anständ'ge Bestien sind es doch,
> Die ganz honett dich überwunden ;
> Doch wir geraten in das Joch
> Von Wölfen, Schweinen und gemeinen Hunden.
>
> Das heult und bellt und grunzt—ich kann
> Ertragen kaum den Duft der Sieger,
> Doch still, Poet, das greift dich an —
> Du bist so krank, und schweigen wäre klüger.

The beasts you fought against were decent and beat you fairly, but we come under the yoke of wolves and swine and vile dogs. They howl and bark and grunt—I can hardly bear the victors' smell. But quiet, Bard, to think about it excites you —you are so ill, silence were wiser.

Heine lived in Passy, then moved into the apartment overlooking a courtyard, No. 50, Rue d'Amsterdam, which has since become legendary. He himself gave it the name ' mattress-grave.' He who had moved so often from one apartment to another in Paris (41, Faubourg Poissonière ; 21 Rue de la Victoire ; 9, Rue de Berlin) now ' settled down.' The only other moves he made were towards the end of his life, went he went to Batignolles for the fresh air, and last of all to the Avenue Matignon, near the Champs Elysées.

It was in the Rue d'Amsterdam that the classic bed of pain was set up. It was here that the mortally sick man entered on a new phase of development ; the body wasted away but new, undreamt-of fields opened out to the hero's spirit and to that of his visitors. The case is rare in the annals of the human spirit, but not wholly unique —there are parallels in Pascal, Proust, Franz Rosenzweig and Kafka. They too, living in sick rooms and to all appearances not having long to wait for death, engaged in protracted, highly intensive intellectual activity in which their soul reached the highest flights. Heine's case is singular, however, in that he assigned an outstanding place to robust health, to *joie de vivre*, both in his system of living and in his system of thought. The others, however, in varying degree but in each case to a much greater extent than Heine, had turned even before their illness to a supersensuous world. Heine of all people was fated to endure the extreme of bodily decay ; he who had so strenuously fought against the desensualized spirit, against the cult of pure spirituality of the ' Nazarenes.' Suddenly brought low to a condition which was the visible opposite of everything he had aspired to and valued—how would he be able to come to terms with his fate ? This was the great question that confronted him since (in his own words) he was no longer ' a divine biped,' no longer ' the freest German since Goethe,' no longer ' a jovial, somewhat corpulent Hellene smiling indulgently at gloomy Nazarenes . . . just a poor, mortally sick Jew, an emaciated image of wretchedness, an unhappy human being.'

Heine answered this question by turning to religion and a personal God. In doing so he kept his political views unchanged. But atheism, which was the logical sequence of Hegel's philosophy, he renounced as decisively as Kierkegaard forsook Hegelianism. It is idle to ask ourselves whether Heine would have indulged in his existential philosophizing had his health remained unimpaired. The question, which Heine himself posed, is not idle because we are uninterested in the answer to it ; quite the contrary, an answer would enable us to see into the remotest depths of the soul. But the question is by its very nature unanswerable. And so we must content ourselves with recording the facts as they actually present themselves to our observation. These facts include, of course, the indications that Heine's renunciation in favour of the concrete was something to which he had always been predisposed. The poet's remarks which we have quoted about sentimentality, about seeing his dead father in the actual brown coat he used to wear, etc., are among such indications.

Let us consider the décor provided for the production of this tremendous transformation. Only sentimental visitors were saddened by the lack of green in the poet's room, the absence of bird-song coming through the windows. To the poet, quiet was more important. It was for this reason he had chosen an apartment over-looking a courtyard. Thick walls kept out the noise from the streets. Unfortunately, the curse of the big city, the piano-tinkler, could not be kept out.

An unquiet grave, death without the privileges of the dead, who have no need to spend money and write letters, let alone books—this is an unhappy state. I've long been measured for my coffin, and for my obituary, too, but I take such a long time dying that I am beginning to find it as tedious as my friends do. However, patience—everything comes to an end. A morning will come when you will find the shutters up on the booth where the puppet-plays of my humour used to delight you.

An ante-chamber led to the poet's room, which was large and not elegant. Two etchings by Robert which he had described comprehensively in his Paris reports—*The Fishers* and *The Reapers*—hung on the walls, as well as a portrait of Mathilde. The curtains were drawn, everything was in a grey half-light. A tapestry screen had been set up away from the window to form a bedroom, even darker than the rest of the room. Here stood the poet's bed. It took some time to get used to the darkness. Beneath the gleaming white bedclothes the wasted body of the poet was barely discernible; it seemed to be without muscles, without flesh, almost without blood. The hands were beautiful, white, and exquisitely formed. The features were calm and composed, with no trace of pain. Heine endured his afflictions with stoical fortitude that called forth com-passion mingled with admiration from his visitors. Only the nights were terrible, without hope, prompting thoughts of suicide which only versifying and morphine enabled him to overcome. He con-stantly reaffirmed his gratitude for the relief derived from this great partnership. 'Opium is also a religion.' 'The Muse has not forsaken me, she accompanies me to the very grave.'

Eight years the last, terrible, hopeless final stage of Heine's disease lasted ; for full eight years, from February, 1848, to February, 1856, Heine was tied to his bed. Occasionally he was able to lie in an armchair. These were the 'good' days. Often, Mme. Jaubert tells us, he lay on 'two mattresses on the floor.' Later on he adopted this system permanently. Scrupulous cleanliness testified to his wife's constant care. It is said that Heine had a feeling of greater mobility lying thus close to the floor, and could more easily reach the books, journals, and papers which were strewn about him ; it was this which decided him, 'a poor, unburied corpse,' to prefer this mode of lying-in-state to all others. Many visitors saw how his nurse would carry him in her broad arms, 'like an eight-year-old child,' from this mattress-grave to his bath or bed. Half-humorously, half-sighing, Heine would say: '*Sic transit gloria mundi!*' 'Without any doubt guessing my thoughts, although he couldn't see me,' wrote Adolf Stahr. 'Tell them in Germany that in Paris they idolize me (*dass man mich in Paris auf Händen trägt*—they carry me on their hands),' Heine impressed on another visitor on one such occasion.

Mathilde came up trumps. 'Her naturally sunny temperament enabled her to feel that each new threatening symptom would pass away, and it was precisely elemental optimism of this kind which proved a boon to Heine' (Laube). 'She's like the angels!' Heine used to say; 'they need no mortgages, they always have ready cash.' Once he exclaimed in delight: 'Ten years happily married! what other German poet can say as much?' And to Campe he wrote:

> The serene consciousness of having lived a fine life fills my soul even in this troublous time and will, I hope, remain with me in my last hours to the very brink of the white abyss—between ourselves, this last is the least terrifying, dying is horrible, not death, if there is indeed a death. Death is perhaps the last superstition.

He told Fanny Lewald of his happy marriage:

> We were bound to each other by no engagement or compulsion from without. Often in my sleepless nights I am frightened at the idea of such bliss, a rapturous shudder passes

through my frame when I think of such overflowing happiness. I've often been facetious and joked about these things, and more often thought about them seriously ; love is not maintained by any hire-agreement, it needs freedom if it is to take root and prosper.

Certain of Heine's biographers have made ludicrous attempts— which I mention purely for the record—to represent all his numerous utterances about his happy married life as mere pose. How easy many writers find it to impugn the integrity of poets whose lives they are inspired to write by an urge which in all consciousness seems inexplicable ; after all, one would have thought that only a love, or at least some understanding of, the poets whose lives they choose to describe would have prompted their undertaking.

Not, of course, that Heine's feelings for Mathilde were always on the same high plane. Where is such unvarying affection to be found! It is quite certain that Mathilde often got on his nerves. It would not have been a matter of indifference to him that she once boxed Dr. Wertheim's ears when he said something about ' better nursing.' Frequently, too, he ' would summon up remembrance of things past.' Then he would long for Amalie, then he would write the poem with which even Meissner, otherwise her loyal partisan, damned Mathilde : ' Verfehlte Liebe, verfehltes Leben '—A failure in love, a failure in life—the poem that is so euphonious and begins in sweetly unself-conscious musing : ' Zuweilen dünkt es mich, als trübe/Geheime Sehnsucht deinen Blick '—Sometimes I think a secret longing casts a shadow on your brow.

Nevertheless, these passing moods are not decisive ; and what can they avail against Heine's telling Houssaye that Juliette (Mathilde) sought with all her strength not to let him go, ' so greatly does she love me ; when I'm on the point of death she weeps so piteously that I awaken in order to drink her tears.' And Mme. Jaubert knew that   ' Her voice was a perpetual charm for Heine. He alluded to it incessantly. Often he assured me that in his long struggle with death this voice had held his soul fast at the very moment when it gathered up its wings for the flight into the unknown.'

On days when his body was racked with pain beyond endurance

he saw no one. We catch no glimpse of Heine's actual physical
sufferings except when it was impossible for him to hide them.
Pride and a deep self-respect sealed his lips. Once his pain left
him and he was able to talk again he regained his natural high
spirits. He would tell his godchild, Alice Arnaut, tales of Paradise,
of the angels who ate cake there and wiped their mouths with
their white wings. ' *Ce qui du reste est bien sale de leur part,*' the
child exclaimed indignantly. ' My wife,' continued Heine—our
informant is Fanny Lewald—

> laughed till the tears ran down her cheeks at the story and
> the child's absorption in the cake-eating angels who used their
> wings as table napkins. (My own pleasure in the telling of the
> story contributed not a little to my wife's merriment, too.)
> The whole of the next night I spent in making up some
> exceedingly gay verses.

He could jest, but his serious opinions and judgments lost
nothing in intensity. His sick-bed pronouncements on Shakespeare
no less than on the ' sweet charm ' of Shakespeare's antipode,
Racine, are of the highest order. He would describe plans he had
formed. He would like to write the ' Life of Jan Steen from his
Pictures.' ' It filled me with the greatest pleasure that in one of
his best pictures he showed his wife, who had often berated him
for his drinking, as a drunken woman.' He toyed also with the idea
of a ' Till Eugenspiegel '—he thought it would have been one of
the best things he had done.

Meanwhile, he composed, night after night, stanzas of the
Lamentations, of *Lazarus,* of the *Hebrew Melodies* that carry us
away by their rare power. Combined with the *Histories,* they form
the greatest of his verse-cycles, the *Romanzero.* His secretary
would come in the morning to find the poem ready fashioned in
the poet's brain. He would dictate it, and then would begin a
process of revision and polishing that would last for hours.
Romanzero is Heine's masterpiece. His description of it—in a letter
to his mother—as very weak must have escaped him in a moment
of depression when his spirits were at their lowest ebb: ' I wrote
it when my strength was already broken.' But to Meissner he said:

> Yes, I know well enough it's beautiful, horribly beautiful!
> It's a cry from the grave, a cry in the night from someone
> buried alive, or even from a corpse, or even from the grave

itself. Oh, yes, German poetry has never heard these accents, could never have been able to hear them, because no poet has ever found himself in such a condition.

His secretary had to read him many medical works dealing with his disease, but an even greater number of theological works and ecclesiastical histories; also the Bible, ' which he knew practically by heart.' ' He wanted to have nothing to do with newspapers; at the most he read the *Journal des Débats*.' Here is the list of books that one secretary read to him in the course of some eight or nine months: *Wilhelm Meister, Wahrheit und Dichtung, Tasso, Faust* (both parts), *Geisterseher*, and practically all of Schiller's dramas.

In particular he esteemed *Wallenstein* very highly. At the same time he did not begrudge taking pains to initiate his secretary into the secrets of the writer's trade. He explained the Why and Wherefore of certain aspects of style to the twenty-year-old youth, even pointing out to him the poetical ' dodges ' which he immediately discerned as they occurred. He drew his attention to the finest nuances of expression and commended to him over and over again the sobriety of the classic authors.

In addition, he enjoyed having travel books read to him. They were a substitute for the far-off world of colour and animation he could not see. Also all Dumas' novels. ' He's entertaining, that mulatto!' he exclaimed. ' He's quite extraordinary. His fantasies give me a rest from my own.' He was grateful for every genuine enrichment. Meissner acquainted him with Schopenhauer's ideas, Fichte's son with Swedenborg's visions. He acknowledged the wit in the writings of his kinsman, Hermann Schiff, but blamed him for

> too harshly exposing the sordid side of Jewish life. The surface filth of the meanest Jewish pedlar often conceals nobility and magnanimity. Often they (the Jews) conceal these splendid qualities purposely, just as in times of oppression they preserved their wealth from covetous eyes behind a screen of poverty.

For the same reason he criticized adversely Auerbach's novel *Poet and Merchant* (on Heine's predecessor who has frequently been noted in these pages, the Breslau poet Kuh). He discussed with a wealth of detail the Jewish types he had seen at the Leipzig Fair: great beauty jostling extreme ugliness. A painter of Biblical subjects ought to study both kinds, he said. One of the

young men he had seen at the fair looked very noble, like the
sorrowing Daniel. 'What contrasts this race produces!' he once
interrupted one of his callers. 'At one time Judas right next to a
Christ. And next to a Jacoby, whom you describe as a paragon
of selflessness, a Ferdinand Lassalle, who is the embodiment of
self-seeking, despite his great talent!'

It is impossible to convey adequately the fullness and the wide
scope of these last discussions. Indications only can be given.
Often the conversation turned on conditions in Germany. Then his
talk would take on a real Socratic irony. He would—apparently—
efface his own personality the better to reveal the outside world in
all its harshness and senseless contradictions. He 'expressed the
most ardent hopes for Germany's future and at the same time
joked about how surprised and frightened the Germans would be
if they ever became free.' Or he would exclaim:

> Oh, I can't write any more, I can't, because we haven't
> a censorship. How can anyone who has always written under
> censorship write without censorship? It would be the end of
> style, of grammar, of morals. Whenever I wrote anything stupid
> before, I thought: Well, the censor will delete it or alter it;
> I relied on the good old censorship. But now—I feel very
> unhappy, I just don't know what to do! I still hope it's all
> untrue and the censorship is still flourishing.

This irony enabled him to endure everything, even the worst, his
own physical helplessness. He described himself as a 'semi-corpse,'
spoke of the day when 'he would have exchanged the painful
grave in the Rue d'Amsterdam for the painless one in the cemetery
of Montmarte.' Such an exchange would be splendid business for
Campe.

Campe treated him badly; the relationship between the two
men was subject to violent fluctuations, like a passionate love-affair.
Heine protested at the relationship being reduced to a purely commercial level. Campe was his friend, he maintained, had obligations
beyond the mere letter of the contract. Campe took his revenge by
leaving all Heine's letters unanswered for three years—a cruel and
senseless torture to inflict on a mortally sick man who was more
than ever dependent on the yield from his books. Eventually relations were restored. 'I already have a monument in Germany,'
quipped Heine, 'the magnificent new offices my publisher has built

out of the profit of my books.' His humour never left him. His
sufferings were reported to have beautified his features; many callers
compared them to Christ's. Heine commented: '*J'ai dans ce
moment un grand succès de moribond.*' Together with sublime
irony there was no lack of the old simple malice. He greeted a
visitor with the remark: 'You find me a little stupid today. Wihl
has just gone: we've exchanged ideas.'

But when one of his faithful callers went away for a lengthy
time, he would weep. He found it hard to say good-bye.

Tears in Heine's eyes (relates Alfred Meissner), in the eyes
of the man whom the world had so often condemned as heart-
less. I couldn't help myself, I was overcome by emotion. . . .
That moment was imprinted on my soul as something eternally
unforgettable. I clasped his hand and pressed it firmly. 'I hope
the interminable death song of the swan of the Rue
d'Amsterdam hasn't bored you too much!' whispered the sick
man, and turned aside.

His brothers Max and Gustav came to see him, his sister
Charlotte, for whom his affection had always been particularly
tender; even his cousin Therese, whom he had once loved, put in
an appearance. His letters to his mother contain outbursts of the
most ardent devotion. Once he writes: 'My dear, good, upright,
and loyal mother, what are the others in comparison with you. We
ought to kiss the floor your foot has trodden on.'

The depressing monotony of the sick-room was masked—it
could hardly have been eliminated—by all this emotional activity.
Many poems portray this leaden existence with its all too
unmistakable intimation of impending death. We read also of
frighteningly eerie scenes like this one: 'One evening in particular
we had become absorbed in a long discussion on German books
of magic, folk-tales and folk-songs. Suddenly Heine seemed to
forget his bodily state completely; in quavering tones he began to
sing the song of Eugene the gallant knight . . .'

And indeed, what a strangely intimate rôle music now began
to play in the life of the erstwhile concert critic, who had not always
performed his duties *con amore*. Fanny Lewald told him that in
Germany his own poems were being sung as folk-songs by high
and low, prentice and soldier. He now heard of this phenomenon
for the first time and rejoiced over every detail with which Fanny

Lewald supplied him. ' He did not know the famous Loreley tune,'
relates Fanny Lewald. The pity of it!

His visitors also told him of Mendelssohn's, Löwe's and
Schubert's musical settings of his poems. He knew only a very few
of them. He liked Löwe's settings best of all ; he said they had
' captivated him ' and that he ' would like to have an instrument
and die playing and singing these melodies.' In 1840 Schumann
sent him the *Heine Lieder-cycle*, Op. 24, without receiving an
answer. It is doubtful whether the pieces ever reached Heine ; the
covering letter was found in his posthumous papers. In 1856 the
Cologne Male Voice Choir undertook a concert tour to Paris. Two
members of the choir (according to another account, a whole section
of the choir's leading members) took the opportunity to visit the
invalid and to sing for him, ' in subdued voices,' settings of his
poems which he did not yet know.

Irony is the term rightly applied to what is too big to grasp—
to what is really unsayable and can only be lived, felt, accomplished—to Socrates' daimon and Kierkegaard's paradox—to the
miracle this side of heaven. Hence we must not be misled by the
irony in Heine's last pronouncements. The irony does not detract
from their gravity ; it is rather that the themes are too grave to
be expressed other than ironically.

' Today I had an extraordinarily comforting dream,' he once
said to Meissner.

It was bright and early in the morning and I was walking
in the cemetery at Montmarte, where I propose being buried
one day—it's quiet and you're not disturbed nearly so much
there as you are at Père Lachaise. The tombstones were
gleaming in the rising sun, and lo! in front of every tombstone
stood a pair of highly polished shoes, women's or men's boots
according to whether the sleepers down below were married
women, spinsters, or men. It was like a big hotel where the
Boots goes from door to door as soon as it is light and neatly
and carefully places the footwear where it belongs. All the
occupants of the graves were still fast asleep, but there was a
magnificent shine on the polished boots, as if they had been
polished by angels, and the whole picture seemed to say:
' Yes, we shall all rise again and begin a new life.'

What particularly distinguishes this description of a dream is
its cheerful, ' bright and early,' gay conversational tone. We feel

that the creed expressed here is an absolutely individual one. The whimsical, tender, serenely confident belief in immortality is highly personal to a unique human being, Heinrich Heine. It has nothing in common with the mysticism of national-German Christianity, although the poet Heine on occasion came close to it. In his book on Börne he says (when discussing Menzel) of those authors who had succumbed to this mysticism: 'Soon they would have incited the rude masses against us with the dark spells of the Middle Ages, and these spells, a mixture of primeval superstition and demonic elemental forces, would have been stronger than all rational arguments.' He himself, however, was proud of retaining his clear rationalism to the end. Along the narrow boundary line separating the sensuous from the supersensuous region he walked steadily forwards with unclouded vision. In this way he drew near to Judaism in the last part of his life, in the same cheerful, serene, ironical manner in which he had proclaimed his belief in immortality in his vision of the cemetery. 'Now that I have to think hourly about my death,' he said to Fanny Lewald, 'I often have very earnest discussions with Jehovah at night, and he has told me: " You may be anything you like, dear doctor, Republican or Socialist—but not an atheist, please." '

The seeds of the change had been sown many years previously. In his *History of Religion and Philosophy* (1834) he opposes spiritualism (meaning the cult of the spiritual), materialism and sensualism to each other. Spiritualism he regards as the insolent claim of the spirit to rule *alone*, seeking pleasure in abstinence and in the denial of the flesh and in pain. Sensualism, on the other hand, he regards with the Saint-Simonists as the *union* of spiritual and sensual postulates, the harmony of spirit and body. He distinguishes sensualism from materialism, in which the spirit, innate ideas, are denied. Materialism, then, is one-sided, just as is spiritualism, only in the opposite direction. Heine rejected the one-sidedness both of spiritualism and materialism. In sensualism he saw the synthesis, the middle path and the harmony which he sought. He identifies sensualism with Spinoza's pantheism: God is everything that is, he is body as well as spirit, 'both are equally divine, and whoever offends against holy matter is as sinful as he who sins against the Holy Ghost.' This doctrine is very clear and goes the right way about attacking one-sidedness—but is wrong,

all the same. We can prove it up to the hilt. In fact, it really does
one good to be able for once not merely to affix the hoary platitude,
'They're complicated' to these admittedly complicated matters, but
in this instance to say in so many words: 'They're wrong, and in
this, that,or the other particular.'

However, let us trace the process of Heine's thoughts a little
further. First he asserts that the bodily and the spiritual have equal
rights and are in fundamental accord. From here it is a step to
the assertion that the bodily matter has been ill-treated hitherto.
The Jews are to blame for this, Heine holds. True, only a few
pages earlier, in talking precisely of Spinoza, the Jew, for whom
matter and spirit were one and in harmony, he had adumbrated
the idea that 'the spirit of the Hebrew prophets rested perhaps
on their distant grandchild.' He forgets this afterwards, though, and
avers:

> The Jews thought of the body as something insignificant,
> as a miserable covering for the *Ruach hakodasch* [*sic,* for
> *hakodesch*], the holy breath, the spirit, and it was this only
> on which they lavished their care and which they held in
> reverence and to which they devoted their cult. Hence they
> became to a unique degree the people of the spirit ; chaste,
> frugal, earnest, abstract, stiff-necked, suited to martyrdom, and
> their sublimest flowering is Jesus Christ.

In this fashion Heine is able to subsume Christianity and
Judaism under the general heading of Nazarenism, with which he
contrasts Hellenism (by which he understands the sensualism he
identified with pantheism). And so he reaches the famous climax
in his book on Börne (there is a similar passage in the *Rabbi von
Bacharach*):

> I say 'Nazarene' to avoid using either 'Jewish' or
> 'Christian,' although the two words are synonymous for me
> and I use them to describe, not a religion, but a temper of
> mind. 'Jews' and 'Christians' are for me words of similar
> meaning and I oppose them to 'Hellenes,' an expression
> which, again, I use to designate, not a particular nation, but
> an intellectual disposition and outlook which may be either
> innate or the result of upbringing. In this sense I would say:
> 'All men are either Jews or Hellenes, people who hate
> imagery and are of an ascetic, spiritualizing temper, or down-
> to-earth people who rejoice in life and in its possibilities of
> self-development.'

And he asks: 'When will there be harmony once more, when will
the world recover from its one-sided cult of the spiritual, the mad
error through which both soul and body fell sick!'

His answer: hitherto there had been over-spiritualisation;
now the time had come to redress the balance by the reverse
process, the 'rehabilitation of matter,' Saint-Simonism. (The
resemblance between this anti-Christian element in Heine and
Nietzsche's anti-Christian doctrine is fortuitous and superficial—
Nietzsche is a different case from Heine altogether. I cannot go
into this here.) Heine says:

> The first thing is to get well, for we are still very weak on
> our pins. The holy vampires of the Middle Ages have sucked
> such a lot of blood out of us. And we must lay rich sin-offerings
> on the altar of matter so that it may forgive the old insults. It
> would indeed be desirable to ordain festivals of games and
> lavish still more extraordinary honours on matter to compen-
> sate it for its past injuries. For Christianity, unable to destroy
> matter, has everywhere dishonoured it, it has degraded the
> noblest pleasures, and the senses had to dissimulate, and
> falsehood and sin resulted.

And he ascribes to pantheism, through making man aware of his
divinity, the power of inspiring him to 'reveal his god-like
qualities,' to 'perform the true epic deeds of true heroism on
this earth.' A revolution, then, but not

> for the Rights of Man for the people, but for the Rights of
> God for men. . . . We are founding a democracy of equally
> glorious, equally sacred, equally inspired gods. You demand
> plain clothes, frugal habits, and insipid pleasures; we, on the
> other hand, demand nectar and ambrosia, purple cloaks, costly
> perfumes, uninhibited revelry, pomp and splendour, laughter
> and dance of girls, music and masque. Restrain your wrath,
> you virtuous Republicans! We shall answer your censorious
> rebukes in the words of Shakespeare's fool: 'Dost thou think,
> because thou art virtuous, there shall be no more cakes and
> ale?'

The voice becomes shrill and then hoarse. The antagonist of one-
sidedness, using the century-old neglect of the flesh as a pretext,
has without noticing it himself lurched into a one-sided cult of the
flesh. Heine's error reflects the happiness of his first years in Paris;
his 'Religion of Joy' has in it something of the joy of the discharged
prisoner. Nevertheless, its ideological anchorage seemed likely to

remain firm for a long time to come, as is mostly the case with errors. 'We want to build the kingdom of heaven here on earth, now' is stridently proclaimed as late as the *Germany* cycle.

Heine's error was twofold: factual and historical. The historical error was due to his interpretation of Judaism.

His factual error. He desired the harmony of matter and spirit. But he failed to see that such a harmony entailed the union of two opposites. He acted as if it were a question of simply joining two phenomena which were in any case closely allied. In reality there is a genuine paradox, the union of incompatibles. Spirit and matter need each other for mutual perfection but are in equal measure in mutual conflict. The spirit must seek to repel matter, matter spirit ; therein consists their life ; therein, and yet also in their finding their way to each other again. Heine harmonizes too quickly, he makes things too easy for himself. Consider merely one thing: the spirit demands justice. In the world of ideas Plato's dictum that they neither suffer nor commit injustice holds good. In the world of matter, however, every organism lives at the expense of the other. A simple, direct linking, therefore, of the kind Heine postulates in his 'democracy of gods' is pure fantasy. 'Wherever a great mind speaks its thought is Golgotha' ; thus Heine sings the crown of thorns that Spinoza, like Jesus, bore. But soon afterwards this truth escapes him again. He does not *want* to realize that there is a conflict. And yet it is essential to live through all the terror of this conflict of body and mind before attempting to undertake the equally mysterious union of the two. Heine was rightly imbued with the feeling that such a union was indispensable, but had no conception of its difficulty. Not till you have despaired of the union as being something as impossible as it is necessary, not till then can the miracle—perhaps—be achieved!

It would seem that Heine's hedonistic outlook long stood in the way of his attaining this final insight. It would have been jollier, admittedly, had body and mind always marched together in friendly harmony instead of sometimes taking quite different paths; if the mind had always prospered in concord with the body and not often flourished at the body's expense. That sort of thing hurts, is opposed to every hedonistic principle, but it reveals the situation in all its grandeur. It was Heine's hedonism that revolted against this larger view. It was in his hedonism, therefore, that he *had* to be deeply injured, in his body, in the husk of matter . . . so that he could attain the necessary insight. I am loth to apply Schopenhauer's 'seeming purposiveness in the life of every human being' in so cruel a context, but—if this sombre dictum has been exemplified anywhere, it surely comes to mind here in Heine's terrible illness more vividly than anywhere else.

It was Heine's illness that led him from the spurious mean (sensualism, pantheism) to the real one. This mean is not abstract, general, and formalistic. It can be grasped only existentially, in the adventure of faith ; it is entirely individual and concrete. It changes from one decisive moment to another, it demands that the whole groping, advancing, living personality be flung into the battle. As long as we deal in generalities, as long as we are not concerned with the highly personal suffering of the individual that mocks all rules and formulas, so long, no doubt, will Hegel's self-motivation of concepts, according to which everything that happens happens reasonably and self-evidently, be sufficient for our understanding of the universe. ' Zu fragmentarisch ist Welt und Leben/Ich will mich zum deutschen Professor begeben/Der weiss das Leben zusammenzusetzen/Und er macht ein verständlich System daraus ;/ Mit seinen Nachtmützen und Schlafrockfetzen/Stopft er die Lücken des Weltenbaus.'—World and life are too fragmentary. I will go to the German professor ; he can put life together and make a comprehensible system of it. With his nightcaps and shreds of dressing-gowns he plugs the gaps in the universe. This scathing criticism of Hegel's philosophy is exactly the line that Kierkegaard was to take later. Heine was the first existential philosopher. His clear understanding, sharpened by his sufferings, of what was concrete, irrational, unique in the individual human being's fate led him to reject the flat, non-committal generality of the Hegelian philosophy. It is in this light that his assertion, repeatedly wrung from him by his sufferings, that he needed a God who could *help* him, is to be understood. He said to Fanny Lewald: ' It is strange that our religions should be universal in character, whereas one's religion ought of all things to be the most individual.' And to Mme. Jaubert, who cross-examined him about his conversion, he said humbly, after much hesitation: ' *Il y a pourtant un coin divin dans l'homme.*' To Ludwig Kalisch he said: ' People's misery is too great. You *have* to believe.'

Heine's conversion did not lead him to the dogma of any particular church, it was not tied to any particular religious denomination. He had not become a believing Catholic or a believing Protestant, contrary to what could be read in German newspapers at the time. A believing Jew ? Not that either. He wanted to ' believe ' *tout court*, wanted to say openly in front of the ' entire upper clergy of atheism,' in front of all the ' fanatical priests of unbelief ' (who certainly exist!) : ' Yes, I have returned to God after having tended swine for a long time with the Hegelians.' This religious confession with its rejection of ' everything churchy,' its dispensing with ' bell-pealing and altar-candles,' occurs in Heine's masterpiece of irony, the ' epilogue ' to the *Romanzero*. He expressed himself similarly in a conversation with Kalisch : ' I have found my way to the good God unaided by church or synagogue. No priest, no rabbi introduced me to him. I made myself known to him myself and he received me kindly. He healed my soul; may he be able to heal my body as well. I should be truly grateful to him for it.'

In a letter he wrote to his old friend Laube in 1850 he says, after developing, in opposition to the ' Hegelian godlessness,' the ' dogma of an actual personal God who exists outside Nature and man's mind ' : ' Hegel has gone down greatly in my estimation, whereas old Moses is doing splendidly.' Did Judaism play some part after all, then, in Heine's new-found piety ? Let us glance first at his piety without reference to any possible Jewish elements in it. It is so marked, this piety, that he would have preferred the second edition of his *History of Religion and Philosophy* not to be printed. As, however, he was not entitled to veto a second edition he wrote a preface revoking the core of the whole book.

I admit frankly that everything in this volume relating particularly to the grand question of God's existence is as wrong as it was ill-considered. Equally ill-considered and wrong was my assertion, in which I followed the school philosophers, that the theory of deism had been utterly destroyed. . . . Deism lives, is alive and very much kicking, is not dead, and the latest German philosophy has killed it least of all. This cobwebby dialectic couldn't lure a dog from the hearth, it couldn't kill a cat, how much less a God.

And he refers satirically to the serpent in the Garden of Eden, ' the little *Privatdozentin* (University lecturer) who six thousand years before Hegel's birth had expounded the entire Hegelian philosophy: to wit, that it was in man that God had attained consciousness of himself.'

The whole change of heart is documented most clearly in the *Confessions*. It flattered my pride, says Heine, when I learnt from Hegel that the good God did not dwell in heaven, but that I myself was the good God here on earth. But in the event it didn't prove possible to put the idea into effect.

> I returned to the fold of God's lowly creatures, and I acknowledged once more the omnipotence of a supreme Being who presides over the destinies of this world and who in future would direct my own earthly affairs. These had become considerably confused in the period when I was my own providence, and I was glad to hand them over to a heavenly superintendent, as it were, whose omniscience really does enable him to look after them much better than I could.

Thus beneath the droll expressions lies a realization of human helplessness in the face of infinity, the ' noble misfortune.' Elsewhere he accounts rather more superficially for his conversion from atheism by denigrating the atheistic standpoint: ' Unwashed journeymen cobblers and tailors presumed to deny in their coarse boarding-house language the existence of God,' and ' atheism began to smell very strongly of cheese, brandy, and tobacco.' But, on the higher level, he refers again to his source of inspiration: ' My eyes were opened simply through reading a book '—the Old Testament, the real ' Temple treasure, which, praise be to God, was not destroyed by flames or the wicked Titus Vespasianus, who came to such a bad end, as the rabbis tell us.'

In particular the story of Nebuchadnezzar captured his imagination ; the king who thought that he himself was the good God but then fell from his high estate and crawled like an animal on the ground and ate grass. So he refers the neo-Hegelians to the Book of Daniel, he commends the story ' not merely to dear Ruge, but also to my much more dyed-in-the-wool friend Marx, and to Messrs. Feuerbach, Daumer, Bruno Bauer, Hengstenberg, and the rest of the crowd, the godless self-Gods.' And he signed one letter ' Nebuchadnezzar II, sometime Royal Prussian atheist, now lotus-flower worshipper.'

His reading of the Bible led him to an understanding of Judaism.
No longer did he dilute it to a simple ' temper ' lacking a national
basis. Previously he himself had not always avoided the mistake,
which he so emphatically condemned, of ' spiritualizing.' Like the
bad politician   that, in typically Jewish fashion, he was, he had
counselled the Poles not to mourn unduly the statehood whose
political reality they had lost, but, ' as once Israel after the fall of
Jerusalem,' to ' raise ' themselves to a purely spiritual existence.
Now, in contrast, his outlook became completely practical. He saw
Moses as legislator to a real community which he remodelled
realiter in accordance with the loftiest moral principles. He
particularly enjoyed listening to his old friend Princess Belgiojoso,
who had just returned from a voyage to the East, when she spoke
of Palestine, a country ' across which he had often travelled in his
mind since the Bible had become his favourite reading.' (Our
informant is Mme. Jaubert.) Now he also understood the ' Jewish
love of freedom,' ' the early greatness of Israel ' in the midst of
nations who held slavery to be just. In Moses he saw a Socialist who,

> as a practical man, sought only to refashion existing customs,
> particularly in relation to property. So instead of grappling with
> the impossible, instead of wildly decreeing the abolition of
> property, he endeavoured to make it more moral, he sought
> to bring property into harmony with morality, with justice
> genuinely based on reason, and he achieved this by introducing
> the year of jubilee whereby all alienated hereditary property,
> which in an agricultural nation always consisted of land,
> reverted to the original owner, no matter in what way the
> property had been alienated originally. This institution was in
> complete contrast to the ' limitation ' of the Romans.

Through his immersion in the study of Moses' social legislation
Heine had already tacitly corrected the second of the two errors
I have noted, the *historical* error, the error of regarding Judaism
as being essentially a ' Nazarene ' religion that flees the world, that
denies the reality of existence here below. What Heine now
expressed, without actually using these words, was the ' here-below
miracle ' of Judaism, the combination of a concrete nationhood
and a universal faith ; a synthesis to which just as much injustice
is done if it is robbed of its national content as if it is deprived of
its universal, metaphysical content. For the substance of Judaism
lies precisely in the ' concretization ' and national revelation of an

infinite idea, in the 'Kingdom of God' as Martin Buber has
derived it from our oldest traditions.

And so Heine's own formulation of this conception now
follows, the words he wrote two years before his death, in those
tremendous *Confessions* whose simplicity and sincerity tug at our
hearts. Here, then, are Heine's concluding words on the Jewish
question, his pæan to Moses ('And he is my best hero' had
already come before, in *Vitzliputzli*), his tribute to the 'master-
builder' who steps on to Sinai (and how small Sinai seems to the
poet when Moses stands on it!):

> Previously I had had no great love for Moses, probably
> because the spirit of Hellenism predominated in me, and I
> could not forgive the legislator of the Jews his hatred of all
> pictorial representation, of all plastic art. I failed to see that
> Moses, in spite of his hostility to art, was nevertheless a great
> artist and possessed a true artistic spirit. Only, in his case, as
> with his Egyptian compatriots, this artistic spirit was directed
> solely to the colossal and the indestructible. But unlike the
> Egyptians he did not fashion his works of art out of brick-
> work and granite but built human pyramids, he sculptured
> human obelisks, he took a poor tribe of shepherds and from it
> created a nation that like the pyramids and the obelisks would
> defy the centuries ; a great, eternal, holy nation, God's nation
> that could serve all the other nations as a pattern, could serve
> all humanity as a prototype ; he created Israel. With greater
> justice than the Roman poet can this artist, the son of Amram
> and Jochebed the midwife, boast of having built a monument
> that will outlast all works made of bronze. Neither of the
> master-builder nor of his work, the Jews, have I spoken with
> sufficient veneration in the past, and no doubt this was again
> due to my Hellenic temperament which found Jewish
> asceticism uncongenial. My predilection for Hellas has
> diminished since then. I see now that the Greeks were only
> handsome youths, whereas the Jews were always men, valiant,
> unyielding men, not merely then but up till now, in spite of
> eighteen centuries of persecution and misery. I have learnt to
> appreciate them better since, and were not all pride of birth a
> foolish contradiction in the champions of revolution and its
> democratic principles the writer of these pages could be proud
> that his ancestors belonged to the noble house of Israel, that
> he is a descendant of the martyrs who gave the world a God
> and a moral code and who have fought and suffered on all the
> battlefields of thought. The history of the Middle Ages and
> even of our modern era has seldom recorded in its daily

chronicles the names of these knights of the holy spirit, for they usually fought with lowered visor. The deeds of the Jews are as little known to the world as their real character. People think they know them because they have seen their beards, but nothing else of theirs ever came to sight and, just as in the Middle Ages so in our own day they are a wandering mystery, a mystery which may be revealed in the day of which the prophet spoke that there would be but one shepherd and one flock and the righteous one who had suffered for the salvation of mankind would be hailed in glory.

Truly, to the man who wrote that, the truth of the words he spoke (in a conversation with Ludwig Kalisch, in 1850) may be granted: 'I make no secret of my Judaism, to which I have not returned, *as I have never left it.*'

Kom-me du bald!

In the middle of June, 1855, a charming young woman entered Heine's apartment at No. 3, Rue de Matignon. She had been in Vienna, where a Viennese admirer of Heine's, the composer Vesque von Püttlingen, had asked her to take the poet some music. She had already accomplished her mission without being permitted to see Heine, whose poems she had admired as the 'vital element of her youth,' when the bell in the adjoining room rang shrilly and a 'somewhat imperious voice' asked her to stay. She entered the dark room and found herself in front of a bed-screen. Then she stood by the invalid's bedside. 'He looked much younger than he really was.' Fascinating features, the face of Christ with the smile of Mephistopheles. Heine extended his hand to her. After a short conversation he gave her a book and invited her to come again. She took the invitation to be purely formal, but soon there came a letter:

Kindest and most delightful of persons! It is a matter of keenest regret to me that I have seen so little of you lately. You have left a very pleasant impression behind you, and I feel a great longing to see you again. Come from tomorrow, if you can ; in any case come as soon as possible. I can receive you at any time of the day, but four o'clock would be best, until—whenever you like. I'm writing to you myself, in spite of my weak eyes, as I haven't a secretary I can rely on at the moment. My ears have been stupefied by all kinds of abominable noises, and I have been very sickly the whole time. I don't know why it is that your affectionate sympathy proves so beneficial to me. Superstitious as I am, I believe that a good fairy has visited me in my hour of sorrow. No, if the fairy was good, the hour was a happy one, too. Or were you a wicked fairy ? I must know soon. Your Heinrich Heine.

Camilla Selden accepted the invitation. And wrote in her memoirs, *The Last Days of Heinrich Heine* (it is a reflection of her good taste that she did not have them published till 1884, a generation after Heine's death): 'From that day onwards my visits ceased only on the bleak February day when the poet was borne to his last resting place.' Eight months then, the last eight months of Heine's life, were filled with the love that now entered the poet's life.

All the efforts of those engaged in Heine research have failed to shed any light on the personality of the lady who wrote several books under the name of Camilla Selden and died in Rouen in 1897. According to her own statement, she was 25 when she made Heine's acquaintance, was born of poor parents and had been adopted by an officer of artillery who later went to America. It is not known for certain what her real name was, Elise Krinitz or Krienitz or von Krinitz, and whether Krinitz was the name of her natural or of her adoptive parents. Charlotte, Heine's sister, says she had been married to a Parisian who after running through her fortune had inveigled her in an adventurous fashion into a mental institution in London. Only with great difficulty had she succeeded in escaping and returning to Paris. What we know of her relationship with Meissner, whose acquaintance she had made before she visited Heine, is confused, too, shadowy and unreal. When Heine got to know her she was divorced and was giving lessons in the German language. Where was she born ? One trail—uncertain—leads to Prague. Charlotte speaks of her as a German, a ' gay child of Swabia ' who combined ' French wit with German

sincerity.' The characterization seems almost to have the force of
a symbol, which was certainly not Charlotte's intention. It rings
all the truer! Did the two divaricating elements that Heine loved,
French reason and German irrationalism, meet at last, in the person
of *La Mouche,* on the poet's deathbed ?

There is much that is wraith-like about this passion on the
edge of the grave. It closes with the vision of the escaping butterflies.
It was heralded by a vision, too ; by the poem *Der Abgekühlte*
which Heine had published four years previously in *Romancero*
and of which *La Mouche* was the clear wish-fulfilment in everything
except possibly the colour of her hair :

> Und ist man tot, so muss man lang
> Im Grabe liegen ; ich bin bang,
> Ja, ich bin bang, das Auferstehen
> Wird nicht so schnell von statten gehen.
>
> Noch einmal, eh' mein Lebenslicht
> Erlöschet, eh' mein Herze bricht—
> Noch einmal möcht' ich vor dem Sterben
> Um Frauenhuld beseligt werben.
>
> Und eine Blonde müsst' es sein,
> Mit Augen sanft wie Mondenschein—
> Denn schlecht bekommen mir am Ende
> Die wild brünetten Sonnenbrände.
>
> Das junge Volk voll Lebenskraft
> Will den Tumult der Leidenschaft,
> Das ist ein Rasen, Schwören, Poltern
> Und wechselseitges Seelenfoltern!
>
> Unjung und nicht mehr ganz gesund,
> Wie ich es bin zu dieser Stund',
> Möcht ich noch einmal lieben, schwärmen
> Und glücklich sein—doch ohne Lärmen.

> And when we're dead, we're dead for good,
> And moulder in the coffin's wood ;
> If truth be told I'm very worried—
> I doubt our resurrection's hurried.
>
> Yet once more ere my soul expires,
> Before my heart of living tires—
> Yet once more do I crave to savour
> The joys of lovely woman's favour.

A blonde I'd choose, with eyes
As soft as moon in bluest skies—
I usually lose all ambitions
Aroused by swarthy sunburnt visions.

When young and strong tempestuous love
Is what we crave all else above ;
Impassioned vows, and noisy sobbing,
Two hearts for ever madly throbbing!

No longer young and far from well,
The selfsame tale I still must tell ;
Still would I love and be attracted,
Seek bliss—but not by noise distracted!

The mysterious newcomer was, in Charlotte's words, a captivating, youthful figure.' ' Of medium height, attractive rather than beautiful. Brown locks framed her finely formed features. Roguish eyes looked out at you over a retroussé nose, and when she spoke or smiled the small lips revealed a row of pearl-like teeth. Her hands and feet were small and dainty, and there was something exceptionally graceful about all her movements.' The sister's verdict—and she was a severe critic—was : ' Extremely charming.'

Mathilde avoided *La Mouche* (so-called by Heine from her signet, on which was engraved a fly). She left the sickroom whenever the other woman came, barely returning her greeting. However, the fact that there were never any violent scenes, of the sort Mathilde usually felt no inhibitions about making, shows that in this case she displayed an instinctive understanding of the situation.

In the early stages of their relationship *La Mouche* tried translating Heine's poems into French. Should I work together with him ? she asked herself half-anxiously, half-joyfully. Her first impressions :

Our loathing of what was humdrum and conventional, ugly or mean ; our hatred of everything that was affected ; the contempt in which we held highfalutin verbiage and sentimental outpourings ; above all, our wholehearted and enthusiastic devotion to the cult of the beautiful—these became the spiritual bonds uniting us.

By and large this is a just characterization of Heine both as poet and man, and reveals its authoress as being of more than average sensitivity. And so they became friends. ' We think alike,' Heine

told her, ' and so I have nothing to hide from you.' Beneath the
grey, sulphurous sky of his physical sufferings and fading energies
the last tender bloom in Heine's life shot up from a rich spiritual soil.

She read to him. Heine liked her pronunciation of German,
and took the opportunity to observe that the German language
was the ' loveliest and most euphonious in the world.' He passed
adverse criticisms on French writers, denouncing in particular
La Sand's inflated, verbose style. She was a blue-stocking. *La
Mouche* protested. But Heine stuck to his guns: ' Let's call a
spade a spade.'

It is very hot in the sick man's room, which is on the fifth floor
overlooking the tree-tops in the avenue. *La Mouche* opens the door
leading to the small balcony which is covered by an awning. Here
Heine would lie propped up on ' good days,' shielded from draughts
by tapestry screens and enjoying through his opera glass the view
of the far-off bustling life in the Champs Elysées below. If over-
long listening to *La Mouche's* reading had tired him out, he would
rest with half-closed eyes, stretch out his arm, and ask *La Mouche*
to put her hand in his. He would press her hand tightly, as if it
were within the power of this woman he loved to snatch him from
the jaws of death. ' Thus did he desire, he said, his voice taking
on a singular sharpness, to cling to his fleeting life.' To cheer him
up, *La Mouche* would ask him to tell her something of his early
life. He responded with alacrity, relating innumerable vivid details.

She had to leave him for a short cure in the Black Forest, on
her doctor's orders. She broke the news to him reluctantly, in
halting words. ' A deep sigh shook the sick man's frame and his
eyes filled with tears. It seemed almost wrong that I should be
thinking of my own health when he was lying at death's door.'

On her return she found him engaged in feverish activity. He was
anxious to complete his memoirs. He wrote furiously, avenging
himself at long last on many an enemy. Only a small, harmless,
though very fine, fragment of these memoirs has reached us, dealing
with his childhood. Heine's *magnum opus,* on which he worked to
the very end, was destroyed. The precise circumstances have been
variously described. It is enough for us that the work has disappeared ; like Byron's memoirs it has gone for ever.

Elise took the place of Heine's secretary when he fell ill. He
dictated letters to her; she read him the proofs of the French version

of the *Travel Sketches*. 'Angrily' he chides her for her incorrect writing of capitals. His heart overflows with tenderness. 'Because we knew each other from the first moment,' wrote *La Mouche* in her memoirs, 'any possibility of a misunderstanding was excluded from the outset, and we could show ourselves to each other as we really were without fear of being misrepresented.' The discreetly feminine remark reveals much more than emerges elsewhere from the restrained narrative of the memoirs. Heine's short letters to her are marked by no such restraint. 'Dear heart,' he writes, and begs his 'lotus-flower' not to expose herself to the inclemencies of his wintry mood. She is the 'last flower' of his 'dreary autumn.' He sends her 'insanely tender greetings.' Similarly in the poem: 'Mein Leib liegt tot im Grab, jedoch/Mein Geist, der ist lebendig noch,/Er wohnt gleich einem Hauskobolde/In deinem Herzchen, meine Holde./Dich fesselt mein Gedankenbann....'—'My body lies dead in its grave, but my spirit lives on. It lives like an elf in your heart, my fair one. My thoughts still cast their spell on you. . . .' And the blazing, daring, hope-abandoning poem, *Die Wahlverlobten* ('The Elective Betrothed'). It is not the poet who dies, but she; she, the beloved, the mortal creature must perish. 'I depart, and you wither alone.' 'Viel anders ist es mit Poeten,/Die kann der Tod nicht gänzlich töten./Uns trifft nicht weltliche Vernichtung,/Wir leben fort im Land der Dichtung,/In Avalun, dem Feenreiche-/Leb wohl auf ewig, schöne Leiche!'—'Far otherwise is it with poets, they can never be wholly slain by Death. Earthly destruction does not affect us, we live on in the world of poesy, in the faery realm of Avalon—farewell for ever, lovely corpse!' In a letter he writes playfully: 'My good, delightful, lovely Mouche, come and buzz round my nose with your tiny wings. I know a song by Mendelssohn with the refrain: Come soon! (*Komme du bald!*). The tune is running through my head all the time: Come soon!'

'Waiting' (*Wartend*) was the title of this song of Mendelssohn's. 'You don't know what the word "waiting" means to Prometheus chained to his rock'—this was the agonized cry with which he greeted her once. But when his condition was too bad he had no wish to see her. 'No school today,' he would write on such occasions. And then again:

How I look forward to seeing you again, my fair Mouche, my soul's desire. The most endearing of musk-cats and at the same time as lovely as an Angora, just the kind I like. For a long time I used to love tiger cats, but that kind is too dangerous and the *empreintes vivantes*[1] they sometimes left on my face were extremely troublesome. Things are still very bad with me, one kind of upset after another and one fit of rage after another —rages at my hopeless plight. I am a dead man who longs for the most ardent pleasures that life can afford. It is horrible.

He still jested occasionally, but often he lapsed into melancholy dreaming, even in her presence—into a doze from which he would awake with a heavy, disconsolate sigh. 'A kind of ecstasy would often come over him when his pains were at their worst ; he would raise his arms and beg for mercy.' He dreamt of his father having his hair dressed and disappearing in a cloud of powder. He wanted to kiss his father's hand. Its fingers were dry twigs, his father himself a hoar-covered, leafless tree. In his poem, *Für die Mouche* ('For Mouche') he sees himself ' with an expression refined by suffering ' lying dead in an open sarcophagus. He describes the bas-reliefs of the stone coffin, the numerous scenes and motifs :

> Die Gegensätze sind hier grell gepaart,
> Des Griechen Lustsinn und der Gottgedanke Judäas.

Diametrical opposites are here shown paired ; the joyousness of the Greek and Judea's God-idea.

At the head of the bier, however, blooms the gloriously coloured passion flower, in whose calix could be seen all the instruments of the crucifixion. ' Like a woman mourning ' the flower bends down and kisses the corpse's hand. ' Du warst die Blume, du geliebtes Kind,/An deinen Küssen musst ich dich erkennen/So zärtlich keine Blumenlippen sind,/So feurig keine Blumenthränen brennen!'—You were that flower, beloved child, I knew you by your kisses. No flower's lips are so tender, no flower's tears burn so fiercely! Neither of them speaks. ' Silence is the chaste blossom of love.'

> Frag, was er strahlet, den Karfunkelstein,
> Frag, was sie duften, Nachtviol'und Rosen —
> Doch frage nie, wovon im Mondenschein
> Die Marterblume und ihr Toter kosen!

Ask the carbuncle what it is that sparkles from it, ask the dame-violet and the rose what fragrance it is that emanates from

[1] A favourite expression of *La Mouche's*.

them, but never ask of what it is that sorrow's flower and her dead swain discourse in the moonlight!

It is his last poem, the last poetical image in a life so rich in poetical imagery.

In February *La Mouche* was confined to her bed with a cold. She hastened to Heine's side only half-recovered.

I did not suspect it would be the last time I should see him among the living. On entering his room I was struck by the ghastly pallor of his lips, and I found him depressed, heavy-hearted, his mood affected by the dreary winter's day. ' You're here at last,' he called out to me. He'd often greeted me with these words ; today, however, he pronounced them in a less affectionate, almost severe tone of voice. So he too misjudged me! The injustice of the rebuke cut me to the quick, nor could I tell so sick a man that I had had to summon up all my strength to get out of bed and come to him. The impossibility of justifying myself tortured me, and I burst into tears. Suddenly, as though he felt my distress, although he could not see my face, he called me to him, and I had to sit on the edge of his bed. He seemed to be deeply moved by the tears which rolled down my pale cheeks. ' Take off your hat, so that I can see you better,' he said. And with a caressing motion he stroked the ribbon of my hat. Impelled by a sudden emotion I pushed back my hat and knelt down at the side of the bed. Was it the memory of past suffering that so agitated me, or the more terrible premonition of coming disaster ? Suffice that I sought in vain to keep back my sobs ; I was no longer able to control my emotions and had perforce to yield to the tumult raging within me. Not a word was spoken, but my friend's hand, which lay on my head, seemed to be raised in blessing over me. This was the last time we were together. I had already gone out of the door and was standing on the landing when the sound of the beloved voice, distinctly audible but as if trembling from anxiety, once more fell upon my ear. ' Till tomorrow, then, you hear ? Don't be late ! '

On Thursday, 14th February, he was racked with violent head-pains. ' I shan't be able to write to my dear mother,' he lamented. The previous day he had told his nurse, with whom he never discussed literary matters otherwise: ' I have only four more days' work to do, and then I shall have finished my task '—alluding in all likelihood to the memoirs. His condition deteriorated. Two doctors ; laudanum, orange-blossom infusions, ice-packs. On Saturday afternoon the nurse heard him whisper ' *schreiben* ' (' write ') three

times. Then he called out: 'Paper—pencil . . .' These were his last
words.

On that 17th day of February, a Sunday (relates Camilla
Selden) I experienced a strange vision when I awoke. At about
eight o'clock in the morning I noticed a peculiar noise in my
room, a kind of skipping and fluttering ; the sort of noise one
hears on summer evenings when butterflies, having come into
a room through an open window, desperately seek their way
out again. I opened my eyes, but quickly closed them again ;
in the morning sunbeams I had glimpsed a black shape that
resembled a gigantic insect, and was struggling to get outside
into the open. I refrain from commenting in any way on this
vision—the only one I have ever had in my life, incidentally—
and mention it solely on account of its singularity. The memory
of it revives ever anew within me on each anniversary of Heine's
death. Although it was cold, and I still did not feel completely
recovered, I nevertheless knocked at the door of my beloved
poet's apartment at ten o'clock in the morning. When I heard
that he had ceased to be I stood for a moment transfixed,
stupefied, as if completely bereft of comprehension ; then I
asked to see him. I was taken into the hushed room where the
corpse, like an effigy lying in its grave, lay in the calm majesty
of death. No trace of human suffering and passion remained
on this cold mortal frame, which in its marvellous beauty
recalled the divine form of the sick son in the *Pilgrimage to
Kevelaar*. In the early hours of morning Death, the great
comforter, had come to the poet's bed to redeem him, but
Death showed itself just to the poet who had loved him and
sung of him, and he fashioned a pale marble countenance
whose regular features recalled the purest masterpieces of Greek
art.

And here we may append some sentences of *La Mouche* in
which, once only, she mentions that which shines between every
line of Heine's letters to her: 'Where could I ever find such a
love ? And the silence of death answered the question for me.
I had thought of everything, excepting only this sudden silence.'

The joyousness of the Greek and Judea's God-idea—even on
the sides of Heine's sarcophagus the diametrical opposites are
juxtaposed. And the last stanzas of the poem regard the conflict
as incapable of resolution.

This view is not shared by the greatest among the sons of men.
They have taught that the conflict must be resolved as far as is

humanly possible; of this they have sung, this they have exemplified
in their lives: Lao-Tse; Plato, whom a Church Father called
Moses Atticus; Moses himself; Goethe and Thomas Aquinas, and
no doubt others throughout the ages. They are mankind's teachers,
the true invisible Church, the *Yeshiva shel Maala,* that Higher
Body of Teachers which the body of teachers on earth may strive
in awe to emulate.

But beside these, who are the great serene exemplars, stand
those who painfully and restlessly but in all sincerity sought without
finding the grand union of opposites and the grand resolution of
conflicting forces. They should be distinguished from those who
arrogantly persisted in propounding false doctrines, however
dazzling.

The time will come when mankind will avenge itself on its real
oppressors and spoliators: those who have been guilty of 'dis-
regarding the boundaries'; those who wish to apply the canons
of arid rationalism to the sacred spheres of eternal beauty and
eternal tragedy, to the divine and to love; and those also who have
imported an irrational dynamic into social questions, instead of
considering them calmly and judicially, not scorning reason in its
legitimate sphere. A truly 'enlightened' mankind will then not so
much bring these despoilers to trial as pass them by without a word.
It will be a mankind 'enlightened' enough to realize that in certain
great momentous departments of life enlightenment is neither
possible nor desirable; a mankind which will know and respect
its limitations, though within these limitations it will strive always
towards self-help and self-improvement. Such a mankind will,
however, think lovingly of those who prepared a path for it. Not
only of those strong characters like Plato, who knew everything
from the first, but of the weaker, hesitating characters; those who
went astray, but were honest enough not to be smug with it all,
who preferred to do what the Philistine contemptuously calls 'going
from one extreme to the other.' In the ranks of these men, who were
never able to bring their questing and their striving for equilibrium
to an end, a pallid countenance will not be wanting, and not only
for his perfect rhythms and images will his portrait be honoured;
his sufferings and his fruitless endeavours will be properly appreciated too.

It will not be wanting, the portrait of Heinrich Heine.

Select Bibliography

HEINE'S WORKS

HEINRICH HEINES SÄMTLICHE WERKE. Herausgegeben von Ernst Elster. Mit Einleitungen, erläuternden Anmerkungen und Verzeichnissen sämtlicher Lesarten. Leipzig and Vienna: Bibliographisches Institut. (No date.) (7 volumes.)

HEINRICH HEINES GESAMMELTE WERKE. Herausgegeben von Gustav Karpeles. Zweite Auflage. Berlin: G. Grote, 1893. (9 volumes; annotated, with a biographical introduction by C. A. Buchheim; includes 784 of Heine's letters.)

HEINES WERKE IN ZEHN BÄNDEN. Unter Mitwirkung von Jonas Fränkel, Ludwig Krähe, Albert Leitzmann, Paul Neuburger, und Julius Petersen. Herausgegeben von Oskar Walzel. Leipzig: Insel-Verlag, 1911-20. (10 volumes plus index volume.)

HEINE'S LETTERS

HEINRICH HEINE: BRIEFE. Erste Gesamtausgabe nach den Handschriften herausgegeben. Eingeleitet und Erläutert von Friedrich Hirth. Mainz: Florian Kupferberg, 1948-53. (5 volumes, Vol. VI to appear shortly.)

HEINE IN ENGLISH TRANSLATION. (See also H. G. Atkins's biography, published in 1929, for an extensive list.)

THE WORKS OF HEINRICH HEINE. Translated by Charles Godfrey Leland, T. Brooksbank, and Margaret Armour. London: William Heinemann, 1892-1905. (12 volumes.)

THE POEMS OF HEINE COMPLETE: Translated in the original metres. With a sketch of Heine's life. By E. A. Bowring. London: Henry G. Bohn, 1861.

PROSE AND POETRY BY HEINRICH HEINE. Translated by various writers and edited by M. M. Bozman. London and Toronto: J. M. Dent and Sons, 1934. (Everyman's Library.)

THE POETRY AND PROSE OF HEINRICH HEINE. Selected and edited with an Introduction by Frederic Ewen. The poetry translated by Louis Untermeyer, Humbert Wolfe, Emma Lazarus, Margaret Armour, and others, including 110 new translations by Aaron Kramer. The prose newly translated by Frederic Ewen. New York: The Citadel Press, 1948.

TRANSLATIONS FROM HEINE

POEMS. By Kathleen Helen Bradley Kirby. London: Langley and Sons, 1949.

HEINE. POEMS AND BALLADS. Translated by Emma Lazarus. With a biographical introduction. New York: Hartsdale House, 1947.

HEINE. THE NORTH SEA AND OTHER POEMS. Translated by William Stirling. German and English. London: Allan Wingate, 1947.

THE POEMS OF HEINRICH HEINE. An English Verse Translation. By Louis Untermeyer. London: Jonathan Cape, 1938.

PORTRAIT OF HEINE. Translations by Humbert Wolfe. German and English. London: Cresset Press, 1930. (Limited edition.)

SELECTED LYRICS OF HEINE. Translated, with a preface, by Humbert Wolfe. German and English. London: John Lane, 1935.

NORTH SEA. Translated by Vernon Watkins. German and English. London: Faber, 1955.

BIOGRAPHIES

ATKINS, H. G. Heine. London: G. Routledge & Sons, 1929.

BAERLEIN, HENRY. Heine: The Strange Guest. London: Geoffrey Bles, 1928.

BROWNE, LEWIS. That Man Heine. (With the collaboration of Elsa Weihl.) New York: The Macmillan Company, 1927.

FEJTO, FRANÇOIS. Heine. A Biography. Translated by Mervyn Savill. London: Allan Wingate, 1946.

MARCUSE, LUDWIG. Heinrich Heine. A Life between Past and Future. Translated from the German by L. Marie Sieveking and Ian F. D. Morrow. London: Sidgwick and Jackson, 1934.

SHARP, WILLIAM. Life of Heinrich Heine. London: Walter Scott, 1888.

STRODTMANN, ADOLF. H. Heines Leben und Werke. Dritte Auflage. Hamburg: Hoffman & Campe, 1884. (2 volumes.)

UNTERMEYER, LOUIS. Heinrich Heine. London: Jonathan Cape, 1938.

VALLENTIN, ANTONINA. Poet in Exile. The Life of Heinrich Heine. Translated by Harrison Brown. London: Victor Gollancz, 1934.

WALTER, H. Heinrich Heine. A Critical Examination of the Poet and His Works. London and Toronto: J. M. Dent & Sons, 1930.

WOLFF, MAX J. Heinrich Heine. (In German.) Munich: Oskar Beck, 1922.

SPECIAL STUDIES, ESSAYS, MEMOIRS, &c.

ARNOLD, MATTHEW. Heinrich Heine. (In " Essays in Criticism," First Series.) London: Macmillan & Company, 1898.

BIEBER, HUGO. Heinrich Heine. Confessio Judaica. Eine Auswahl aus seinen Dichtungen, Schriften und Briefen. Berlin: Welt-Verlag, 1925.

ELIOT, GEORGE. Essays and Leaves from a Note-book. (" German Wit: Heinrich Heine.") Edinburgh and London: W. Blackwood & Sons, 1884.

EMBDEN, LUDWIG v. Heinrich Heines Familienleben. Hamburg: Hoffman u. Campe, 1892.

FAIRLEY, BARKER. Heinrich Heine. An Interpretation. Oxford: Oxford University Press, 1954. (A study of certain recurring images and *motifs* in Heine.)

HEYMANN, FRITZ. Der Chevalier von Geldern. Amsterdam: Querido, 1937.

HIRTH, FRIEDRICH. Heinrich Heine. Bausteine zu einer Biographie. Mainz: Florian Kupferberg, 1950.

HIRTH, FRIEDRICH. Heinrich Heine und seine Französischen Freunde. Mainz: Florian Kupferberg, 1950.

HOUBEN, H. H. Gespräche mit Heine. Zum erstenmal gesammelt und herausgegeben. Frankfurt am Main: Literarische Anstalt Rütten & Loening, 1926.

HUFFER, HERMANN. Heinrich Heine. Gesammelte Aufsätze Herausgegeben von Ernst Elster. Berlin: Georg Bondi, 1908.

KAUFFMANN, DAVID. Aus Heinrich Heines Ahnensaal. Breslau: S. Schottlaender, 1896.

LEWALD, AUGUST. Aquarelle aus dem Leben. Mannheim: Heinrich Hoff, 1837.

LEWALD, AUGUST. Gesammelte Schriften. Leipzig: F. A. Brockhaus, 1844-45.

LEWALD, FANNY. Erinnerungen an Heinrich Heine. In " Zwölf Bilder nach dem Leben." Berlin: Otto Janke, 1888.

MEISSNER, ALFRED. Heinrich Heine: Erinnerungen. Hamburg: Hoffman und Campe, 1856.

MEISSNER, ALFRED. Die Matratzengruft: Erinnerung an Heinrich Heine. Herausgegeben von Georg Weberknecht. Stuttgart R. Lutz, 1921.

MEYER, FRIEDRICH. Verzeichnis einer Heinrich Heine-Bibliothek. Leipzig: Dyksche Buchhandlung, 1905.

ROSE, WILLIAM. Heinrich Heine. Two Studies of his Thought and Feeling. Oxford: Clarendon Press. London: Cumberlege, 1956.

SELDEN, CAMILLA. Heinrich Heine's Last Days. Newly translated from the French by Mary Thiddall. London: T. Fisher Unwin, 1898.

STAHR, ADOLF. Zwei Monate in Paris. Oldenburg: Schulze'sche Buchhandlung, 1851.

STOESSINGER, FELIX. Heinrich Heine. Mein wertvollstes Vermächtnis (Religion, Leben, Dichtung). Zürich: Manesse Verlag, 1950.

STRODTMANN, ADOLF. Heinrich Heine's Wirken und Streben, dargestellt an seinen Werken. Hamburg: Gustav Karl Würgar, 1857.

TABAK, ISRAEL. Judaic Lore in Heine. The Heritage of a Poet. Baltimore: The John Hopkins Press, 1948.

VICTOR, W. Marx und Heine. Tatsache und Spekulation in der Darstellung ihrer Beziehungen. Berlin: Bruno Henschel und Sohn, 1951.

VICTOR, WALTHER. Mathilde. Ein Leben um Heinrich Heine. Leipzig, Wien: E. P. Tal u. Co. Verlag, 1931.

WEBER, HILMAR H. The Heine Collection in the Harvard College Library. Reprinted from the Harvard Library Notes, December 1935. Cambridge, Massachusetts, 1935.

WITRIOL, J. Heine the Jew. In "The Jewish Monthly," July, 1950. London: The Anglo-Jewish Association.

Index